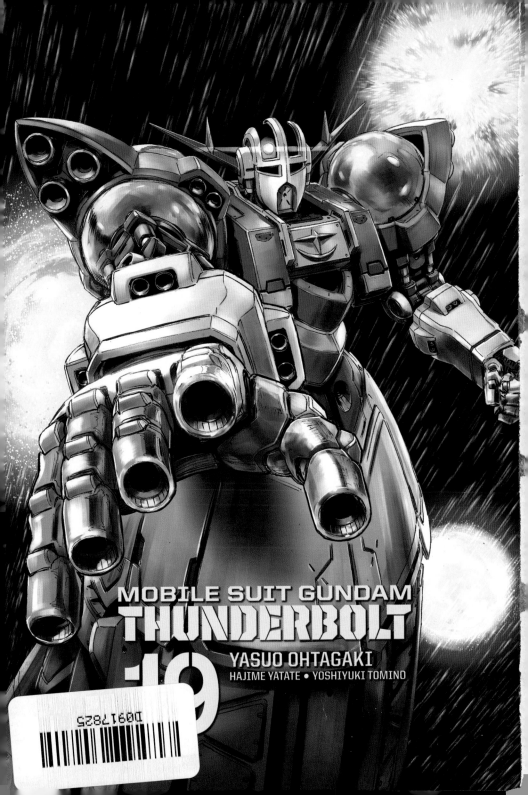

MOBILE SUIT GUNDAM THUNDERBOLT

19

YASUO OHTAGAKI

HAJIME YATATE • YOSHIYUKI TOMINO

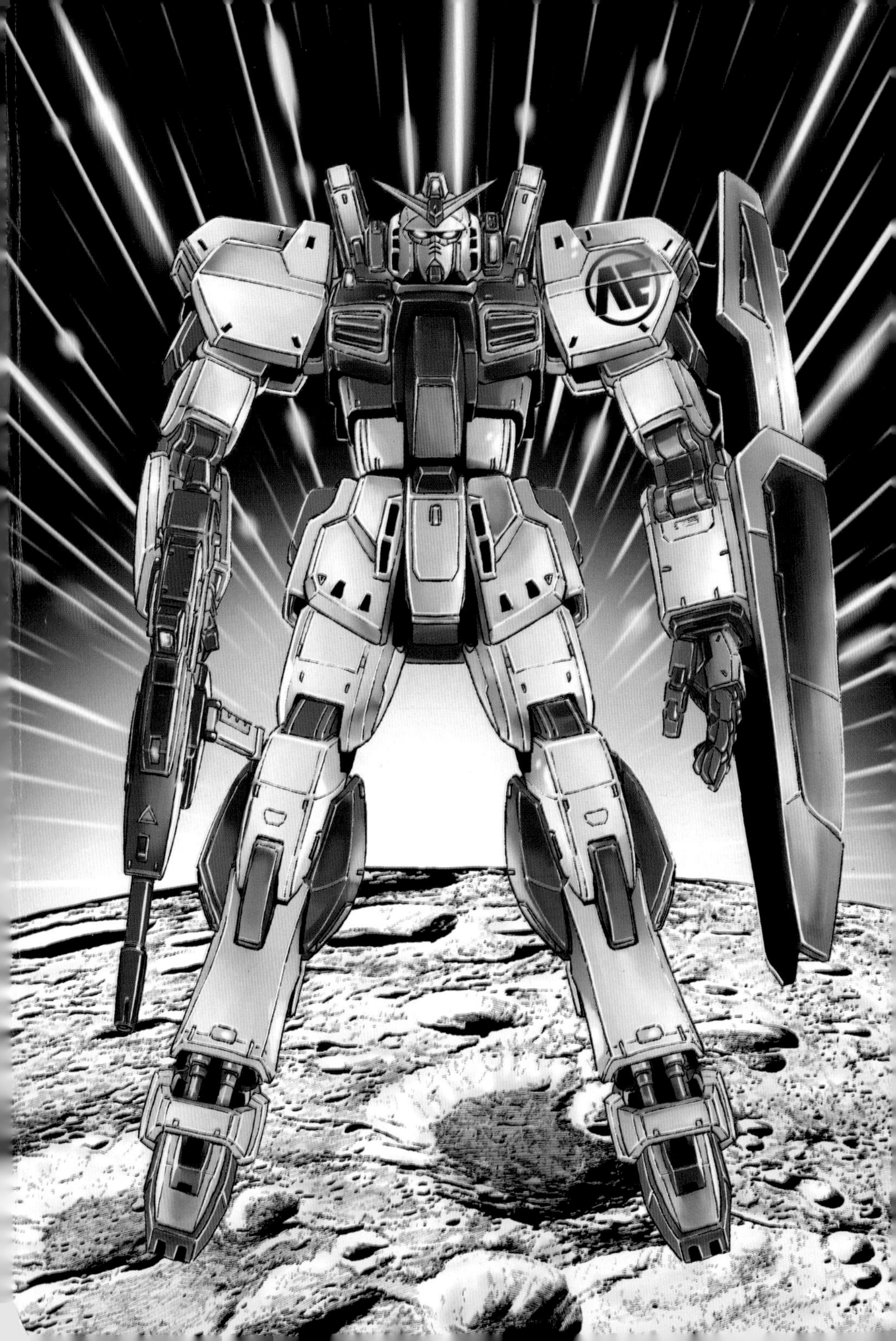

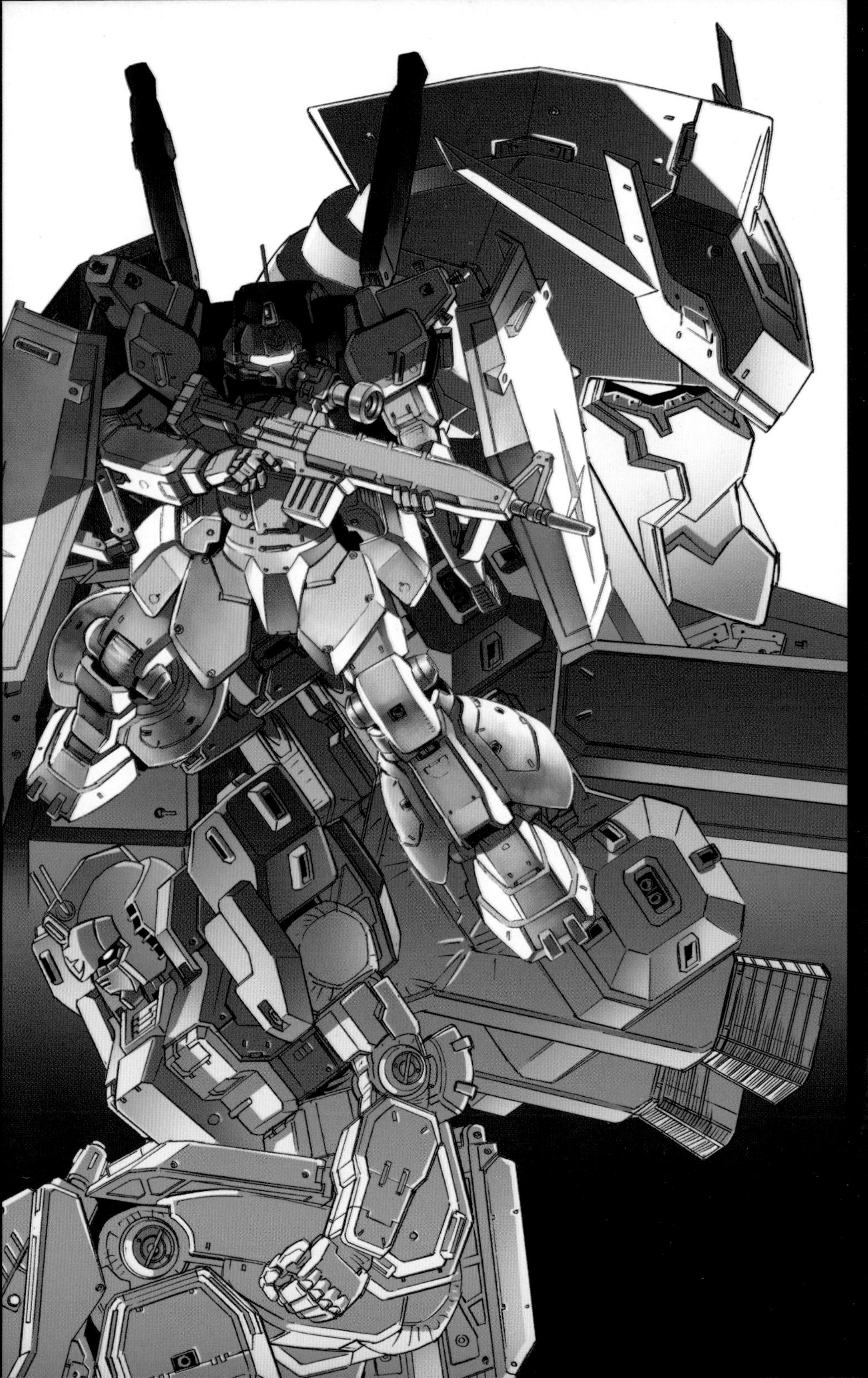

MOBILE SUIT GUNDAM
THUNDERBOLT
19

THE TERRARIUM ON THE MOON

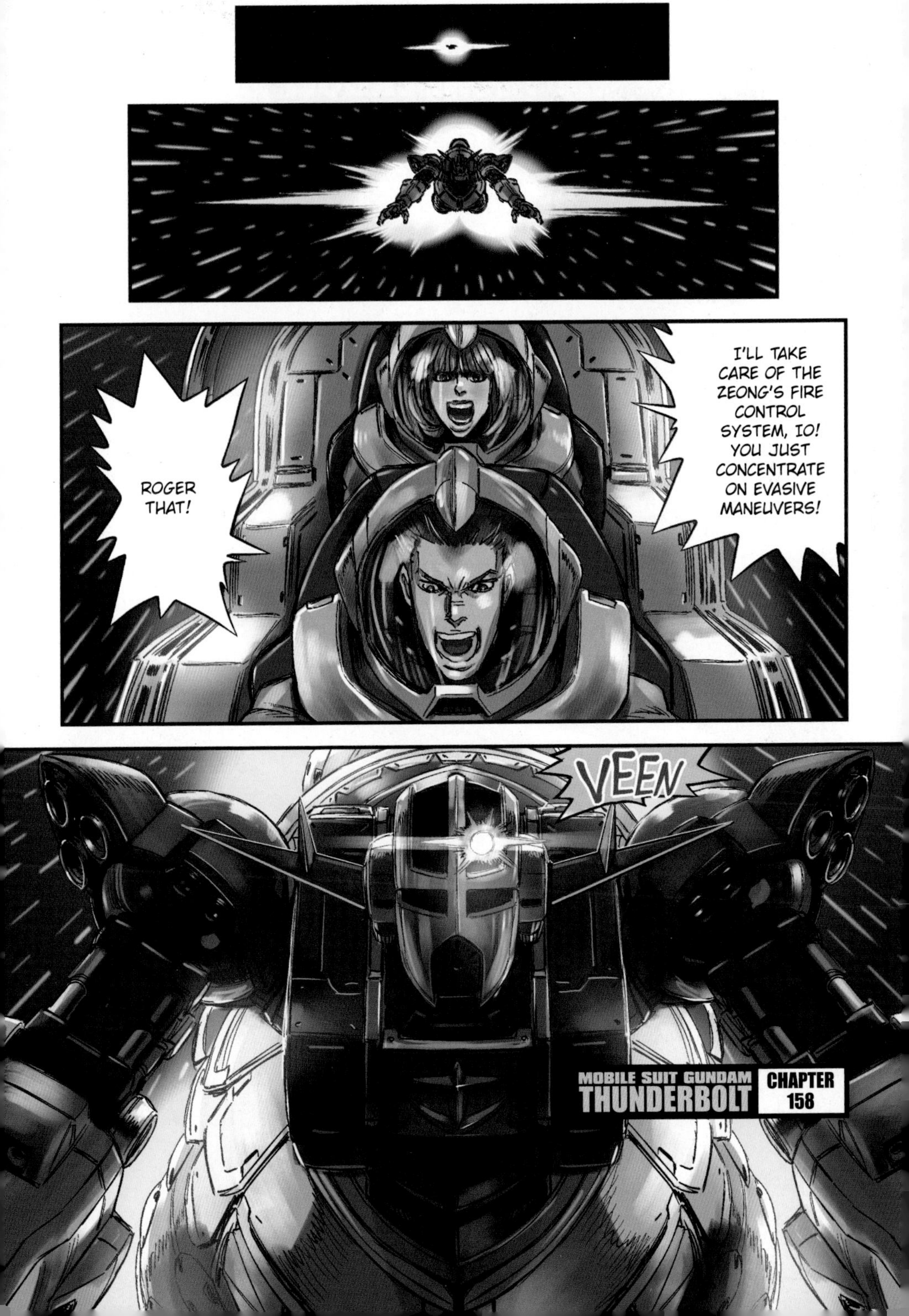
I'LL TAKE CARE OF THE ZEONG'S FIRE CONTROL SYSTEM, IO! YOU JUST CONCENTRATE ON EVASIVE MANEUVERS!
ROGER THAT!
VEEN
MOBILE SUIT GUNDAM THUNDERBOLT
CHAPTER 158

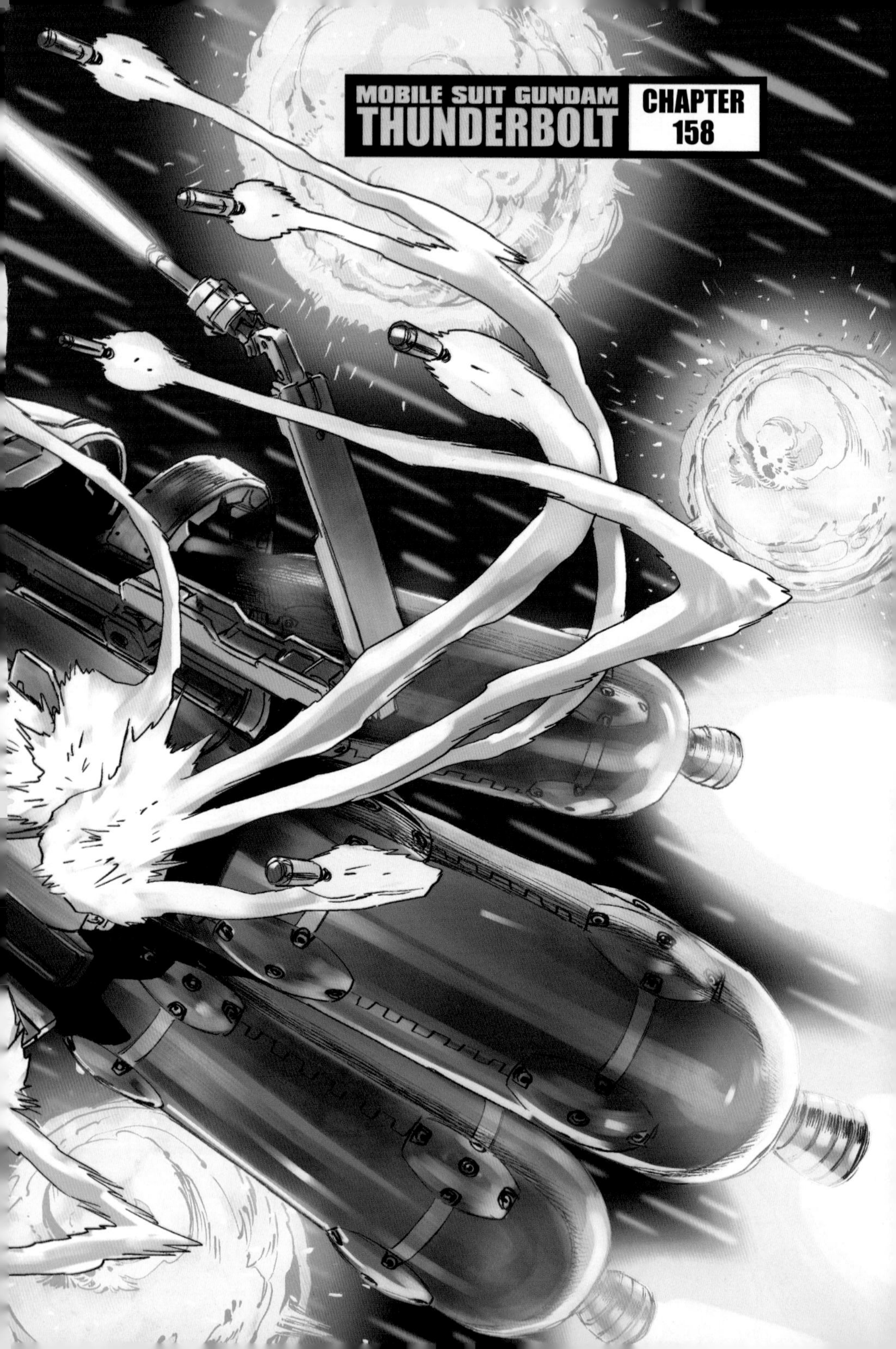
MOBILE SUIT GUNDAM THUNDERBOLT
CHAPTER 158

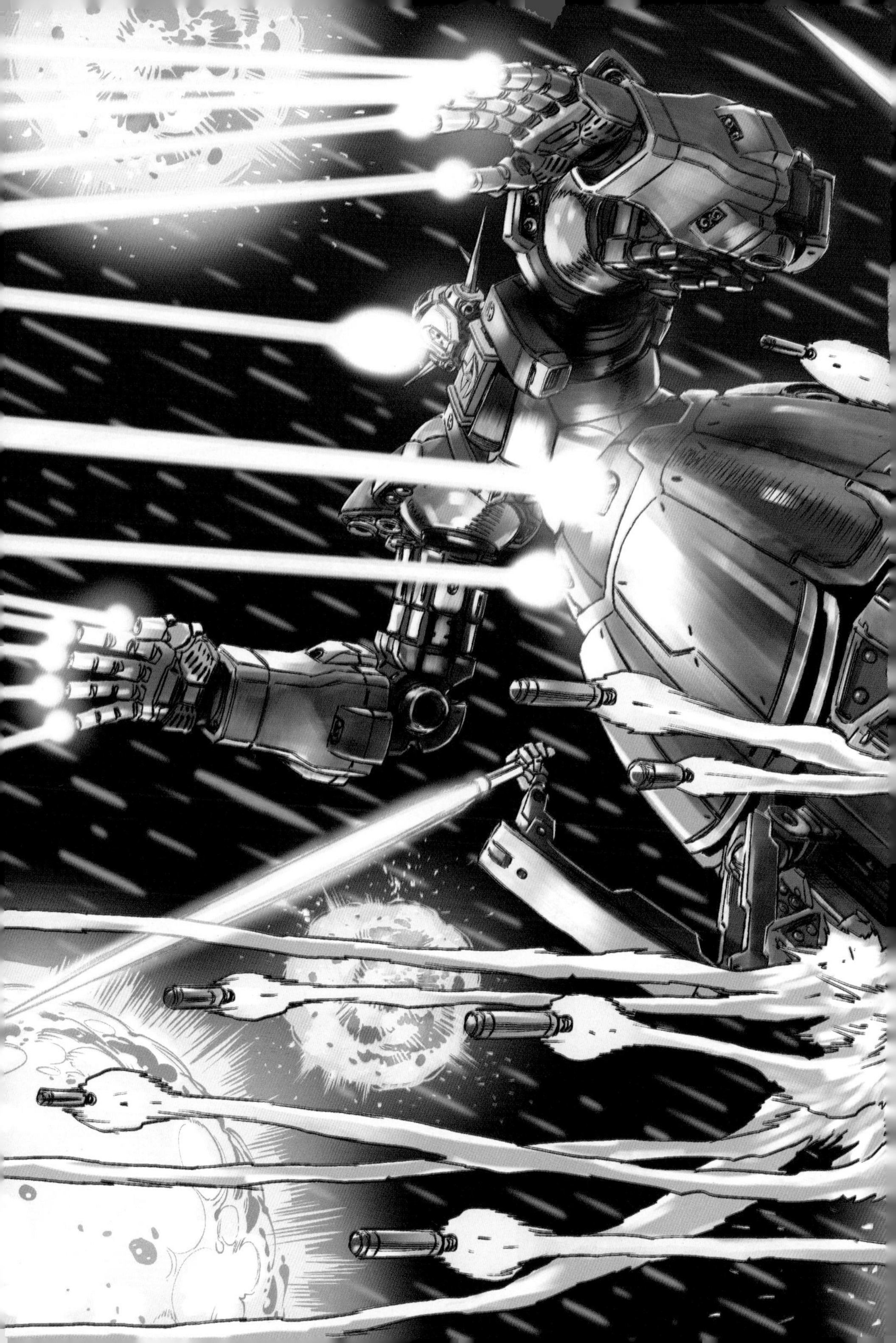

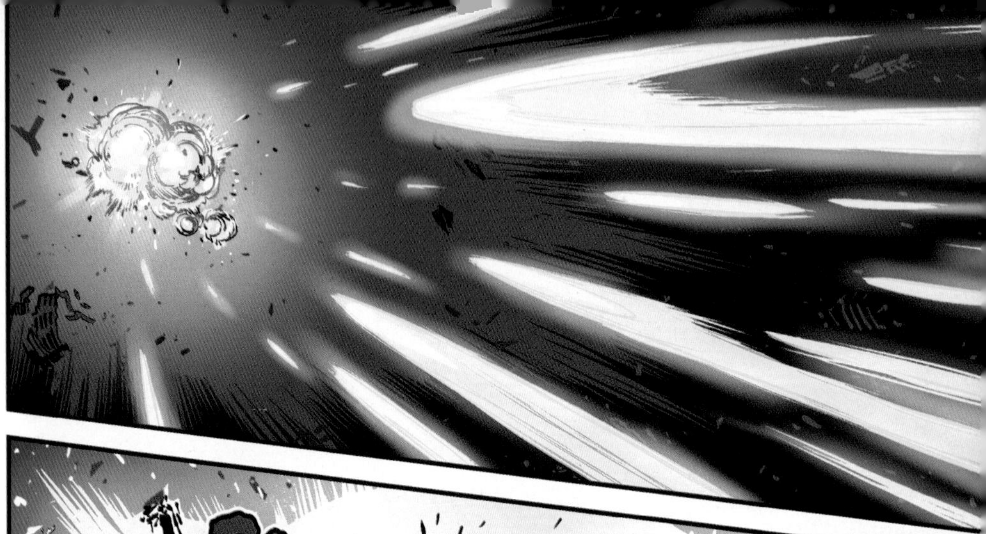

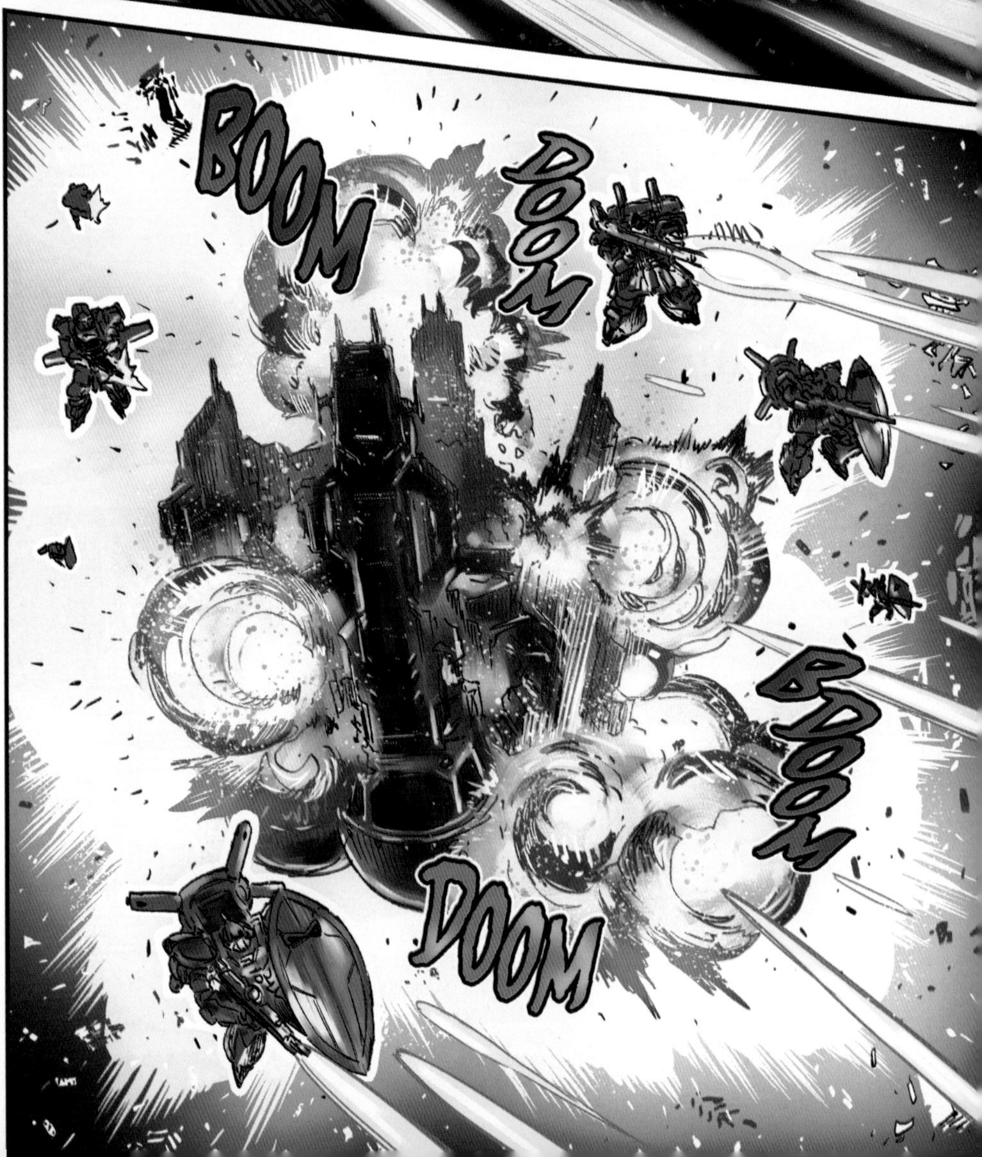
DOOM
BOOM
BDOOM
DOOM

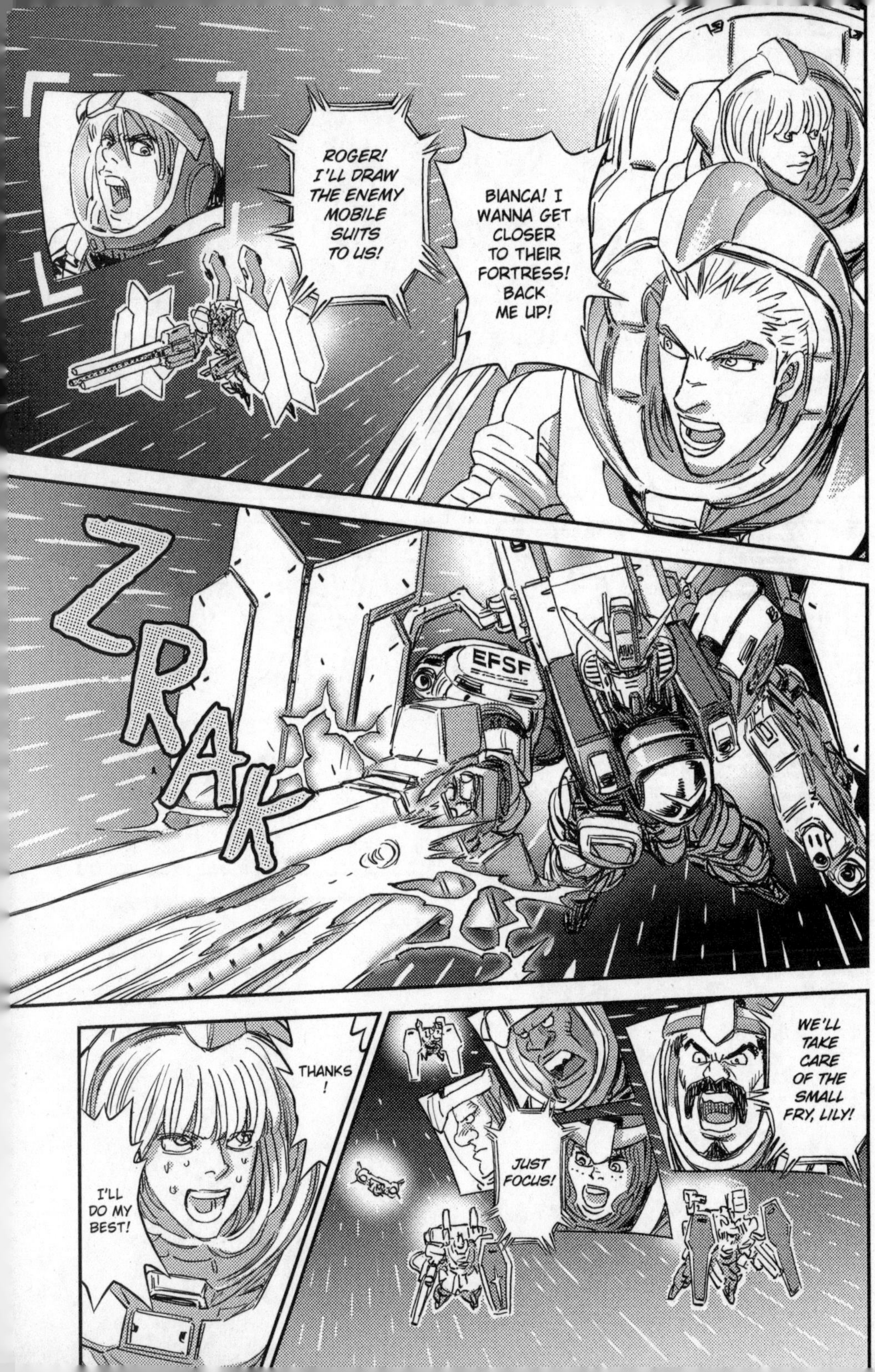
BIANCA! I WANNA GET CLOSER TO THEIR FORTRESS! BACK ME UP!
ROGER! I'LL DRAW THE ENEMY MOBILE SUITS TO US!
EFSF
ZRAK
WE'LL TAKE CARE OF THE SMALL FRY, LILY!
JUST FOCUS!
THANKS!
I'LL DO MY BEST!

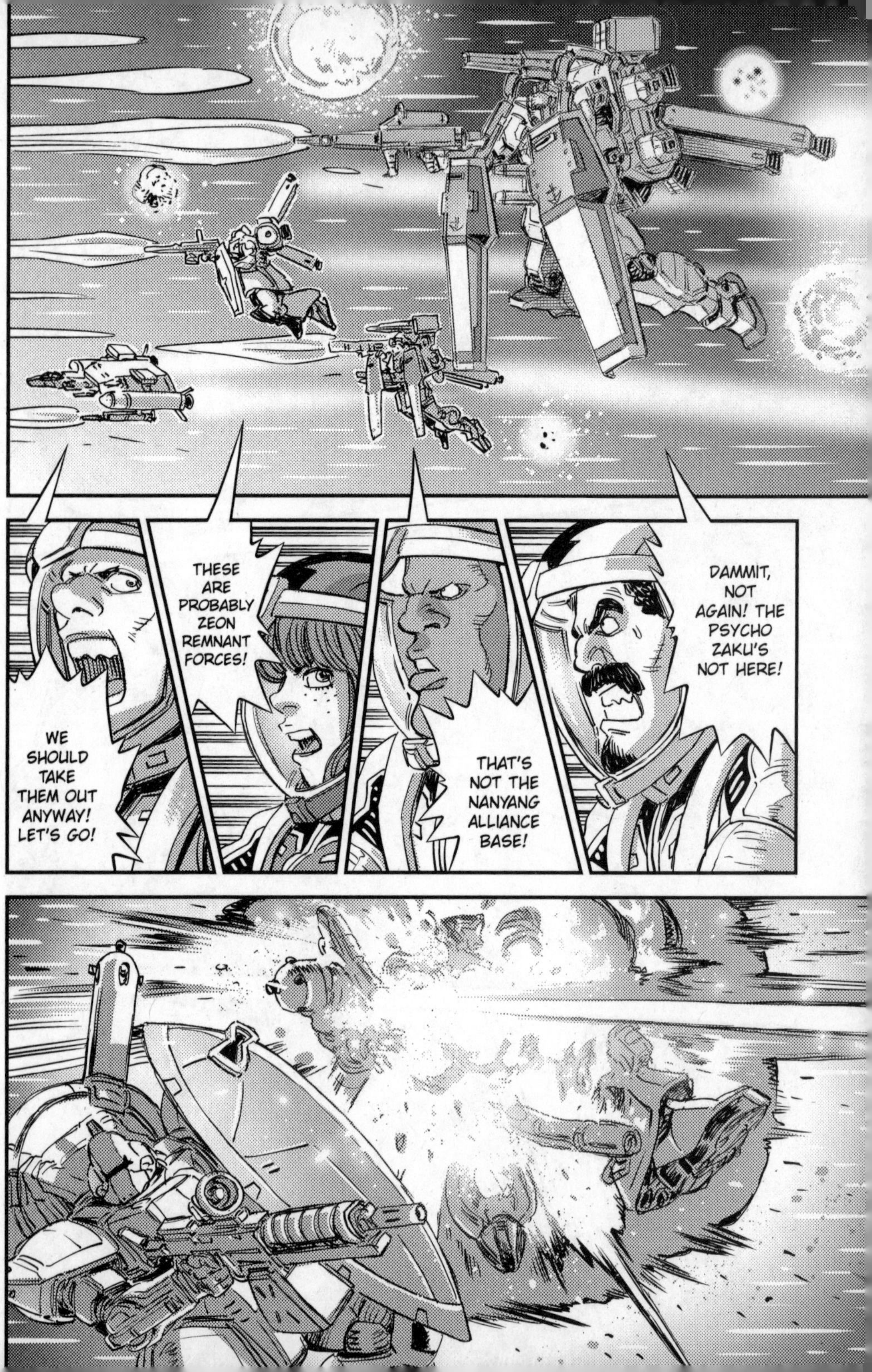
DAMMIT, NOT AGAIN! THE PSYCHO ZAKU'S NOT HERE!
THAT'S NOT THE NANYANG ALLIANCE BASE!
THESE ARE PROBABLY ZEON REMNANT FORCES!
WE SHOULD TAKE THEM OUT ANYWAY! LET'S GO!

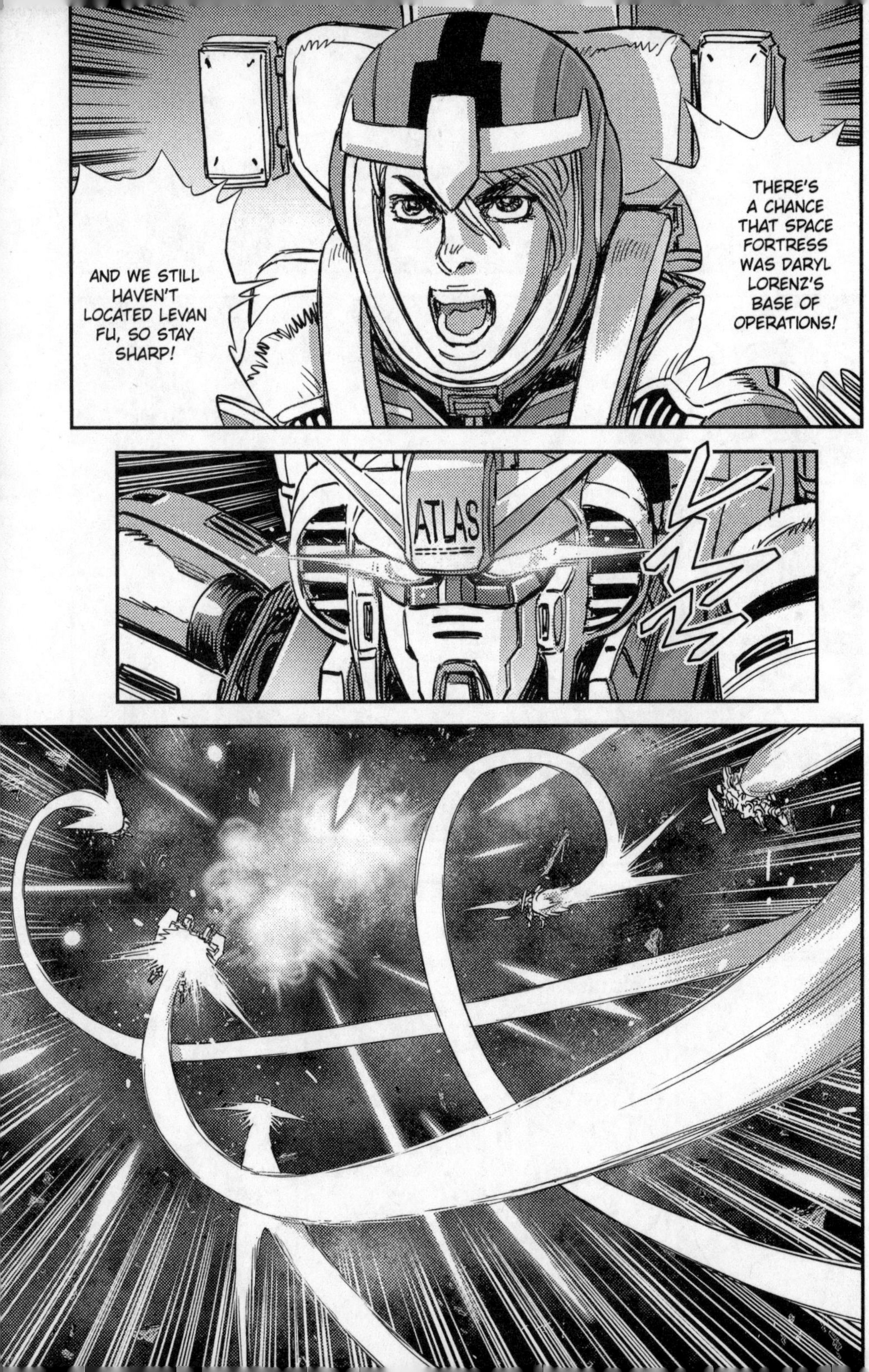
THERE'S A CHANCE THAT SPACE FORTRESS WAS DARYL LORENZ'S BASE OF OPERATIONS!
AND WE STILL HAVEN'T LOCATED LEVAN FU, SO STAY SHARP!
ATLAS
VMM

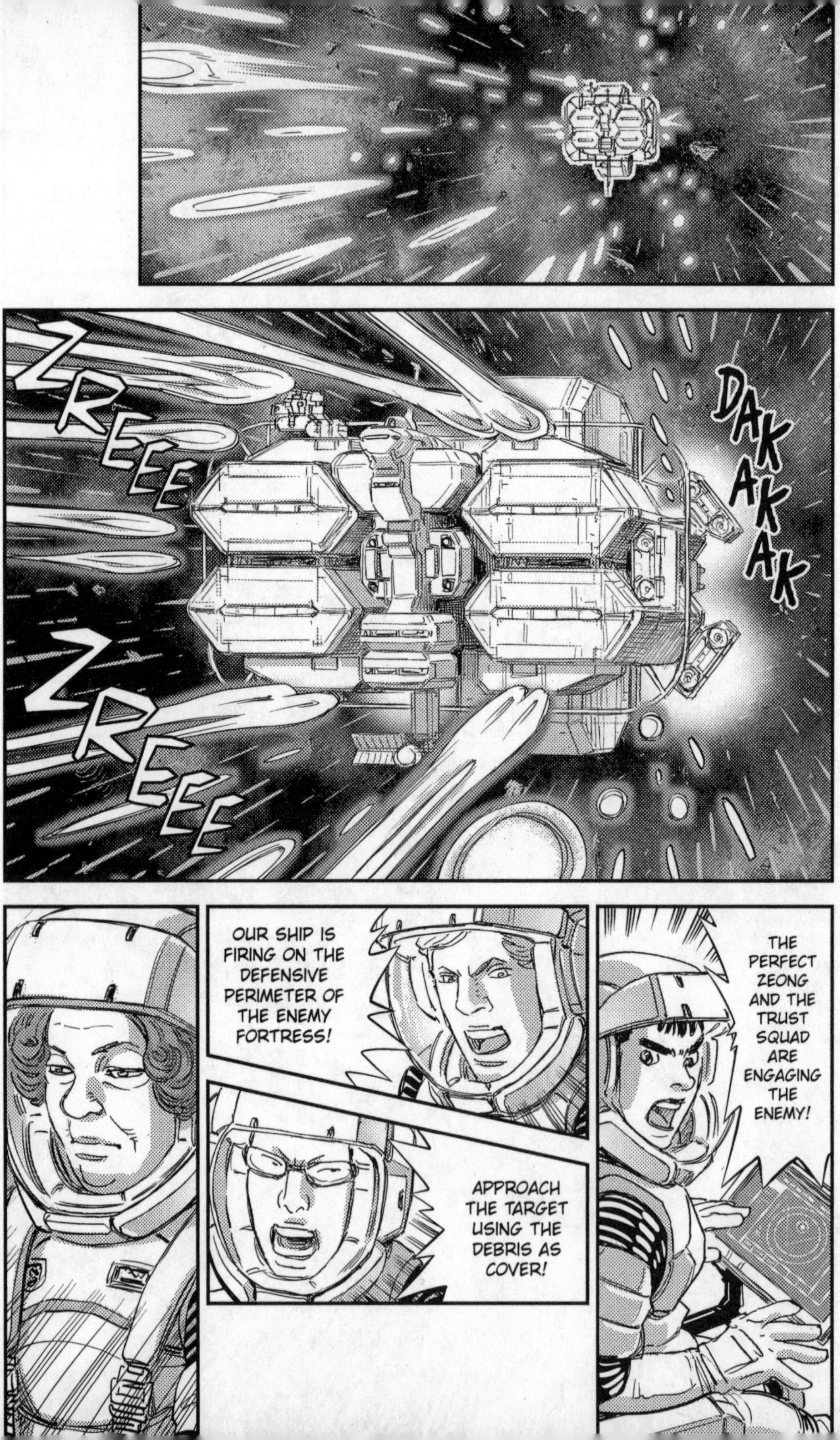
DAKAKAK
ZREEEE
ZREEEE
THE PERFECT ZEONG AND THE TRUST SQUAD ARE ENGAGING THE ENEMY!
OUR SHIP IS FIRING ON THE DEFENSIVE PERIMETER OF THE ENEMY FORTRESS!
APPROACH THE TARGET USING THE DEBRIS AS COVER!

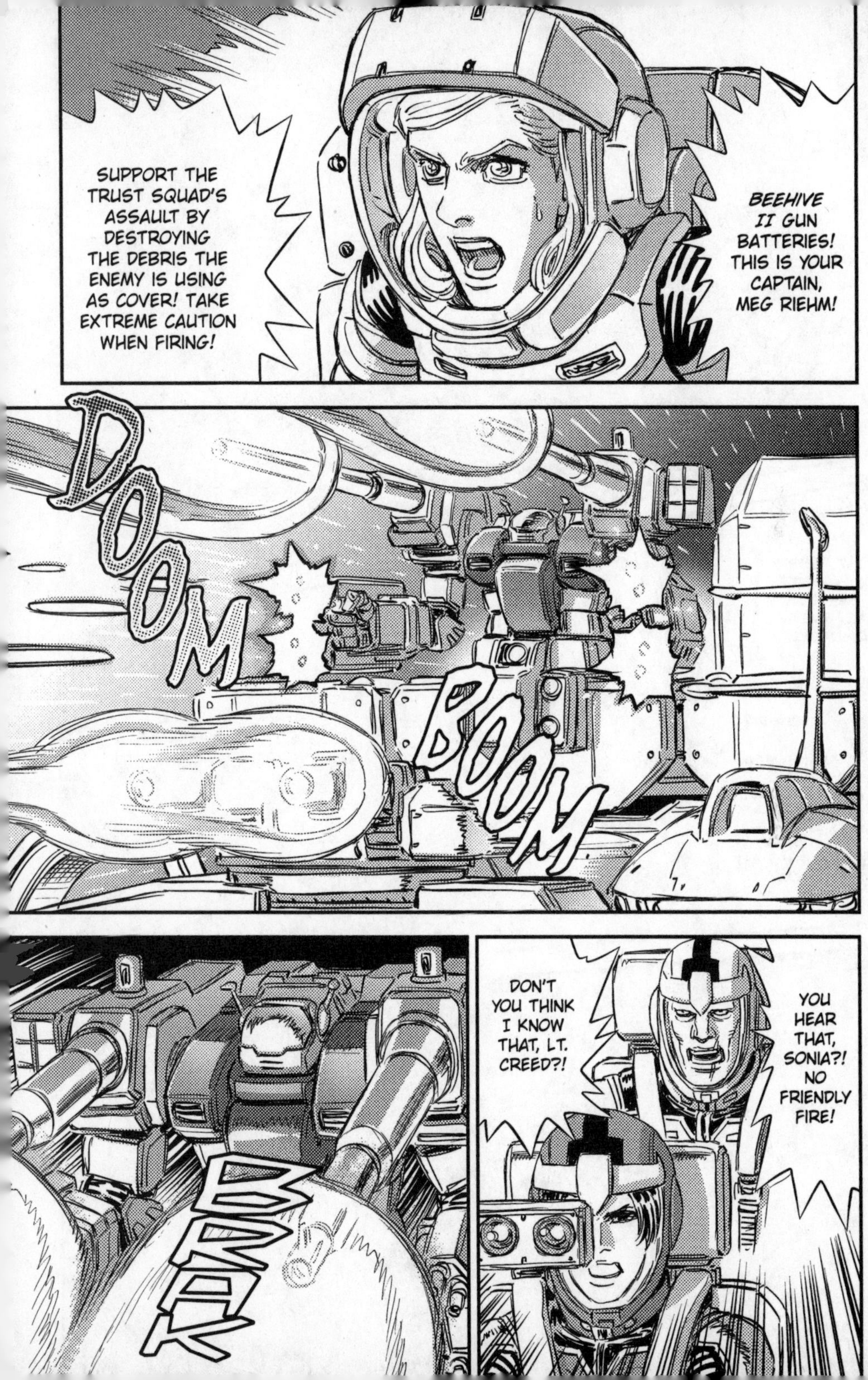
BEEHIVE II GUN BATTERIES! THIS IS YOUR CAPTAIN, MEG RIEHM!
SUPPORT THE TRUST SQUAD'S ASSAULT BY DESTROYING THE DEBRIS THE ENEMY IS USING AS COVER! TAKE EXTREME CAUTION WHEN FIRING!
DOOOM
BOOM
YOU HEAR THAT, SONIA?! NO FRIENDLY FIRE!
DON'T YOU THINK I KNOW THAT, LT. CREED?!

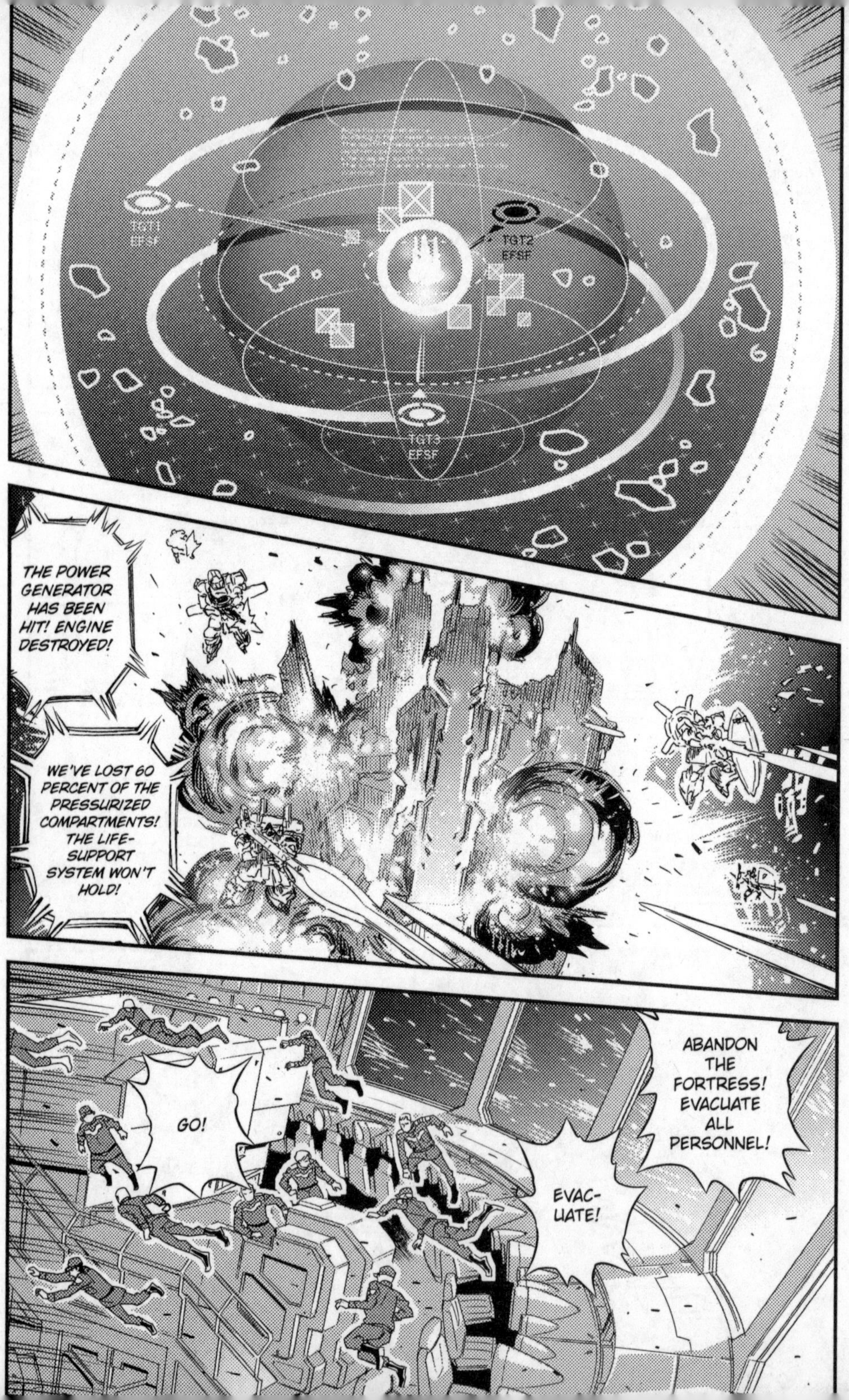
TGT2
EFSF
TGT1
EFSF
TGT3
EFSF
THE POWER GENERATOR HAS BEEN HIT! ENGINE DESTROYED!
WE'VE LOST 60 PERCENT OF THE PRESSURIZED COMPARTMENTS! THE LIFE-SUPPORT SYSTEM WON'T HOLD!
ABANDON THE FORTRESS! EVACUATE ALL PERSONNEL!
GO!
EVAC-UATE!

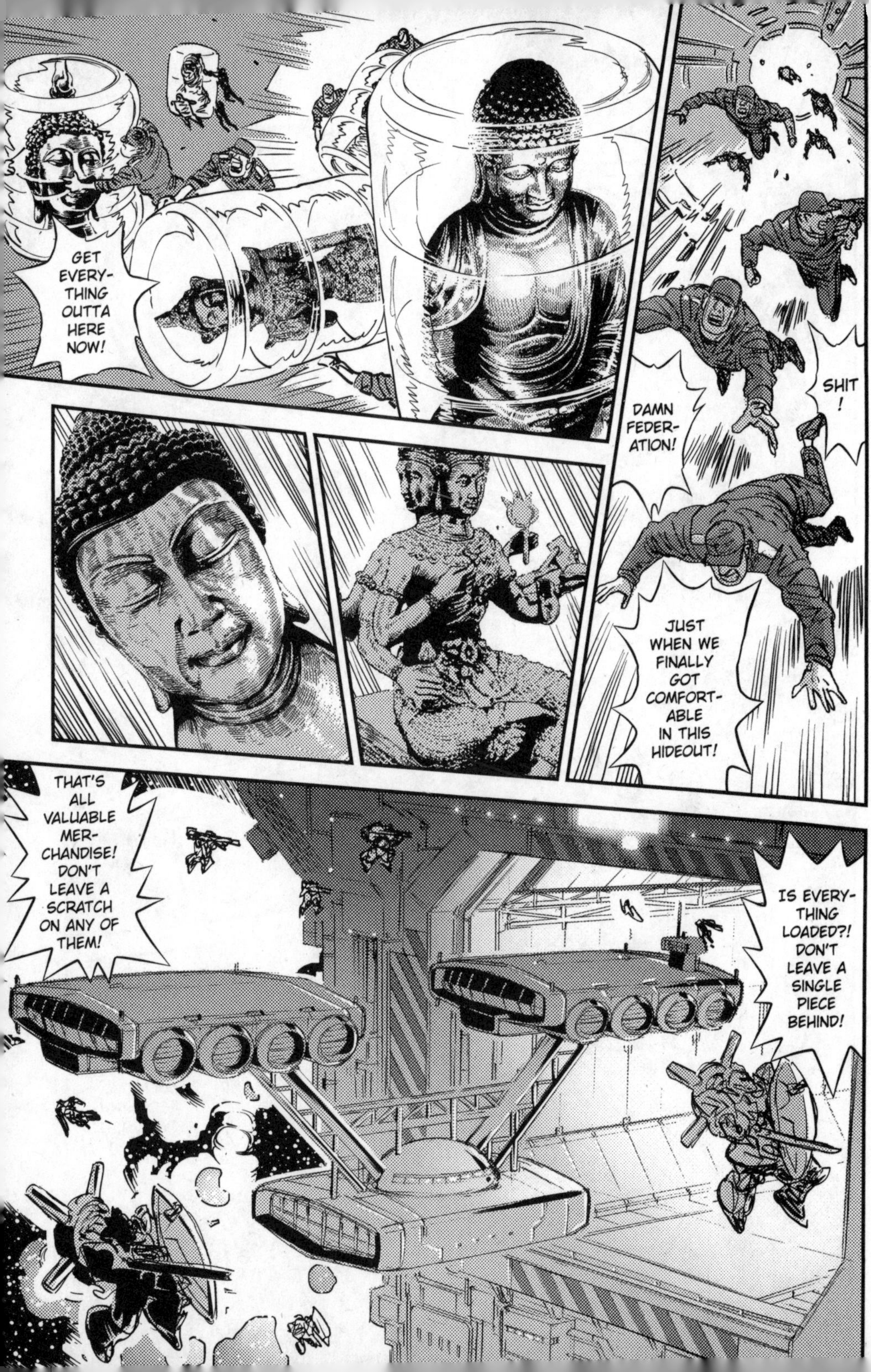
SHIT!
DAMN FEDERATION!
JUST WHEN WE FINALLY GOT COMFORTABLE IN THIS HIDEOUT!
GET EVERYTHING OUTTA HERE NOW!
IS EVERYTHING LOADED?! DON'T LEAVE A SINGLE PIECE BEHIND!
THAT'S ALL VALUABLE MERCHANDISE! DON'T LEAVE A SCRATCH ON ANY OF THEM!

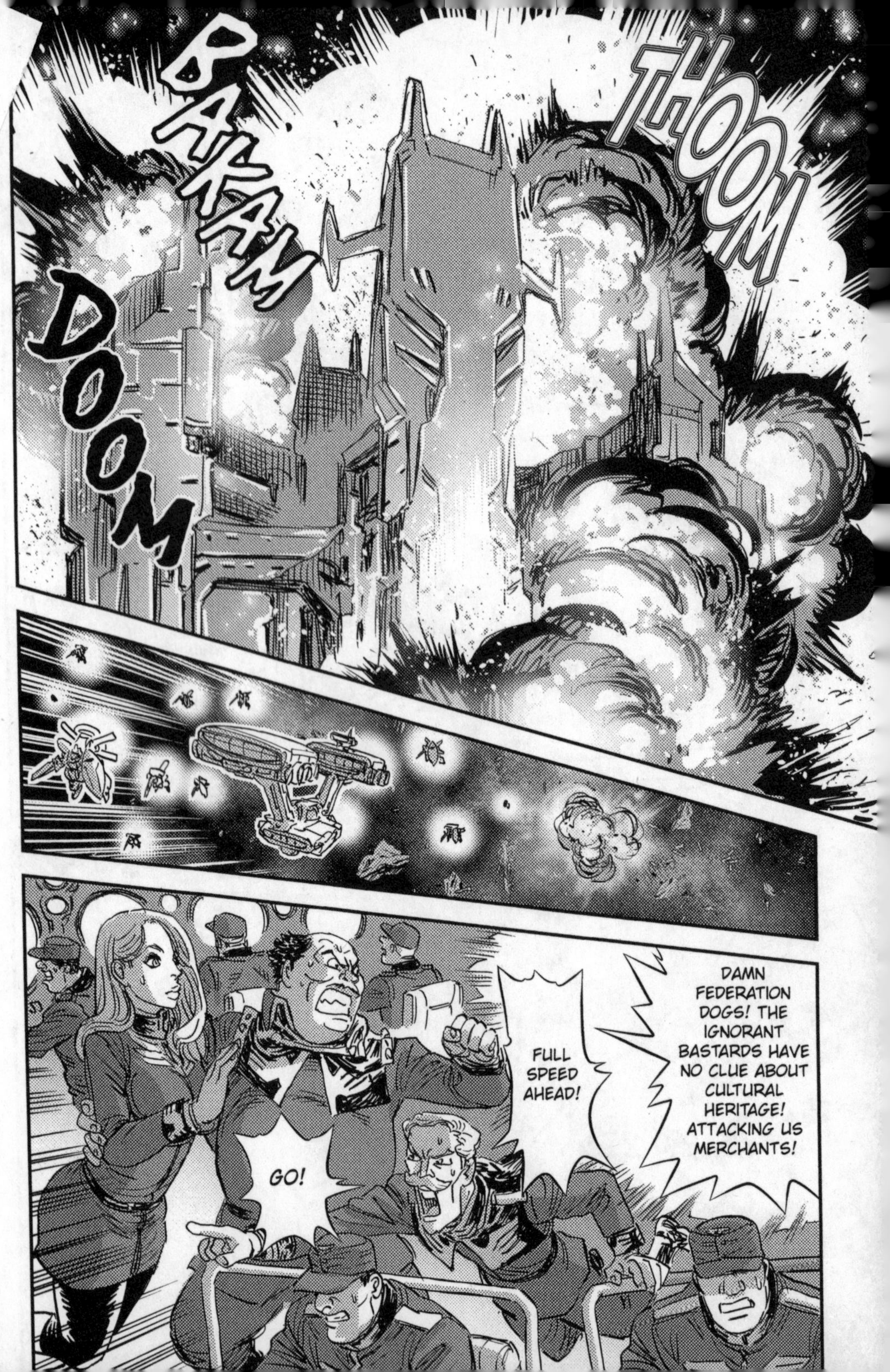
THOOM
BAKAM
DOOM
DAMN FEDERATION DOGS! THE IGNORANT BASTARDS HAVE NO CLUE ABOUT CULTURAL HERITAGE! ATTACKING US MERCHANTS!
FULL SPEED AHEAD!
GO!

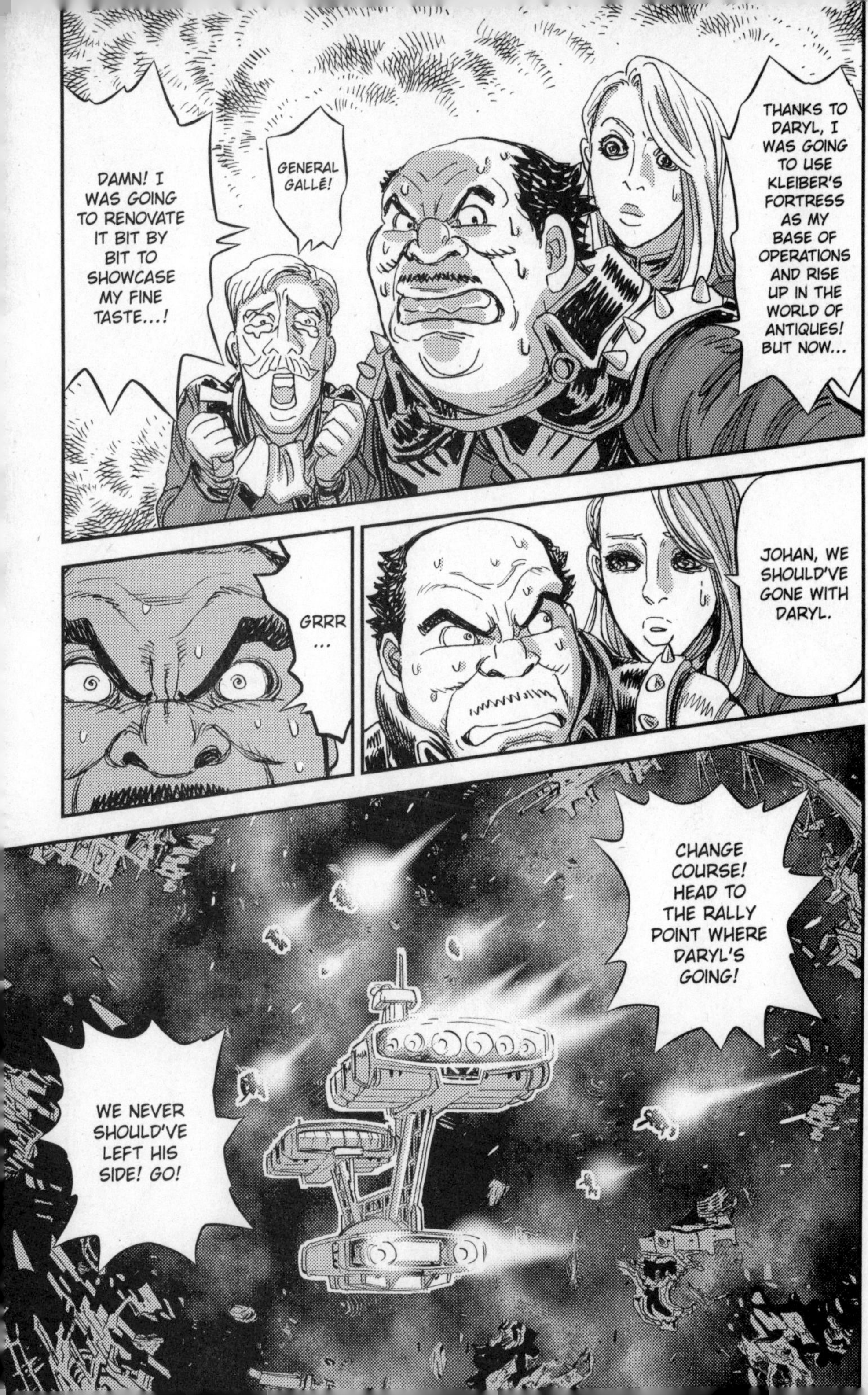
THANKS TO DARYL, I WAS GOING TO USE KLEIBER'S FORTRESS AS MY BASE OF OPERATIONS AND RISE UP IN THE WORLD OF ANTIQUES! BUT NOW...
GENERAL GALLÉ!
DAMN! I WAS GOING TO RENOVATE IT BIT BY BIT TO SHOWCASE MY FINE TASTE...!
JOHAN, WE SHOULD'VE GONE WITH DARYL.
GRRR ...
CHANGE COURSE! HEAD TO THE RALLY POINT WHERE DARYL'S GOING!
WE NEVER SHOULD'VE LEFT HIS SIDE! GO!

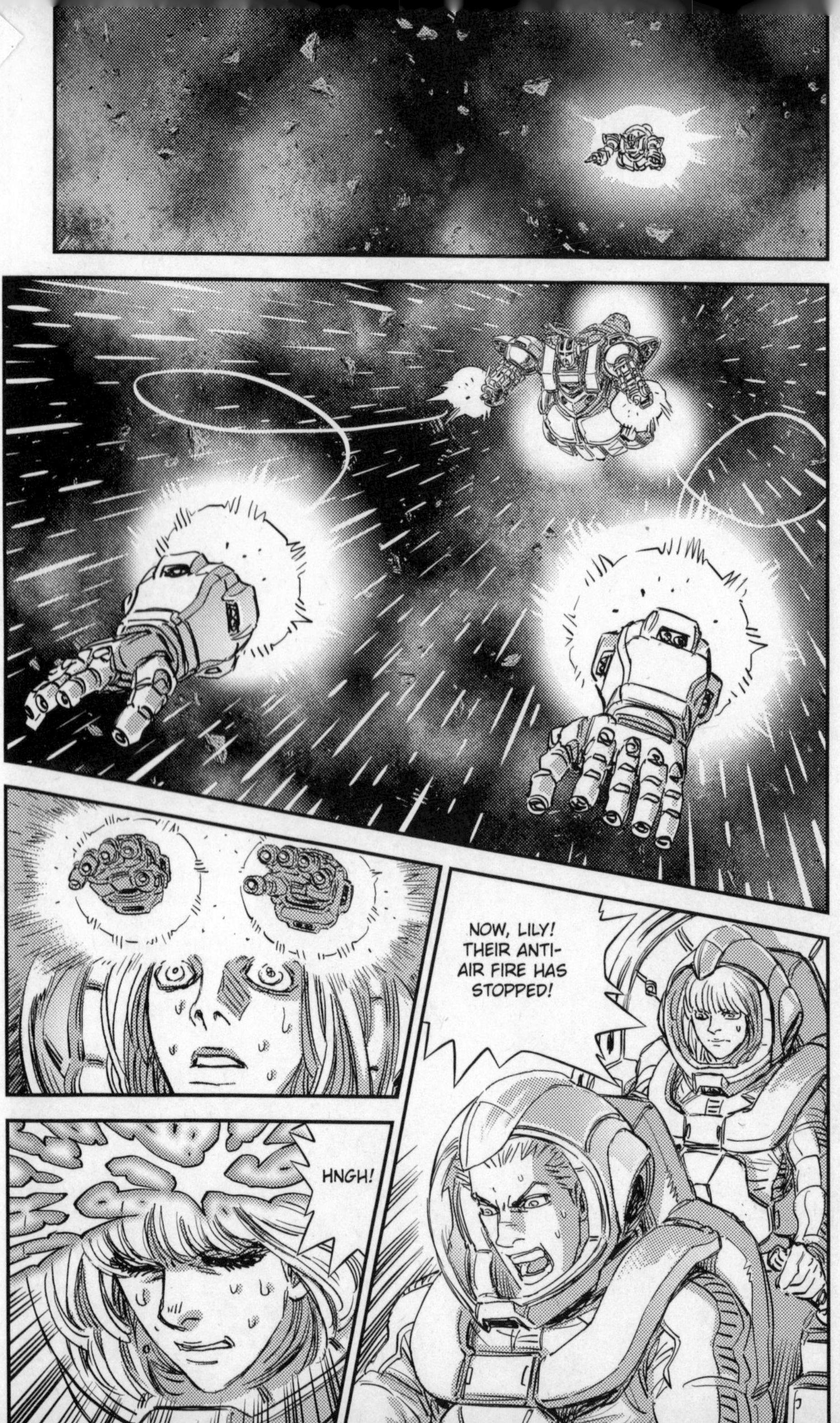
NOW, LILY! THEIR ANTI-AIR FIRE HAS STOPPED!
HNGH!

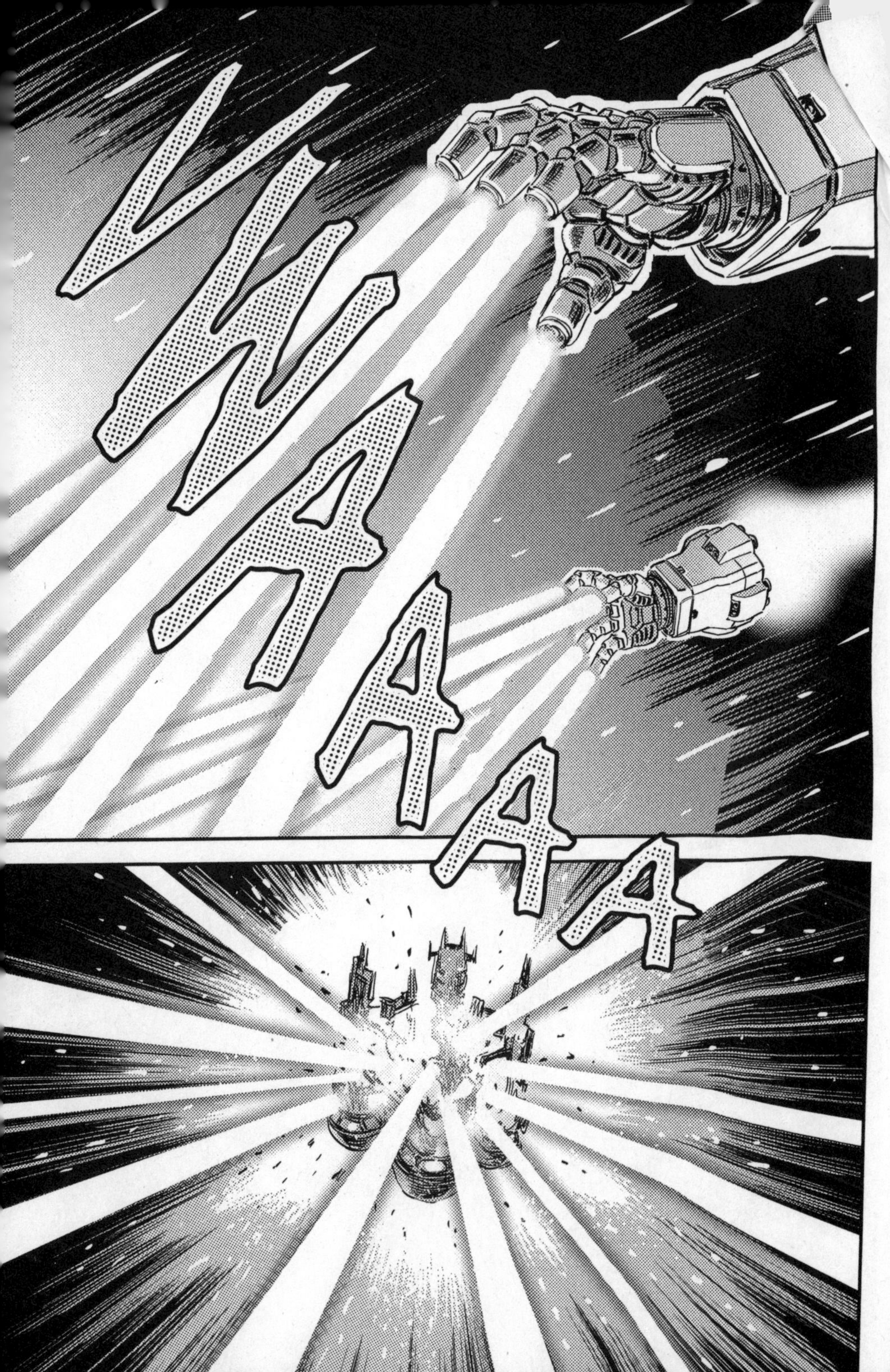
WHAAAAA

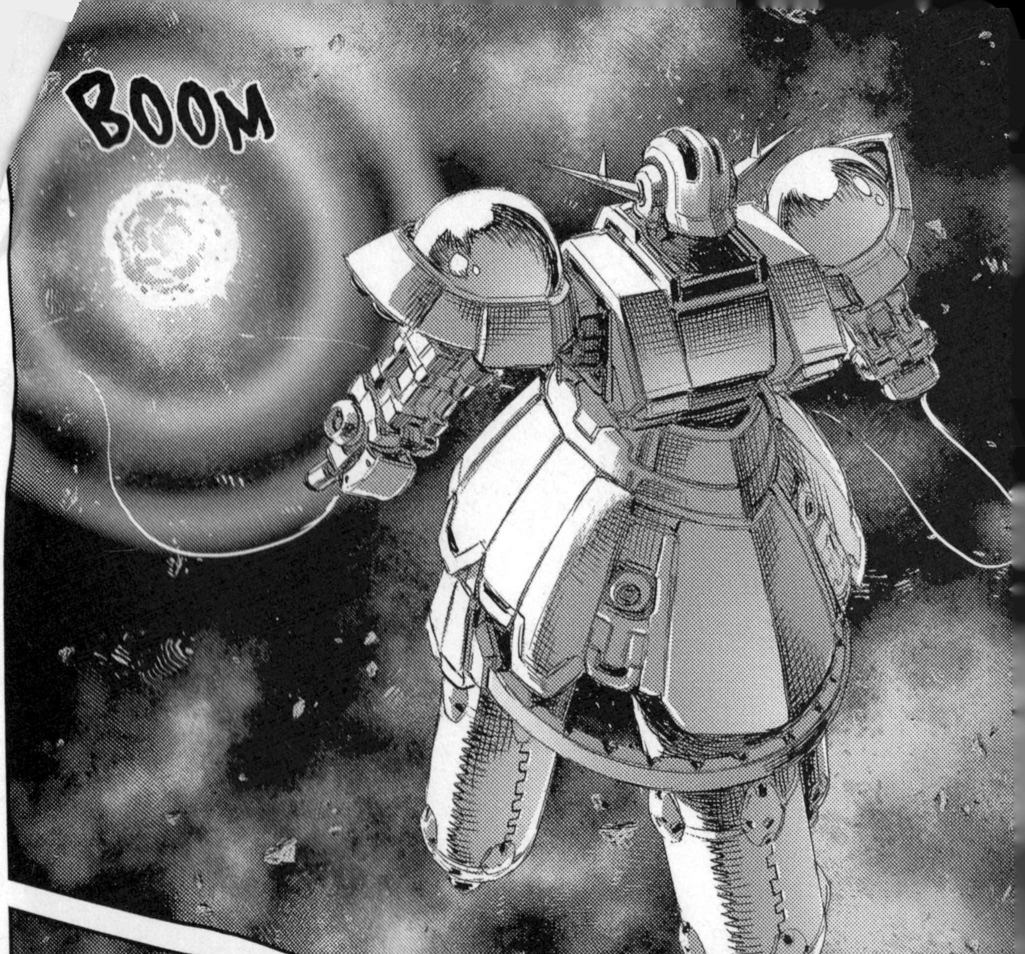
BOOM

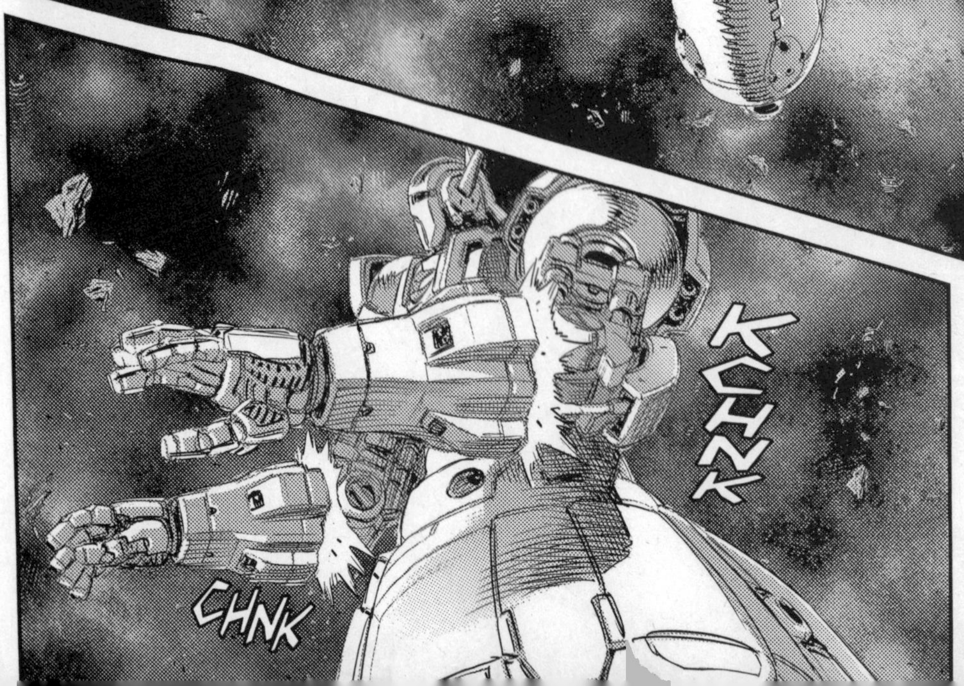
KCHNK
CHNK

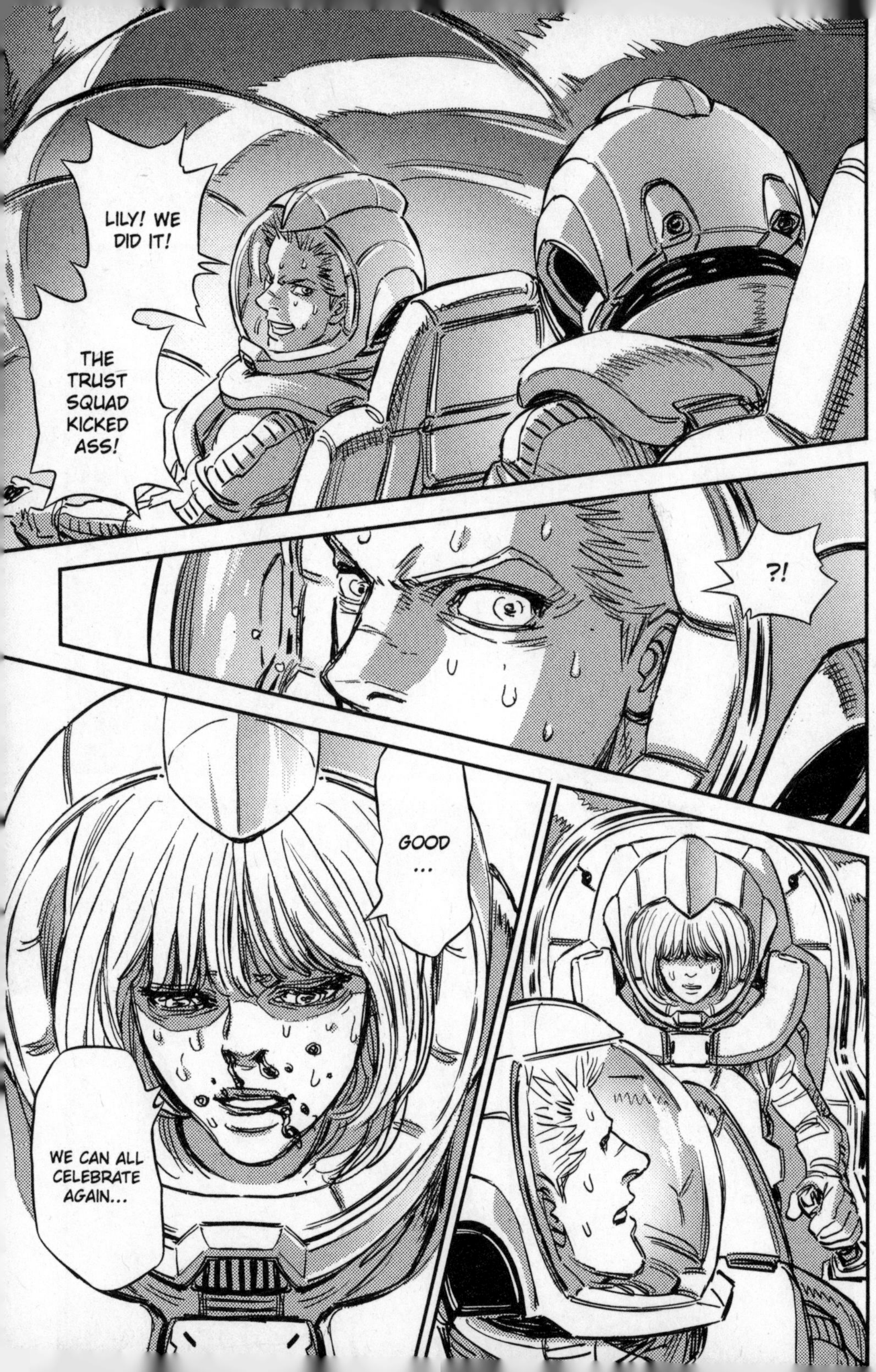

LILY! WE DID IT!
THE TRUST SQUAD KICKED ASS!
?!
GOOD ...
WE CAN ALL CELEBRATE AGAIN...

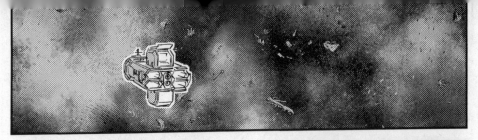

OPEN THE AFT HATCH!

DECK CREW, PREPARE FOR MOBILE SUIT RECOVERY!

THE ZEONG'S BACK! MEDICS STAND BY!

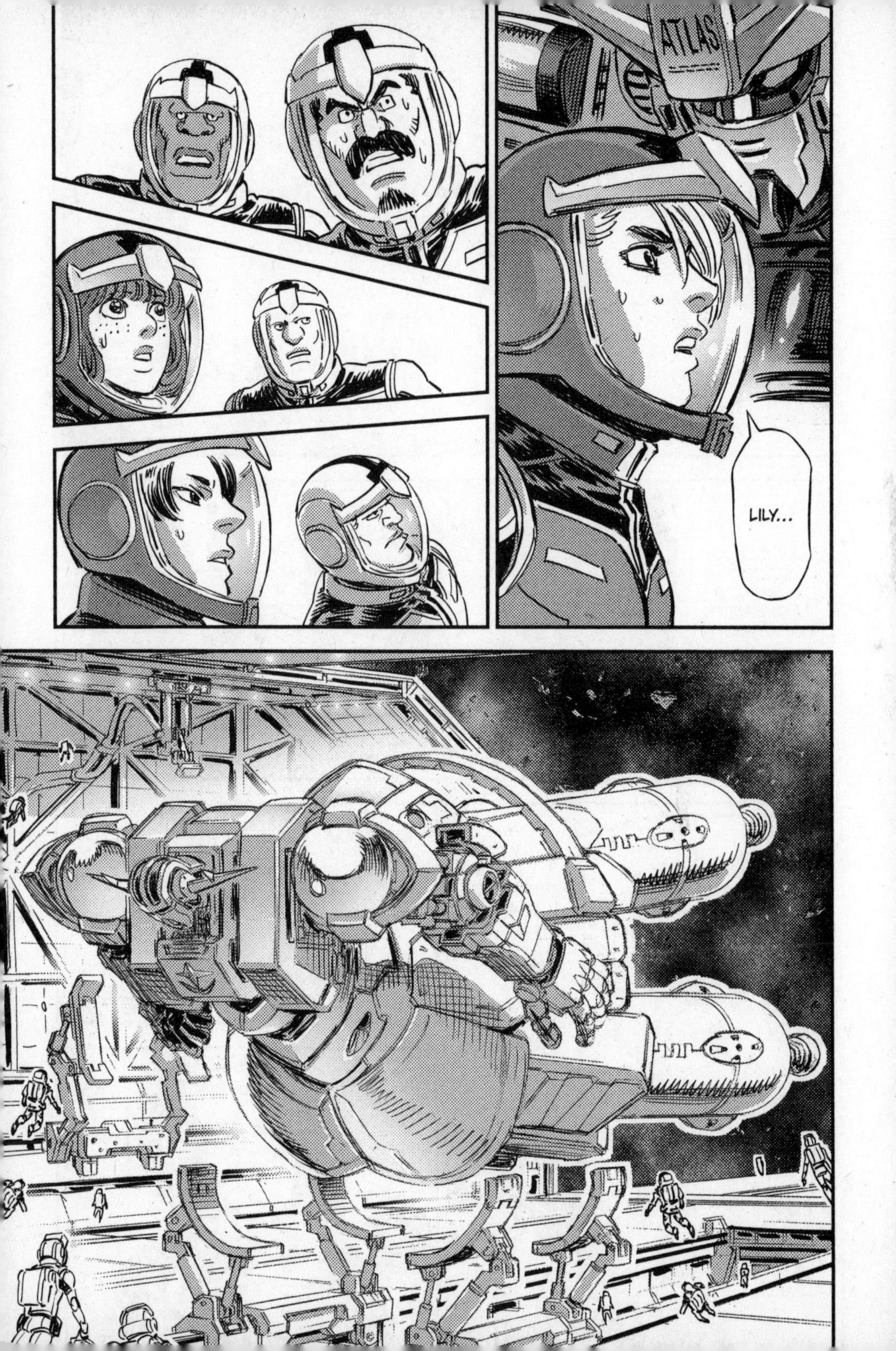
ATLAS
LILY...

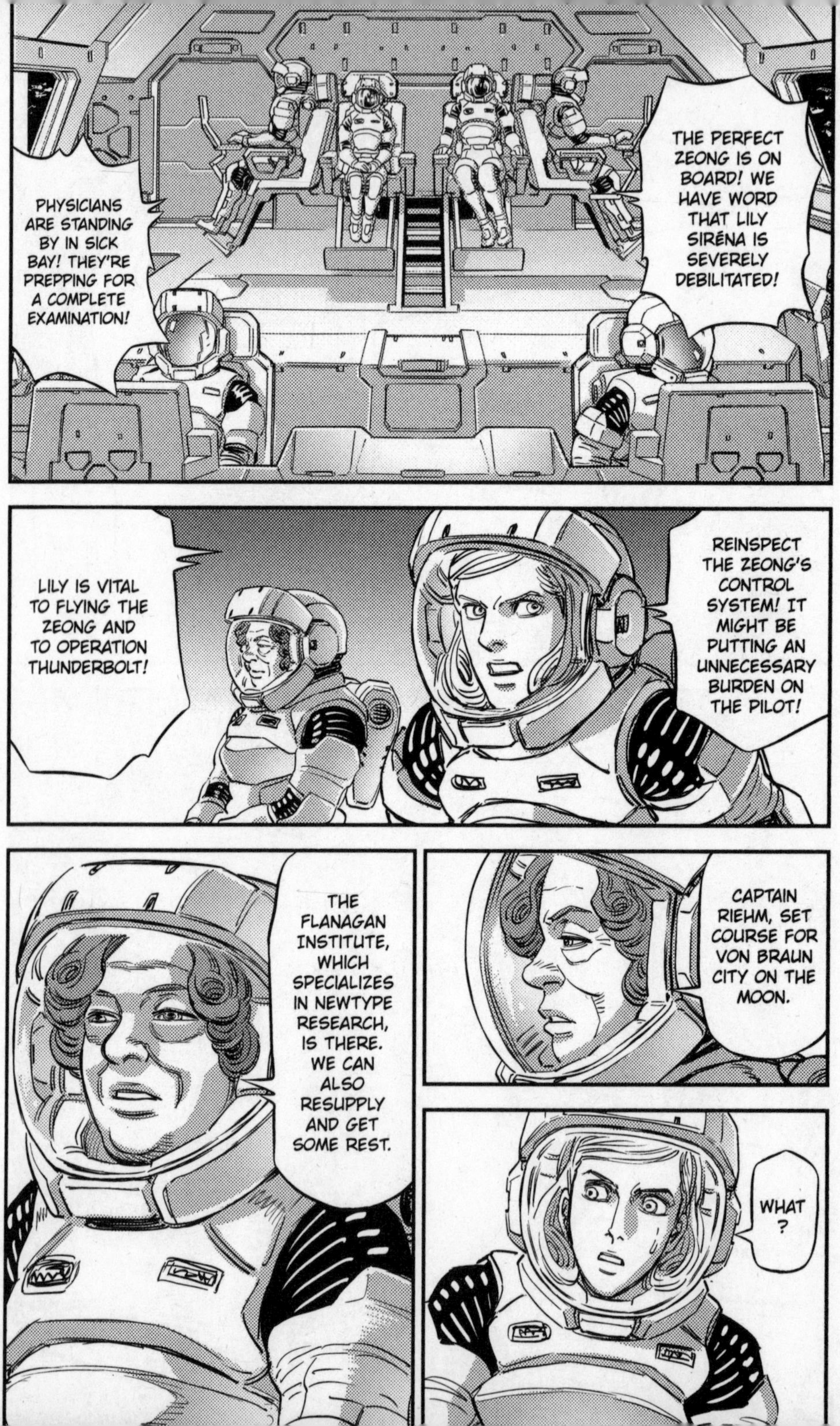
THE PERFECT ZEONG IS ON BOARD! WE HAVE WORD THAT LILY SIRÉNA IS SEVERELY DEBILITATED!
PHYSICIANS ARE STANDING BY IN SICK BAY! THEY'RE PREPPING FOR A COMPLETE EXAMINATION!
REINSPECT THE ZEONG'S CONTROL SYSTEM! IT MIGHT BE PUTTING AN UNNECESSARY BURDEN ON THE PILOT!
LILY IS VITAL TO FLYING THE ZEONG AND TO OPERATION THUNDERBOLT!
CAPTAIN RIEHM, SET COURSE FOR VON BRAUN CITY ON THE MOON.
WHAT?
THE FLANAGAN INSTITUTE, WHICH SPECIALIZES IN NEWTYPE RESEARCH, IS THERE. WE CAN ALSO RESUPPLY AND GET SOME REST.

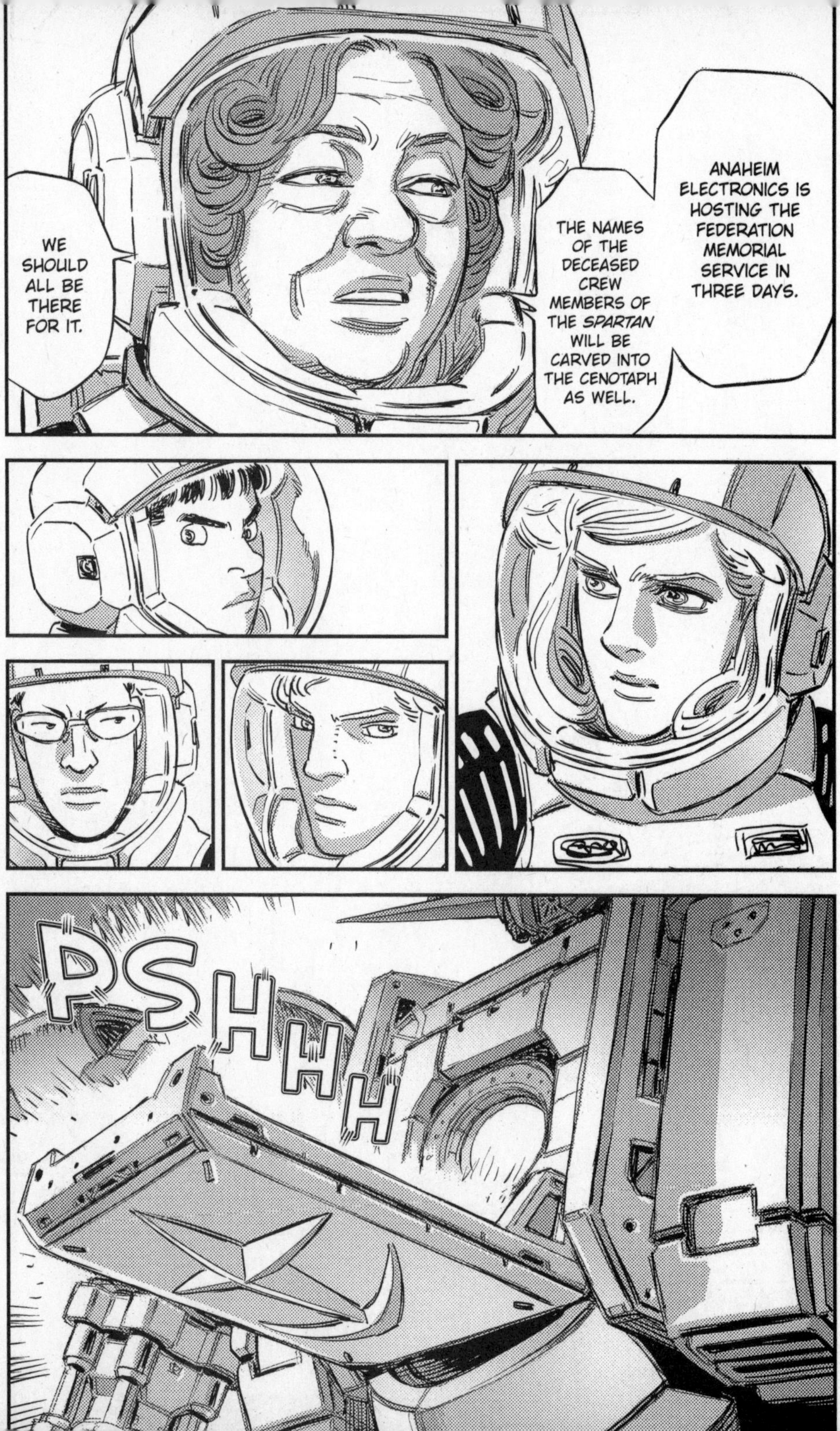
ANAHEIM ELECTRONICS IS HOSTING THE FEDERATION MEMORIAL SERVICE IN THREE DAYS.
THE NAMES OF THE DECEASED CREW MEMBERS OF THE *SPARTAN* WILL BE CARVED INTO THE CENOTAPH AS WELL.
WE SHOULD ALL BE THERE FOR IT.
PSHHHH

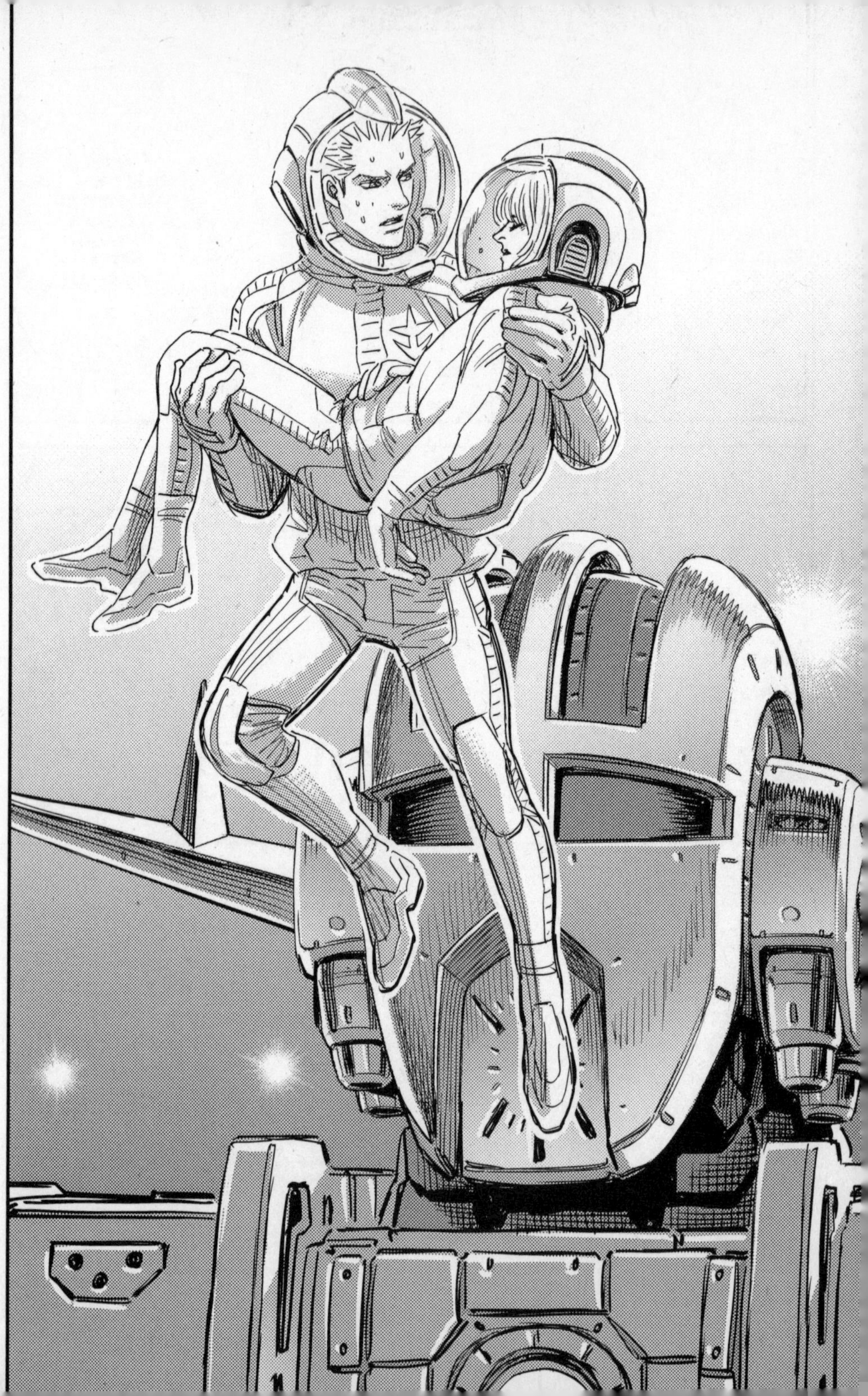

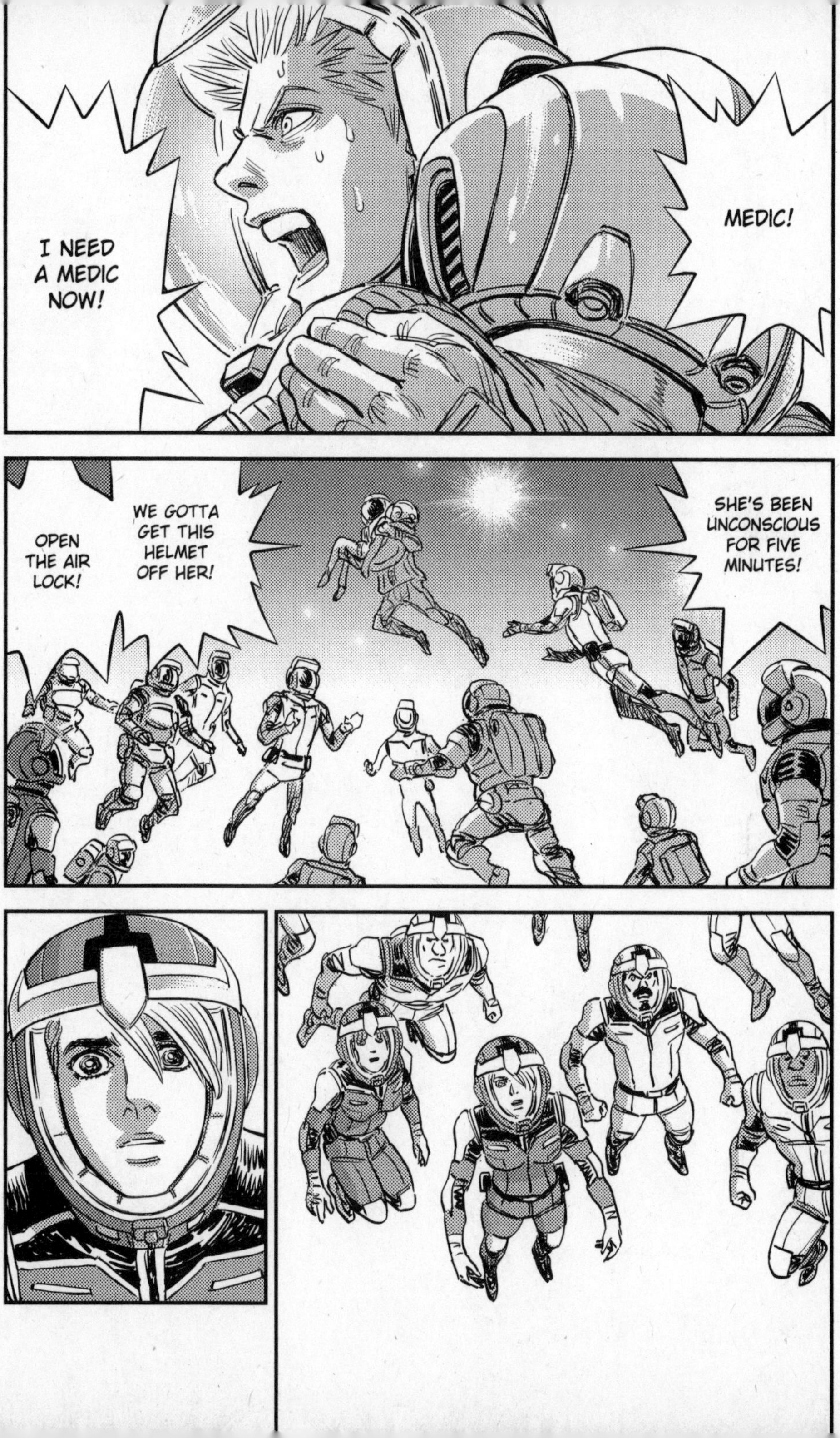
MEDIC!
I NEED A MEDIC NOW!
SHE'S BEEN UNCONSCIOUS FOR FIVE MINUTES!
WE GOTTA GET THIS HELMET OFF HER!
OPEN THE AIR LOCK!

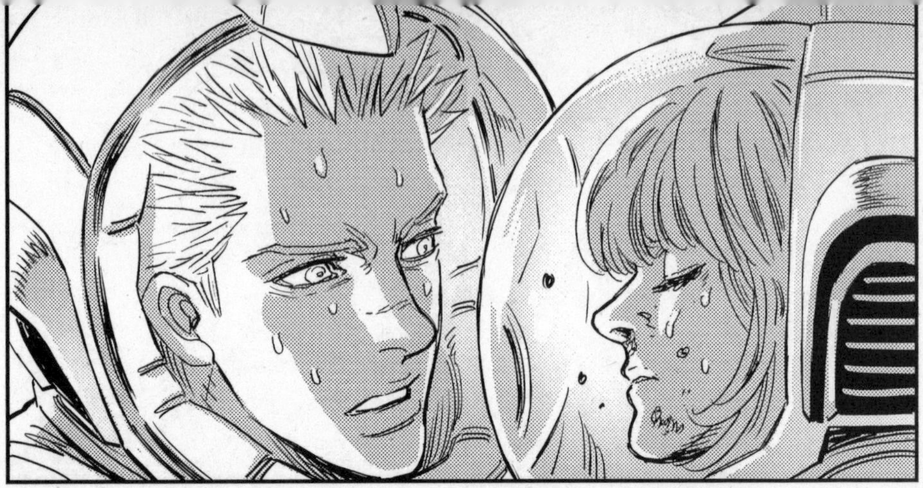

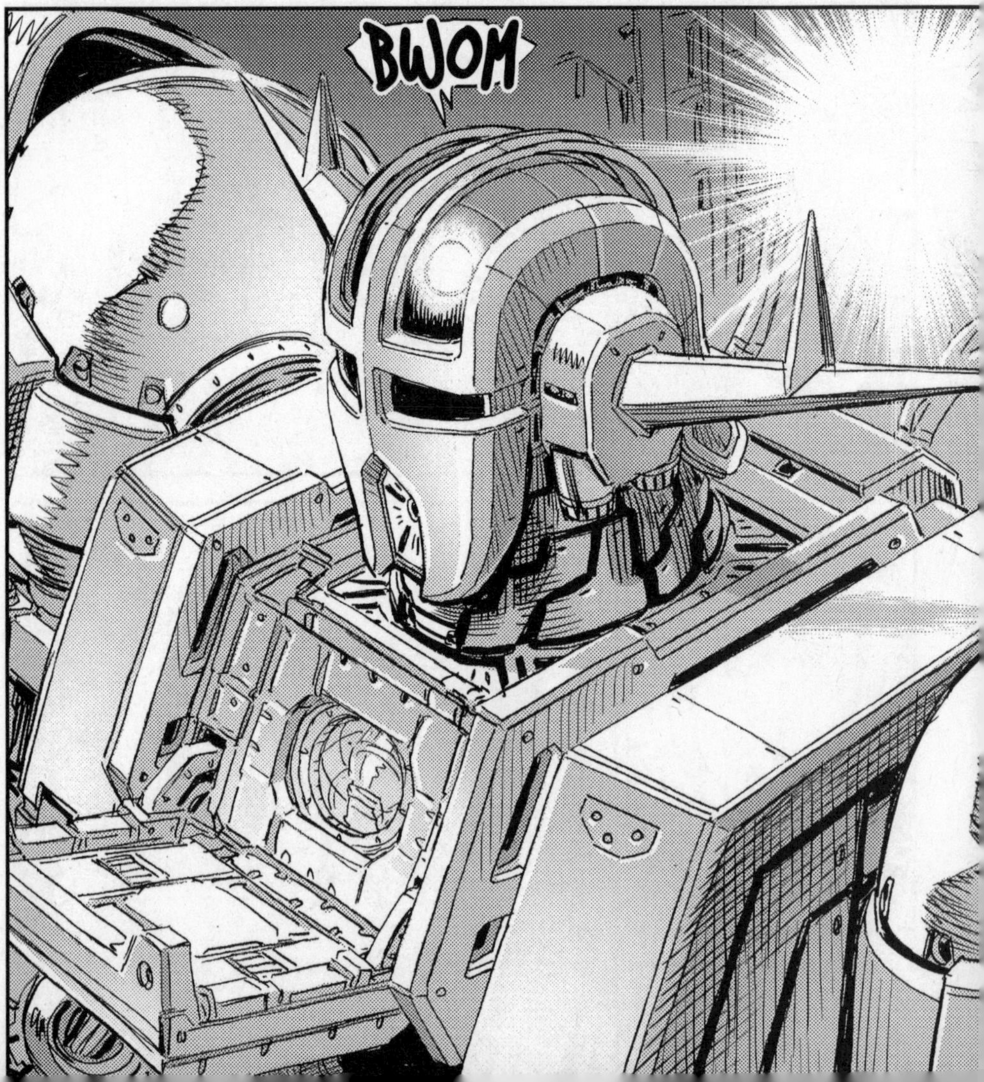
BWOM

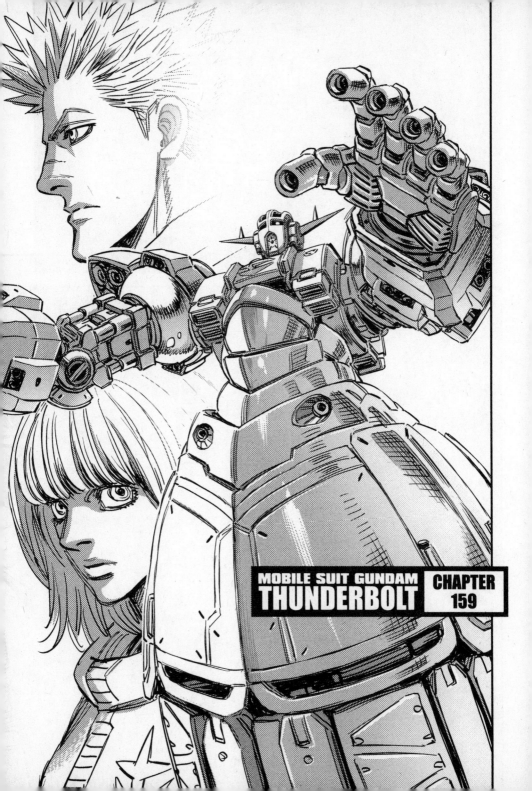

MOBILE SUIT GUNDAM
THUNDERBOLT

CHAPTER
159

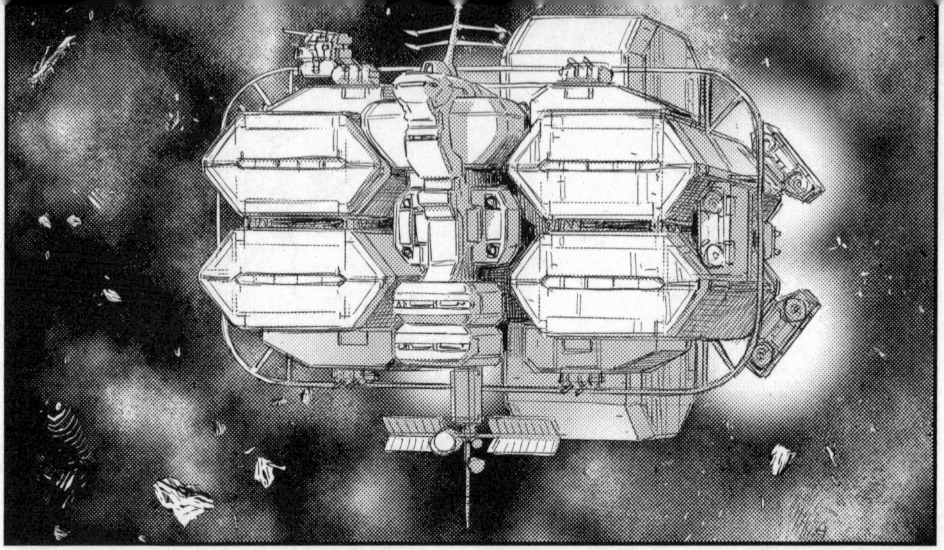
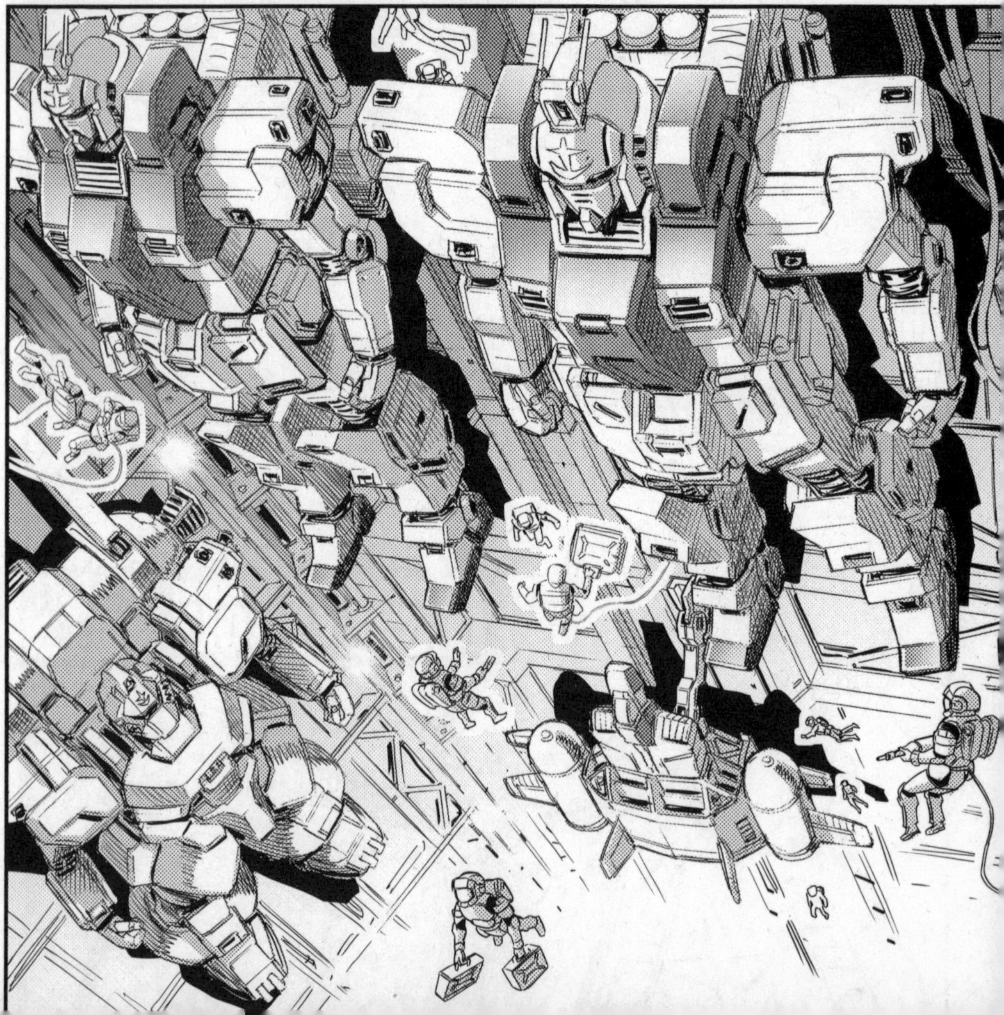

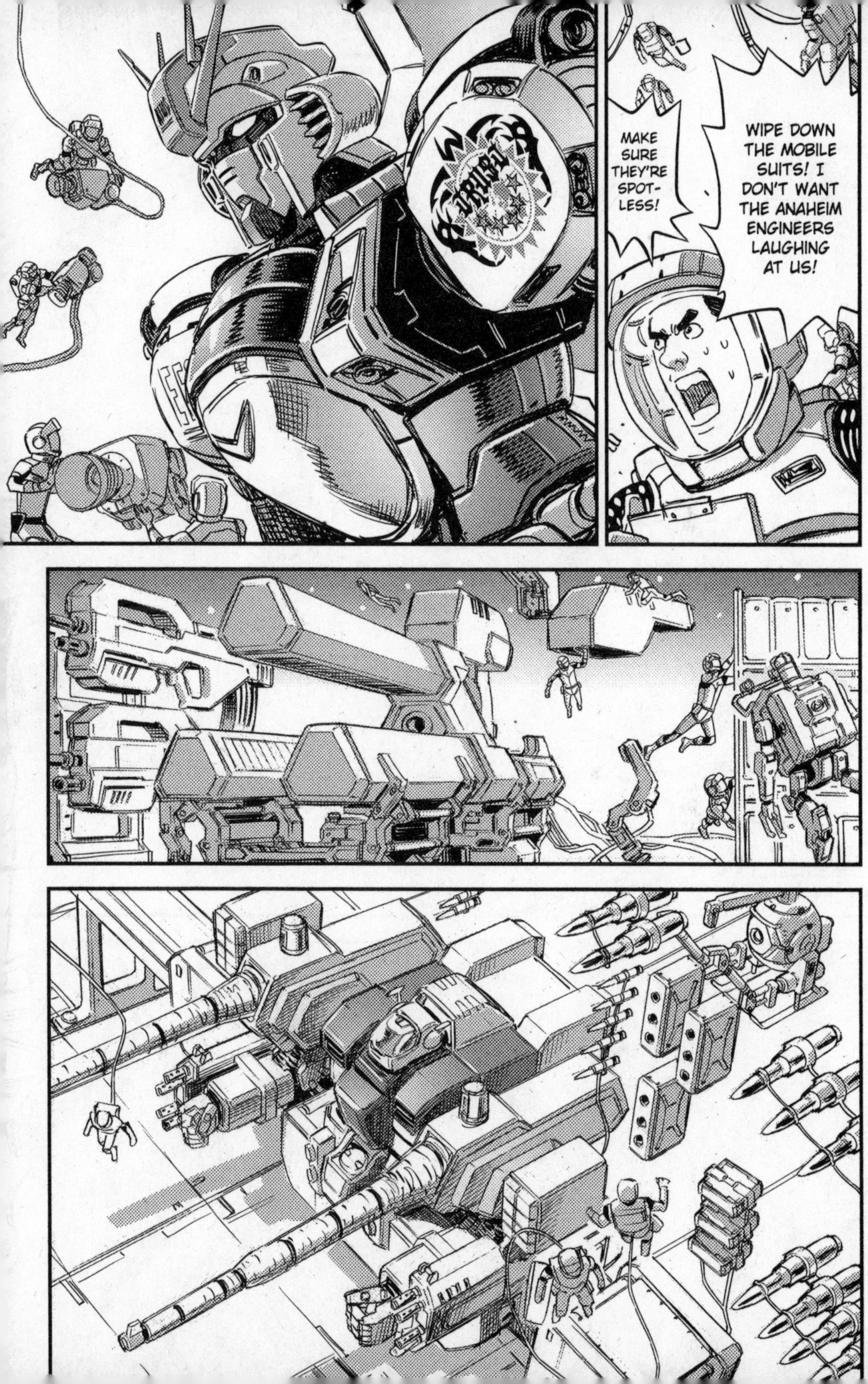
WIPE DOWN THE MOBILE SUITS! I DON'T WANT THE ANAHEIM ENGINEERS LAUGHING AT US!
MAKE SURE THEY'RE SPOT-LESS!

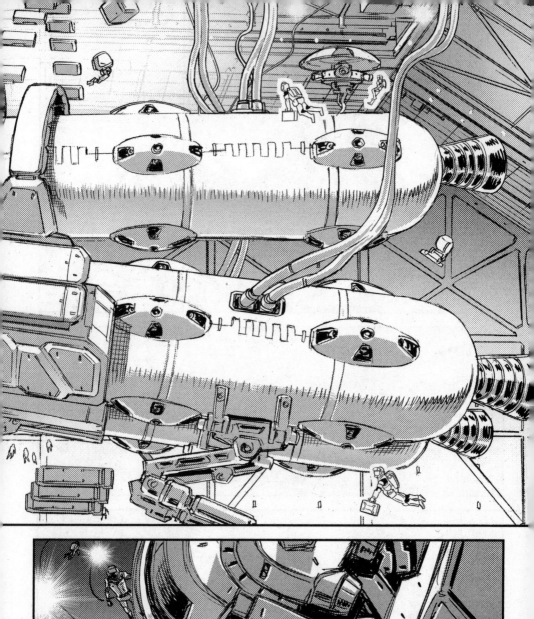

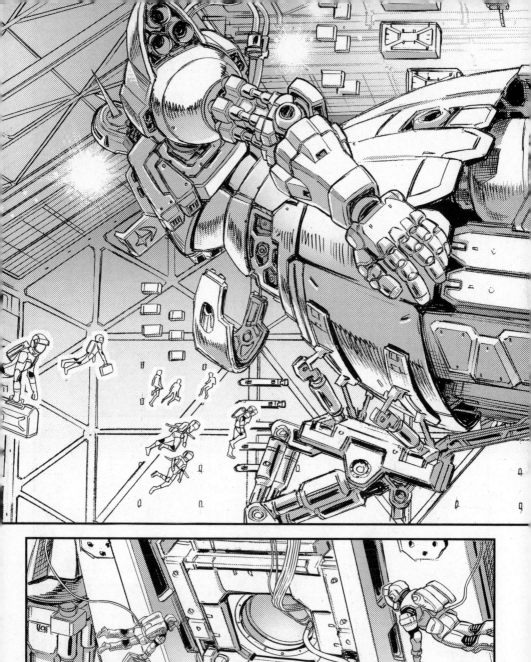
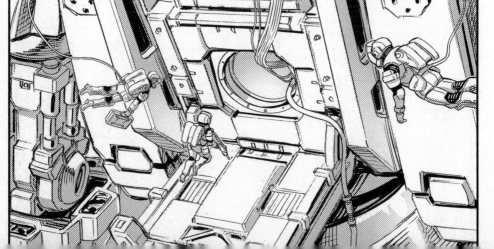

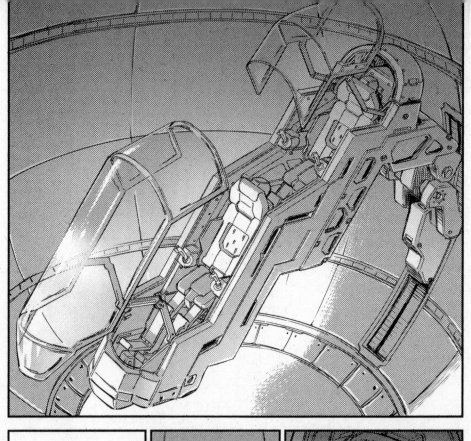

SICK BAY

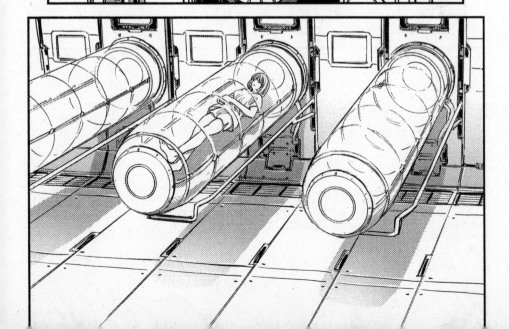

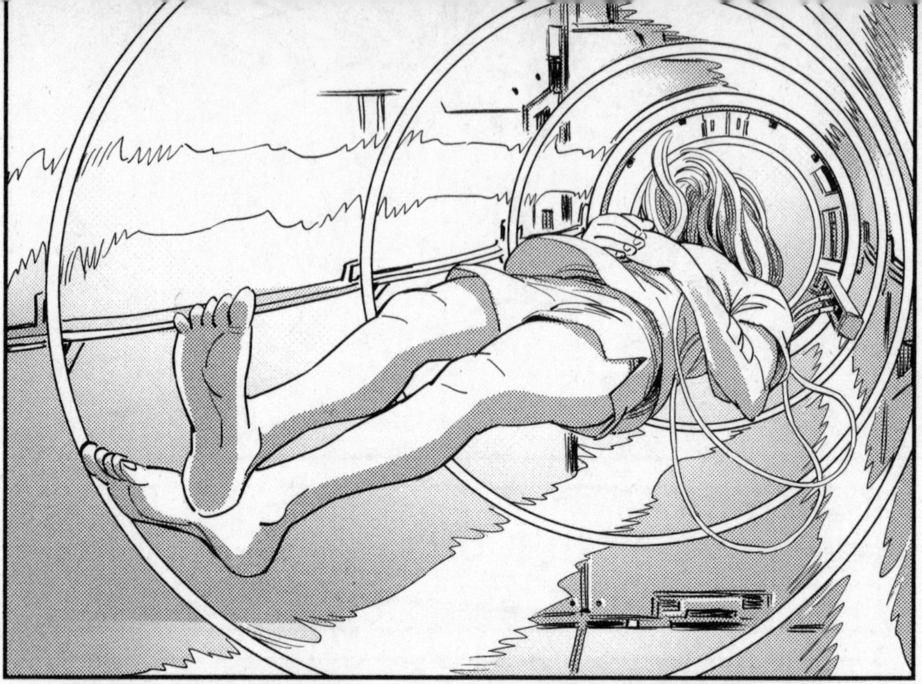

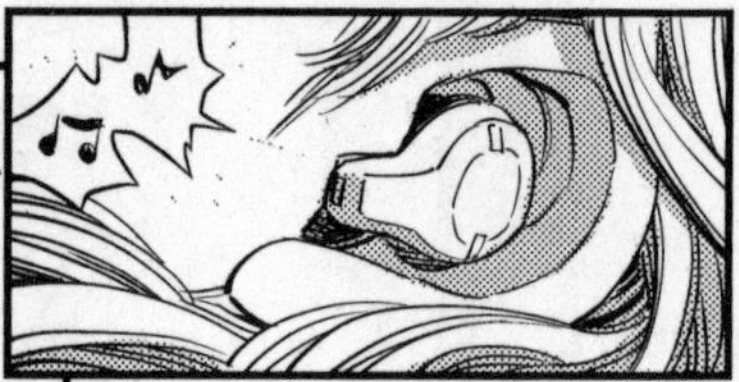

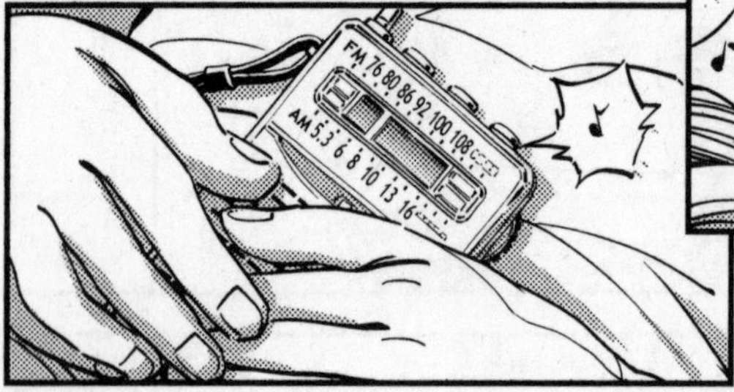
FM 76 80 86 92 100 108
AM 5.3 6 8 10 13 16

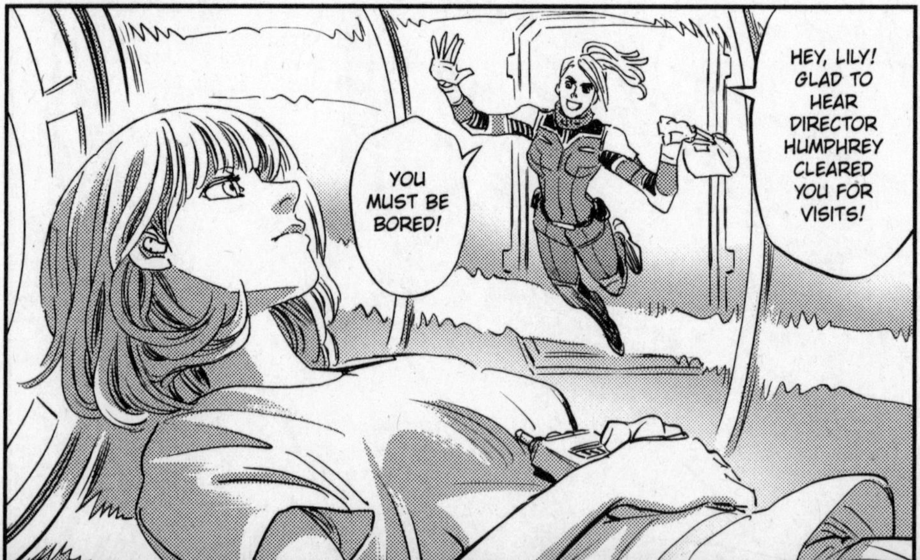
HEY, LILY! GLAD TO HEAR DIRECTOR HUMPHREY CLEARED YOU FOR VISITS!
YOU MUST BE BORED!

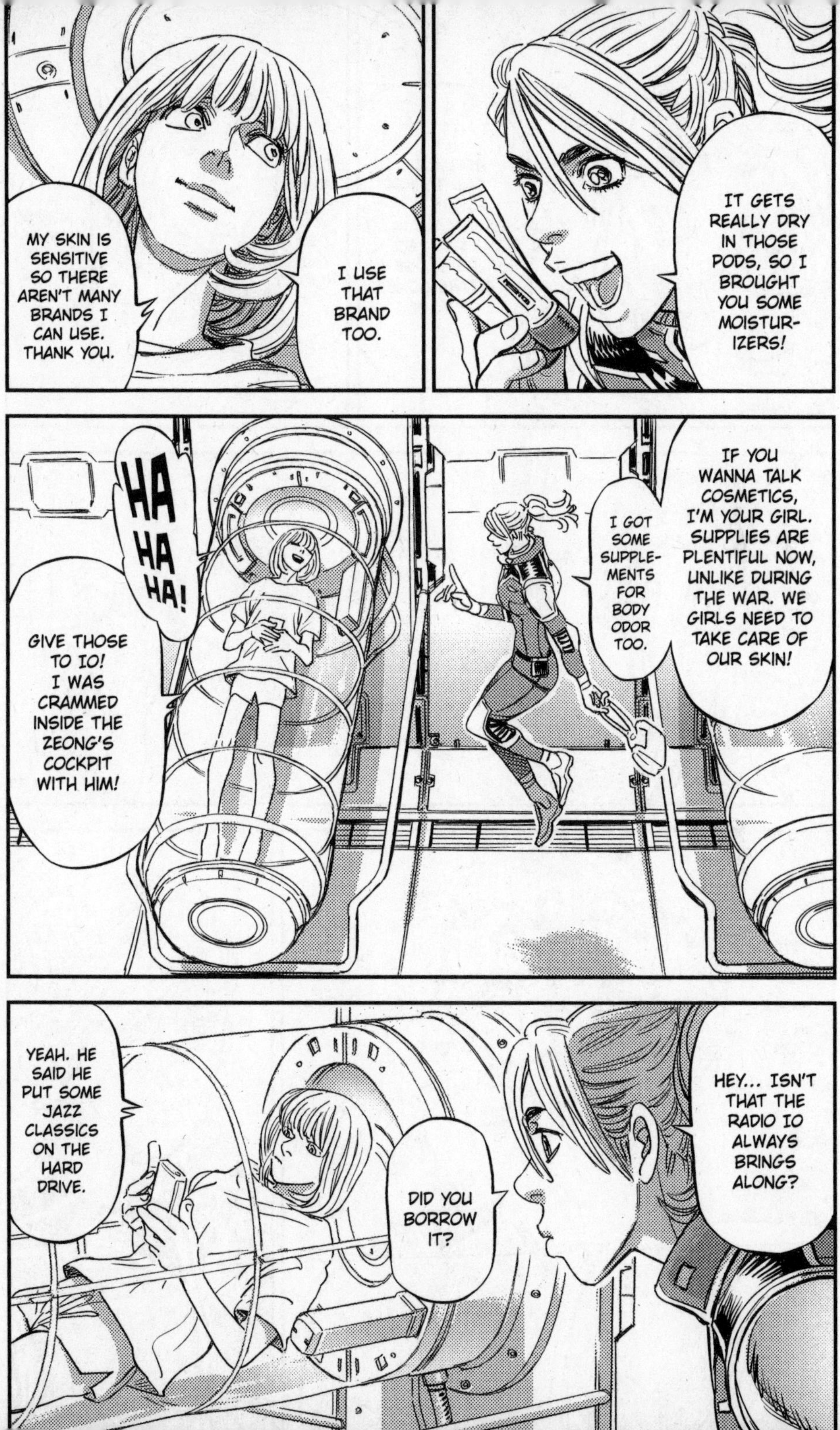
IT GETS REALLY DRY IN THOSE PODS, SO I BROUGHT YOU SOME MOISTUR-IZERS!
I USE THAT BRAND TOO.
MY SKIN IS SENSITIVE SO THERE AREN'T MANY BRANDS I CAN USE. THANK YOU.
IF YOU WANNA TALK COSMETICS, I'M YOUR GIRL. SUPPLIES ARE PLENTIFUL NOW, UNLIKE DURING THE WAR. WE GIRLS NEED TO TAKE CARE OF OUR SKIN!
I GOT SOME SUPPLE-MENTS FOR BODY ODOR TOO.
HA HA HA!
GIVE THOSE TO IO! I WAS CRAMMED INSIDE THE ZEONG'S COCKPIT WITH HIM!
HEY... ISN'T THAT THE RADIO IO ALWAYS BRINGS ALONG?
DID YOU BORROW IT?
YEAH. HE SAID HE PUT SOME JAZZ CLASSICS ON THE HARD DRIVE.

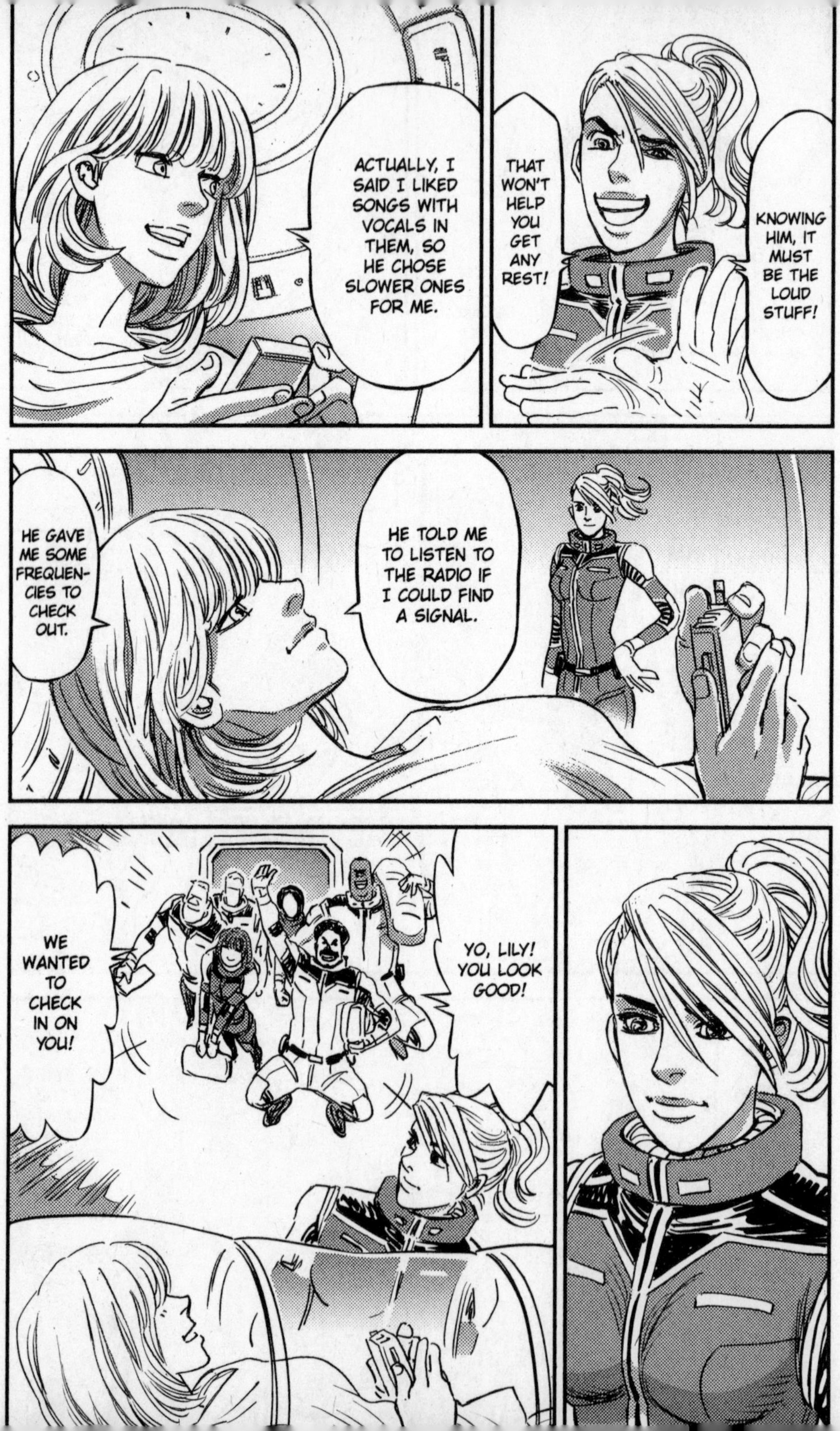
KNOWING HIM, IT MUST BE THE LOUD STUFF!
THAT WON'T HELP YOU GET ANY REST!
ACTUALLY, I SAID I LIKED SONGS WITH VOCALS IN THEM, SO HE CHOSE SLOWER ONES FOR ME.
HE TOLD ME TO LISTEN TO THE RADIO IF I COULD FIND A SIGNAL.
HE GAVE ME SOME FREQUENCIES TO CHECK OUT.
YO, LILY! YOU LOOK GOOD!
WE WANTED TO CHECK IN ON YOU!

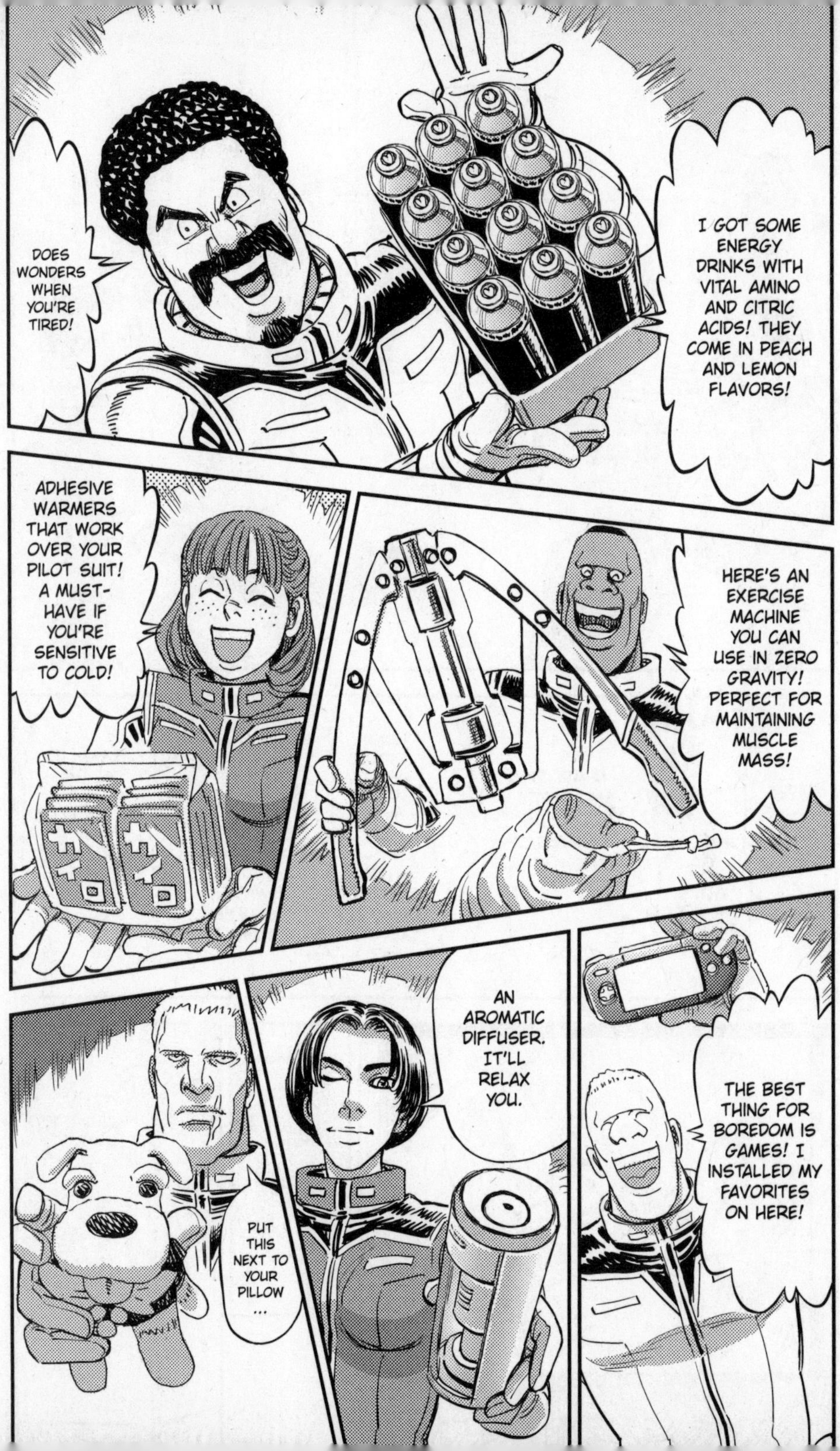
I GOT SOME ENERGY DRINKS WITH VITAL AMINO AND CITRIC ACIDS! THEY COME IN PEACH AND LEMON FLAVORS!
DOES WONDERS WHEN YOU'RE TIRED!
HERE'S AN EXERCISE MACHINE YOU CAN USE IN ZERO GRAVITY! PERFECT FOR MAINTAINING MUSCLE MASS!
ADHESIVE WARMERS THAT WORK OVER YOUR PILOT SUIT! A MUST-HAVE IF YOU'RE SENSITIVE TO COLD!
THE BEST THING FOR BOREDOM IS GAMES! I INSTALLED MY FAVORITES ON HERE!
AN AROMATIC DIFFUSER. IT'LL RELAX YOU.
PUT THIS NEXT TO YOUR PILLOW ...

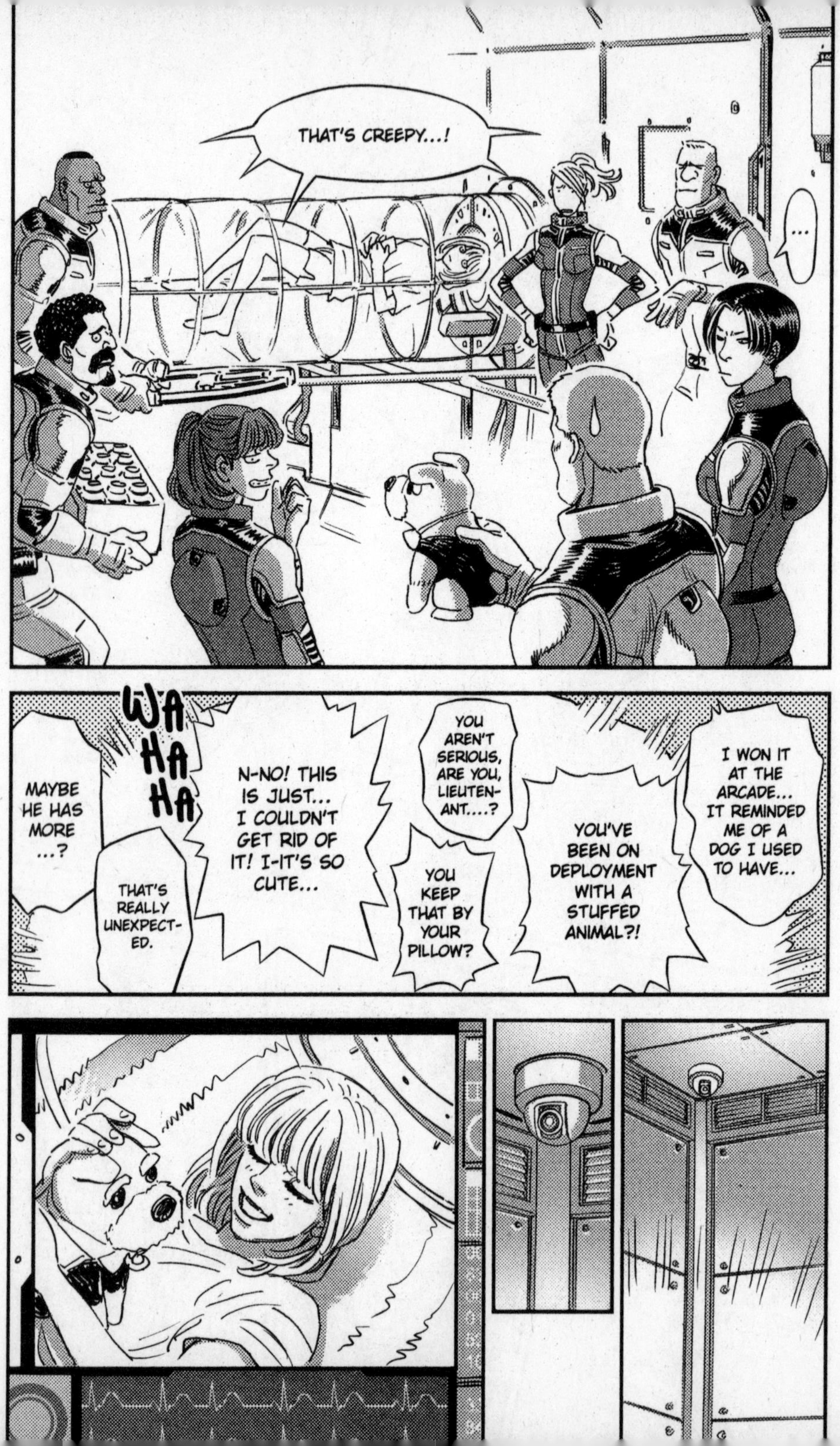
...
THAT'S CREEPY...!
I WON IT AT THE ARCADE... IT REMINDED ME OF A DOG I USED TO HAVE...
YOU'VE BEEN ON DEPLOYMENT WITH A STUFFED ANIMAL?!
YOU AREN'T SERIOUS, ARE YOU, LIEUTEN-ANT....?
YOU KEEP THAT BY YOUR PILLOW?
N-NO! THIS IS JUST... I COULDN'T GET RID OF IT! I-IT'S SO CUTE...
WA HA HA
MAYBE HE HAS MORE ...?
THAT'S REALLY UNEXPECT-ED.

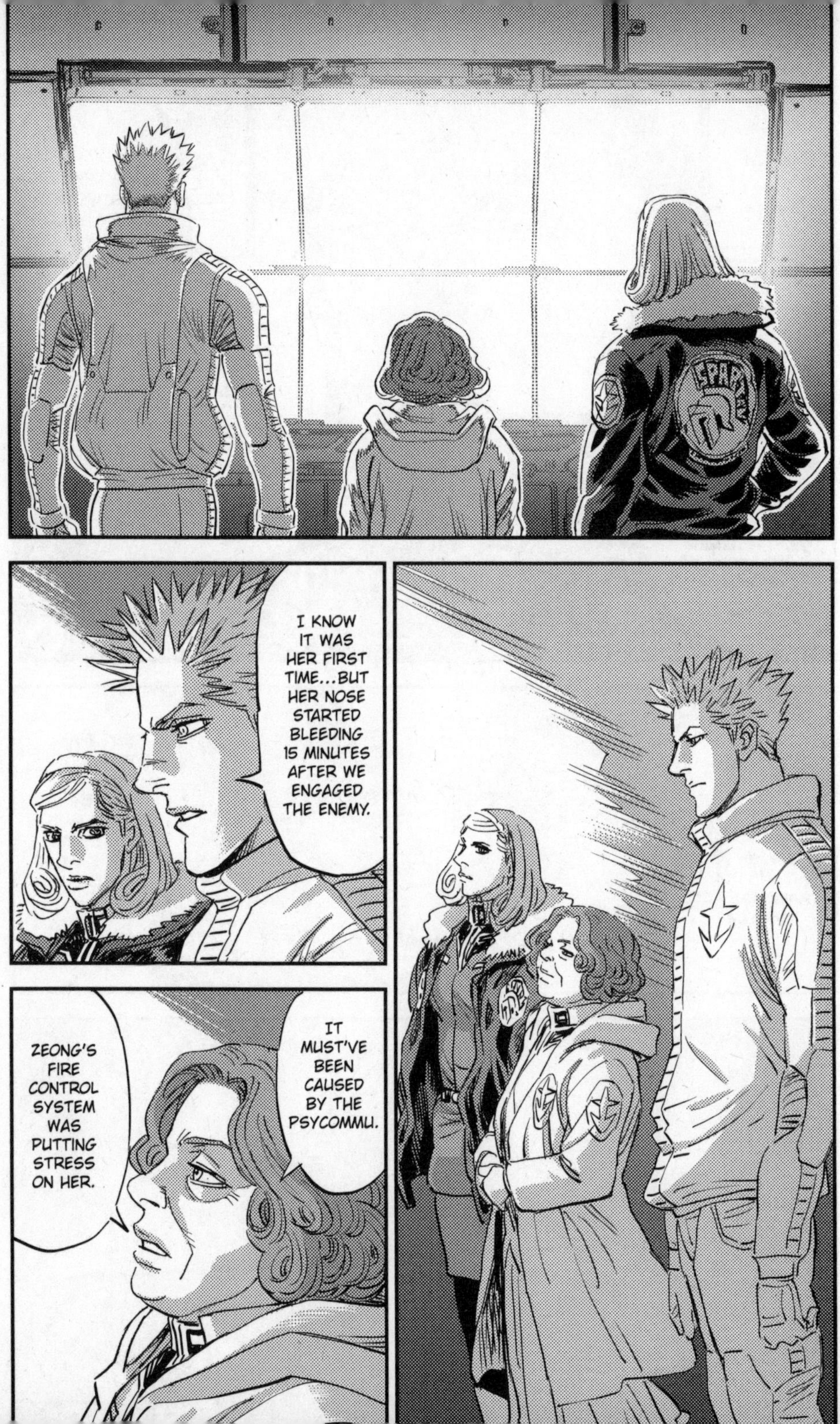
I KNOW IT WAS HER FIRST TIME...BUT HER NOSE STARTED BLEEDING 15 MINUTES AFTER WE ENGAGED THE ENEMY.
IT MUST'VE BEEN CAUSED BY THE PSYCOMMU.
ZEONG'S FIRE CONTROL SYSTEM WAS PUTTING STRESS ON HER.

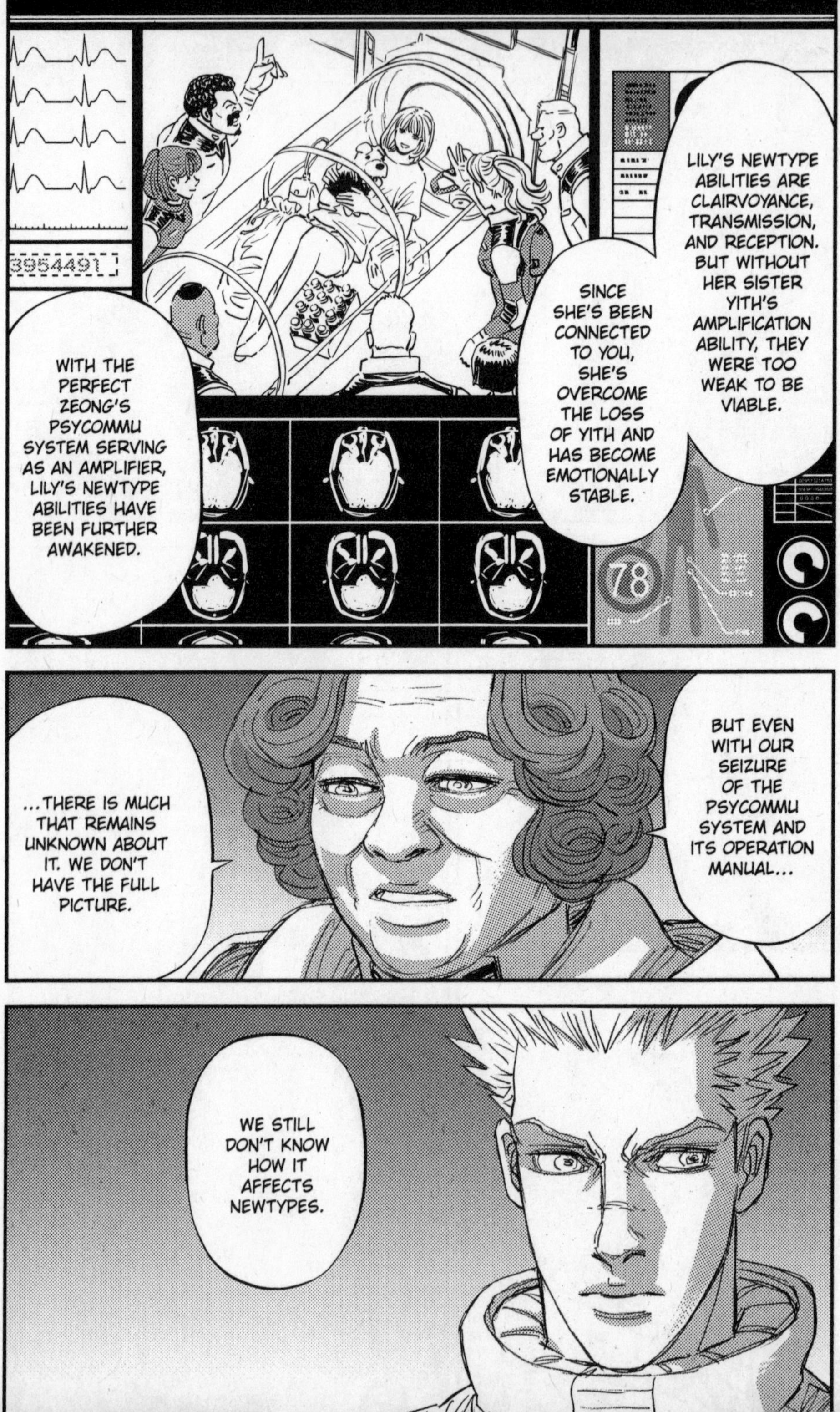
LILY'S NEWTYPE ABILITIES ARE CLAIRVOYANCE, TRANSMISSION, AND RECEPTION. BUT WITHOUT HER SISTER YITH'S AMPLIFICATION ABILITY, THEY WERE TOO WEAK TO BE VIABLE.
SINCE SHE'S BEEN CONNECTED TO YOU, SHE'S OVERCOME THE LOSS OF YITH AND HAS BECOME EMOTIONALLY STABLE.
78
WITH THE PERFECT ZEONG'S PSYCOMMU SYSTEM SERVING AS AN AMPLIFIER, LILY'S NEWTYPE ABILITIES HAVE BEEN FURTHER AWAKENED.
3954491
BUT EVEN WITH OUR SEIZURE OF THE PSYCOMMU SYSTEM AND ITS OPERATION MANUAL...
...THERE IS MUCH THAT REMAINS UNKNOWN ABOUT IT. WE DON'T HAVE THE FULL PICTURE.
WE STILL DON'T KNOW HOW IT AFFECTS NEWTYPES.

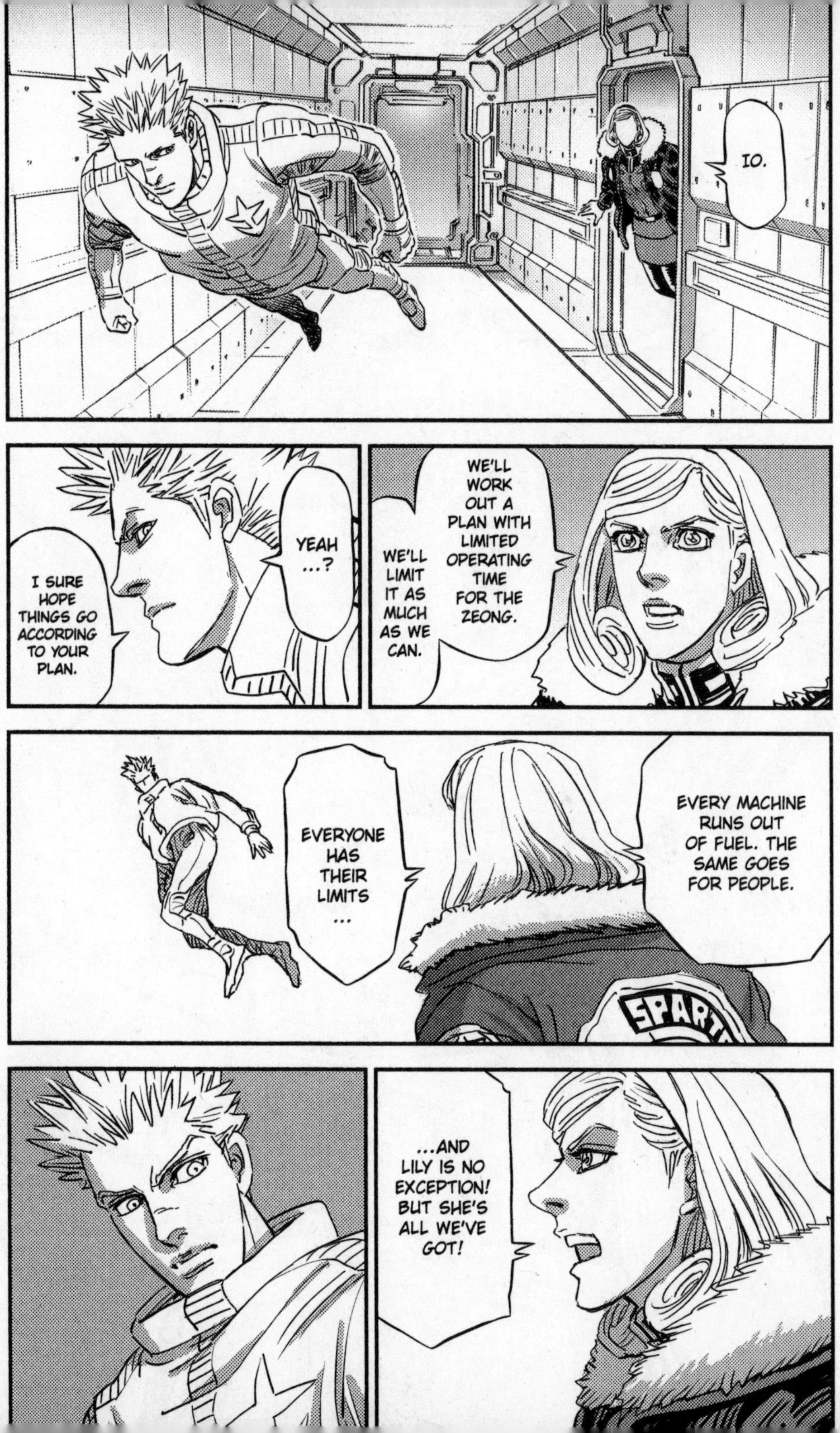
IO.
WE'LL WORK OUT A PLAN WITH LIMITED OPERATING TIME FOR THE ZEONG.
WE'LL LIMIT IT AS MUCH AS WE CAN.
YEAH ...?
I SURE HOPE THINGS GO ACCORDING TO YOUR PLAN.
EVERY MACHINE RUNS OUT OF FUEL. THE SAME GOES FOR PEOPLE.
EVERYONE HAS THEIR LIMITS ...
...AND LILY IS NO EXCEPTION! BUT SHE'S ALL WE'VE GOT!

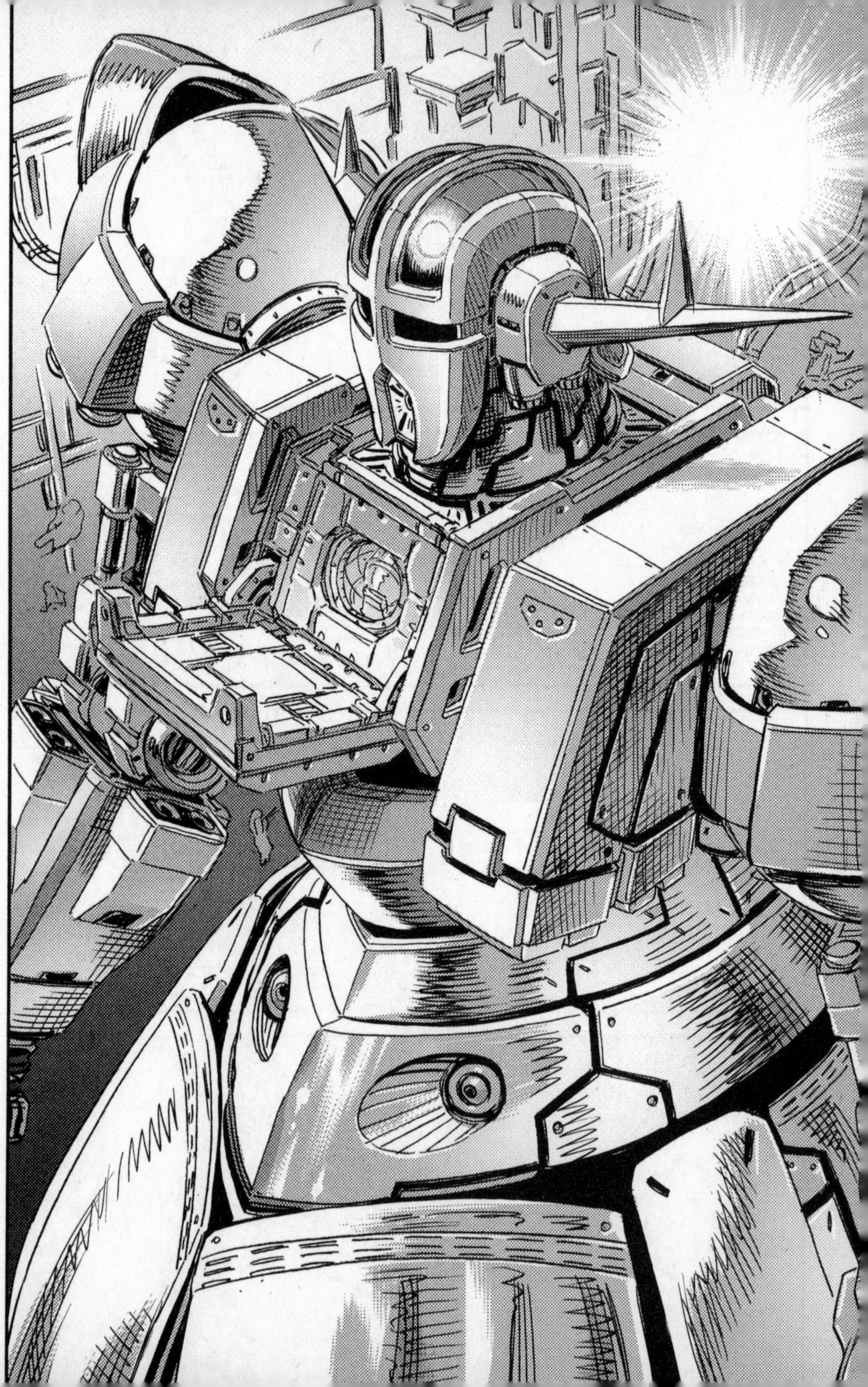

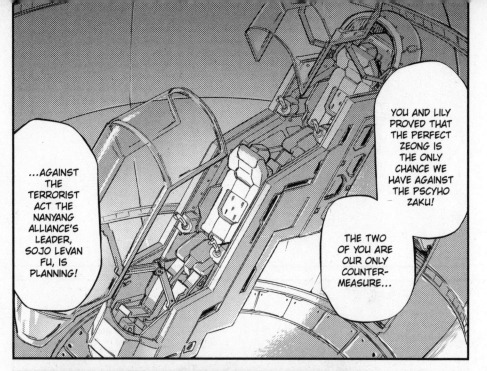

YOU AND LILY PROVED THAT THE PERFECT ZEONG IS THE ONLY CHANCE WE HAVE AGAINST THE PSCYHO ZAKU!
THE TWO OF YOU ARE OUR ONLY COUNTER-MEASURE...
...AGAINST THE TERRORIST ACT THE NANYANG ALLIANCE'S LEADER, SOJO LEVAN FU, IS PLANNING!
EVEN IF ZEON'S PSYCOMMU SYSTEM IS AN UNKNOWN TECHNOLOGY HIDDEN INSIDE A BLACK BOX...
IT'S THE ONLY CHOICE WE HAVE!
WE MAY LOSE LILY... BUT THAT'S THE ONLY WAY WE'LL GET DARYL LORENZ!

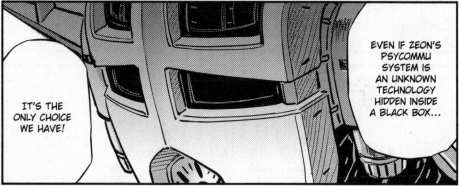

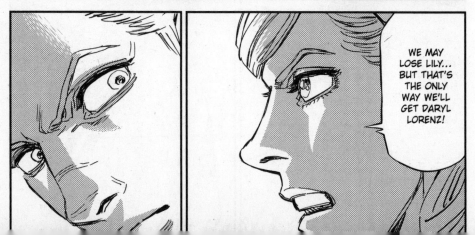

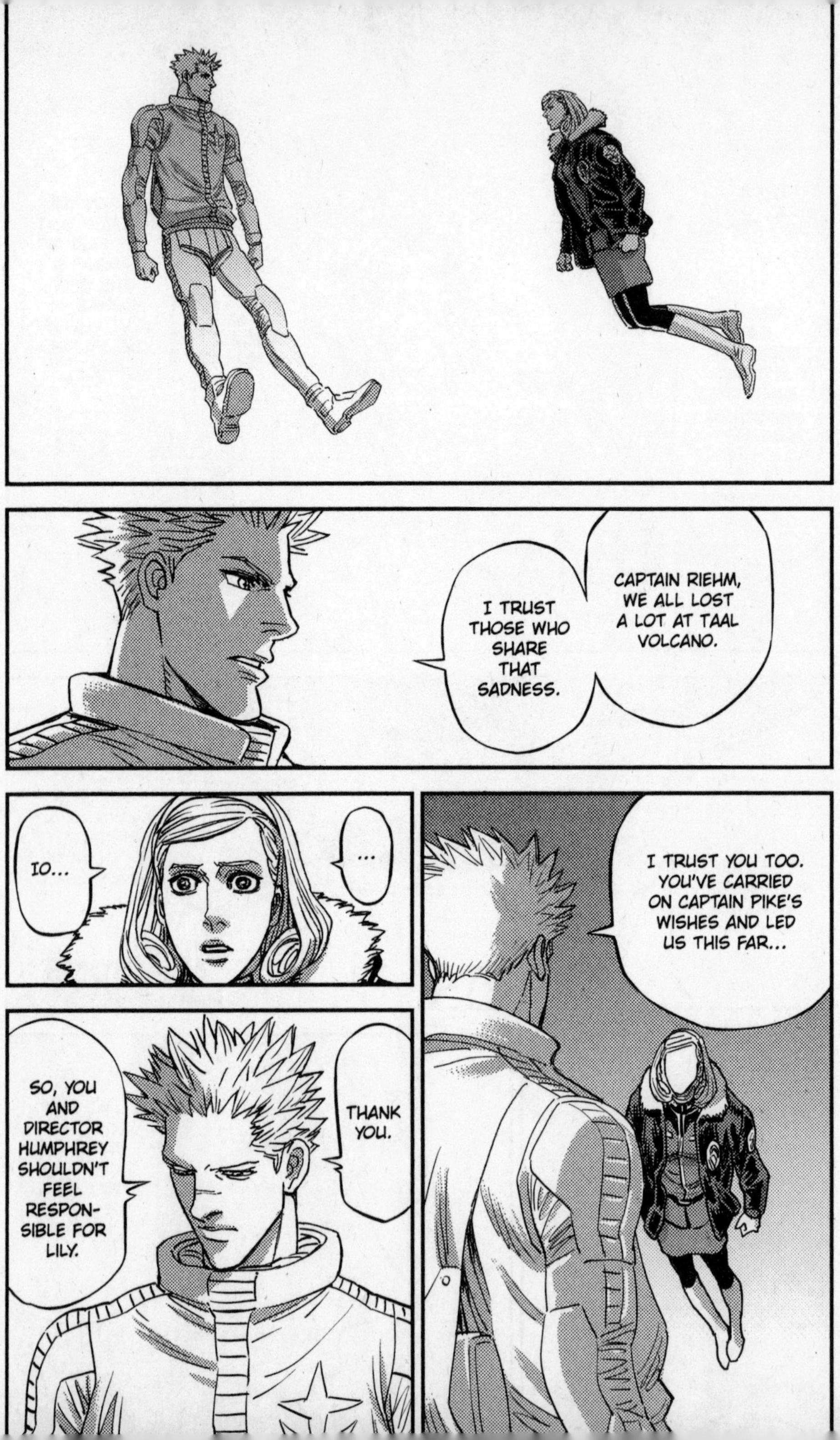
CAPTAIN RIEHM, WE ALL LOST A LOT AT TAAL VOLCANO.
I TRUST THOSE WHO SHARE THAT SADNESS.
I TRUST YOU TOO. YOU'VE CARRIED ON CAPTAIN PIKE'S WISHES AND LED US THIS FAR...
...
IO...
THANK YOU.
SO, YOU AND DIRECTOR HUMPHREY SHOULDN'T FEEL RESPONSIBLE FOR LILY.

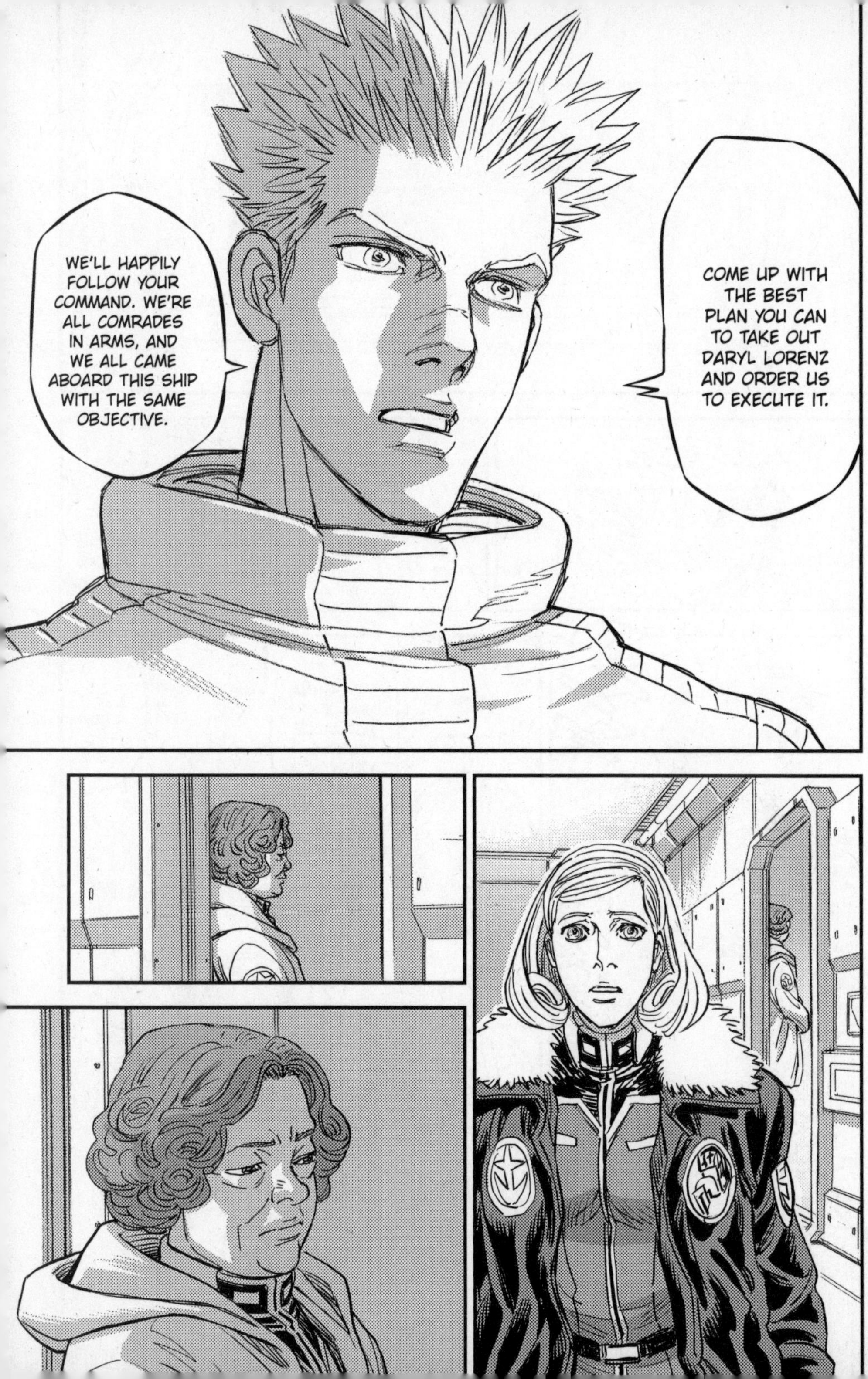
COME UP WITH THE BEST PLAN YOU CAN TO TAKE OUT DARYL LORENZ AND ORDER US TO EXECUTE IT.
WE'LL HAPPILY FOLLOW YOUR COMMAND. WE'RE ALL COMRADES IN ARMS, AND WE ALL CAME ABOARD THIS SHIP WITH THE SAME OBJECTIVE.

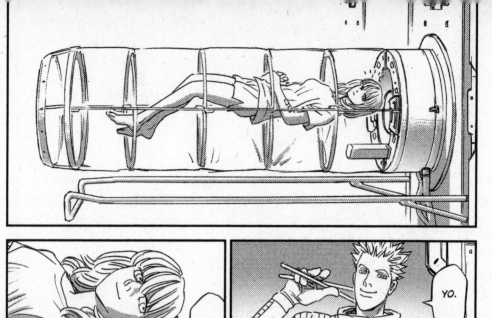

HEY.

YO.

I'M GONNA SEE IF IT ACTUALLY WORKS. YOU WANNA SEE?

I GOT A NEW TOY.

SURE. WHAT IS IT?

SHHK

CHOK

SNAP

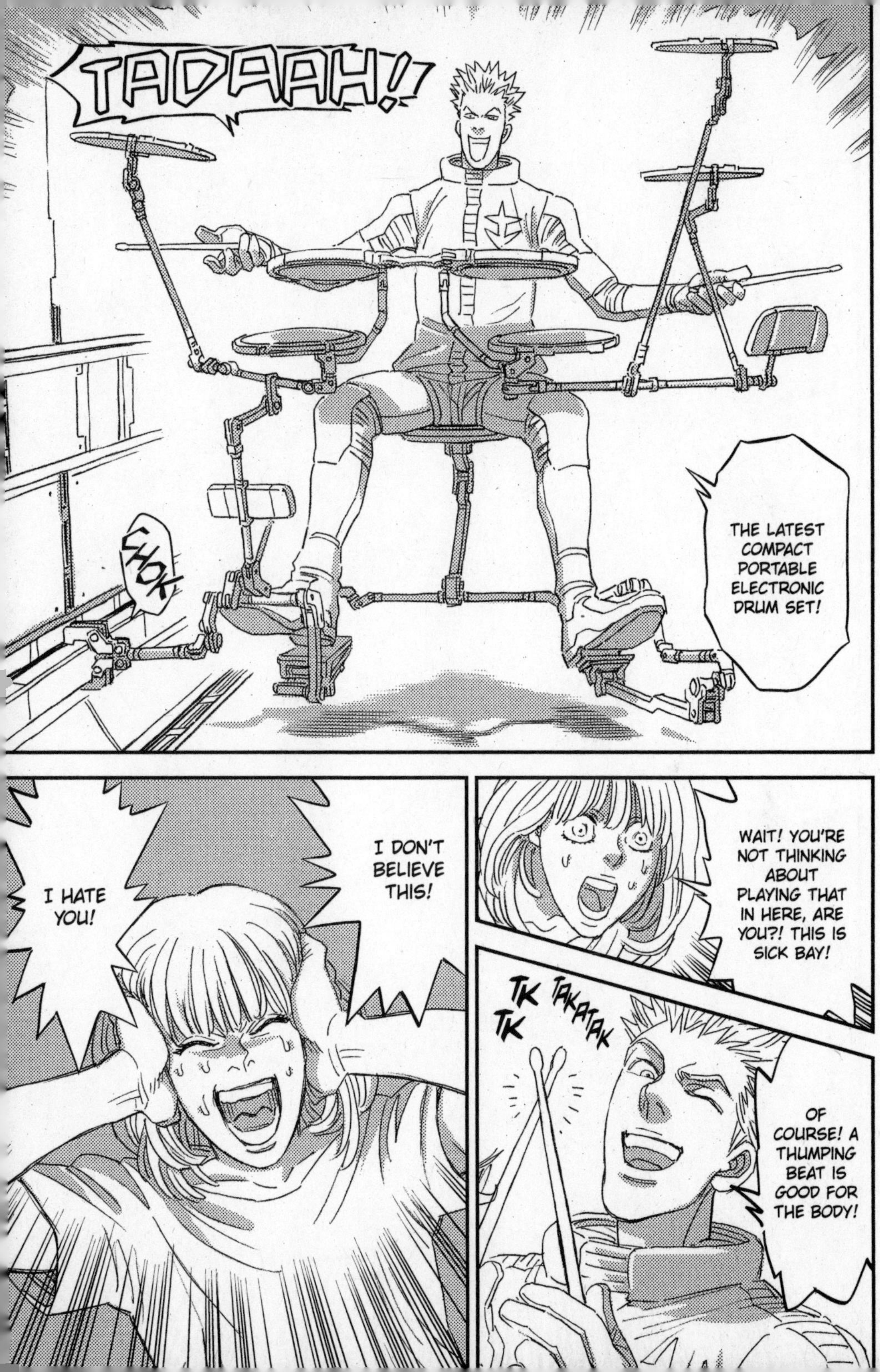
TADAAH!!
THE LATEST COMPACT PORTABLE ELECTRONIC DRUM SET!
CHOK
WAIT! YOU'RE NOT THINKING ABOUT PLAYING THAT IN HERE, ARE YOU?! THIS IS SICK BAY!
TK TK TAKATAK
OF COURSE! A THUMPING BEAT IS GOOD FOR THE BODY!
I DON'T BELIEVE THIS!
I HATE YOU!

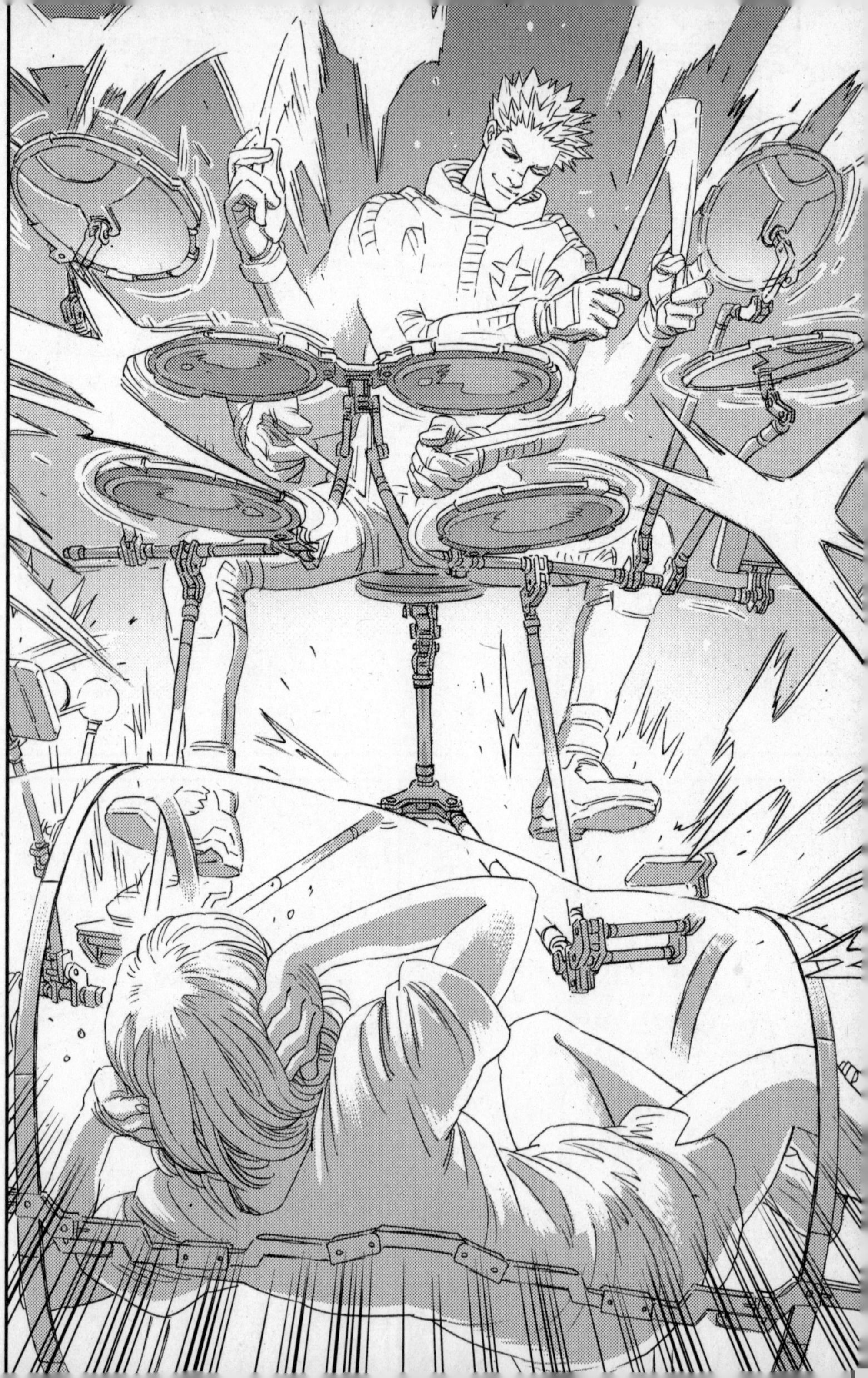

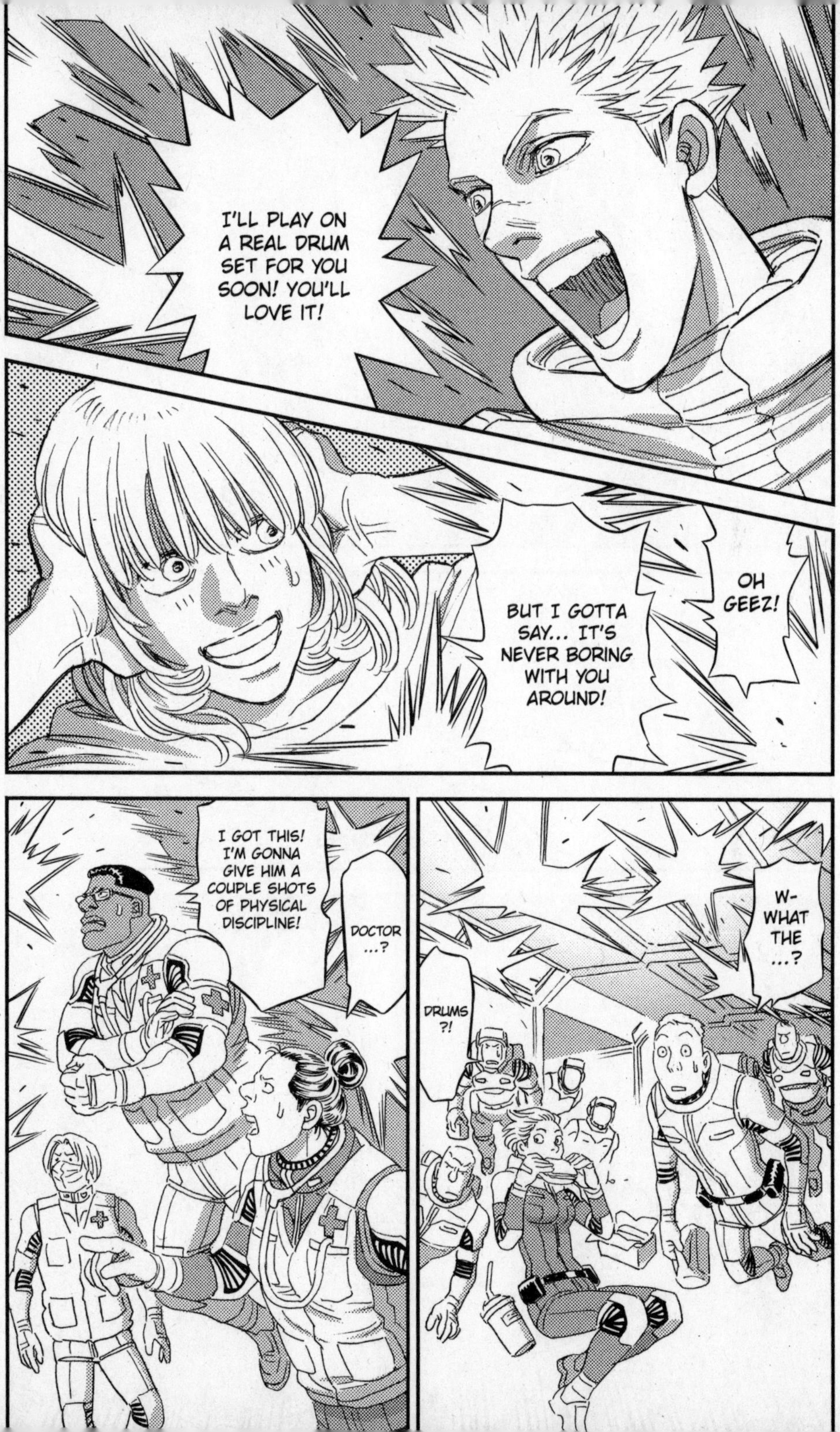
I'LL PLAY ON A REAL DRUM SET FOR YOU SOON! YOU'LL LOVE IT!
OH GEEZ!
BUT I GOTTA SAY... IT'S NEVER BORING WITH YOU AROUND!
W-WHAT THE ...?
DRUMS ?!
I GOT THIS! I'M GONNA GIVE HIM A COUPLE SHOTS OF PHYSICAL DISCIPLINE!
DOCTOR ...?

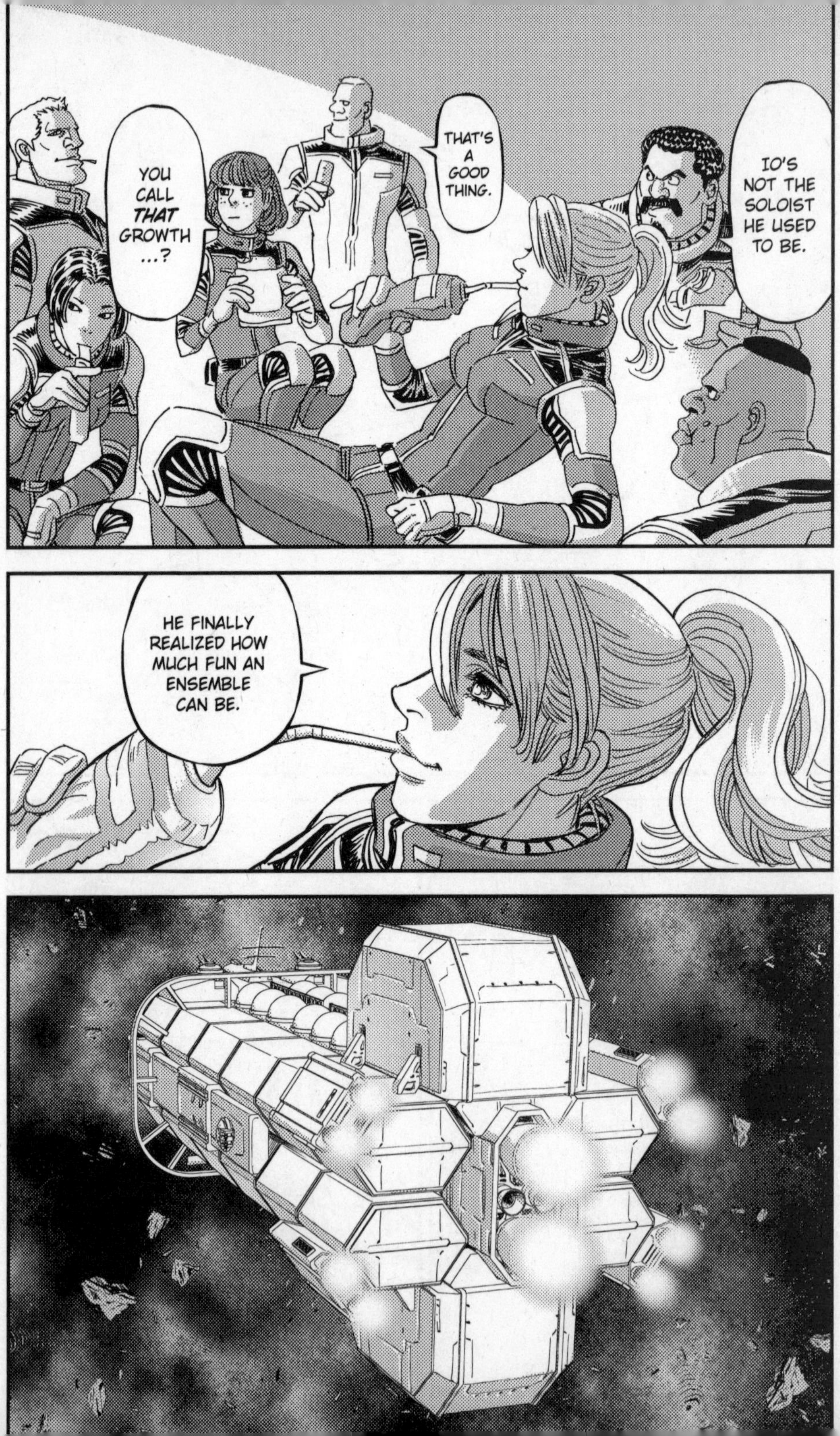
IO'S NOT THE SOLOIST HE USED TO BE.
THAT'S A GOOD THING.
YOU CALL *THAT* GROWTH ...?
HE FINALLY REALIZED HOW MUCH FUN AN ENSEMBLE CAN BE.

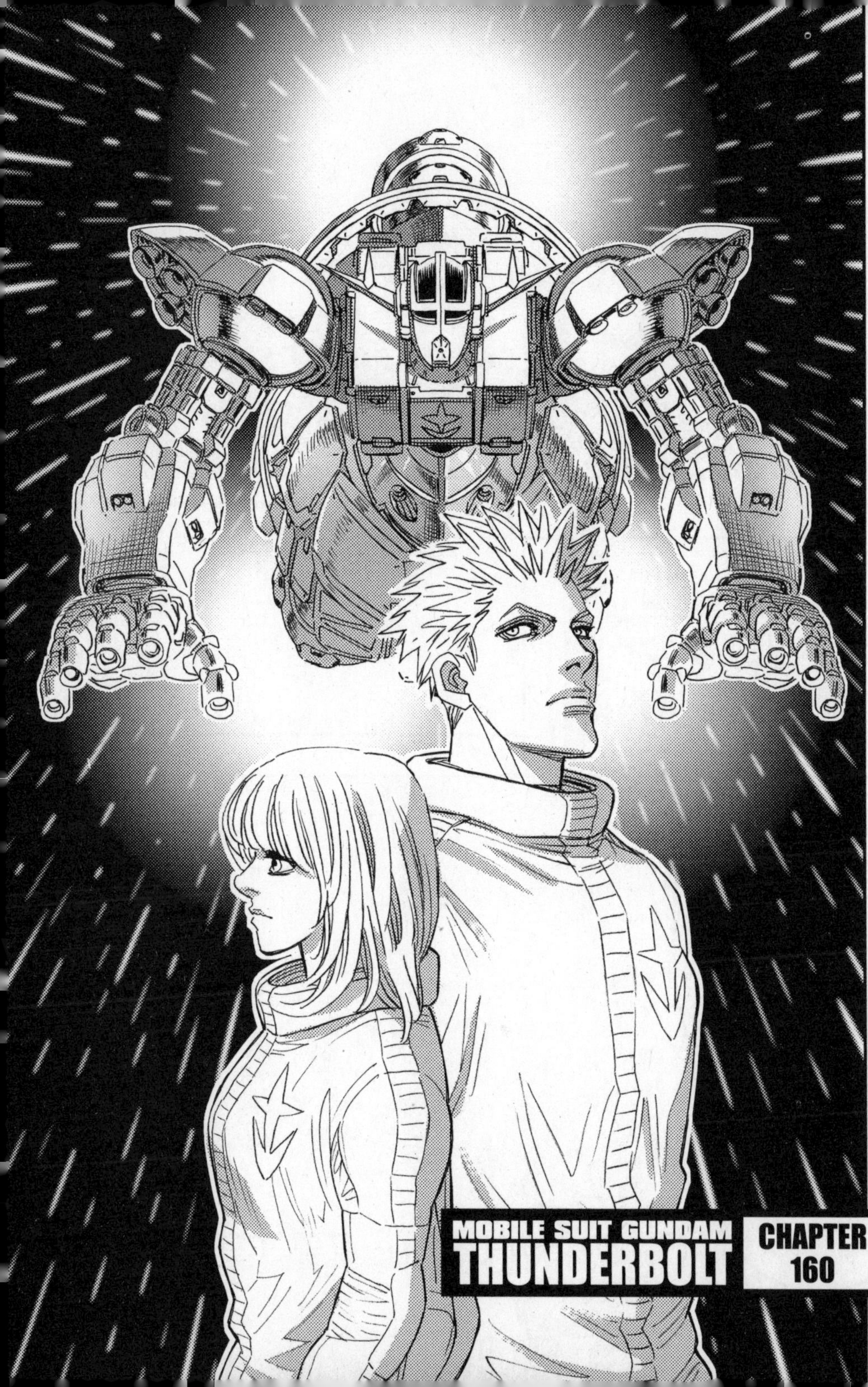
MOBILE SUIT GUNDAM
THUNDERBOLT
CHAPTER 160

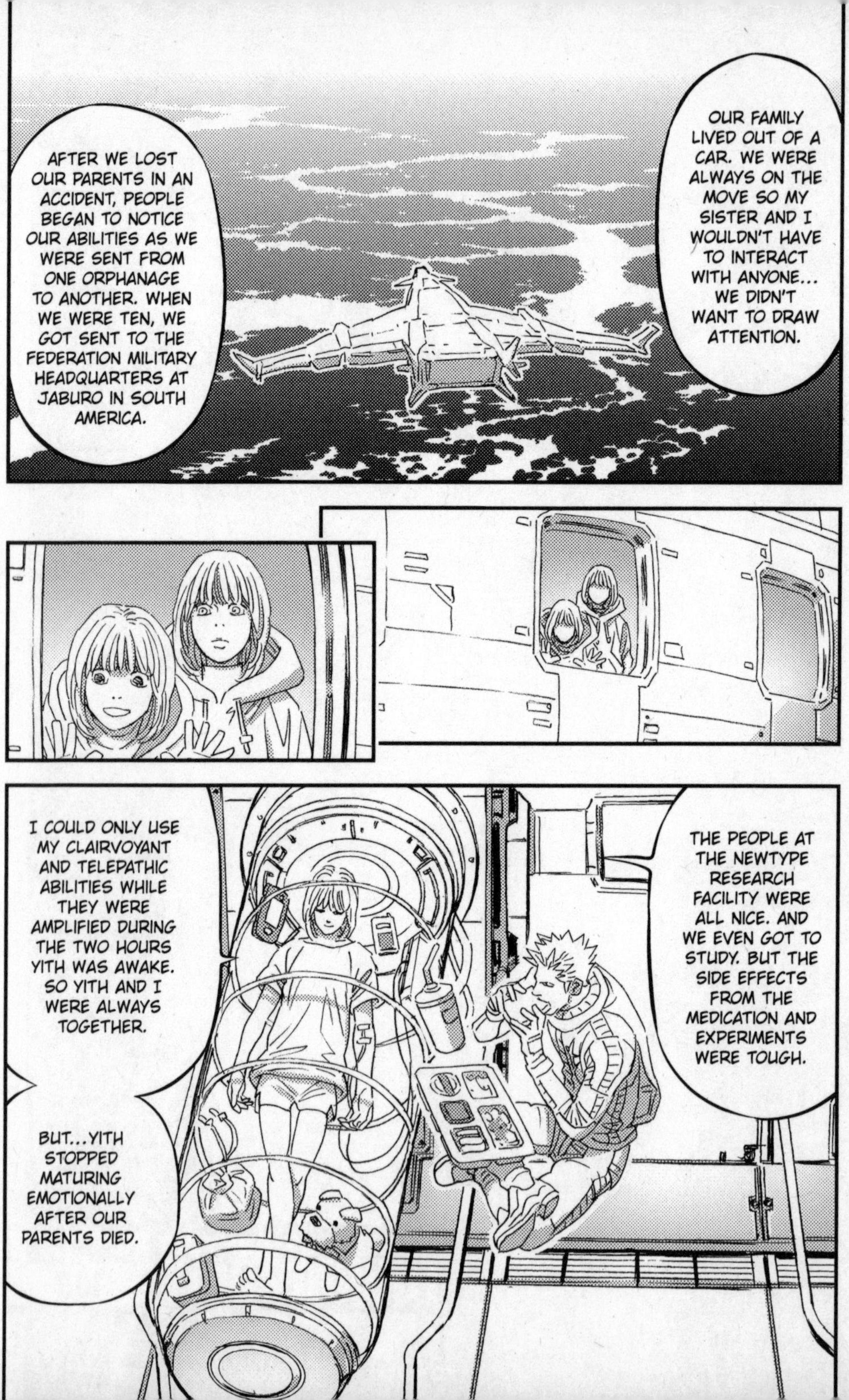
OUR FAMILY LIVED OUT OF A CAR. WE WERE ALWAYS ON THE MOVE SO MY SISTER AND I WOULDN'T HAVE TO INTERACT WITH ANYONE... WE DIDN'T WANT TO DRAW ATTENTION.
AFTER WE LOST OUR PARENTS IN AN ACCIDENT, PEOPLE BEGAN TO NOTICE OUR ABILITIES AS WE WERE SENT FROM ONE ORPHANAGE TO ANOTHER. WHEN WE WERE TEN, WE GOT SENT TO THE FEDERATION MILITARY HEADQUARTERS AT JABURO IN SOUTH AMERICA.
THE PEOPLE AT THE NEWTYPE RESEARCH FACILITY WERE ALL NICE. AND WE EVEN GOT TO STUDY. BUT THE SIDE EFFECTS FROM THE MEDICATION AND EXPERIMENTS WERE TOUGH.
I COULD ONLY USE MY CLAIRVOYANT AND TELEPATHIC ABILITIES WHILE THEY WERE AMPLIFIED DURING THE TWO HOURS YITH WAS AWAKE. SO YITH AND I WERE ALWAYS TOGETHER.
BUT...YITH STOPPED MATURING EMOTIONALLY AFTER OUR PARENTS DIED.

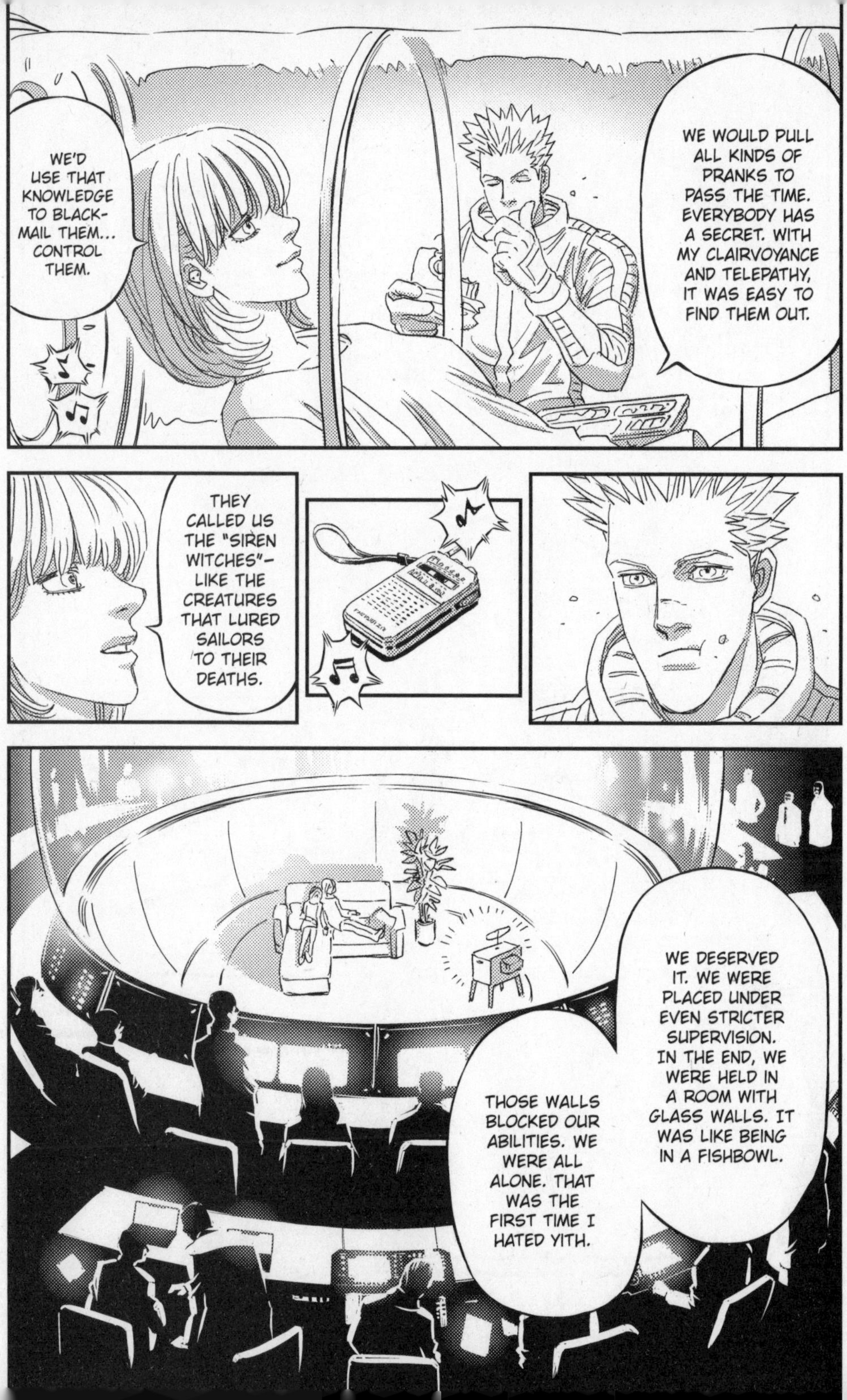
WE WOULD PULL ALL KINDS OF PRANKS TO PASS THE TIME. EVERYBODY HAS A SECRET. WITH MY CLAIRVOYANCE AND TELEPATHY, IT WAS EASY TO FIND THEM OUT.
WE'D USE THAT KNOWLEDGE TO BLACK-MAIL THEM... CONTROL THEM.
THEY CALLED US THE "SIREN WITCHES"—LIKE THE CREATURES THAT LURED SAILORS TO THEIR DEATHS.
WE DESERVED IT. WE WERE PLACED UNDER EVEN STRICTER SUPERVISION. IN THE END, WE WERE HELD IN A ROOM WITH GLASS WALLS. IT WAS LIKE BEING IN A FISHBOWL.
THOSE WALLS BLOCKED OUR ABILITIES. WE WERE ALL ALONE. THAT WAS THE FIRST TIME I HATED YITH.

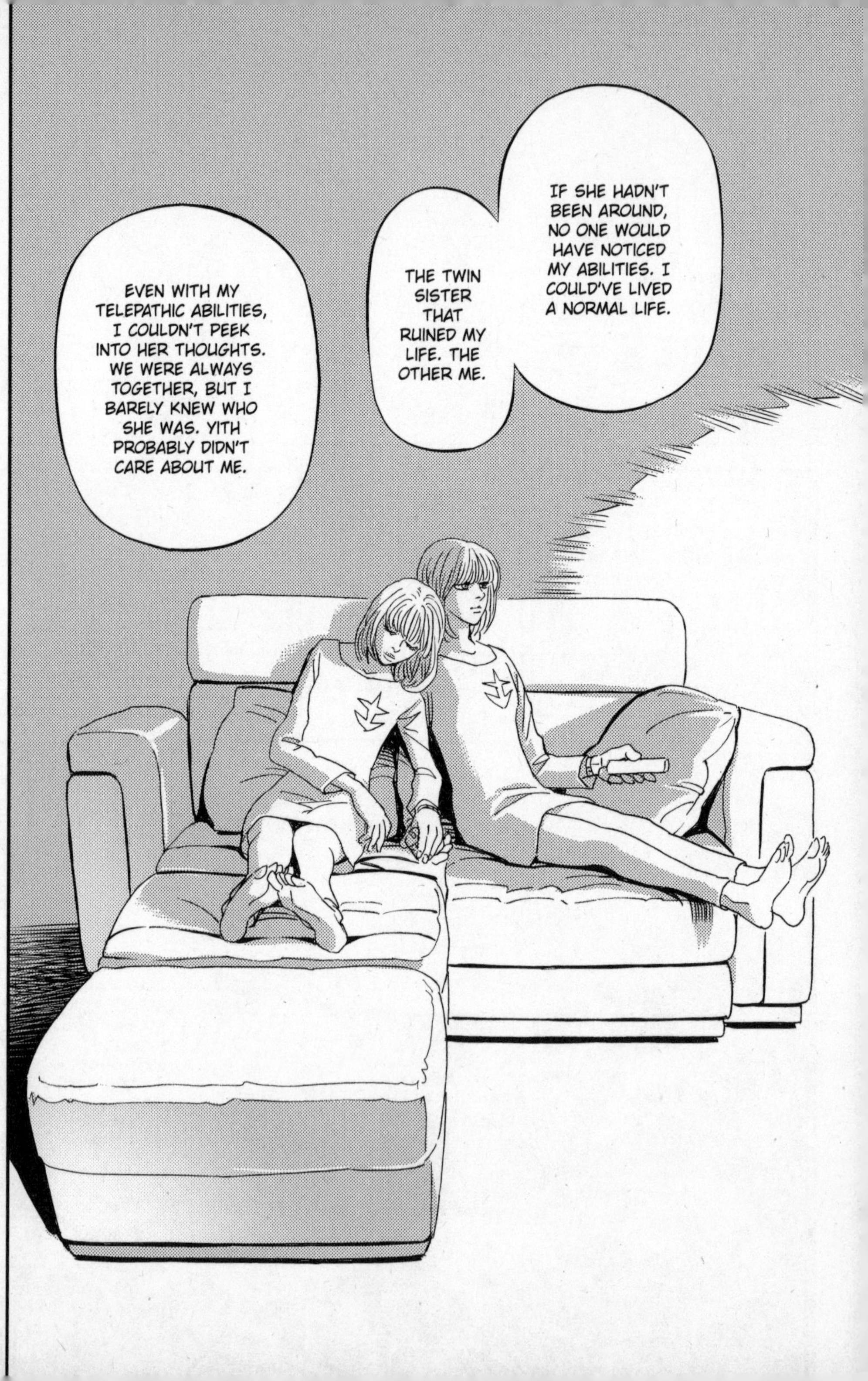
IF SHE HADN'T BEEN AROUND, NO ONE WOULD HAVE NOTICED MY ABILITIES. I COULD'VE LIVED A NORMAL LIFE.
THE TWIN SISTER THAT RUINED MY LIFE. THE OTHER ME.
EVEN WITH MY TELEPATHIC ABILITIES, I COULDN'T PEEK INTO HER THOUGHTS. WE WERE ALWAYS TOGETHER, BUT I BARELY KNEW WHO SHE WAS. YITH PROBABLY DIDN'T CARE ABOUT ME.

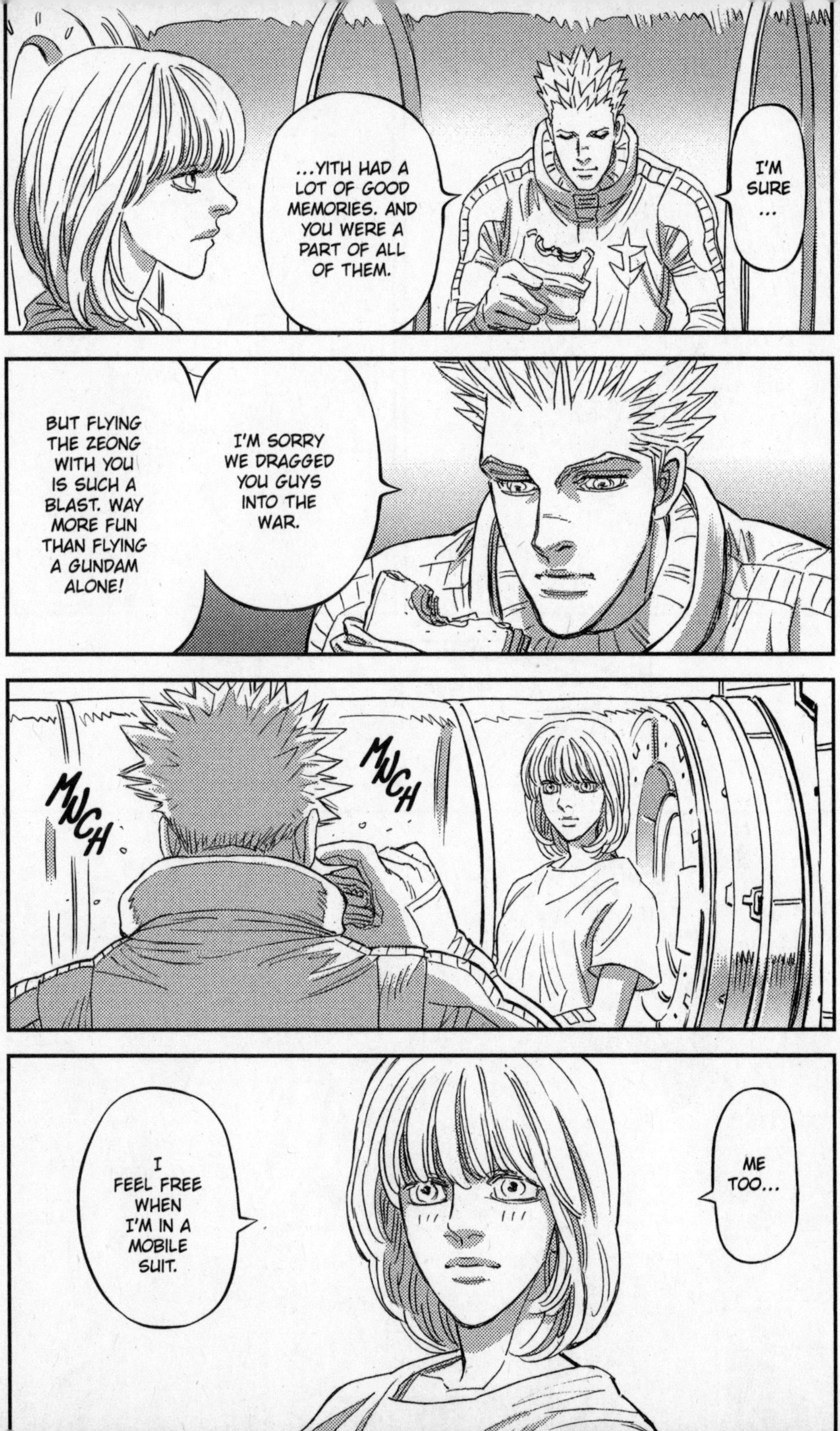
I'M SURE ...
...YITH HAD A LOT OF GOOD MEMORIES. AND YOU WERE A PART OF ALL OF THEM.
I'M SORRY WE DRAGGED YOU GUYS INTO THE WAR.
BUT FLYING THE ZEONG WITH YOU IS SUCH A BLAST. WAY MORE FUN THAN FLYING A GUNDAM ALONE!
MUNCH
MUNCH
ME TOO...
I FEEL FREE WHEN I'M IN A MOBILE SUIT.

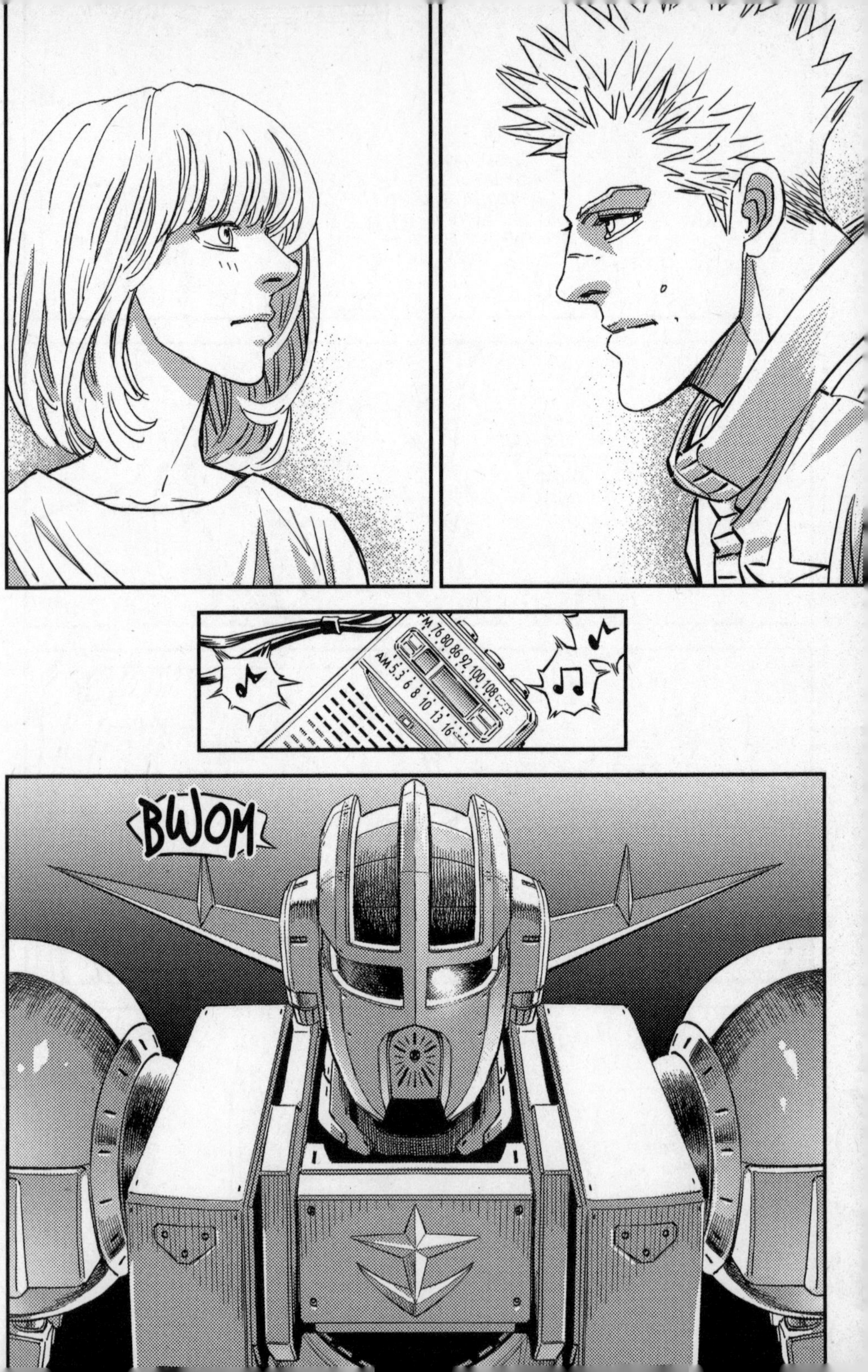
FM 76 80 86 92 100 108
AM 5.3 6 8 10 13 16
BWOM

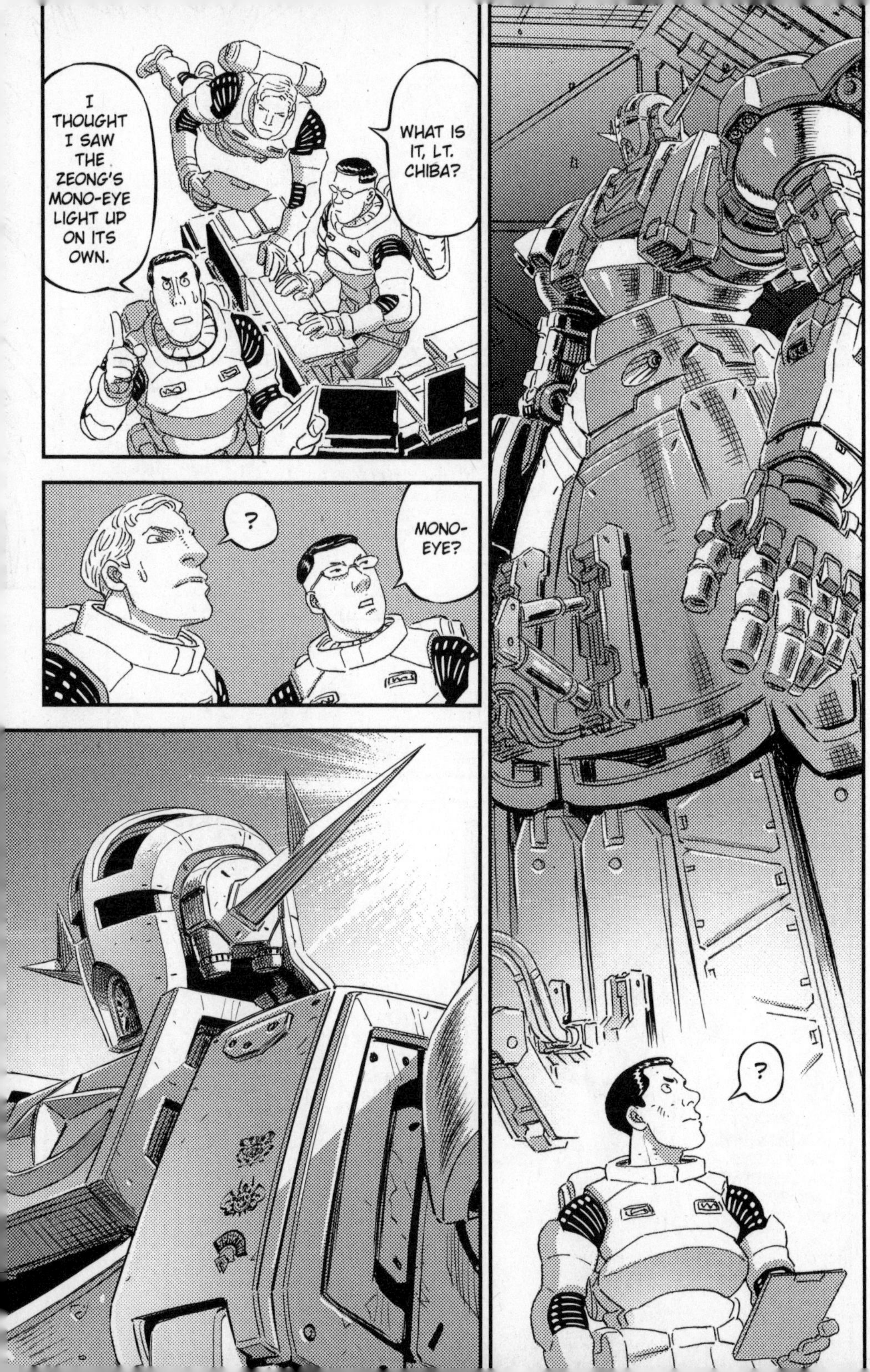
?
WHAT IS IT, LT. CHIBA?
I THOUGHT I SAW THE ZEONG'S MONO-EYE LIGHT UP ON ITS OWN.
MONO-EYE?
?

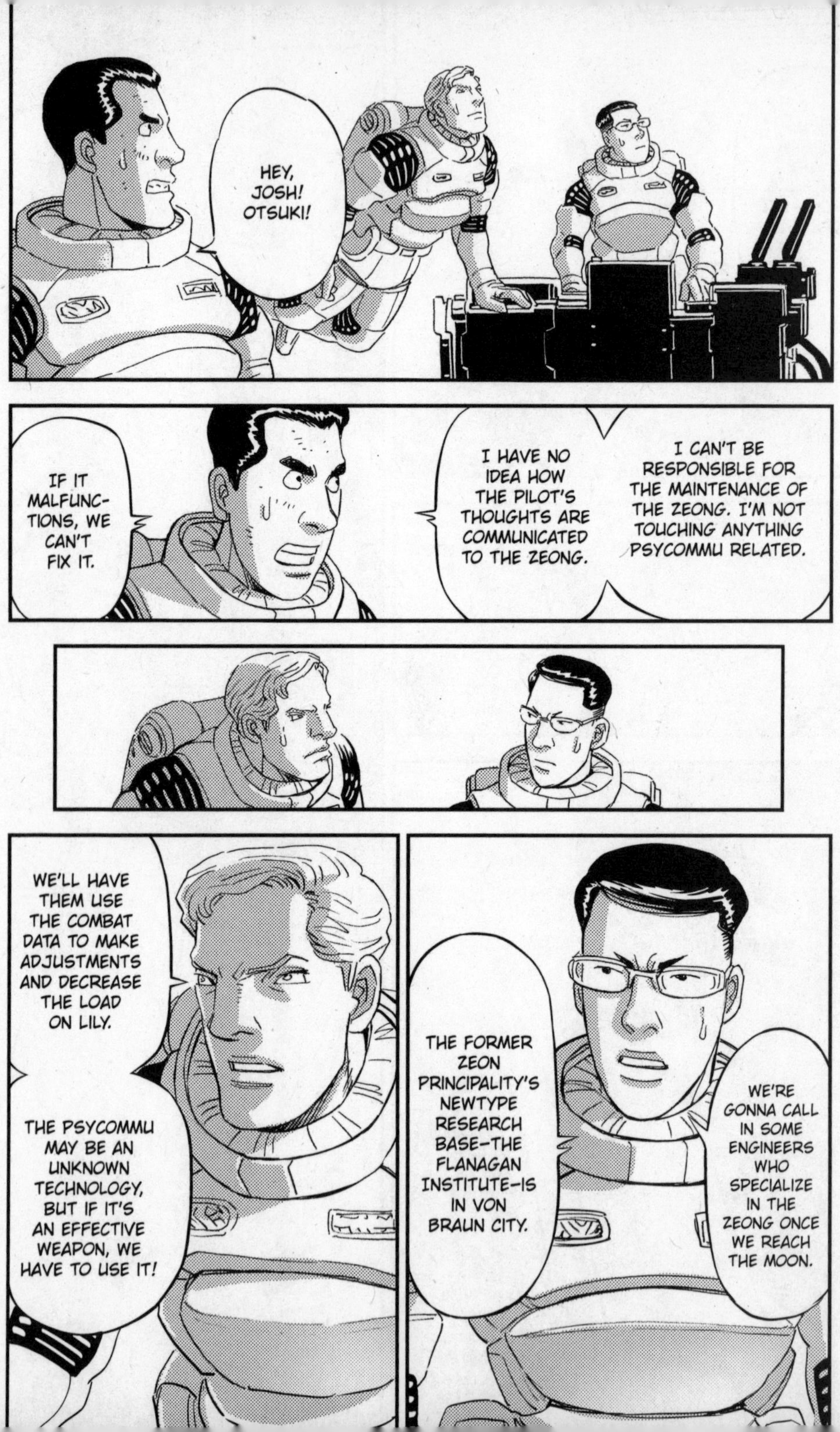
HEY, JOSH! OTSUKI!
I CAN'T BE RESPONSIBLE FOR THE MAINTENANCE OF THE ZEONG. I'M NOT TOUCHING ANYTHING PSYCOMMU RELATED.
I HAVE NO IDEA HOW THE PILOT'S THOUGHTS ARE COMMUNICATED TO THE ZEONG.
IF IT MALFUNC-TIONS, WE CAN'T FIX IT.
WE'RE GONNA CALL IN SOME ENGINEERS WHO SPECIALIZE IN THE ZEONG ONCE WE REACH THE MOON.
THE FORMER ZEON PRINCIPALITY'S NEWTYPE RESEARCH BASE—THE FLANAGAN INSTITUTE—IS IN VON BRAUN CITY.
WE'LL HAVE THEM USE THE COMBAT DATA TO MAKE ADJUSTMENTS AND DECREASE THE LOAD ON LILY.
THE PSYCOMMU MAY BE AN UNKNOWN TECHNOLOGY, BUT IF IT'S AN EFFECTIVE WEAPON, WE HAVE TO USE IT!

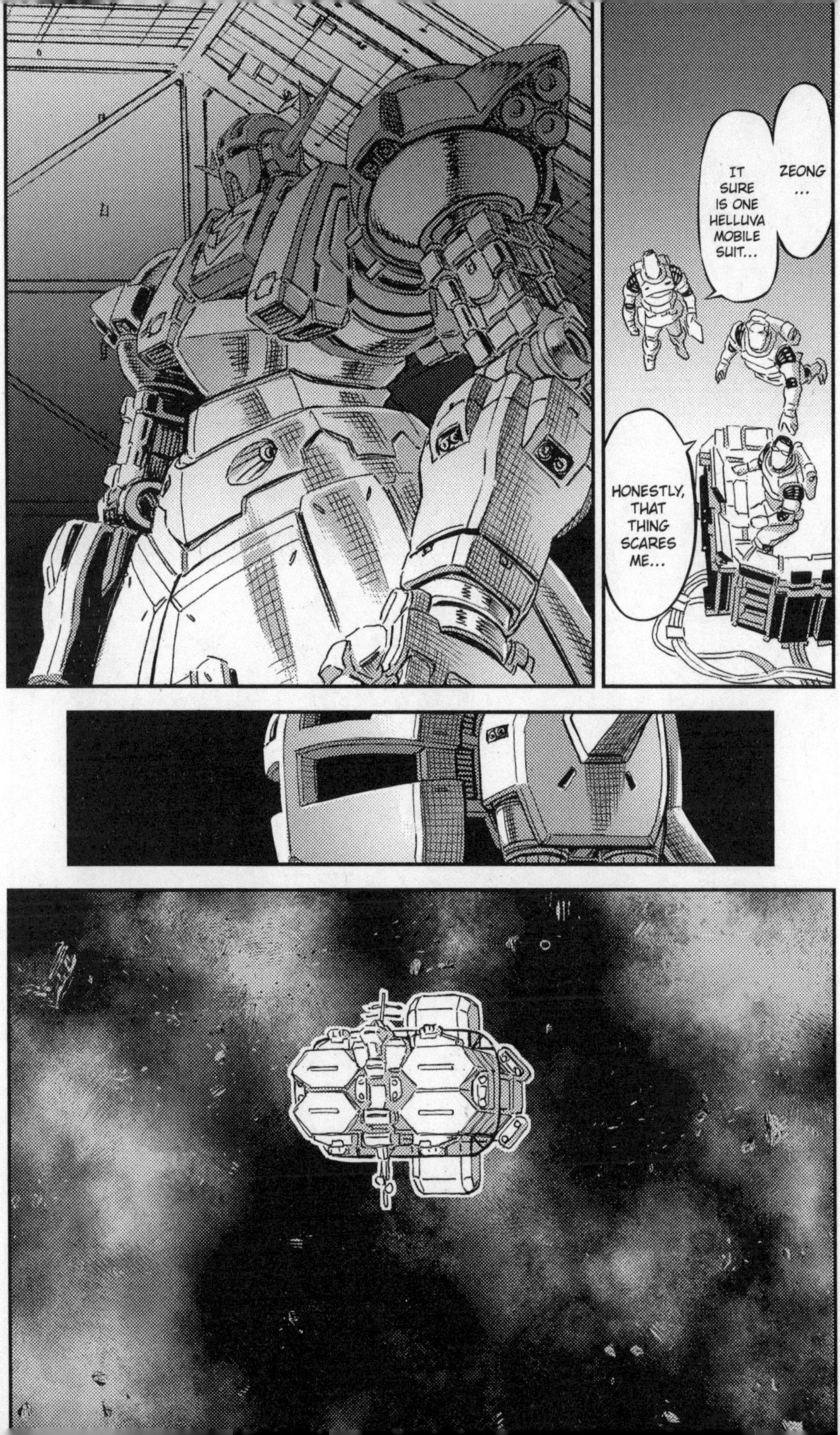
ZEONG...
IT SURE IS ONE HELLUVA MOBILE SUIT...
HONESTLY, THAT THING SCARES ME...

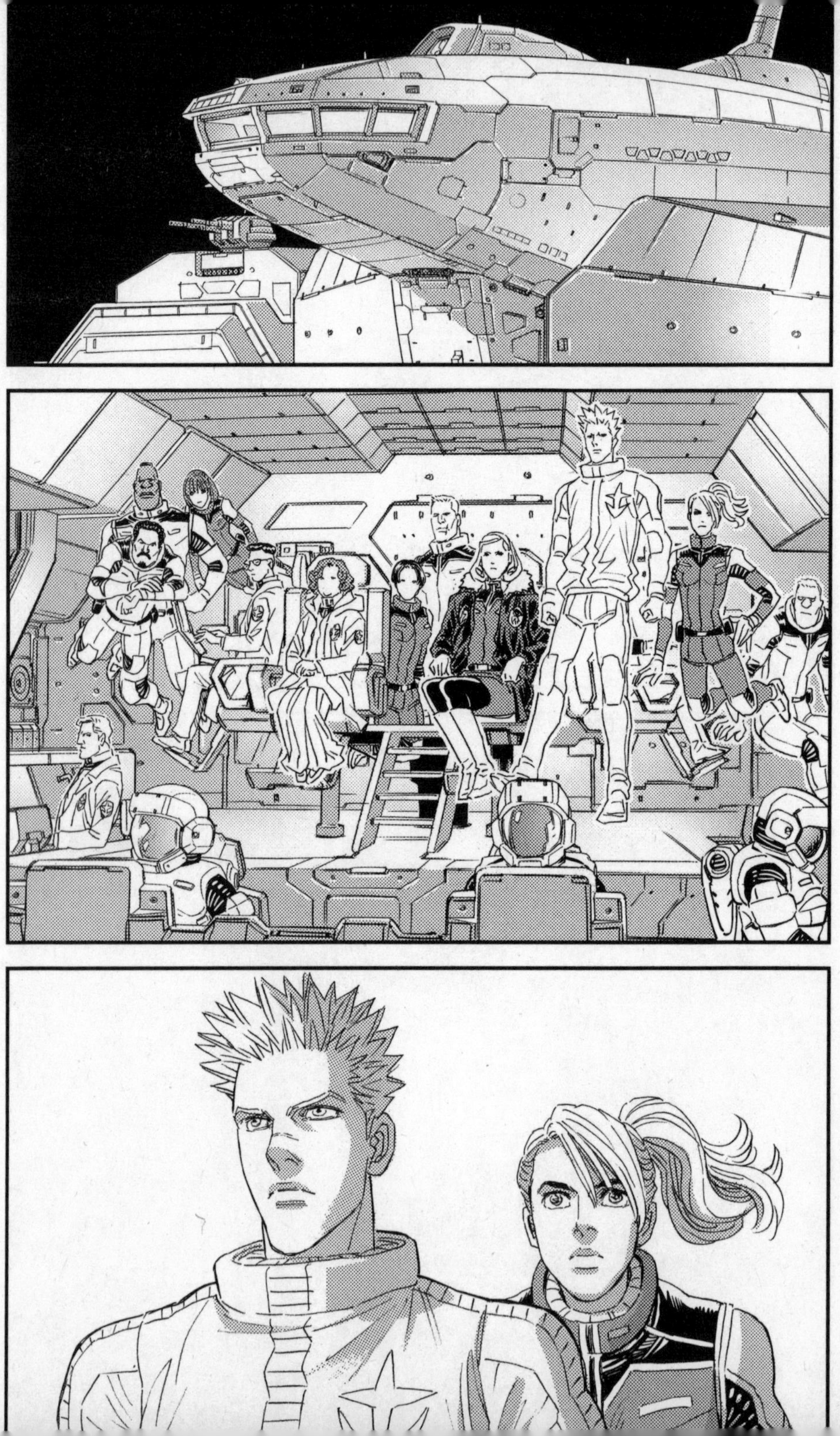

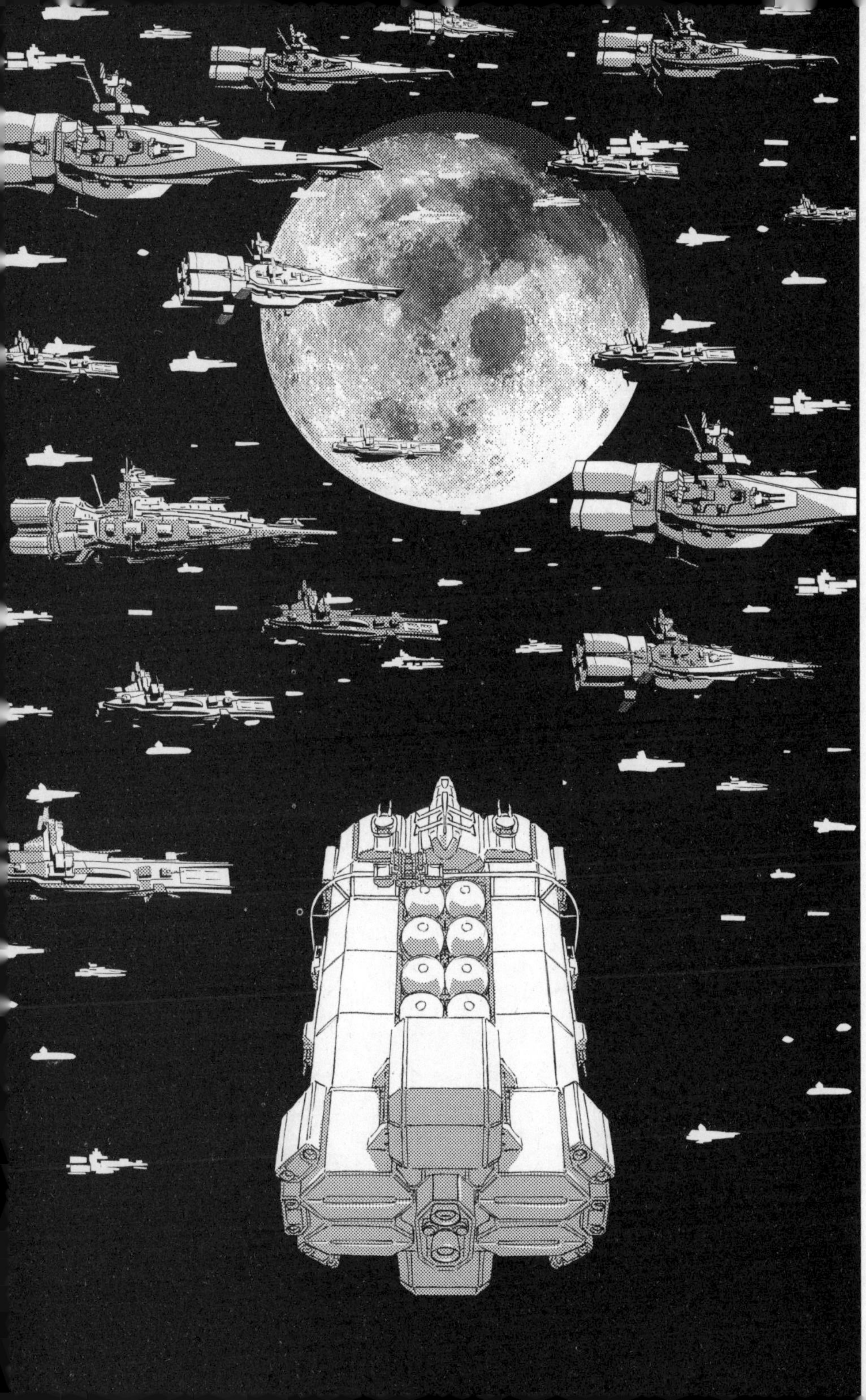

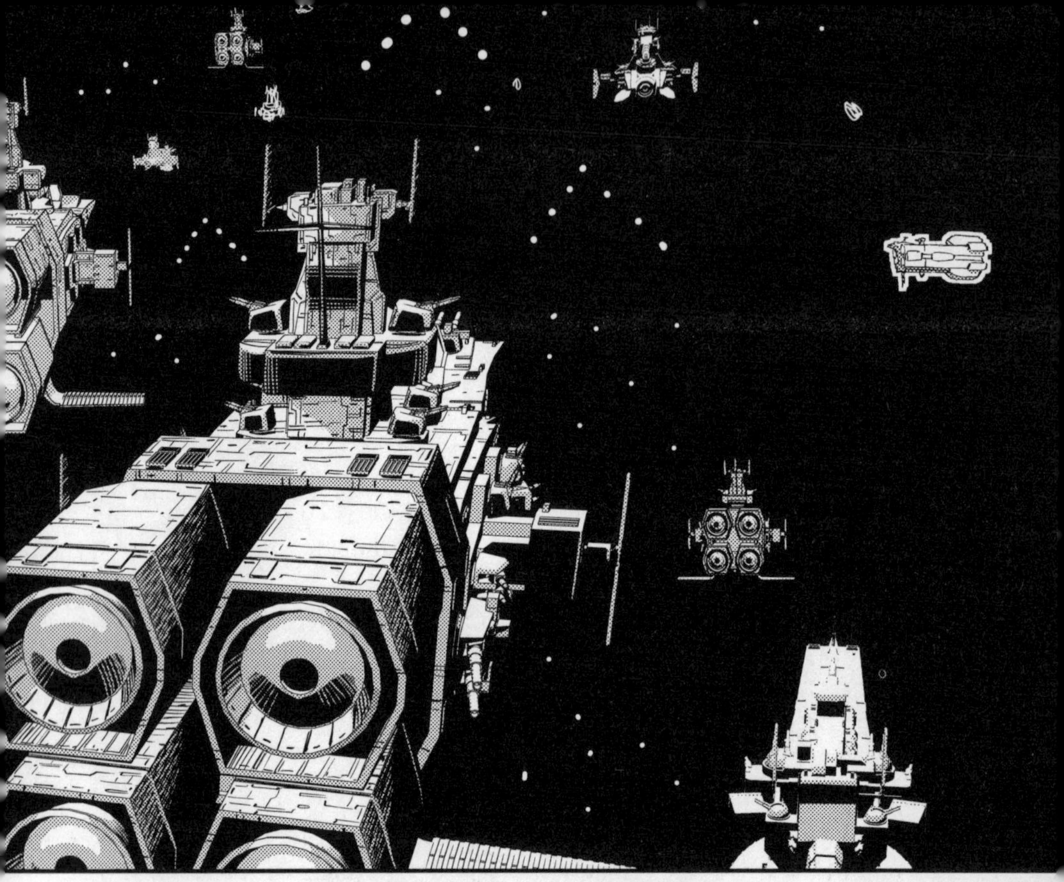

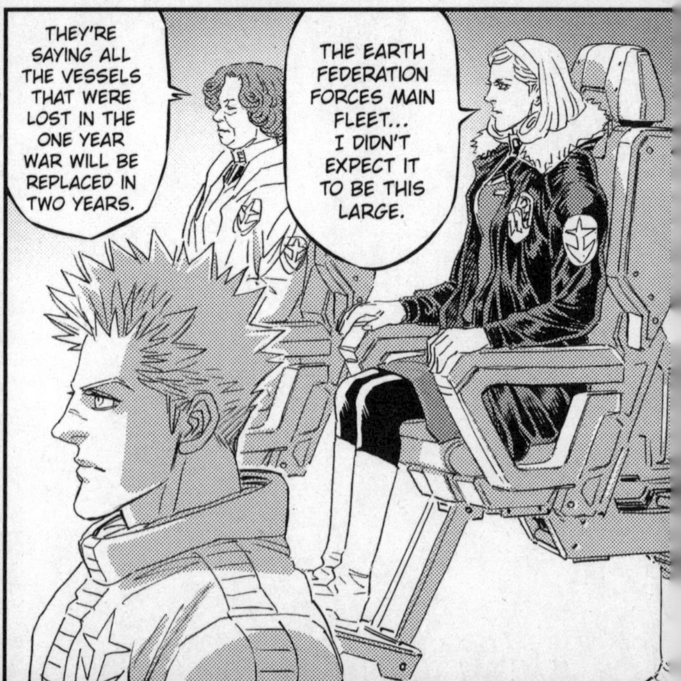
THE EARTH FEDERATION FORCES MAIN FLEET... I DIDN'T EXPECT IT TO BE THIS LARGE.
THEY'RE SAYING ALL THE VESSELS THAT WERE LOST IN THE ONE YEAR WAR WILL BE REPLACED IN TWO YEARS.

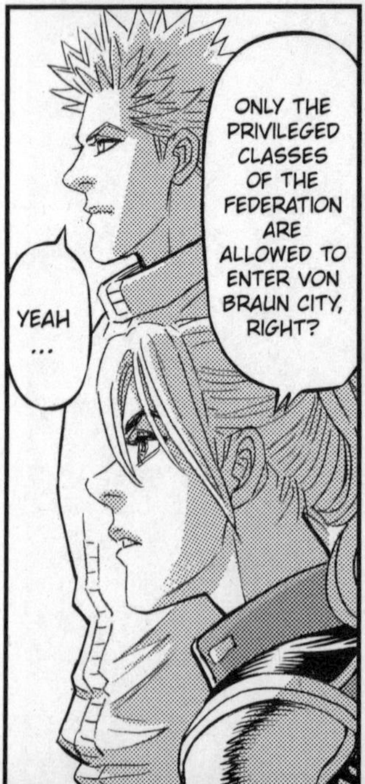
ONLY THE PRIVILEGED CLASSES OF THE FEDERATION ARE ALLOWED TO ENTER VON BRAUN CITY, RIGHT?
YEAH ...

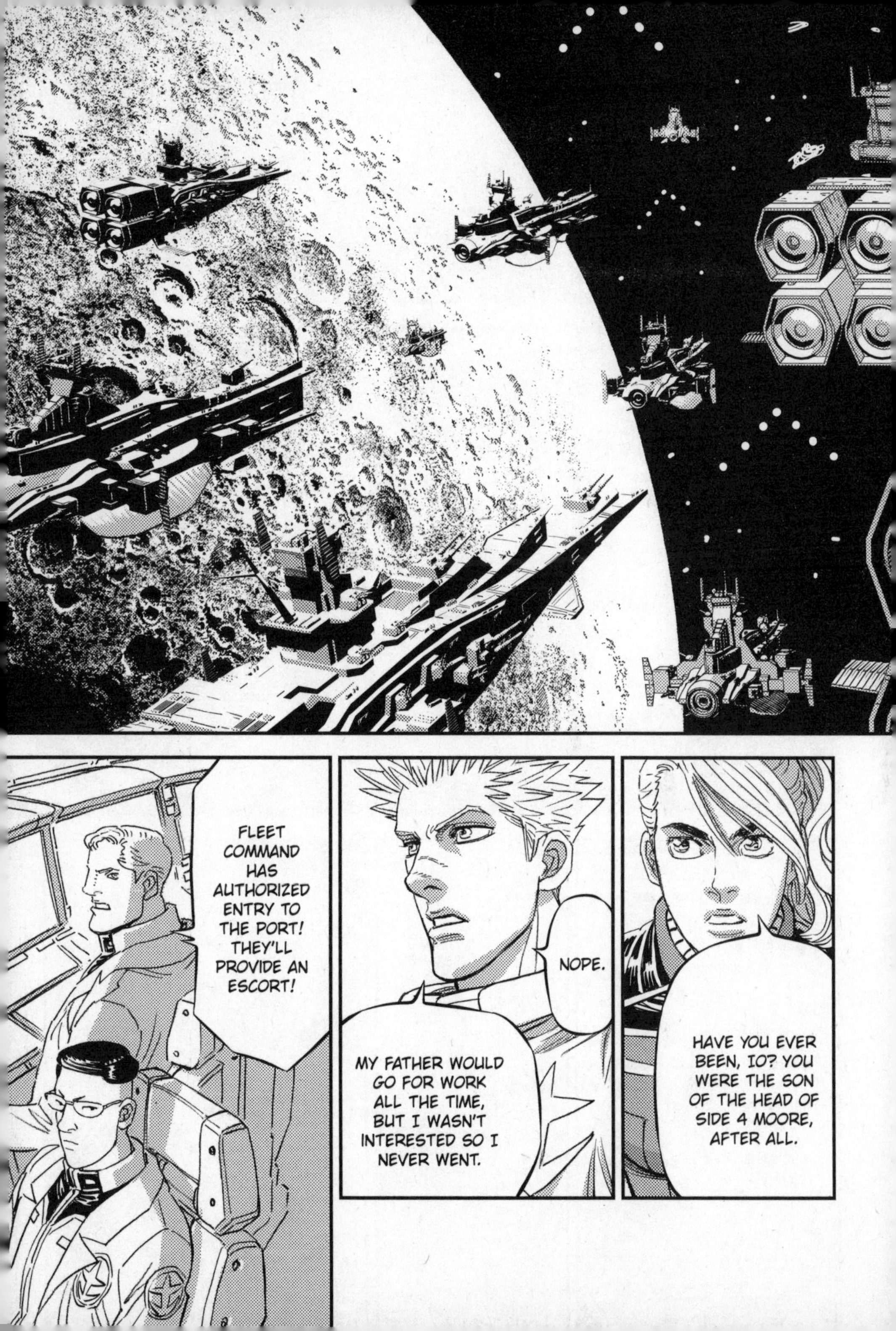
HAVE YOU EVER BEEN, IO? YOU WERE THE SON OF THE HEAD OF SIDE 4 MOORE, AFTER ALL.
NOPE.
MY FATHER WOULD GO FOR WORK ALL THE TIME, BUT I WASN'T INTERESTED SO I NEVER WENT.
FLEET COMMAND HAS AUTHORIZED ENTRY TO THE PORT! THEY'LL PROVIDE AN ESCORT!

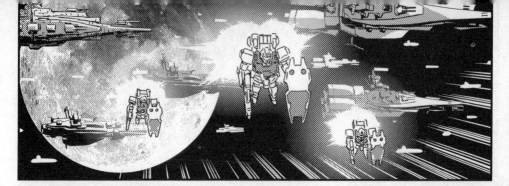

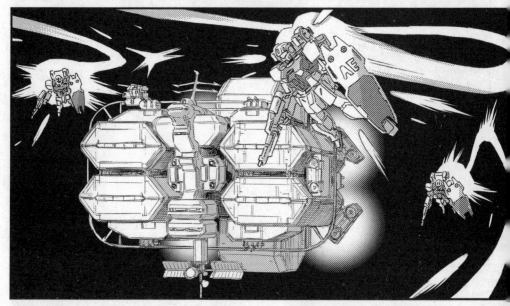

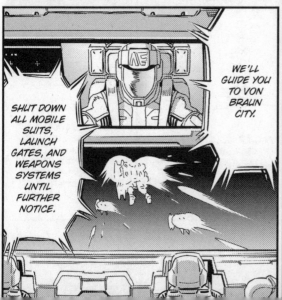

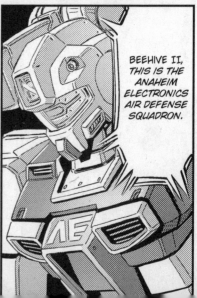

BEEHIVE II, THIS IS THE ANAHEIM ELECTRONICS AIR DEFENSE SQUADRON.
WE'LL GUIDE YOU TO VON BRAUN CITY.
SHUT DOWN ALL MOBILE SUITS, LAUNCH GATES, AND WEAPONS SYSTEMS UNTIL FURTHER NOTICE.

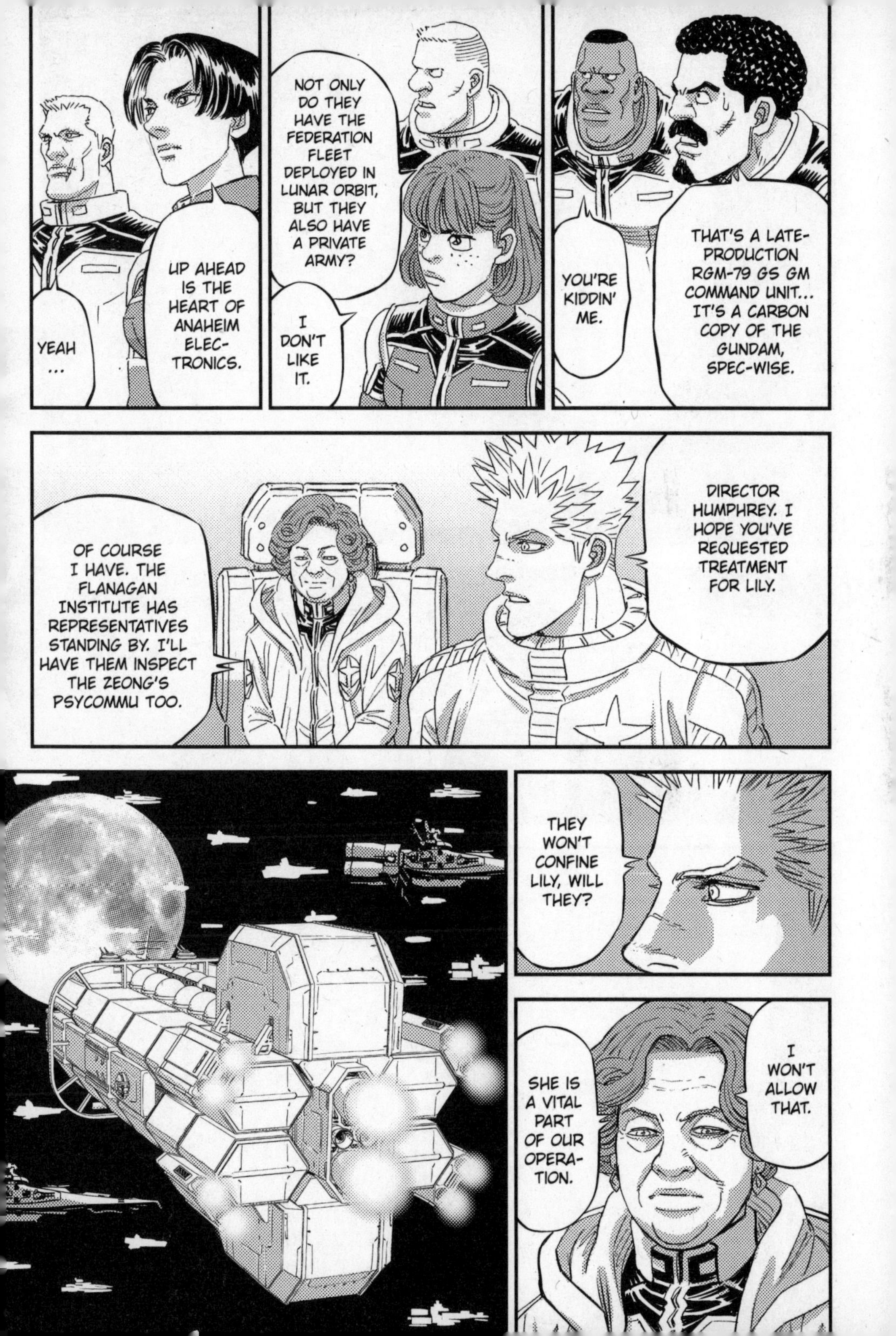
THAT'S A LATE-PRODUCTION RGM-79 GS GM COMMAND UNIT... IT'S A CARBON COPY OF THE GUNDAM, SPEC-WISE.
YOU'RE KIDDIN' ME.
NOT ONLY DO THEY HAVE THE FEDERATION FLEET DEPLOYED IN LUNAR ORBIT, BUT THEY ALSO HAVE A PRIVATE ARMY?
I DON'T LIKE IT.
UP AHEAD IS THE HEART OF ANAHEIM ELEC-TRONICS.
YEAH ...
DIRECTOR HUMPHREY. I HOPE YOU'VE REQUESTED TREATMENT FOR LILY.
OF COURSE I HAVE. THE FLANAGAN INSTITUTE HAS REPRESENTATIVES STANDING BY. I'LL HAVE THEM INSPECT THE ZEONG'S PSYCOMMU TOO.
THEY WON'T CONFINE LILY, WILL THEY?
I WON'T ALLOW THAT.
SHE IS A VITAL PART OF OUR OPERA-TION.

WE'VE ENTERED ORBIT.

HEADING TO THE FAR SIDE OF THE MOON.

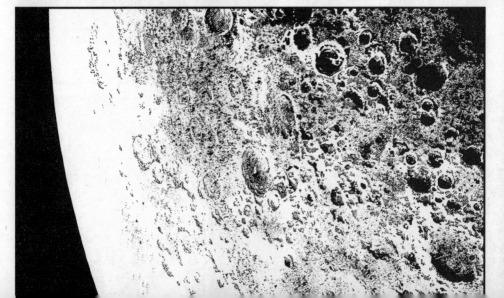

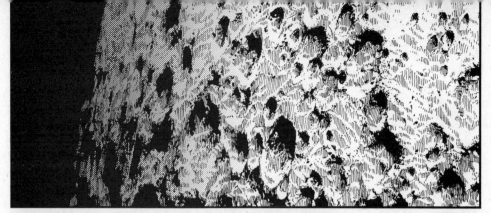

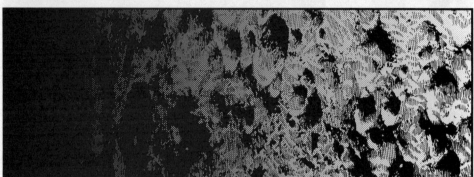

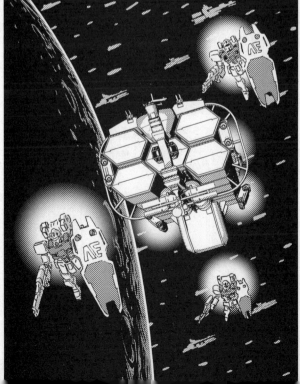

THE GATE-WAY TO HEAVEN, EH ...?

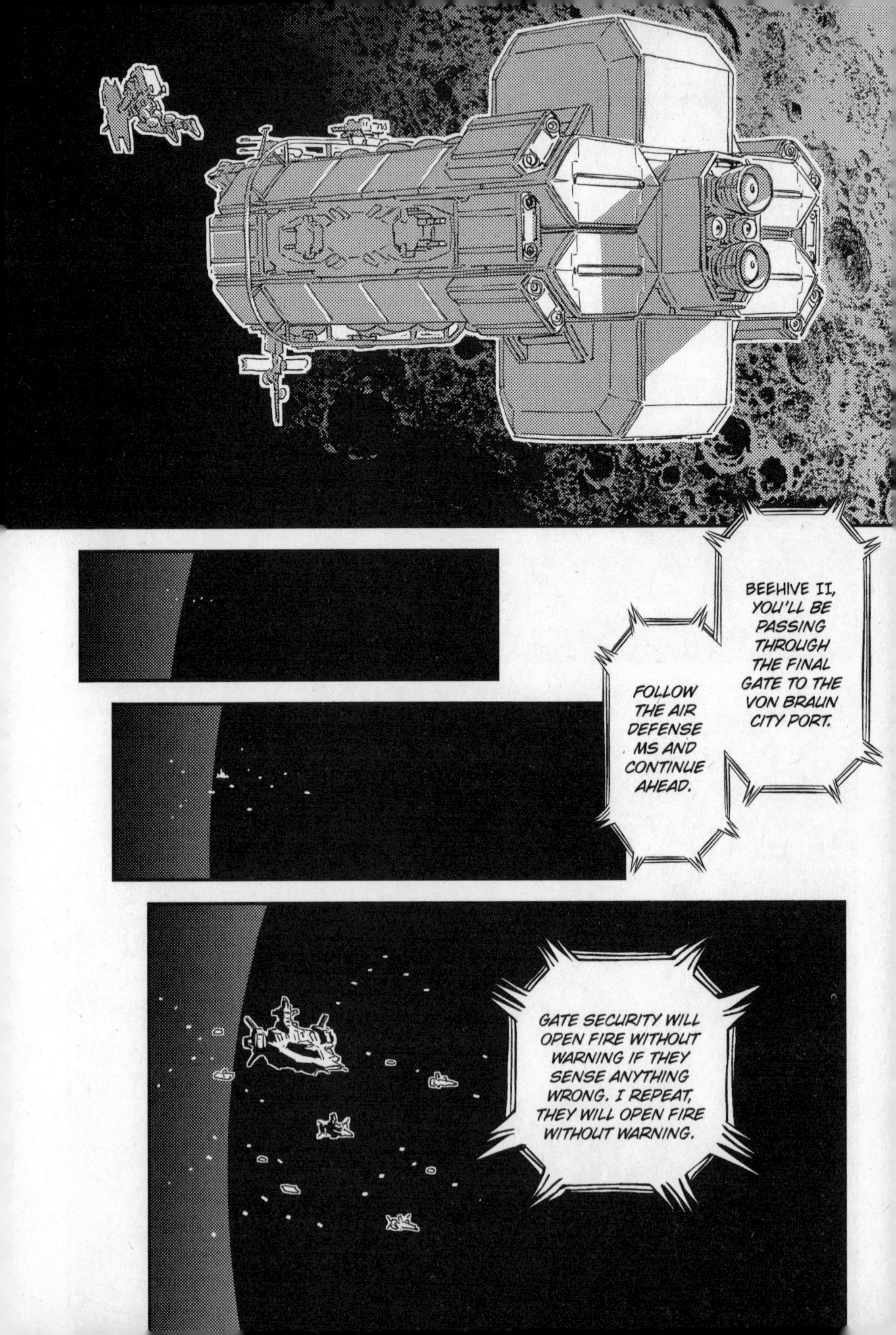
BEEHIVE II, YOU'LL BE PASSING THROUGH THE FINAL GATE TO THE VON BRAUN CITY PORT.
FOLLOW THE AIR DEFENSE MS AND CONTINUE AHEAD.
GATE SECURITY WILL OPEN FIRE WITHOUT WARNING IF THEY SENSE ANYTHING WRONG. I REPEAT, THEY WILL OPEN FIRE WITHOUT WARNING.

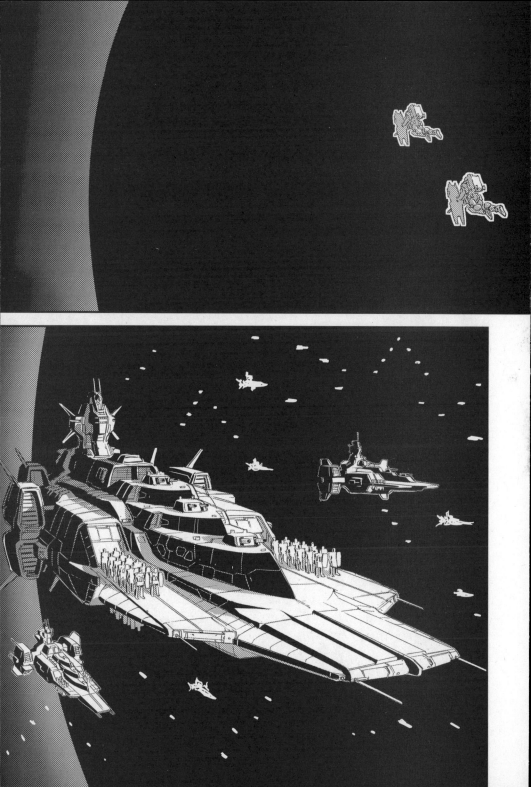

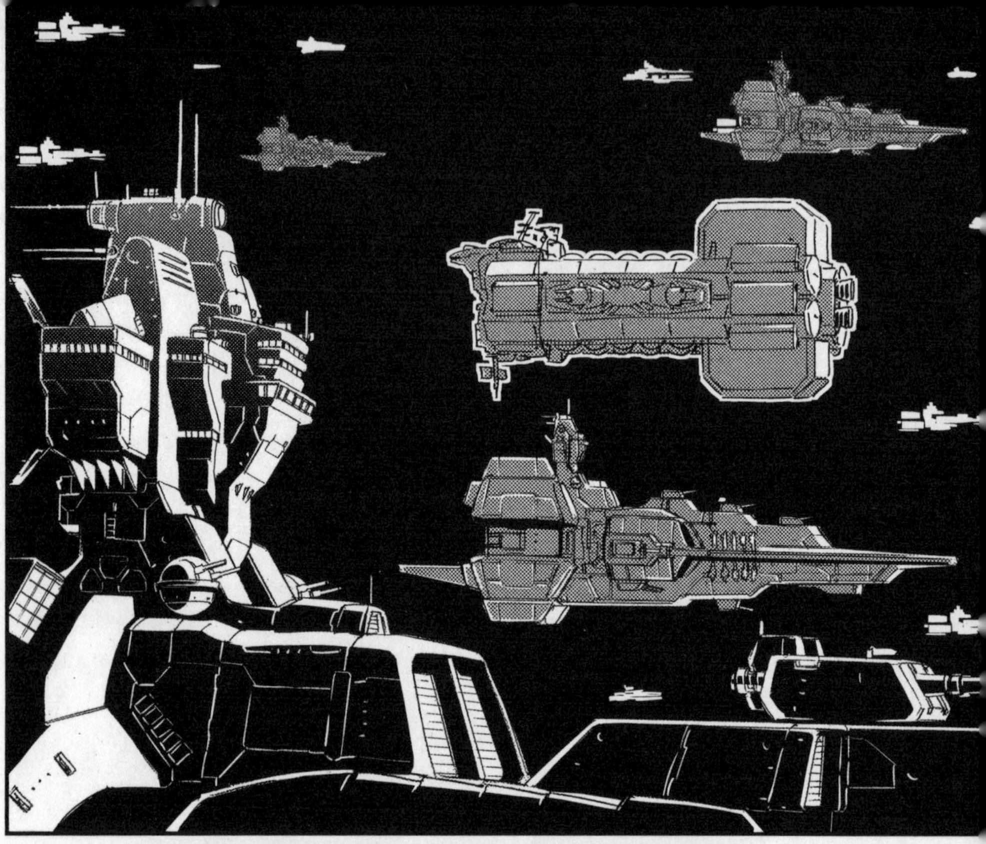

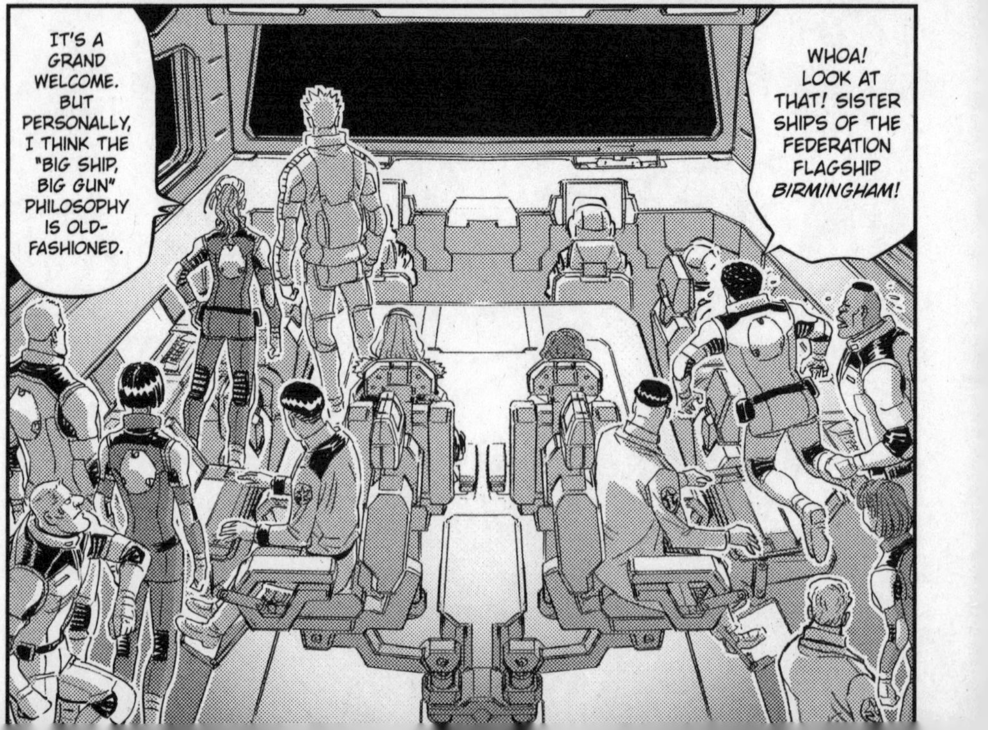
WHOA! LOOK AT THAT! SISTER SHIPS OF THE FEDERATION FLAGSHIP *BIRMINGHAM*!
IT'S A GRAND WELCOME. BUT PERSONALLY, I THINK THE "BIG SHIP, BIG GUN" PHILOSOPHY IS OLD-FASHIONED.

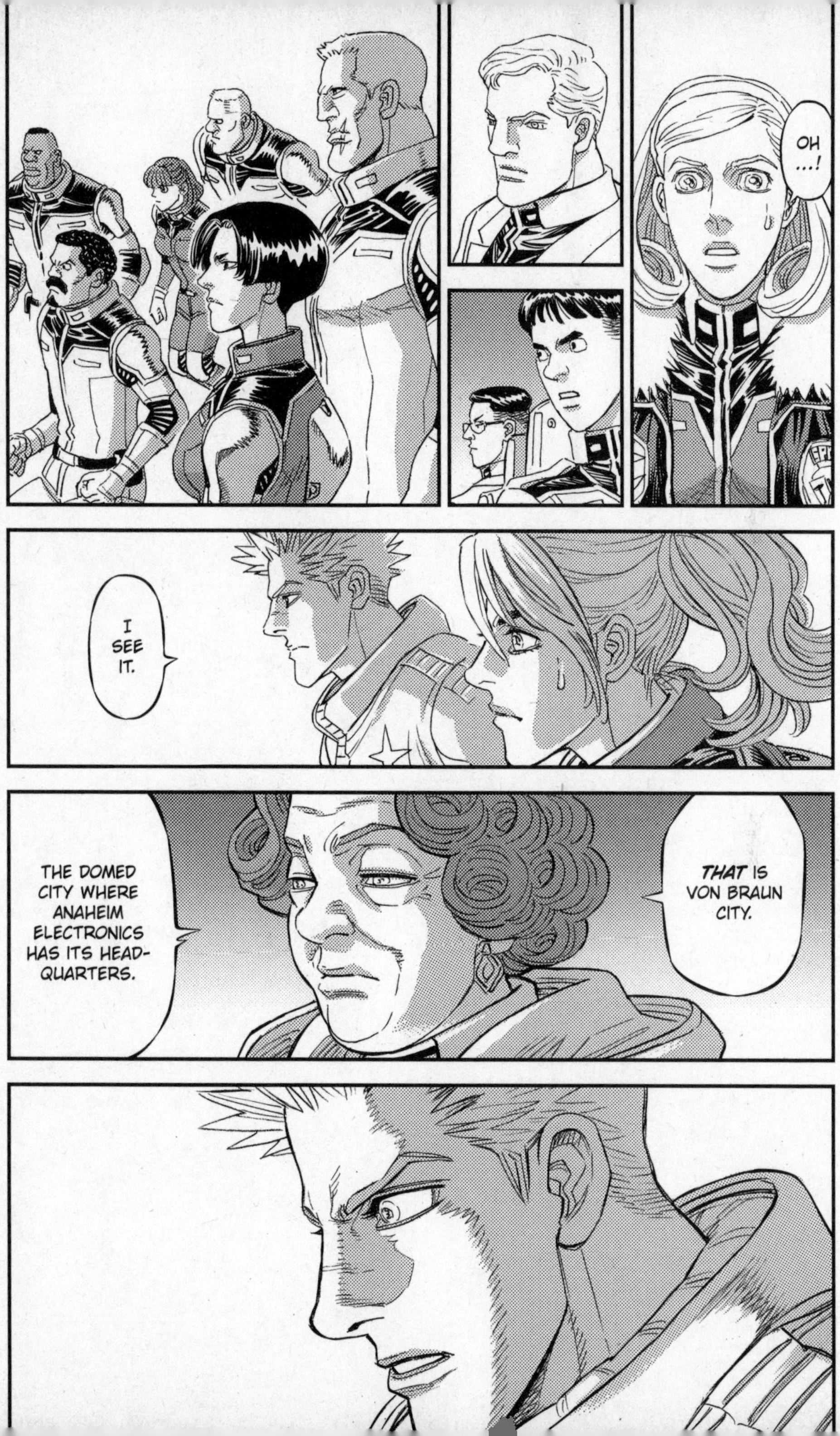
OH ...!
I SEE IT.
THAT IS VON BRAUN CITY.
THE DOMED CITY WHERE ANAHEIM ELECTRONICS HAS ITS HEAD-QUARTERS.

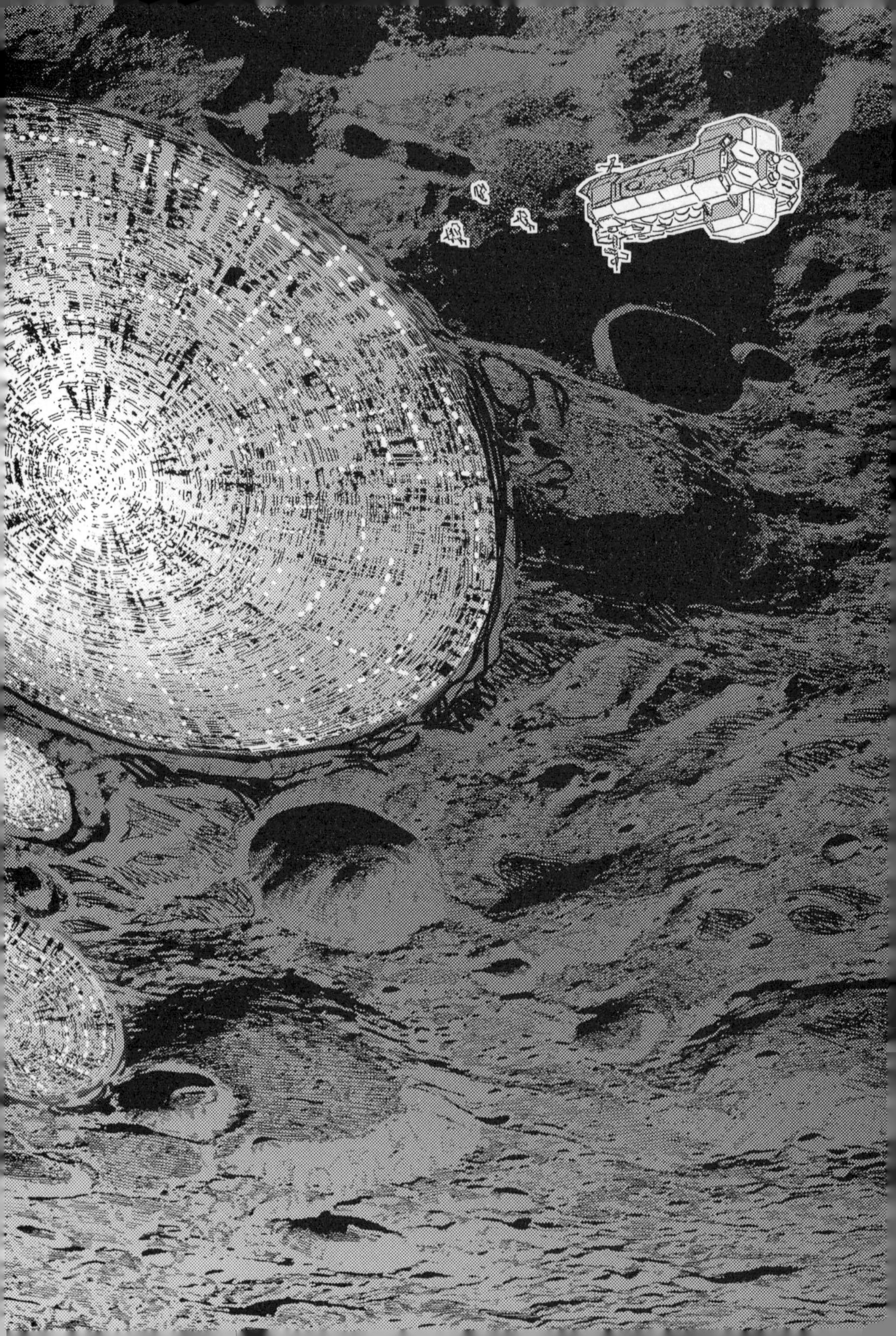

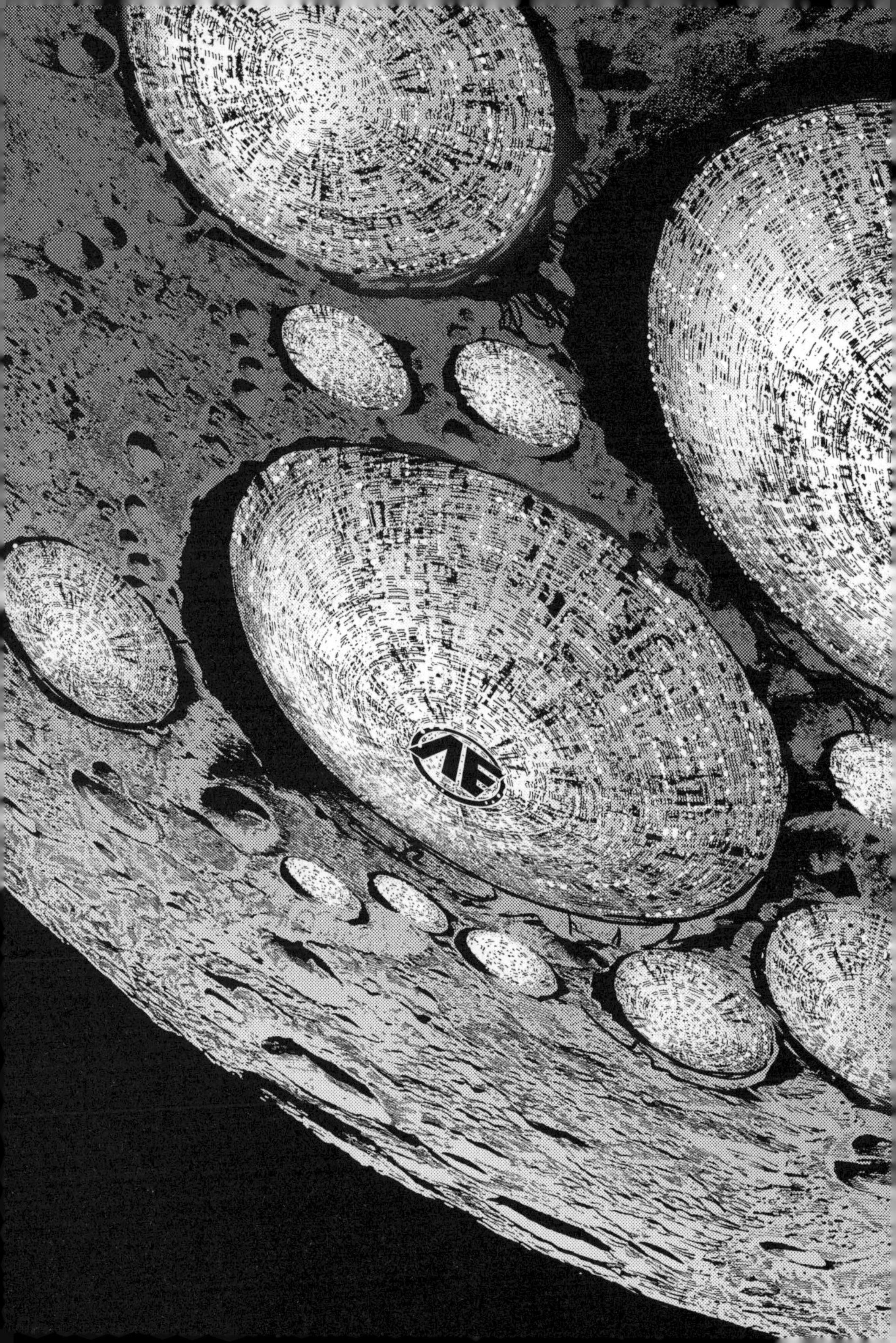

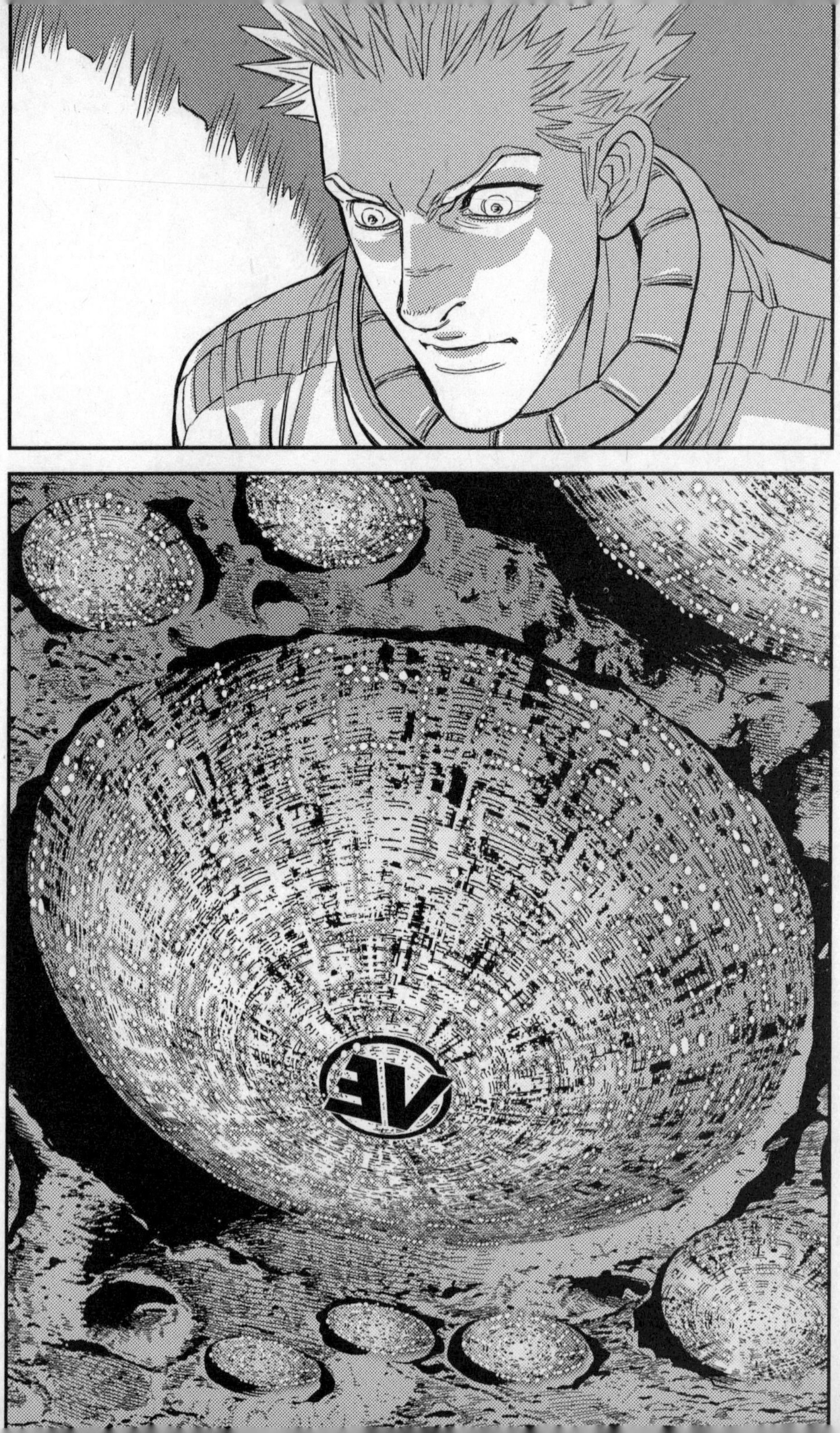

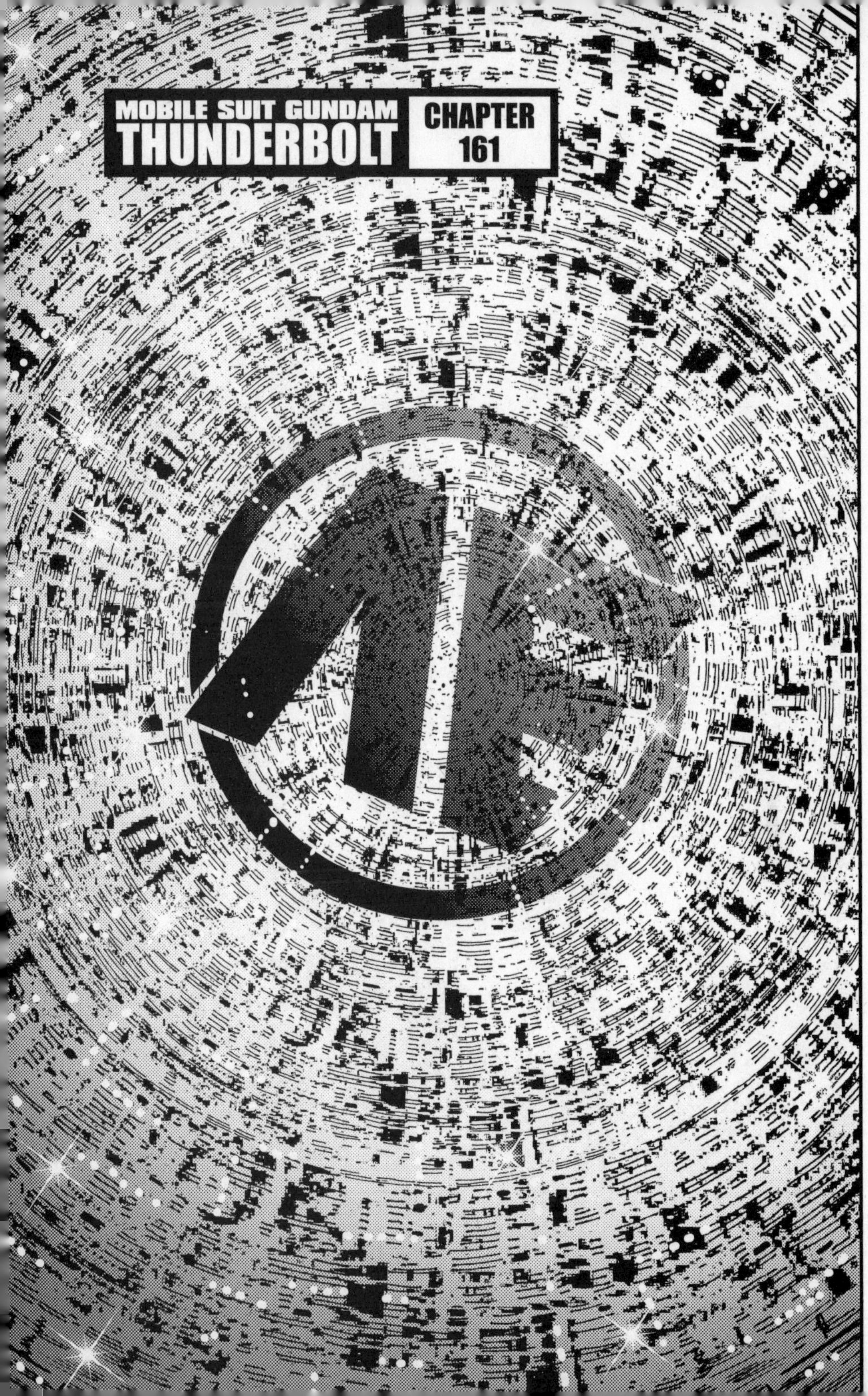
MOBILE SUIT GUNDAM
THUNDERBOLT
CHAPTER
161

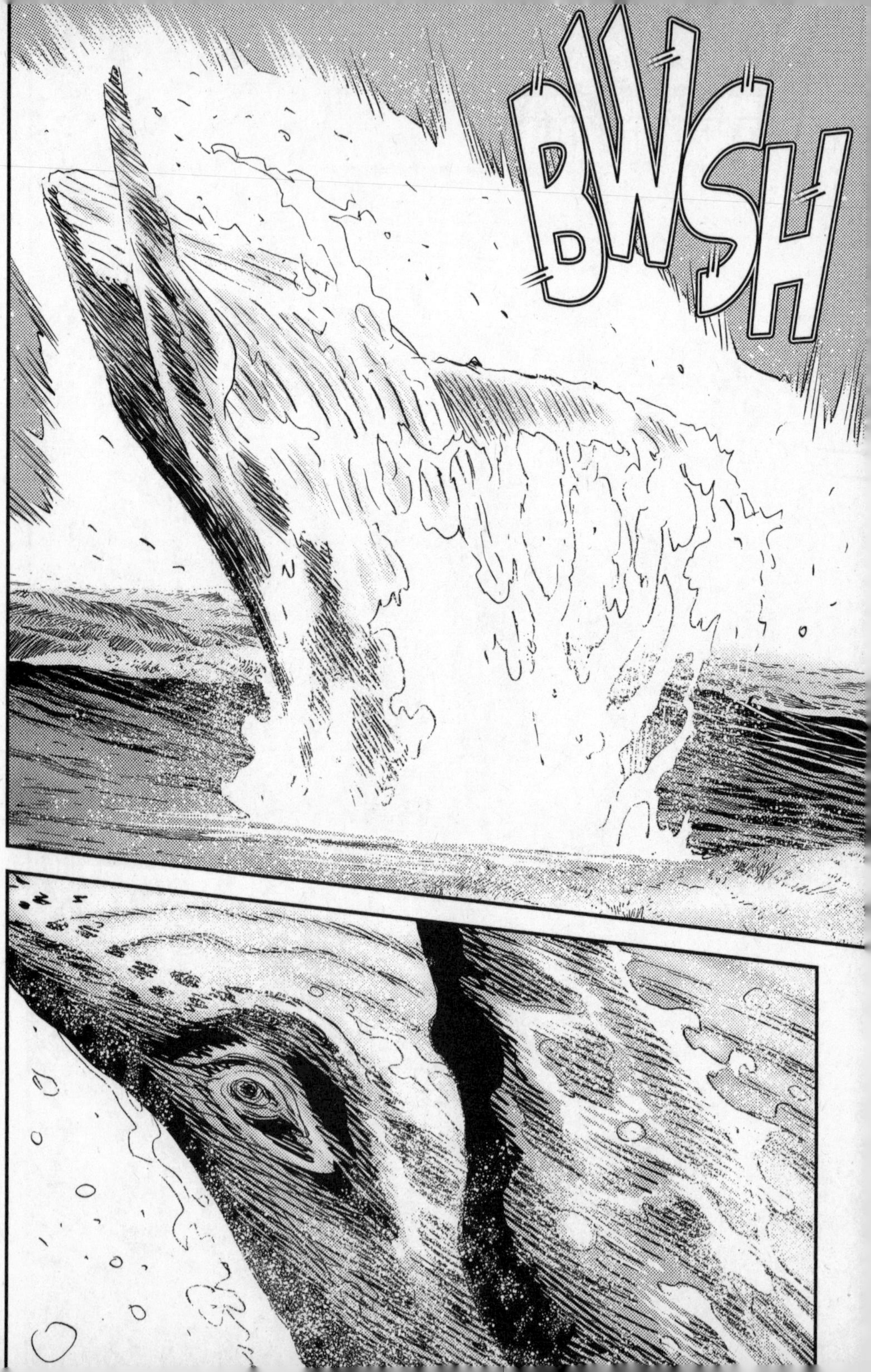
BWSH

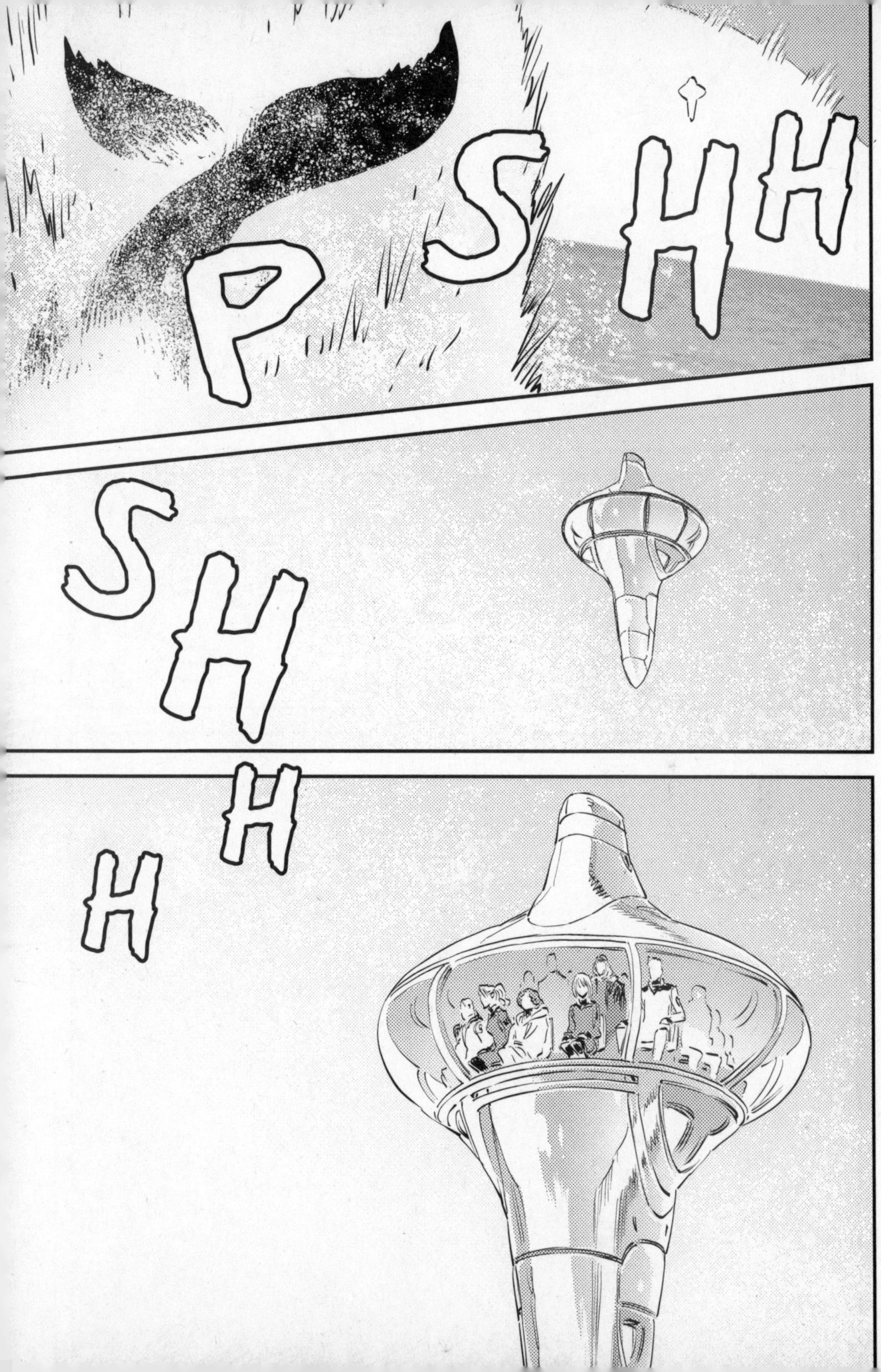
PSHH
SH
HH

NO WAY!

A WHALE ?!

WHAT THE ...?

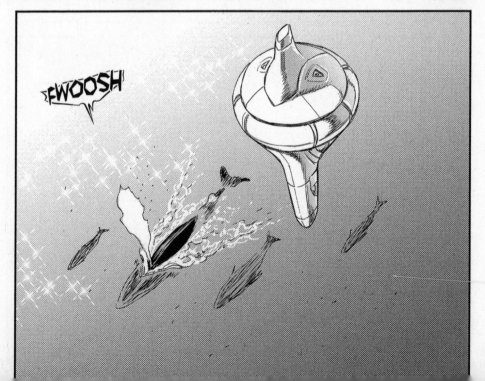

FWOOSH

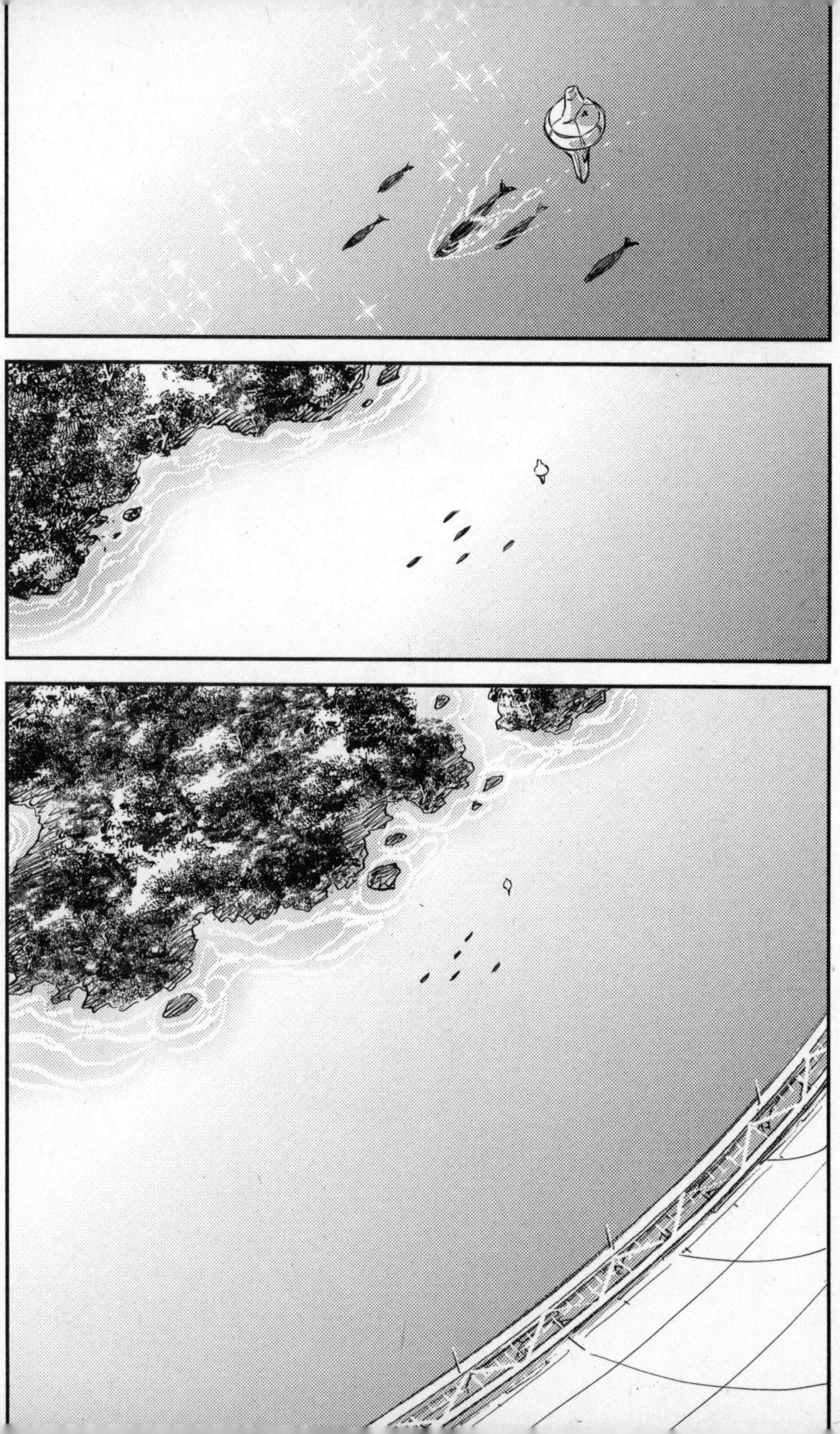

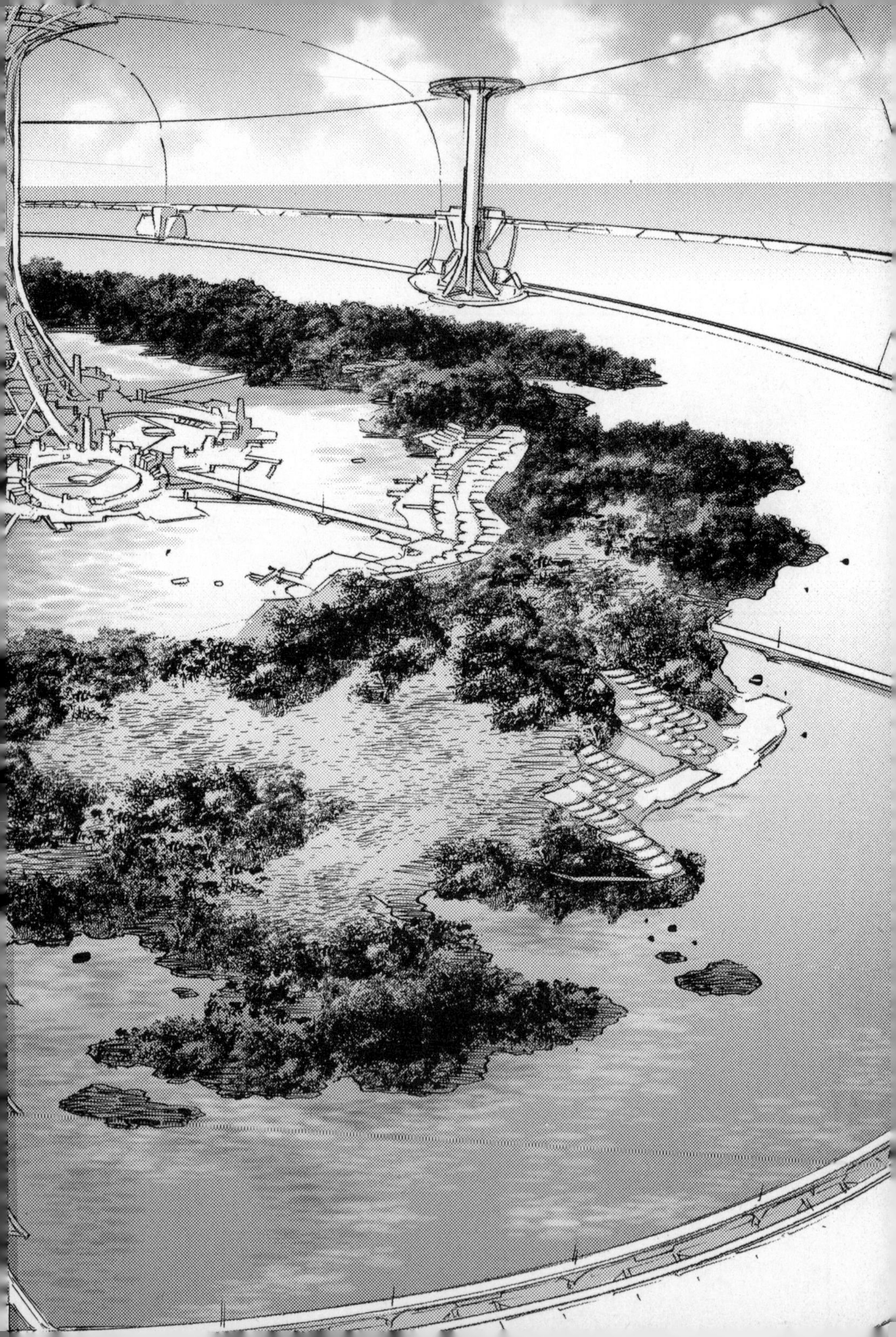

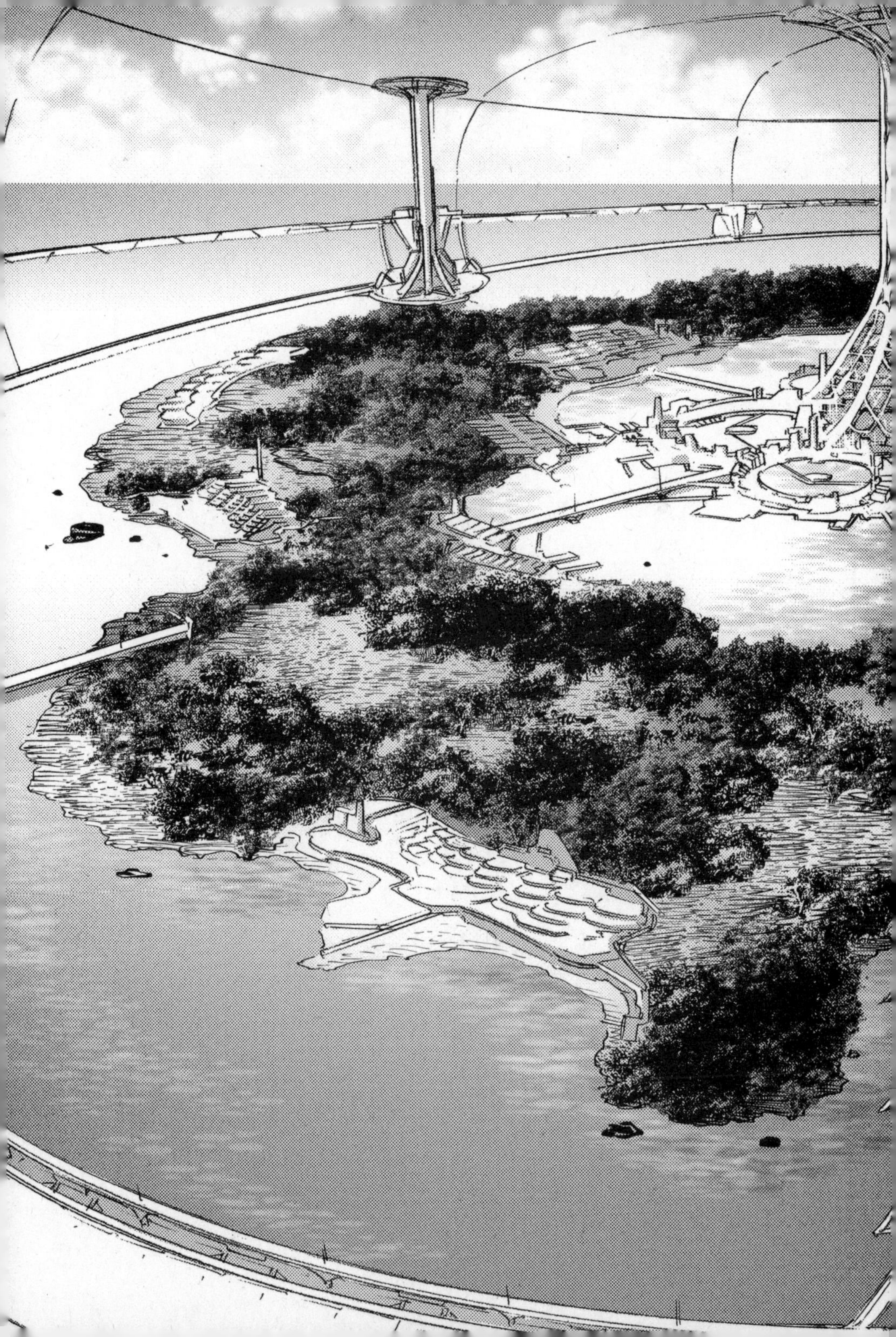

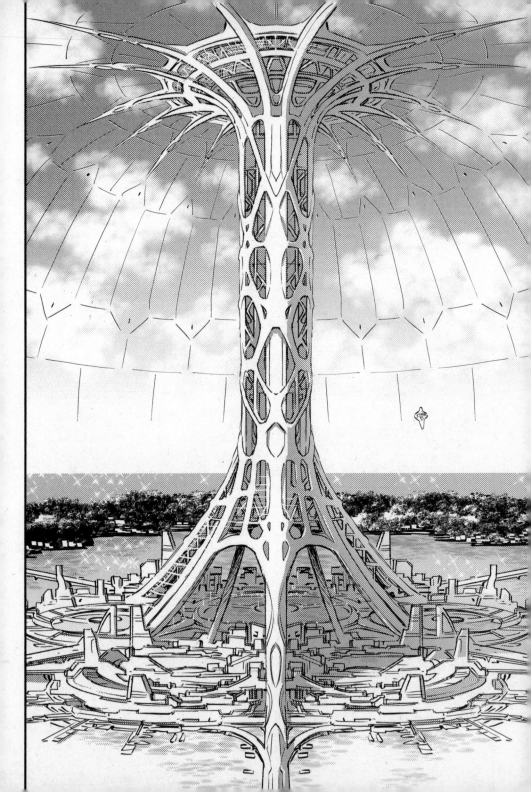

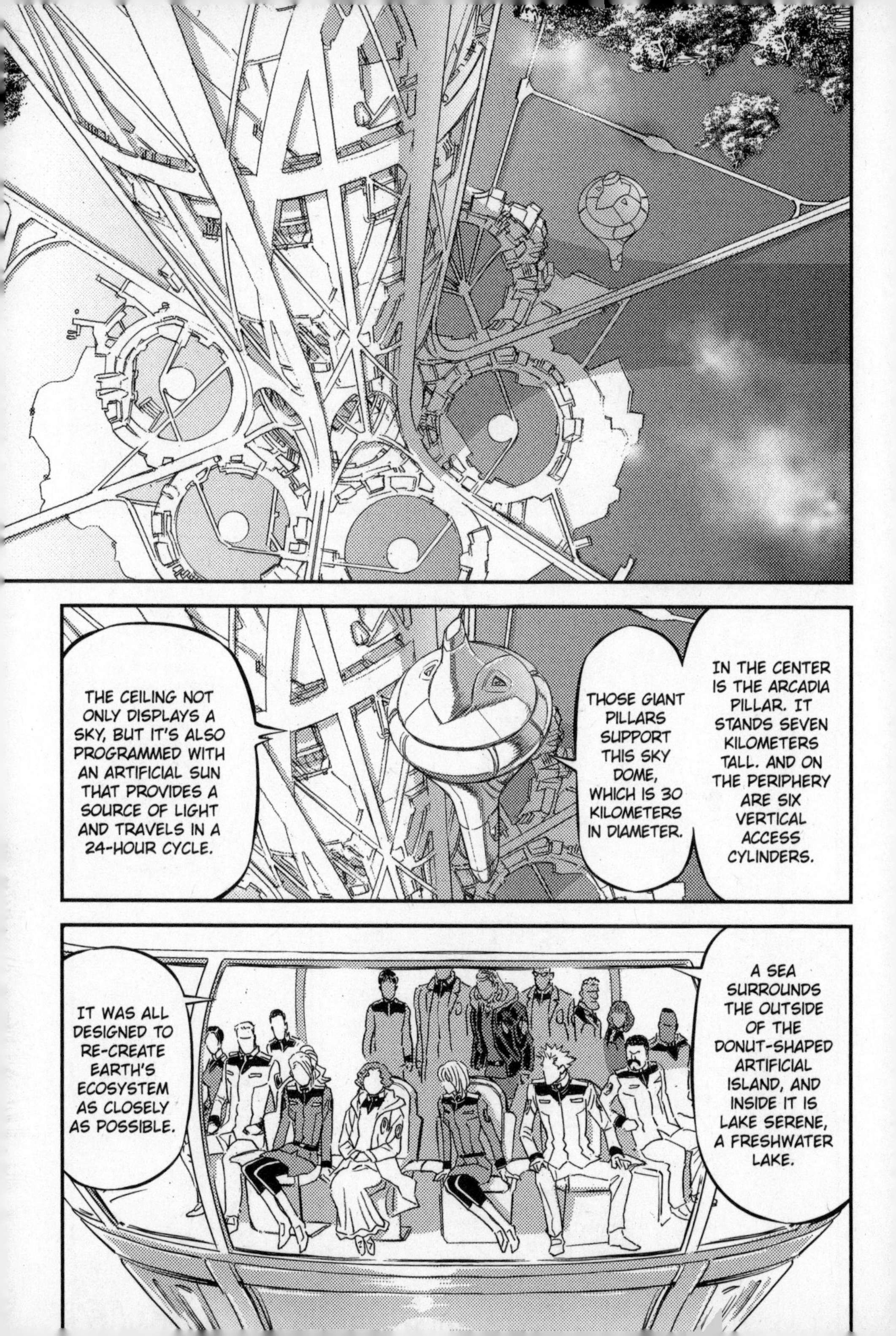
IN THE CENTER IS THE ARCADIA PILLAR. IT STANDS SEVEN KILOMETERS TALL. AND ON THE PERIPHERY ARE SIX VERTICAL ACCESS CYLINDERS.
THOSE GIANT PILLARS SUPPORT THIS SKY DOME, WHICH IS 30 KILOMETERS IN DIAMETER.
THE CEILING NOT ONLY DISPLAYS A SKY, BUT IT'S ALSO PROGRAMMED WITH AN ARTIFICIAL SUN THAT PROVIDES A SOURCE OF LIGHT AND TRAVELS IN A 24-HOUR CYCLE.
A SEA SURROUNDS THE OUTSIDE OF THE DONUT-SHAPED ARTIFICIAL ISLAND, AND INSIDE IT IS LAKE SERENE, A FRESHWATER LAKE.
IT WAS ALL DESIGNED TO RE-CREATE EARTH'S ECOSYSTEM AS CLOSELY AS POSSIBLE.

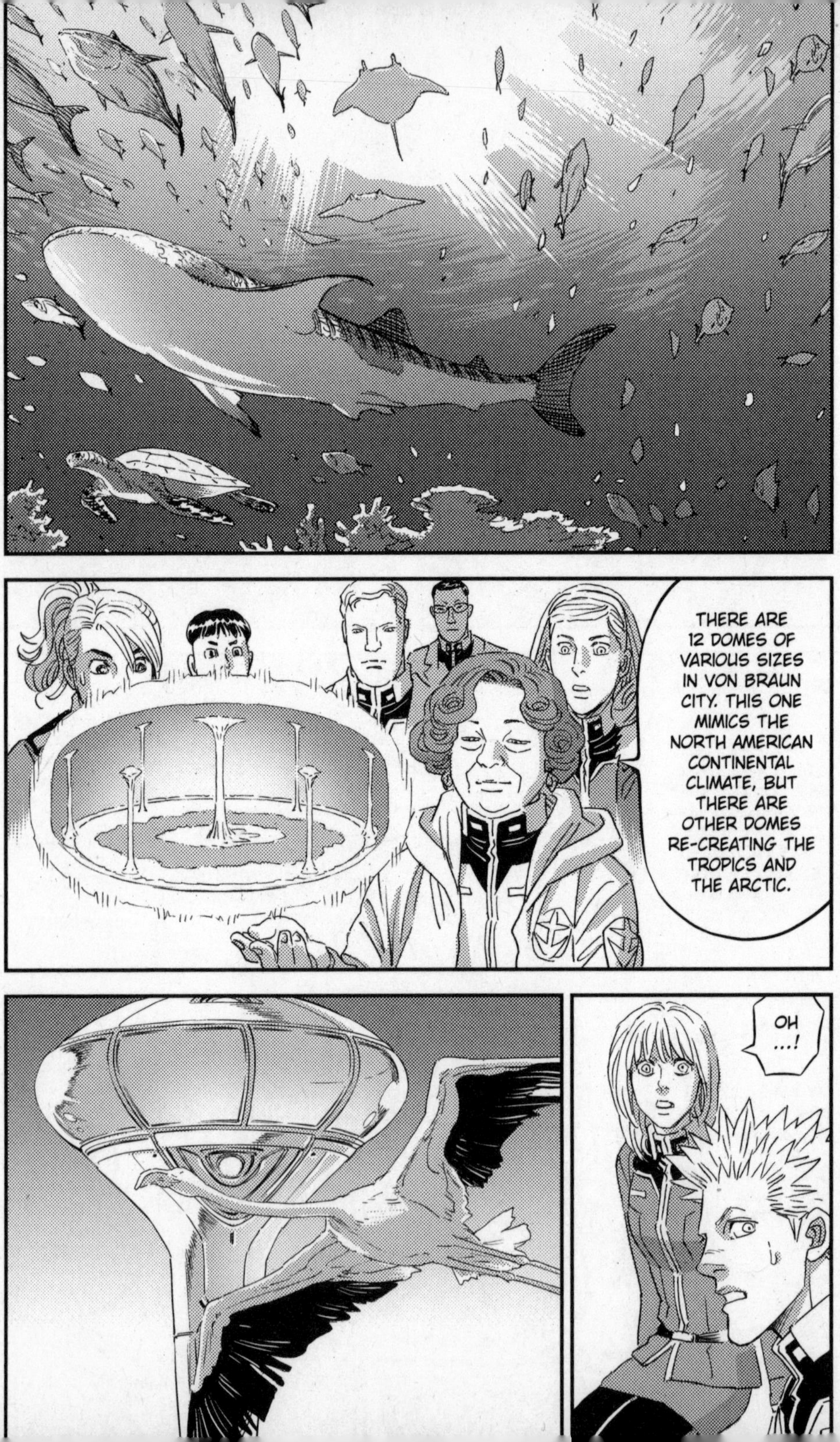
THERE ARE 12 DOMES OF VARIOUS SIZES IN VON BRAUN CITY. THIS ONE MIMICS THE NORTH AMERICAN CONTINENTAL CLIMATE, BUT THERE ARE OTHER DOMES RE-CREATING THE TROPICS AND THE ARCTIC.
OH ...!

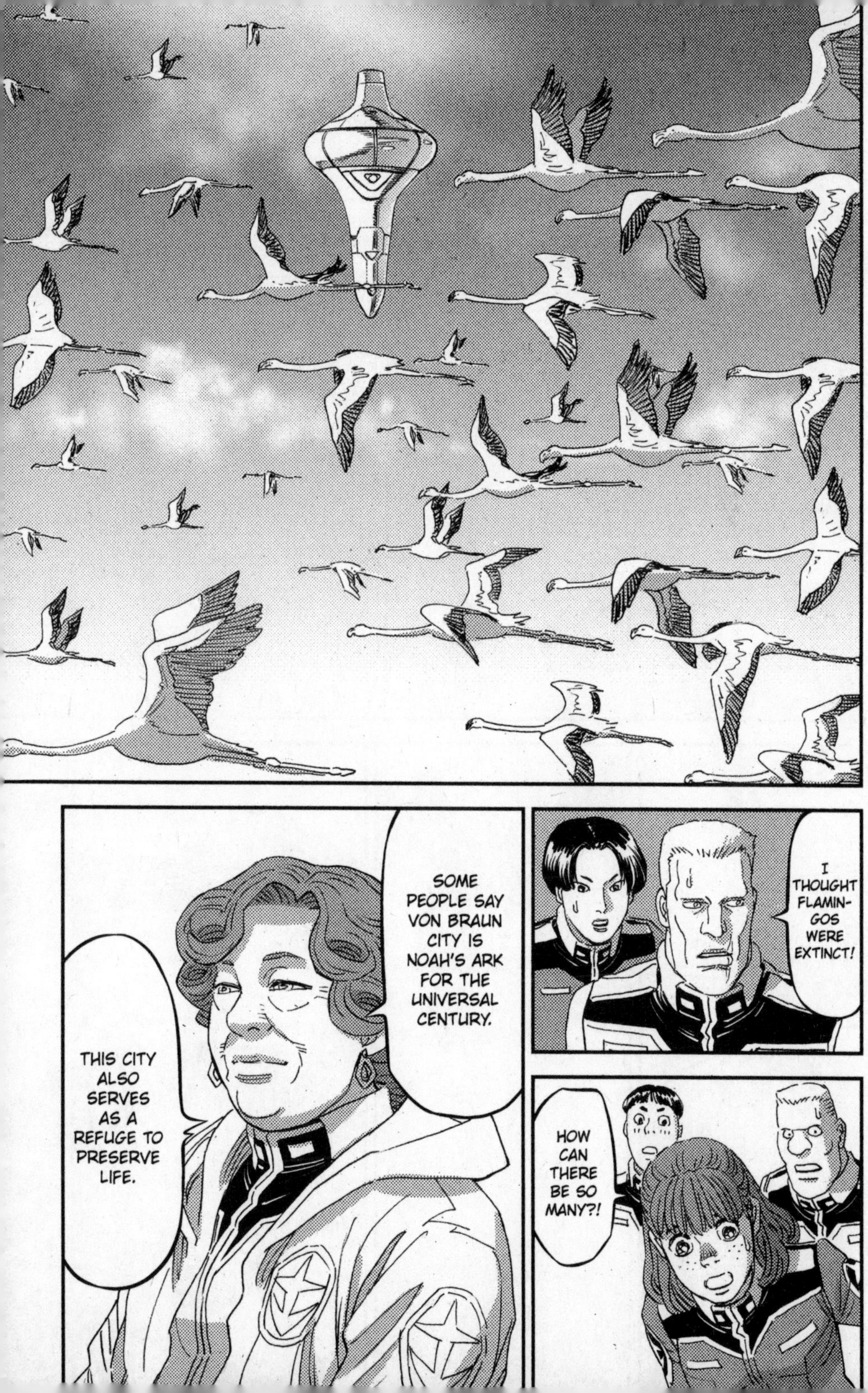
I THOUGHT FLAMIN-GOS WERE EXTINCT!
HOW CAN THERE BE SO MANY?!
SOME PEOPLE SAY VON BRAUN CITY IS NOAH'S ARK FOR THE UNIVERSAL CENTURY.
THIS CITY ALSO SERVES AS A REFUGE TO PRESERVE LIFE.

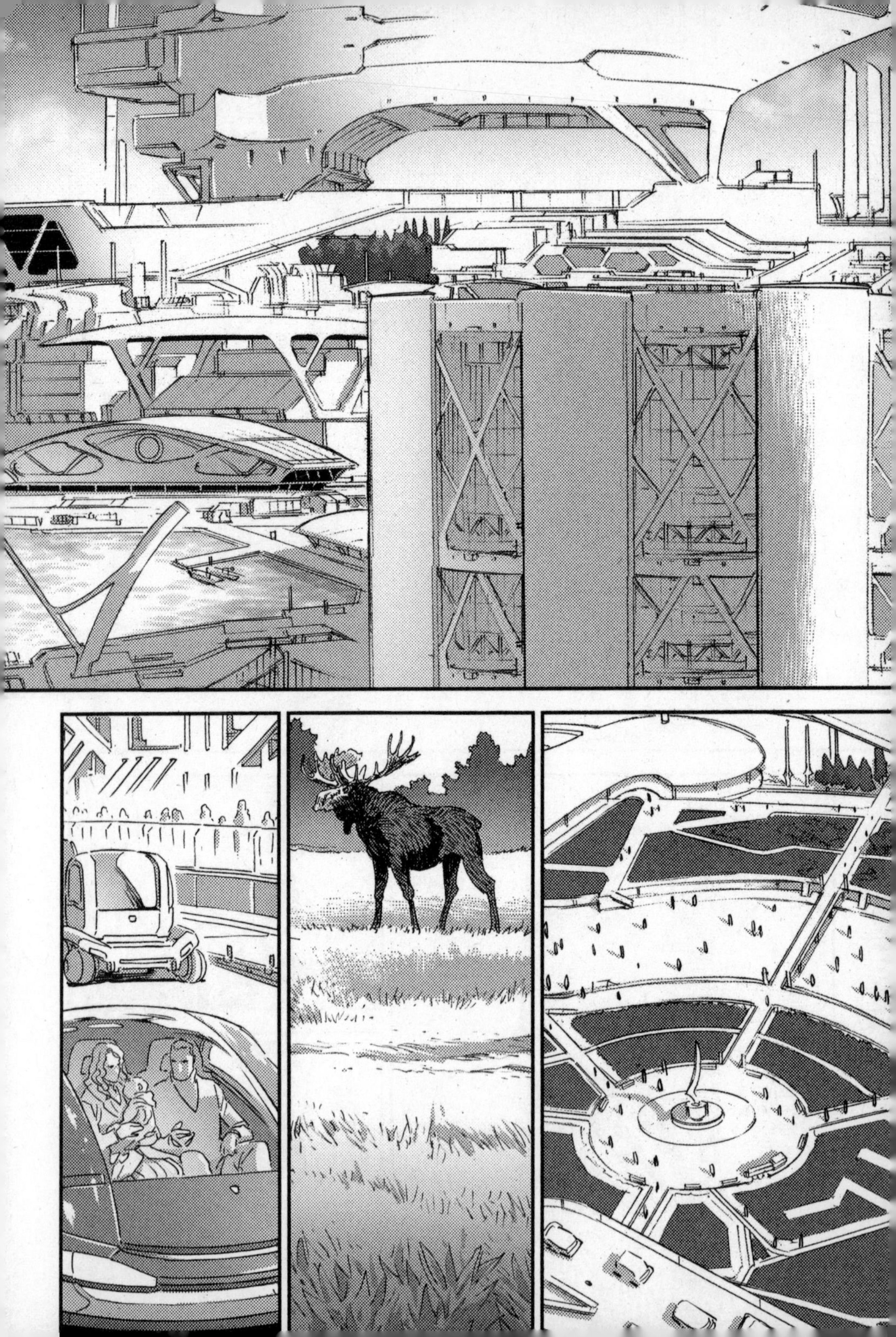

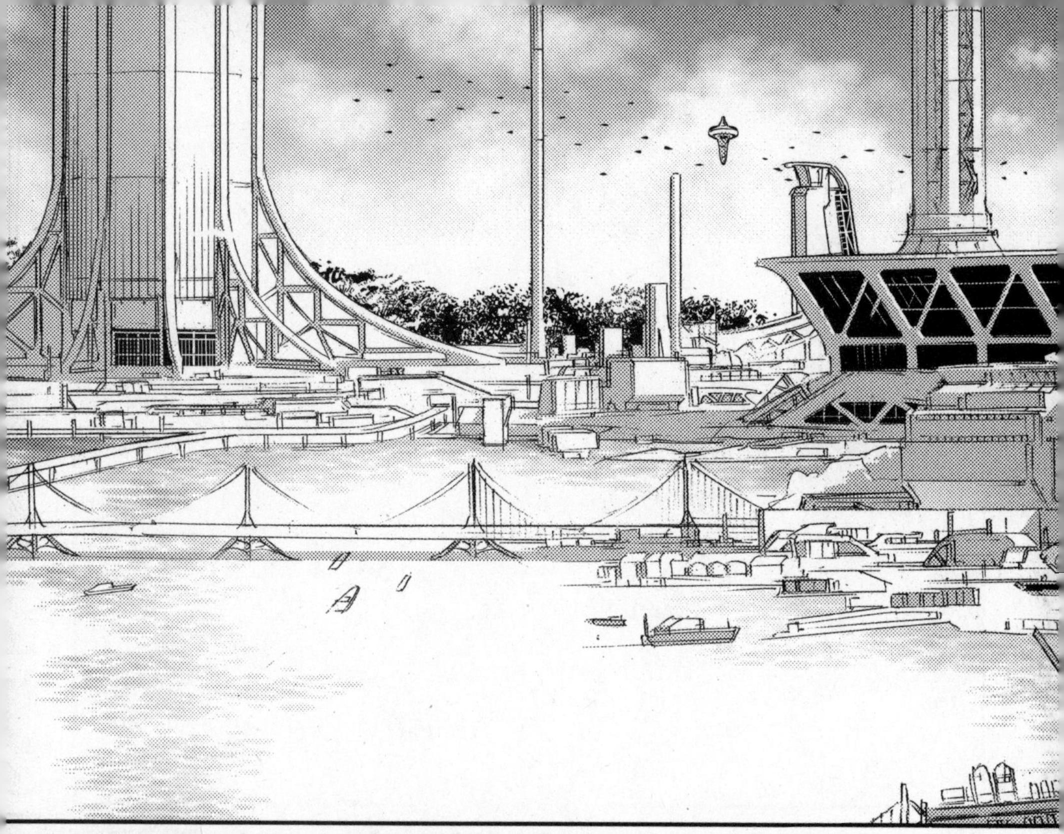
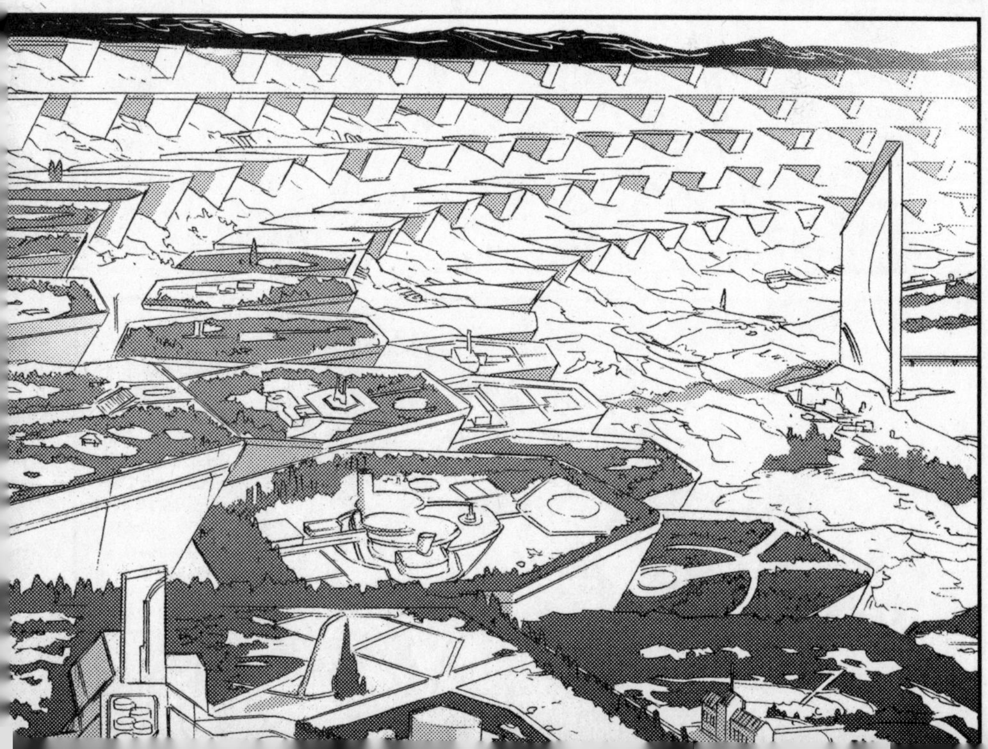

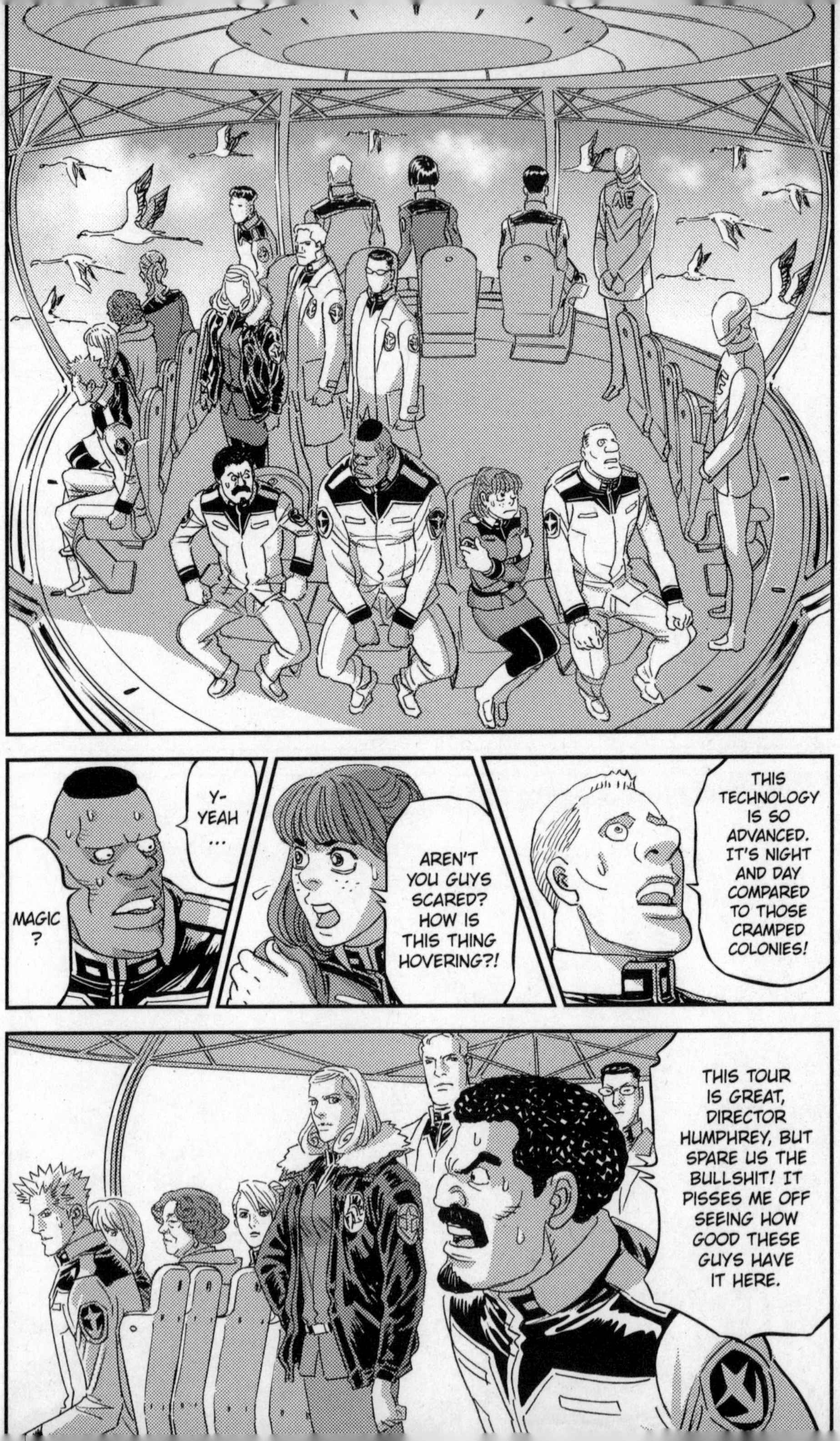
THIS TECHNOLOGY IS SO ADVANCED. IT'S NIGHT AND DAY COMPARED TO THOSE CRAMPED COLONIES!
AREN'T YOU GUYS SCARED? HOW IS THIS THING HOVERING?!
Y-YEAH...
MAGIC?
THIS TOUR IS GREAT, DIRECTOR HUMPHREY, BUT SPARE US THE BULLSHIT! IT PISSES ME OFF SEEING HOW GOOD THESE GUYS HAVE IT HERE.

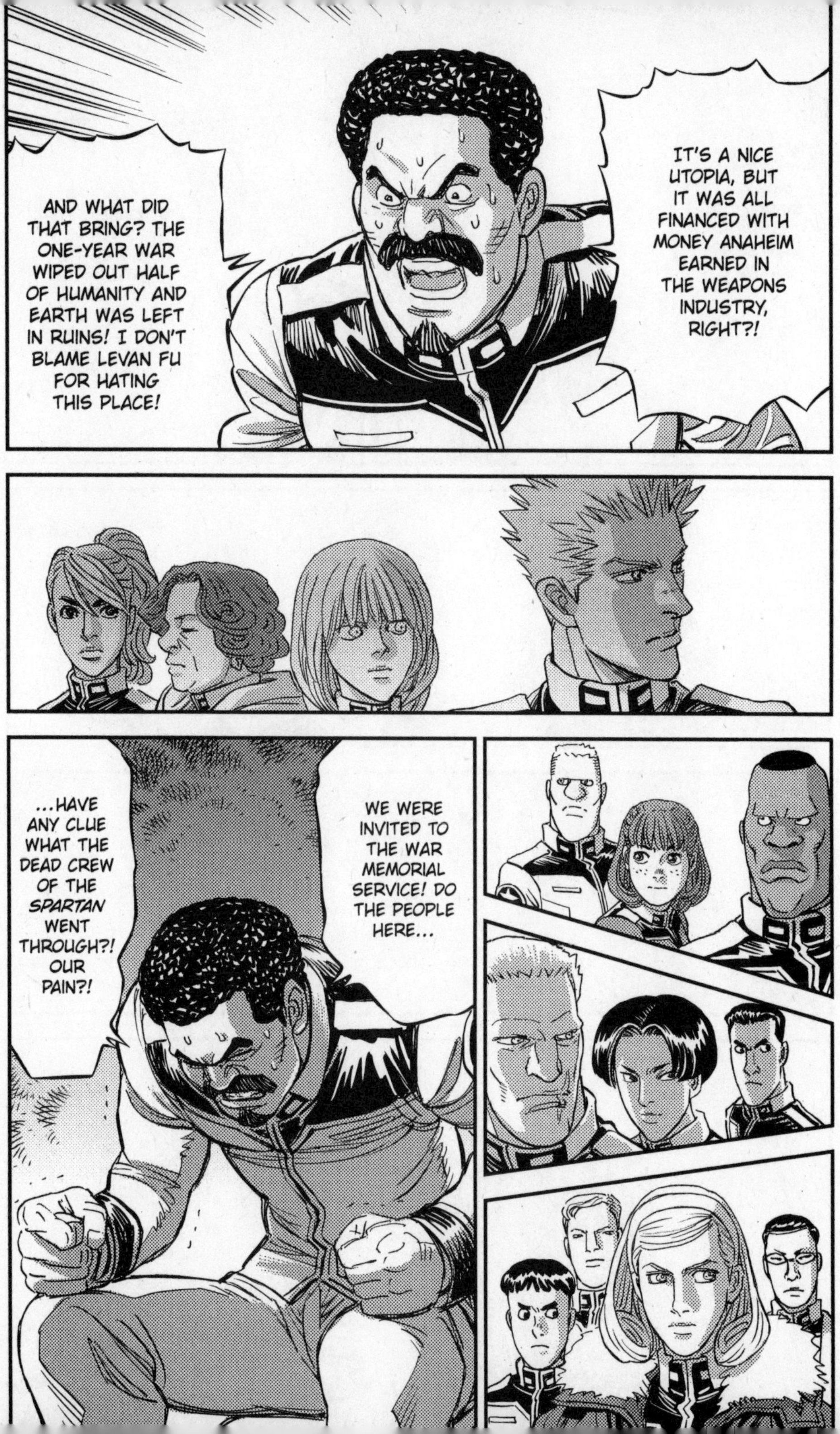
IT'S A NICE UTOPIA, BUT IT WAS ALL FINANCED WITH MONEY ANAHEIM EARNED IN THE WEAPONS INDUSTRY, RIGHT?!
AND WHAT DID THAT BRING? THE ONE-YEAR WAR WIPED OUT HALF OF HUMANITY AND EARTH WAS LEFT IN RUINS! I DON'T BLAME LEVAN FU FOR HATING THIS PLACE!
WE WERE INVITED TO THE WAR MEMORIAL SERVICE! DO THE PEOPLE HERE...
...HAVE ANY CLUE WHAT THE DEAD CREW OF THE *SPARTAN* WENT THROUGH?! OUR PAIN?!

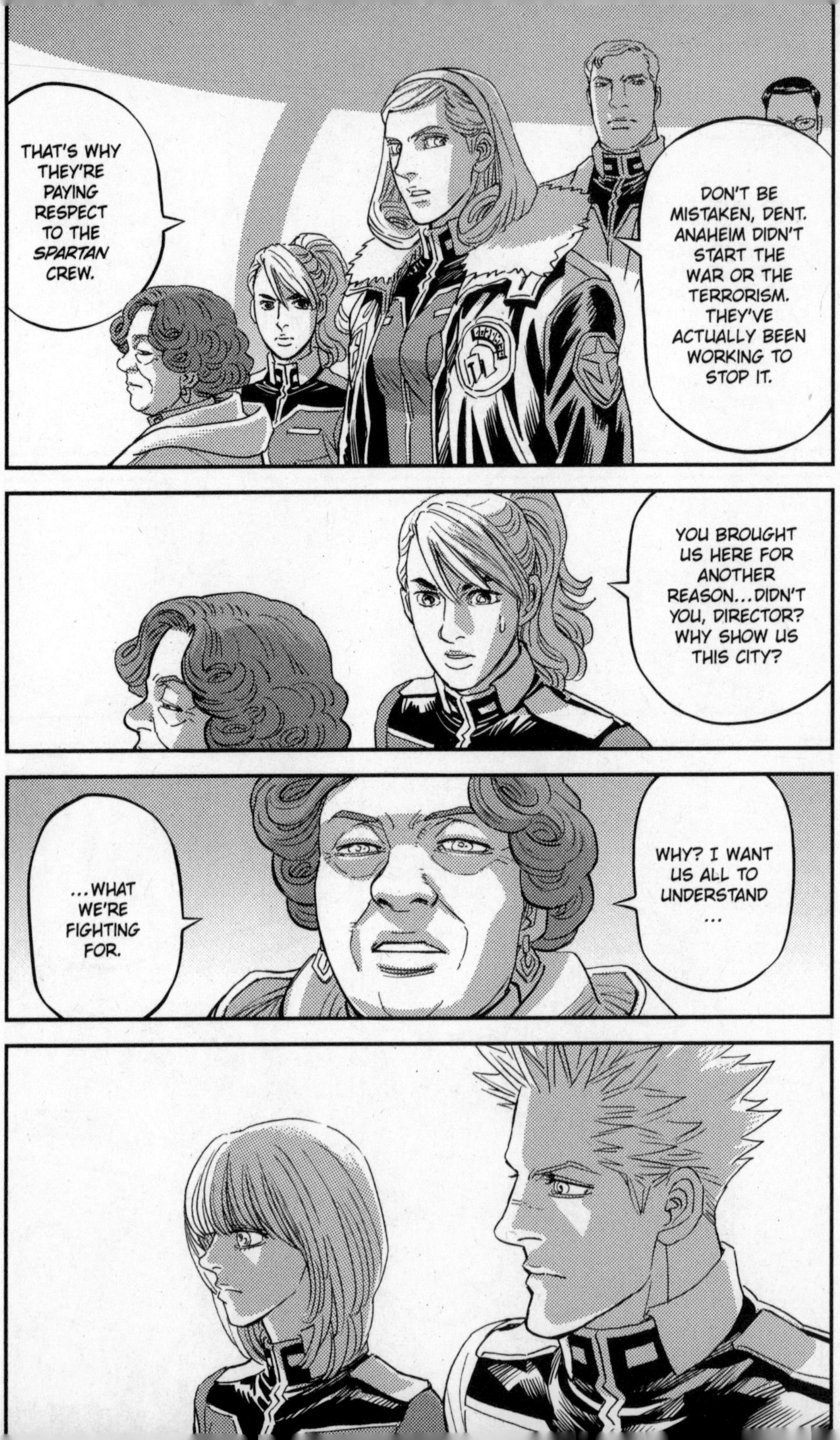
THAT'S WHY THEY'RE PAYING RESPECT TO THE *SPARTAN* CREW.
DON'T BE MISTAKEN, DENT. ANAHEIM DIDN'T START THE WAR OR THE TERRORISM. THEY'VE ACTUALLY BEEN WORKING TO STOP IT.
YOU BROUGHT US HERE FOR ANOTHER REASON...DIDN'T YOU, DIRECTOR? WHY SHOW US THIS CITY?
WHY? I WANT US ALL TO UNDERSTAND ...
...WHAT WE'RE FIGHTING FOR.

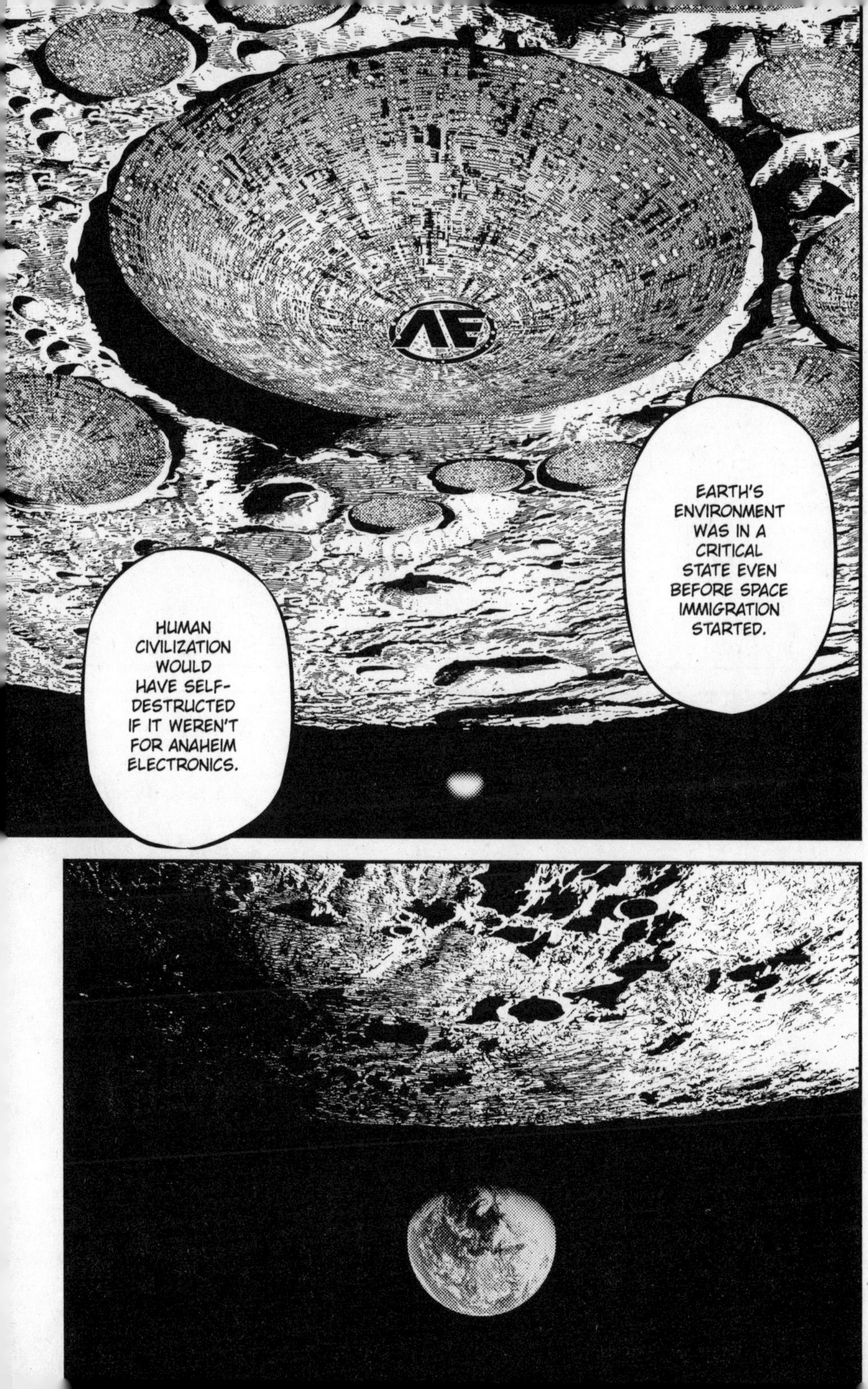
EARTH'S ENVIRONMENT WAS IN A CRITICAL STATE EVEN BEFORE SPACE IMMIGRATION STARTED.
HUMAN CIVILIZATION WOULD HAVE SELF-DESTRUCTED IF IT WEREN'T FOR ANAHEIM ELECTRONICS.

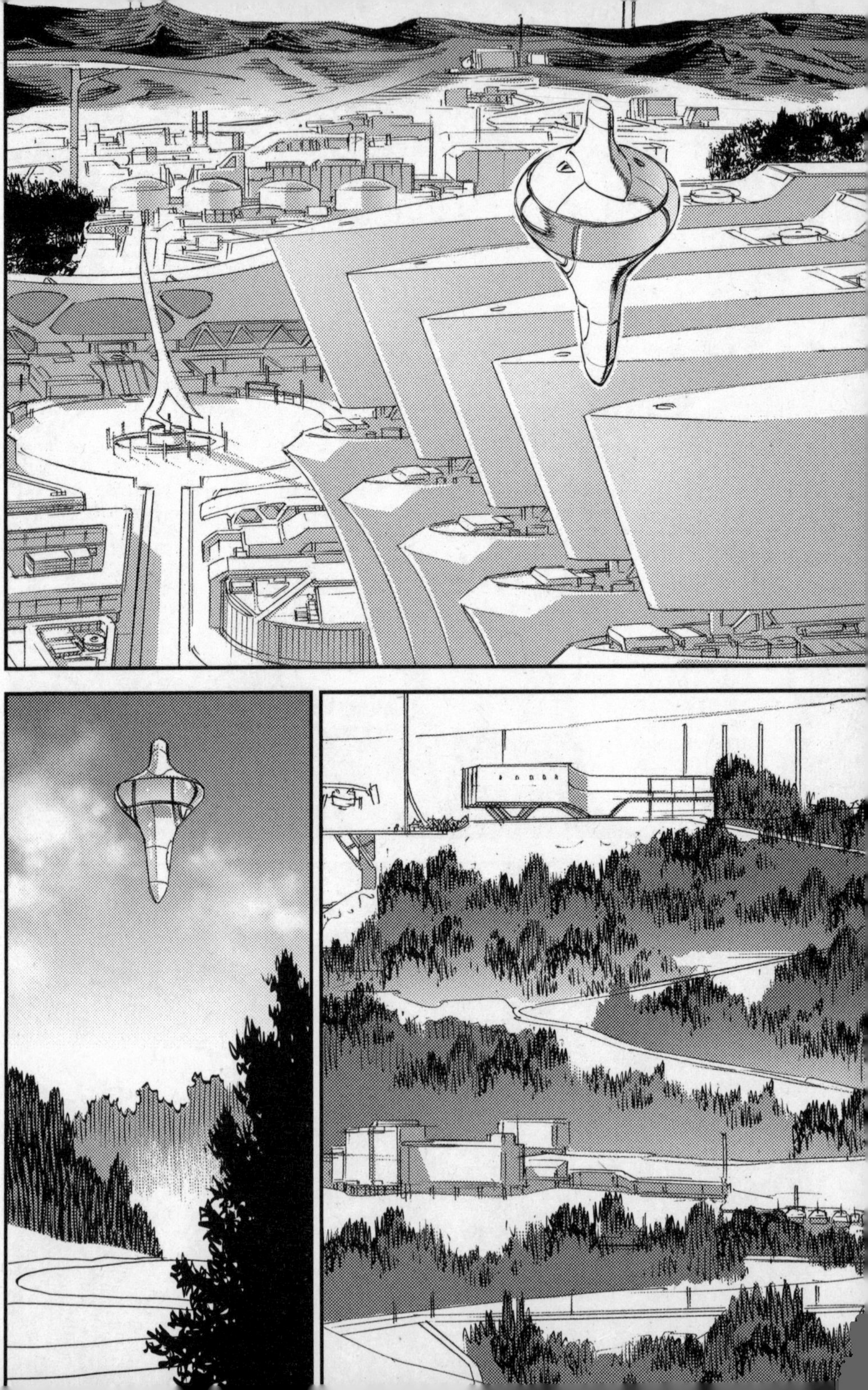

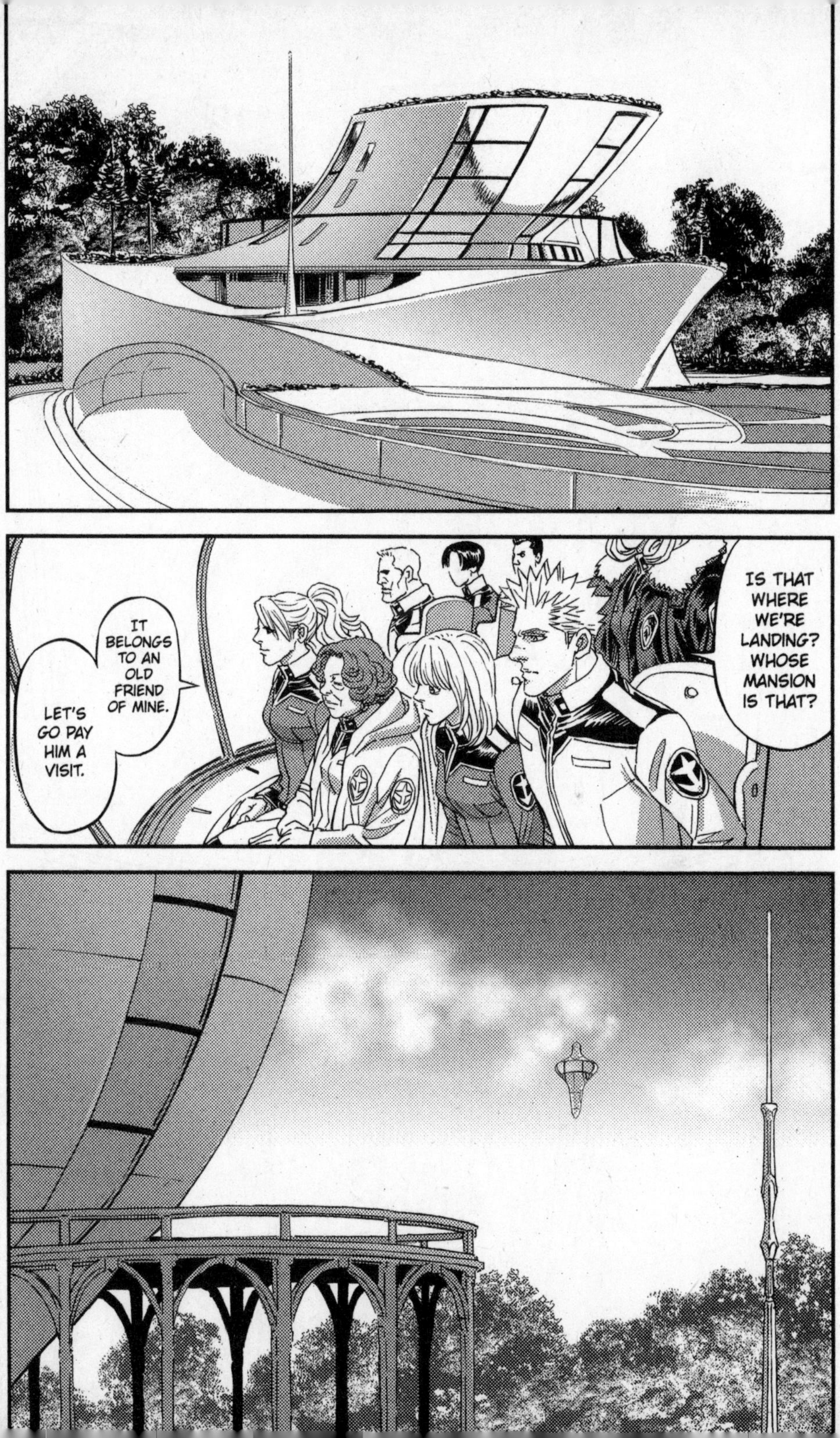
IS THAT WHERE WE'RE LANDING? WHOSE MANSION IS THAT?
IT BELONGS TO AN OLD FRIEND OF MINE.
LET'S GO PAY HIM A VISIT.

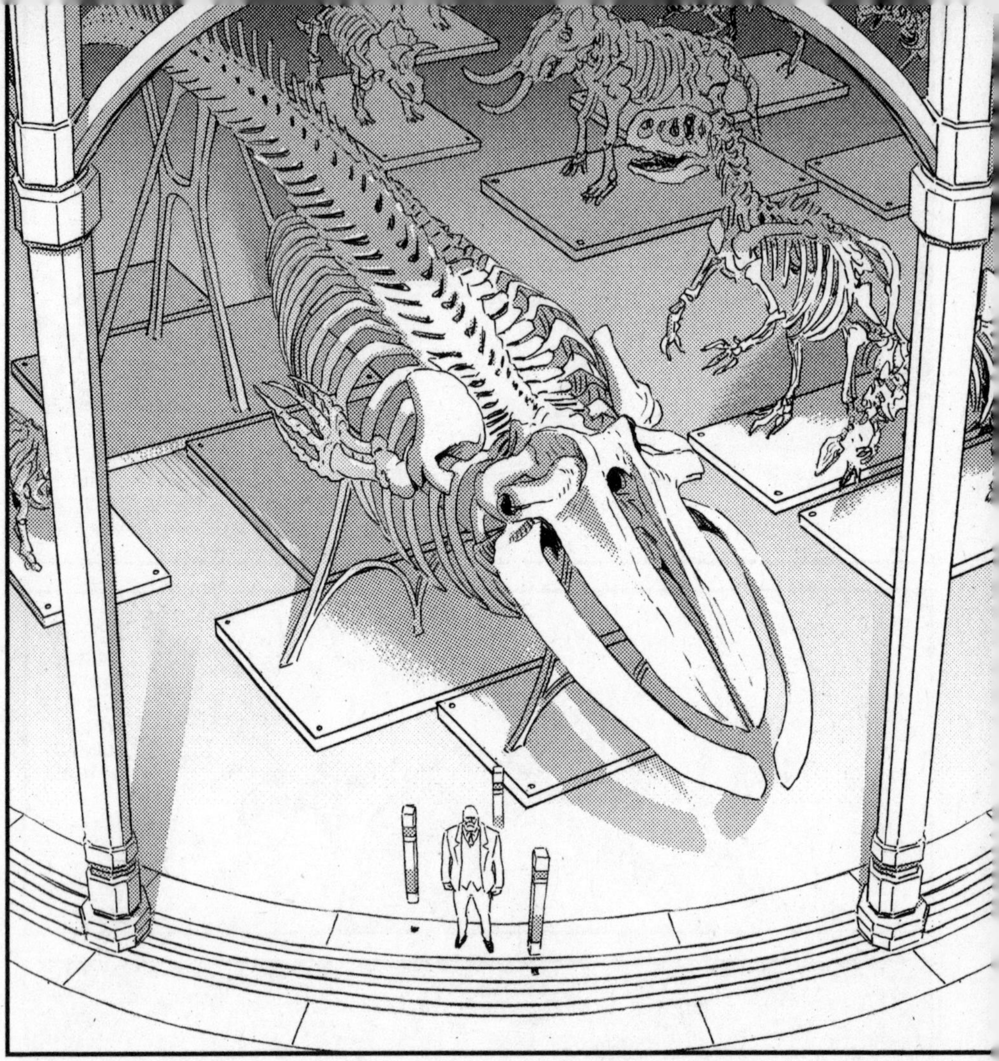
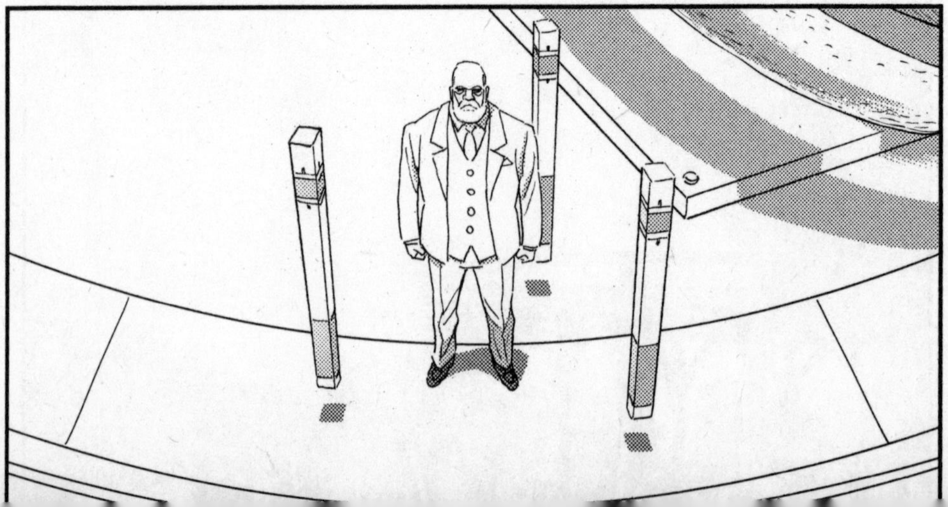

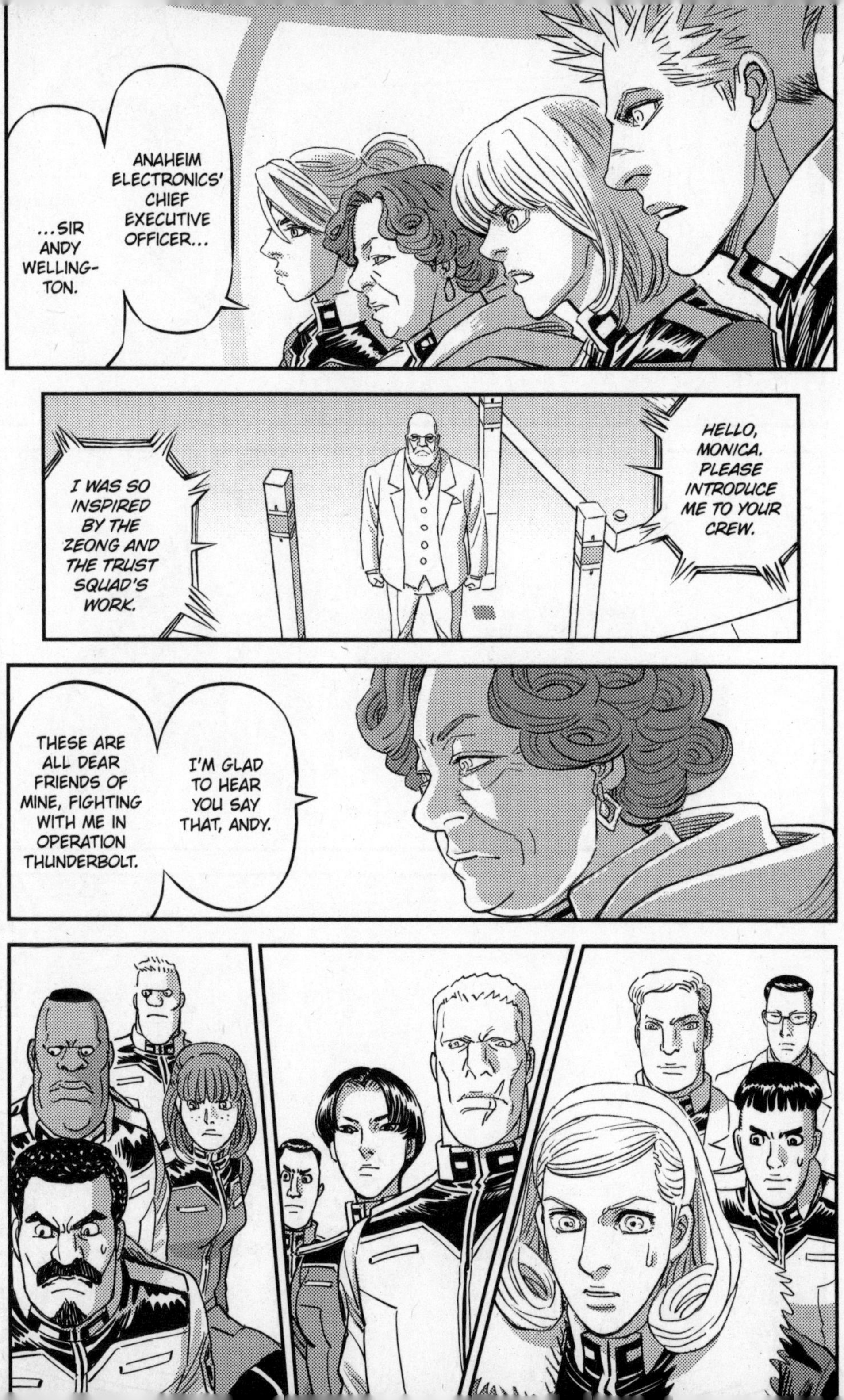
ANAHEIM ELECTRONICS' CHIEF EXECUTIVE OFFICER...
...SIR ANDY WELLING-TON.
HELLO, MONICA. PLEASE INTRODUCE ME TO YOUR CREW.
I WAS SO INSPIRED BY THE ZEONG AND THE TRUST SQUAD'S WORK.
I'M GLAD TO HEAR YOU SAY THAT, ANDY.
THESE ARE ALL DEAR FRIENDS OF MINE, FIGHTING WITH ME IN OPERATION THUNDERBOLT.

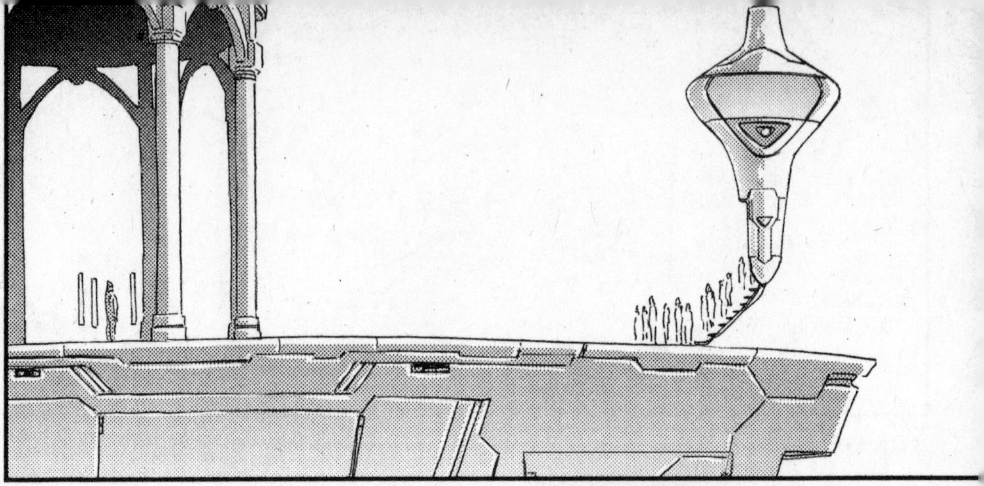
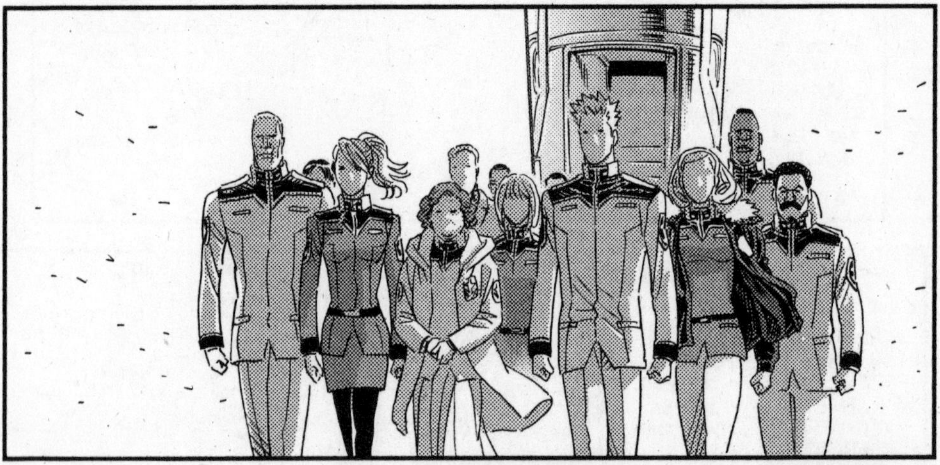
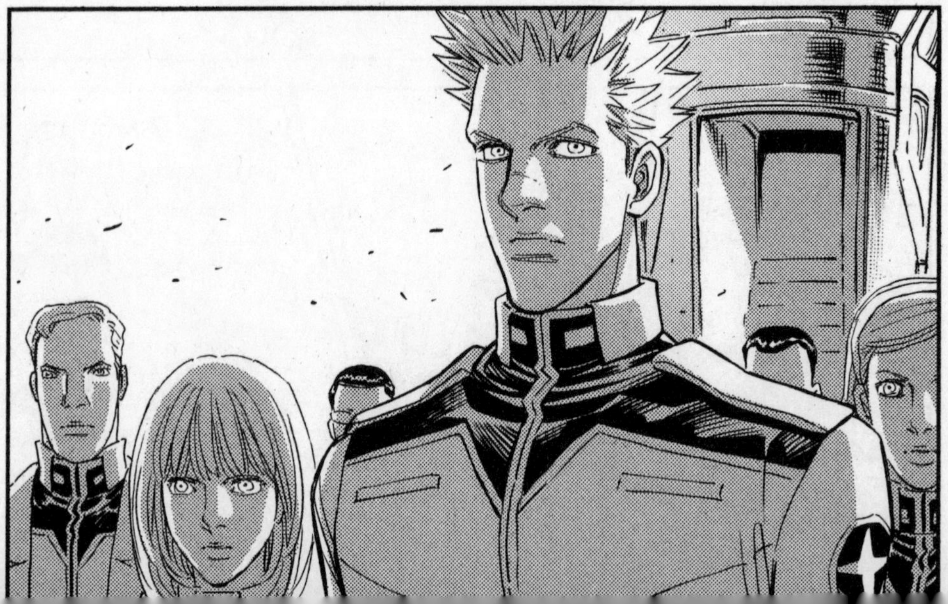

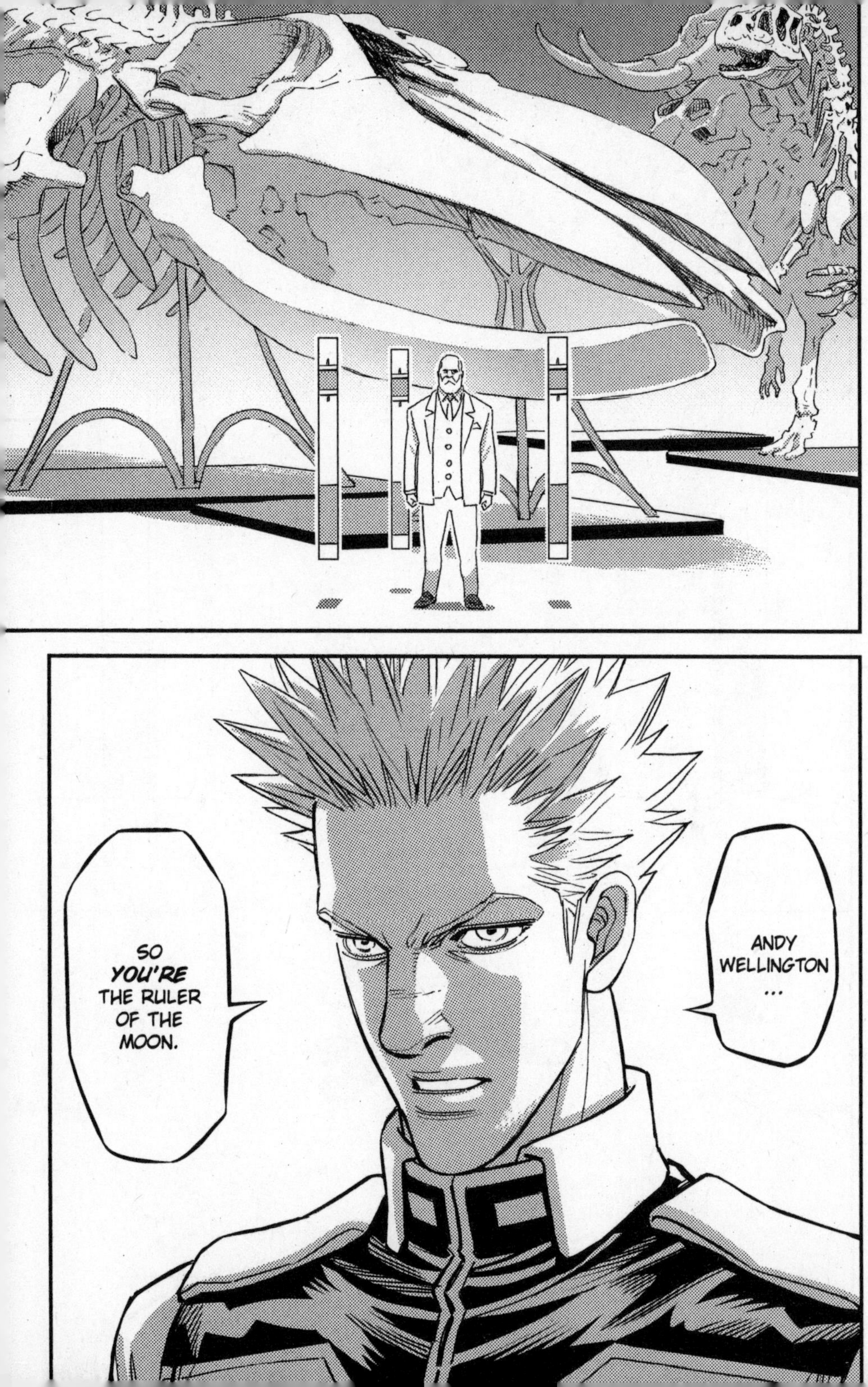
ANDY WELLINGTON ...
SO *YOU'RE* THE RULER OF THE MOON.

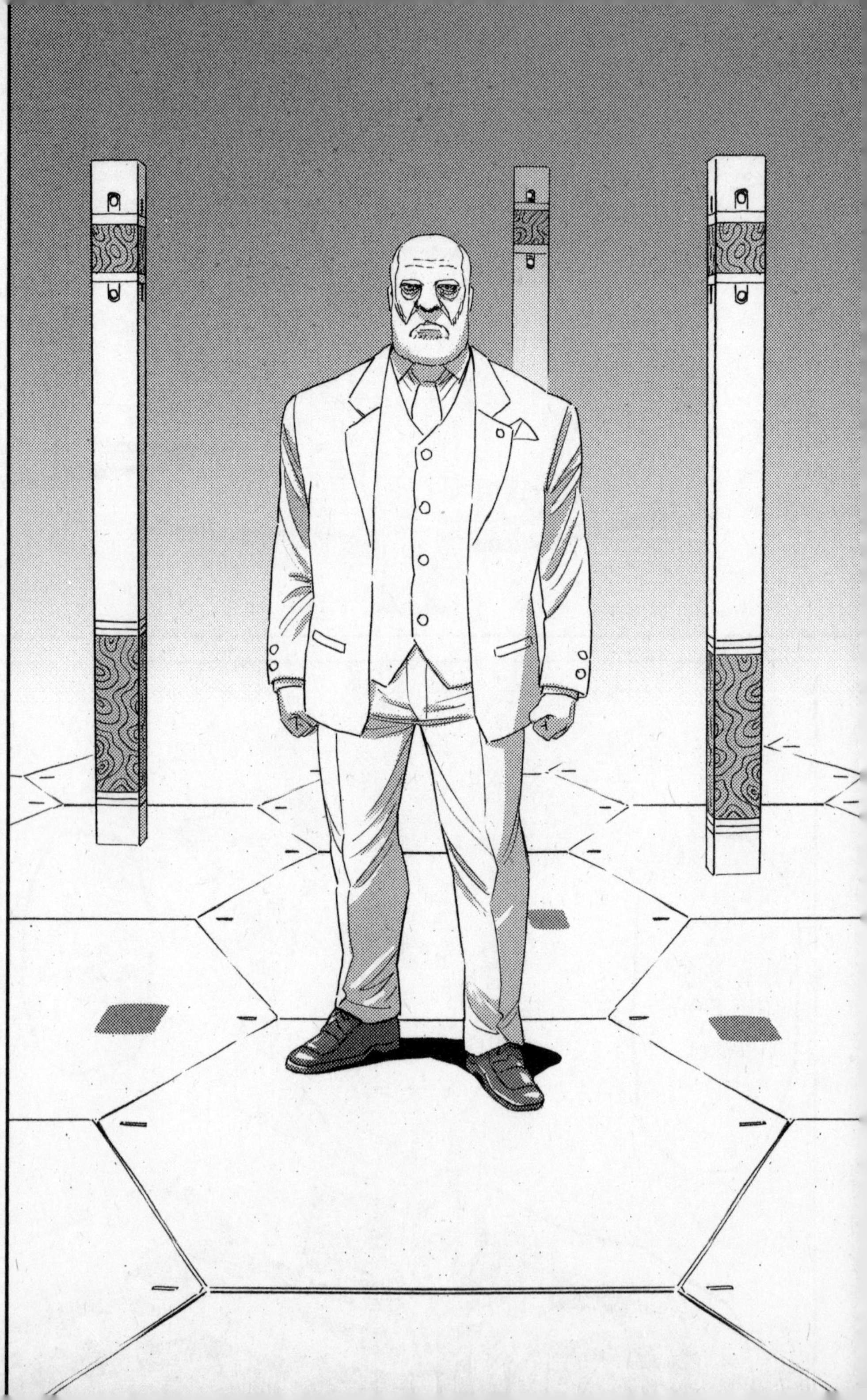

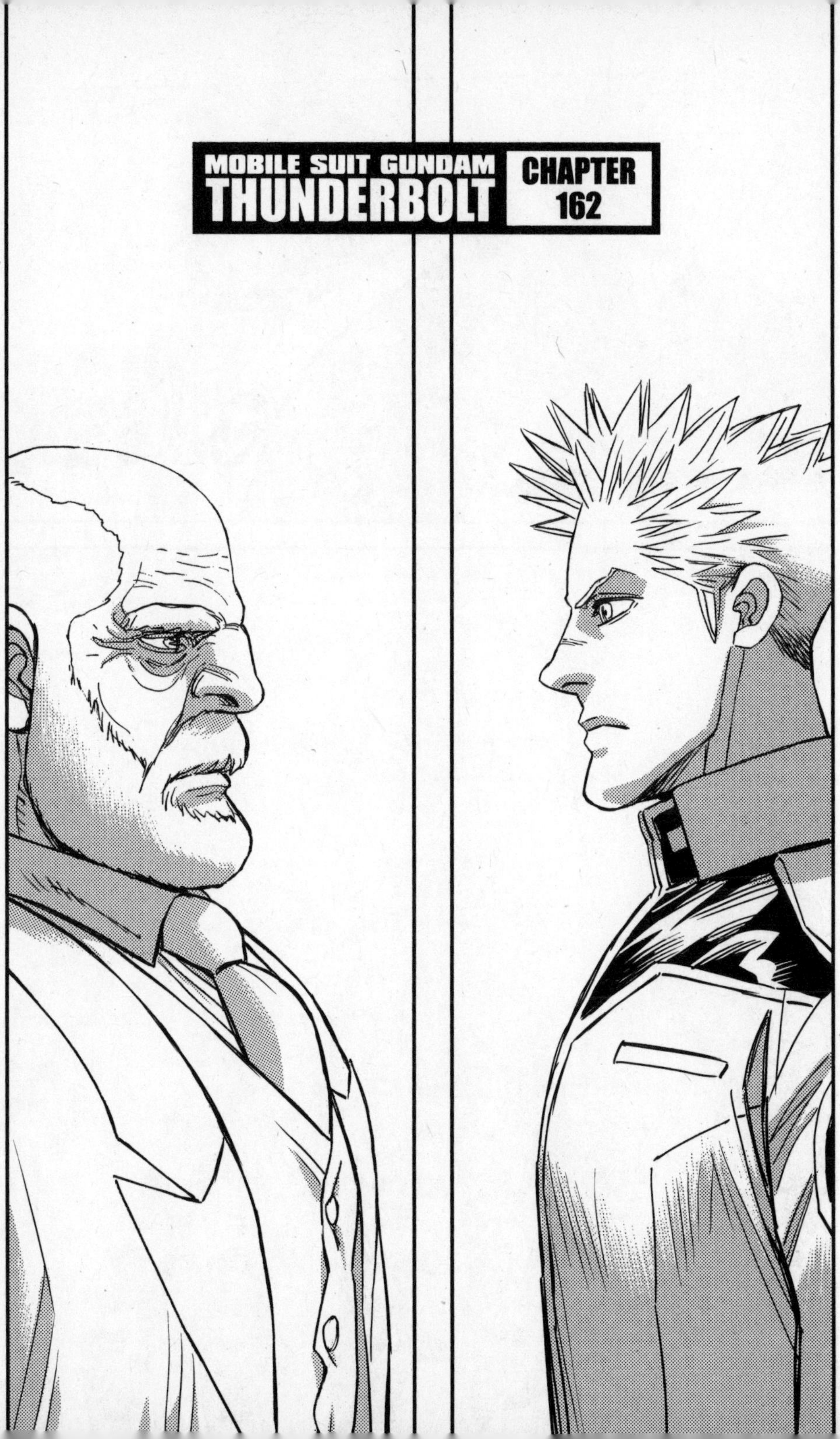
MOBILE SUIT GUNDAM
THUNDERBOLT
CHAPTER
162

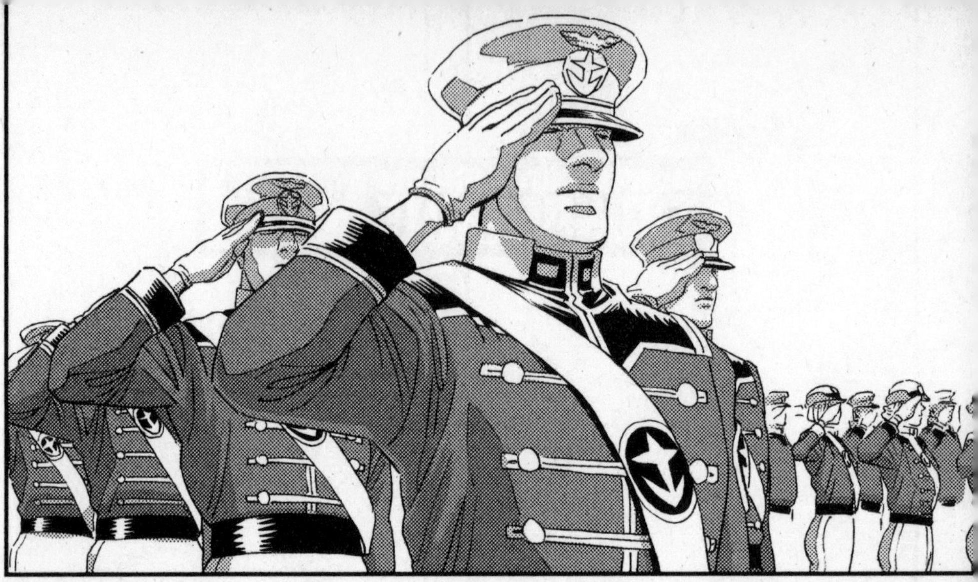
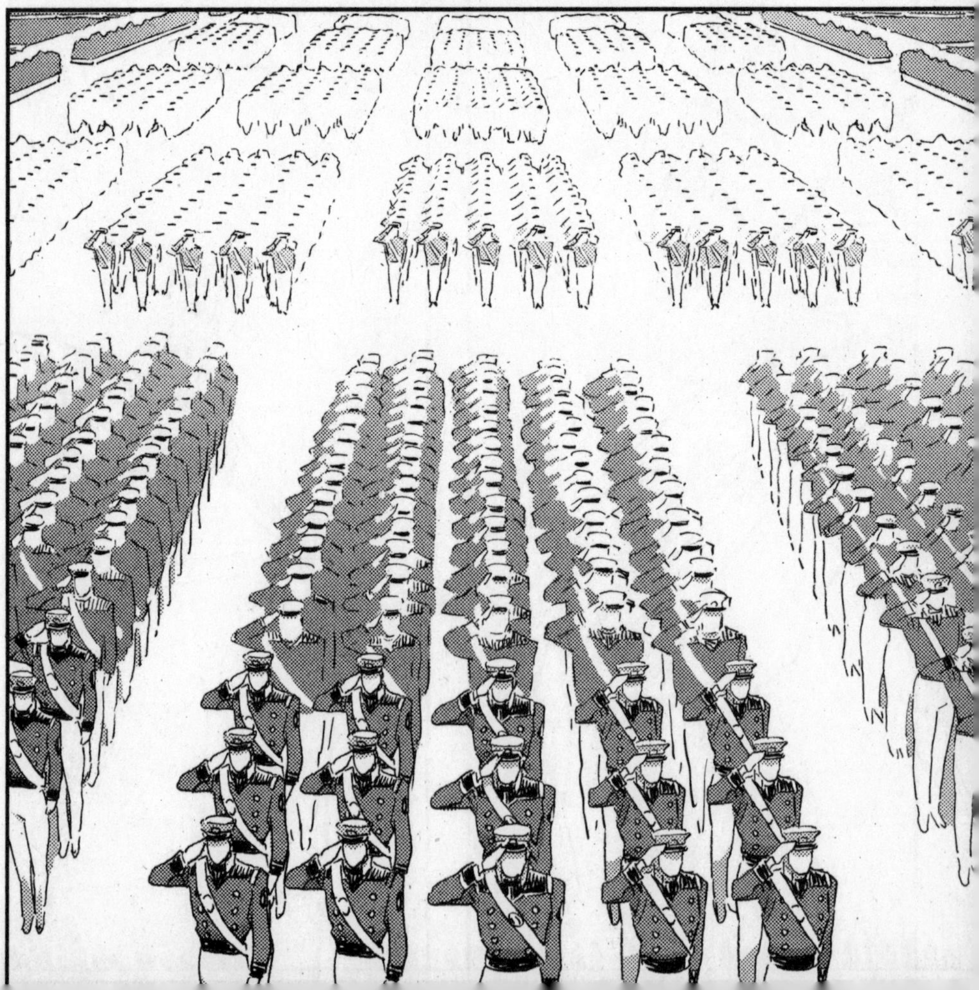

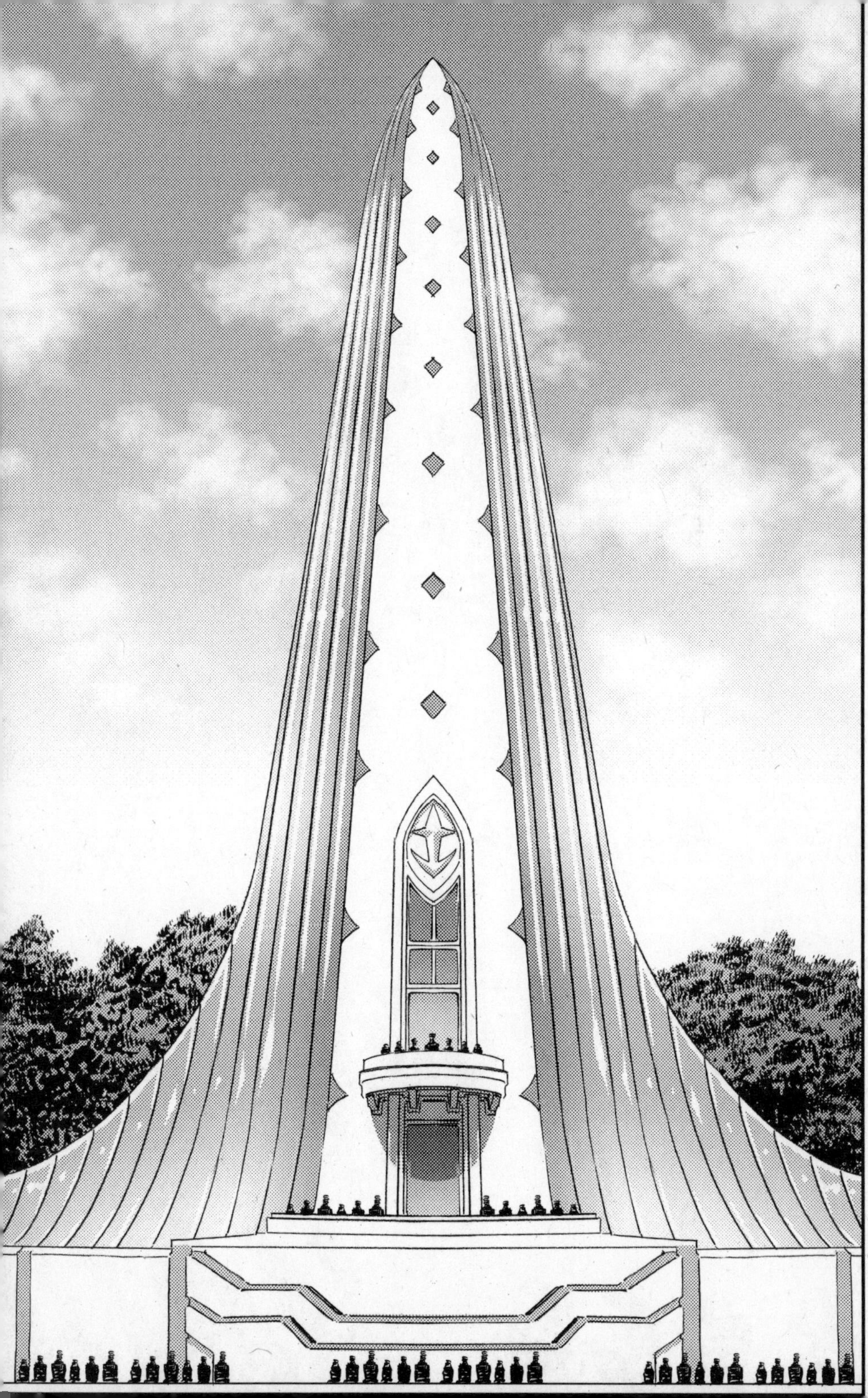

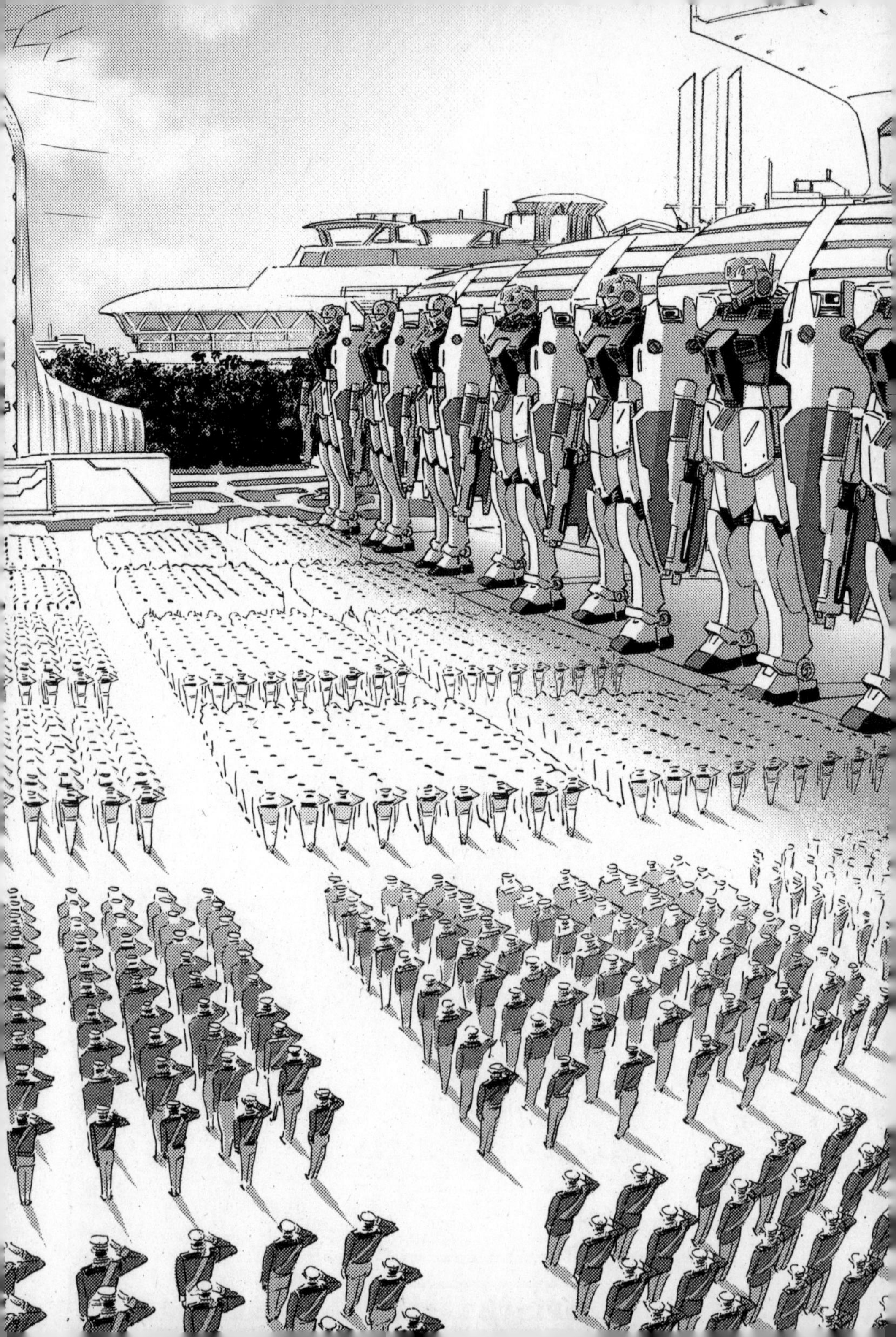

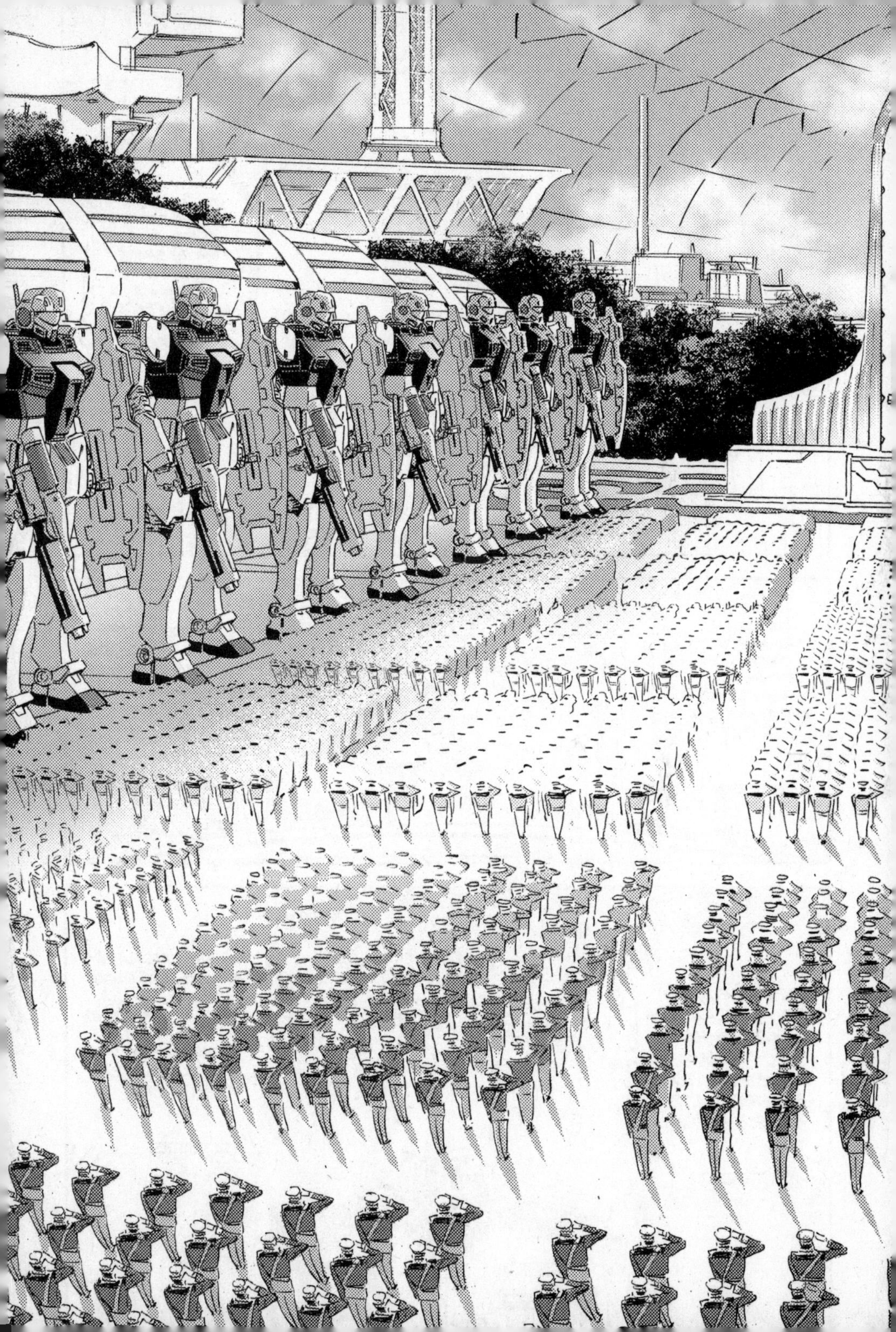

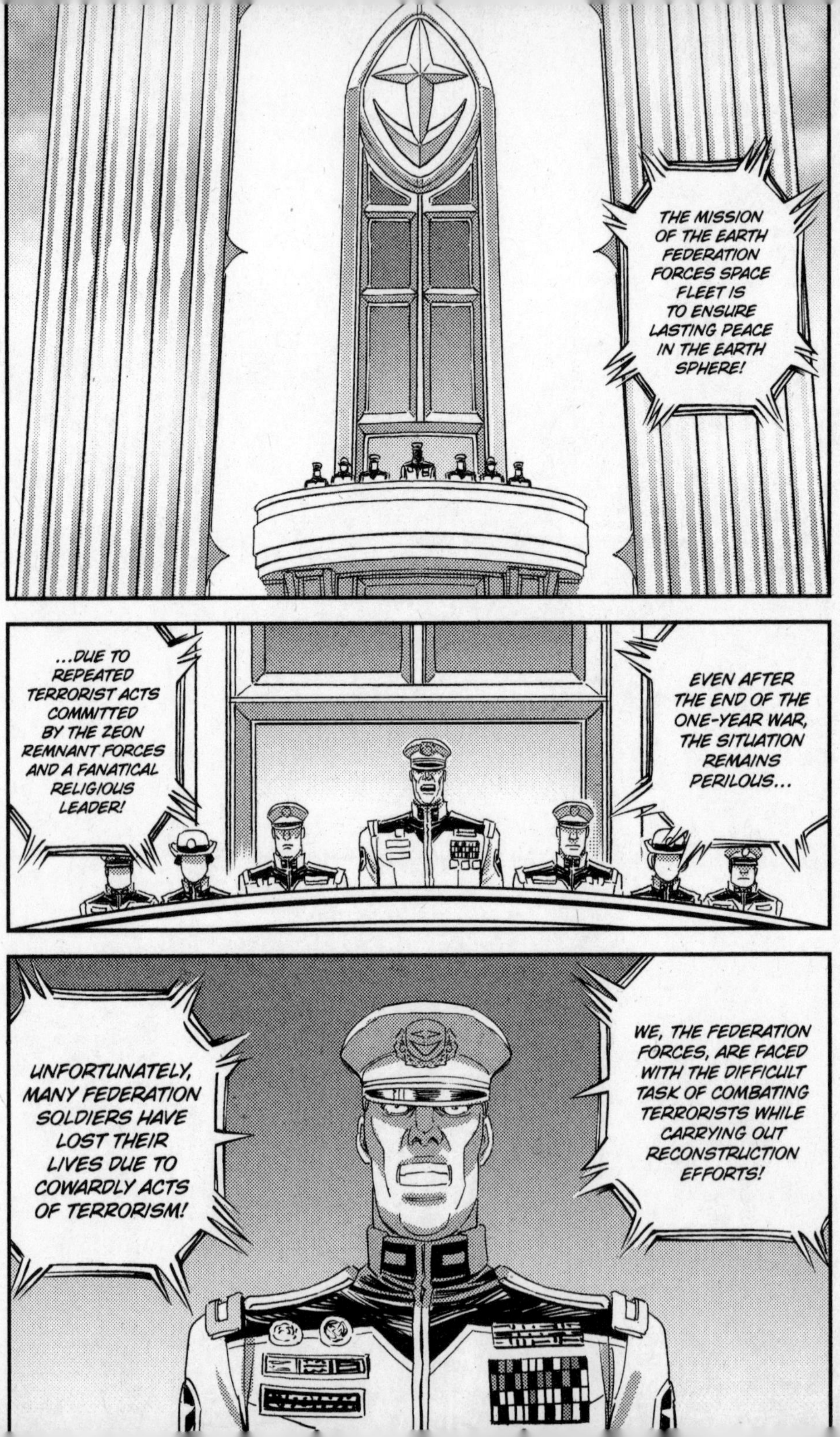
THE MISSION OF THE EARTH FEDERATION FORCES SPACE FLEET IS TO ENSURE LASTING PEACE IN THE EARTH SPHERE!
EVEN AFTER THE END OF THE ONE-YEAR WAR, THE SITUATION REMAINS PERILOUS...
...DUE TO REPEATED TERRORIST ACTS COMMITTED BY THE ZEON REMNANT FORCES AND A FANATICAL RELIGIOUS LEADER!
WE, THE FEDERATION FORCES, ARE FACED WITH THE DIFFICULT TASK OF COMBATING TERRORISTS WHILE CARRYING OUT RECONSTRUCTION EFFORTS!
UNFORTUNATELY, MANY FEDERATION SOLDIERS HAVE LOST THEIR LIVES DUE TO COWARDLY ACTS OF TERRORISM!

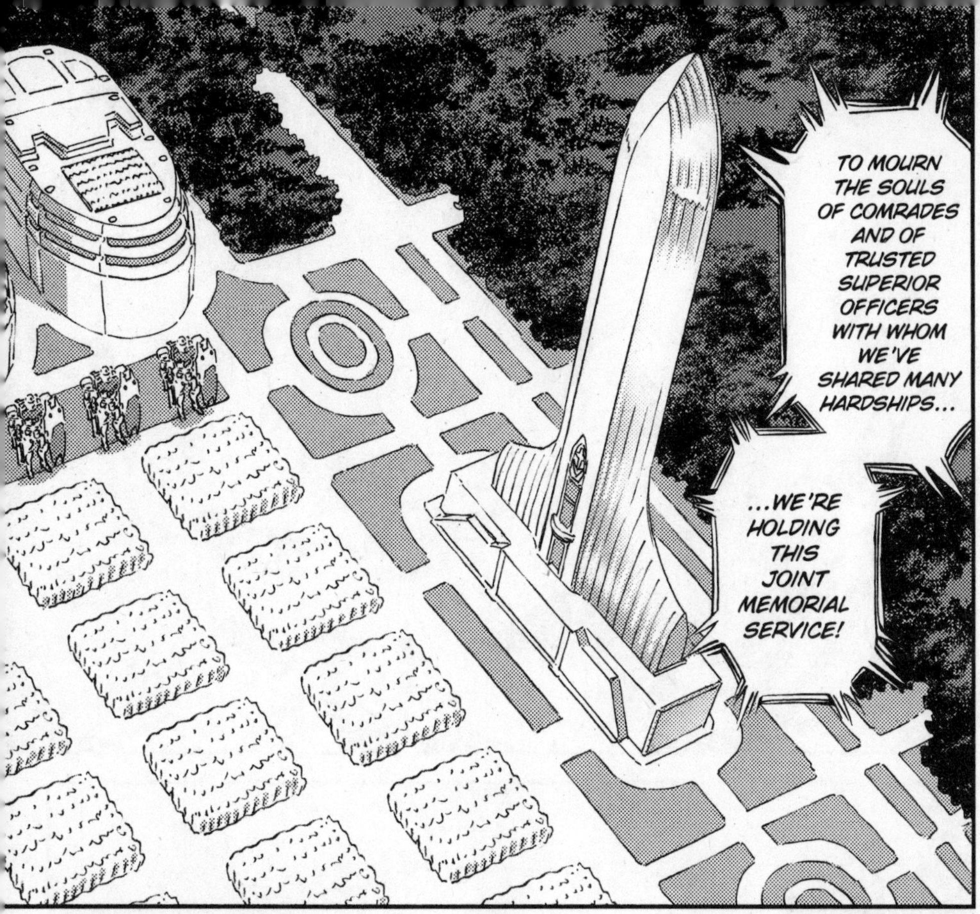
TO MOURN THE SOULS OF COMRADES AND OF TRUSTED SUPERIOR OFFICERS WITH WHOM WE'VE SHARED MANY HARDSHIPS...
...WE'RE HOLDING THIS JOINT MEMORIAL SERVICE!
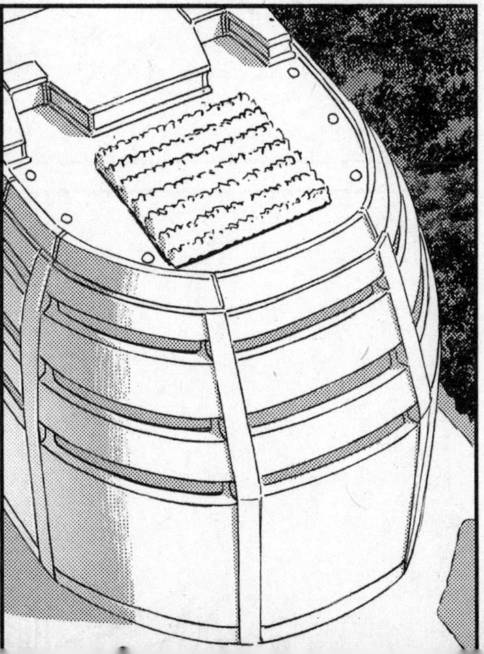
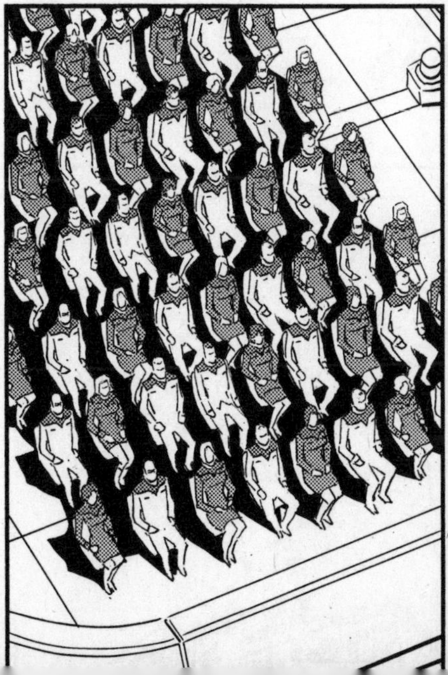

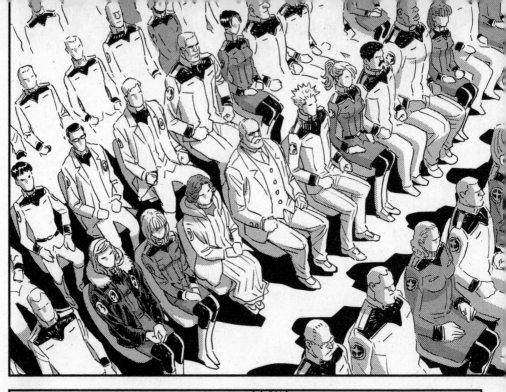

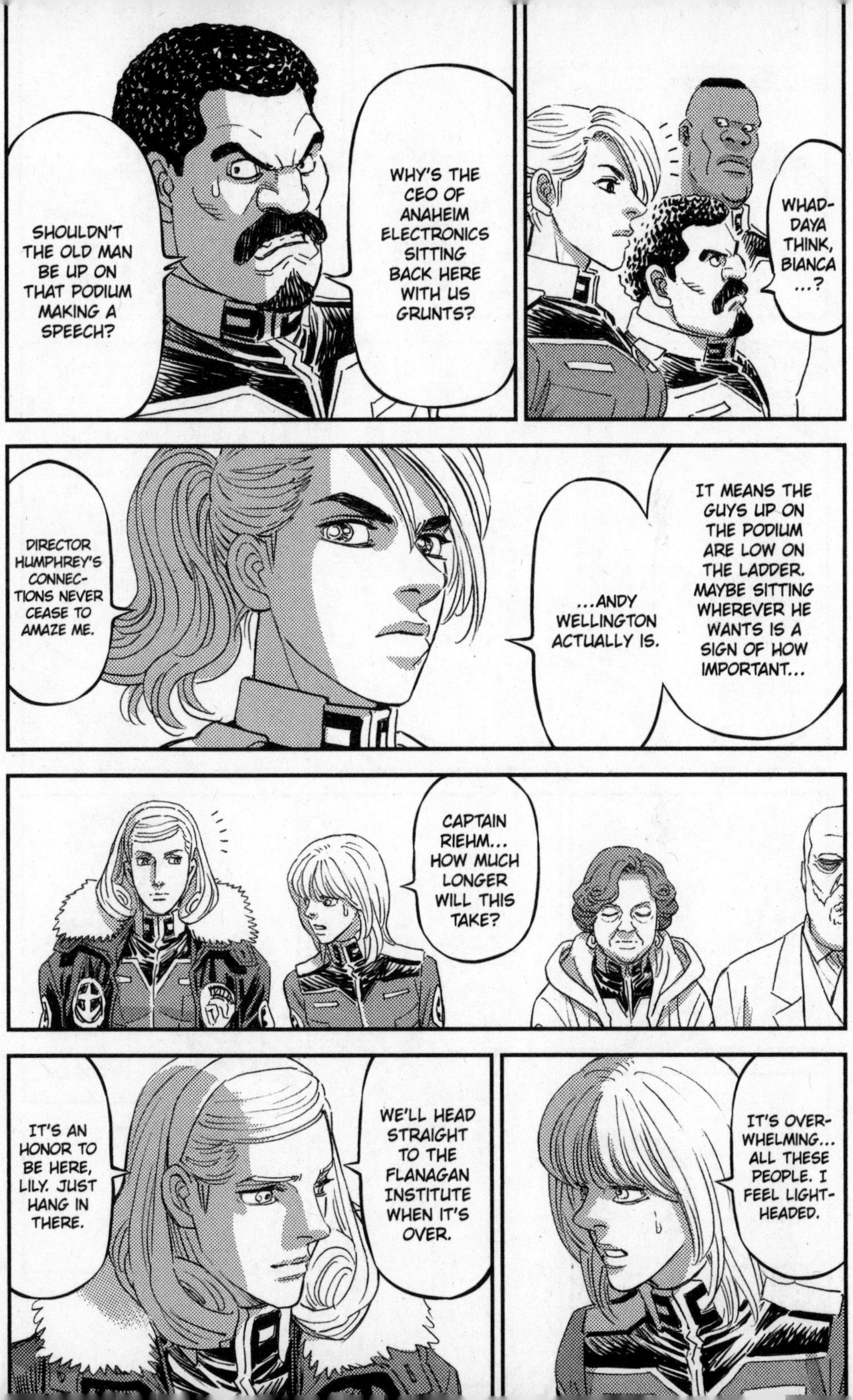
WHAD-DAYA THINK, BIANCA ...?
WHY'S THE CEO OF ANAHEIM ELECTRONICS SITTING BACK HERE WITH US GRUNTS?
SHOULDN'T THE OLD MAN BE UP ON THAT PODIUM MAKING A SPEECH?
IT MEANS THE GUYS UP ON THE PODIUM ARE LOW ON THE LADDER. MAYBE SITTING WHEREVER HE WANTS IS A SIGN OF HOW IMPORTANT...
...ANDY WELLINGTON ACTUALLY IS.
DIRECTOR HUMPHREY'S CONNEC-TIONS NEVER CEASE TO AMAZE ME.
CAPTAIN RIEHM... HOW MUCH LONGER WILL THIS TAKE?
IT'S OVER-WHELMING... ALL THESE PEOPLE. I FEEL LIGHT-HEADED.
WE'LL HEAD STRAIGHT TO THE FLANAGAN INSTITUTE WHEN IT'S OVER.
IT'S AN HONOR TO BE HERE, LILY. JUST HANG IN THERE.

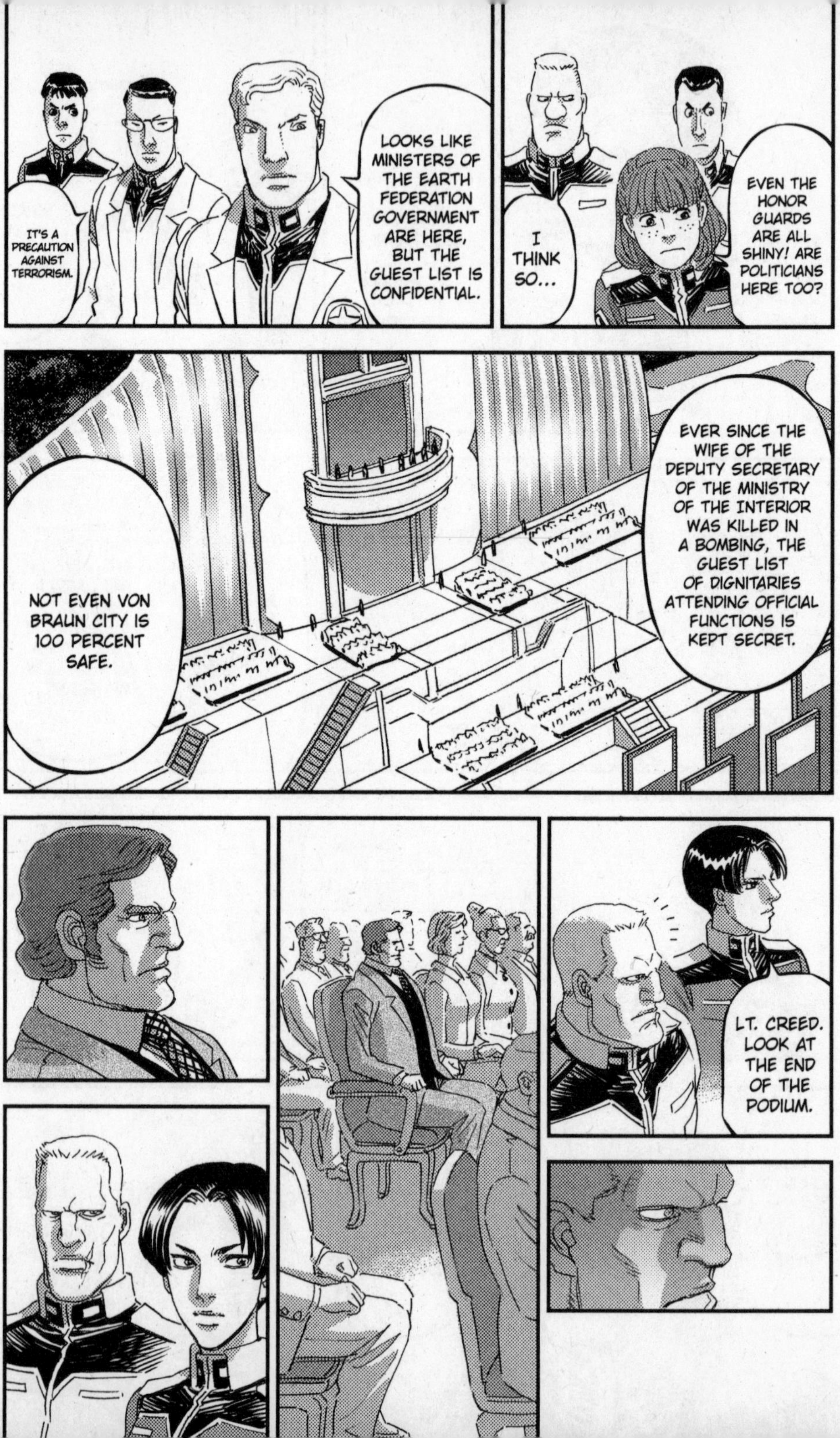
EVEN THE HONOR GUARDS ARE ALL SHINY! ARE POLITICIANS HERE TOO?
I THINK SO...
LOOKS LIKE MINISTERS OF THE EARTH FEDERATION GOVERNMENT ARE HERE, BUT THE GUEST LIST IS CONFIDENTIAL.
IT'S A PRECAUTION AGAINST TERRORISM.
EVER SINCE THE WIFE OF THE DEPUTY SECRETARY OF THE MINISTRY OF THE INTERIOR WAS KILLED IN A BOMBING, THE GUEST LIST OF DIGNITARIES ATTENDING OFFICIAL FUNCTIONS IS KEPT SECRET.
NOT EVEN VON BRAUN CITY IS 100 PERCENT SAFE.
LT. CREED. LOOK AT THE END OF THE PODIUM.

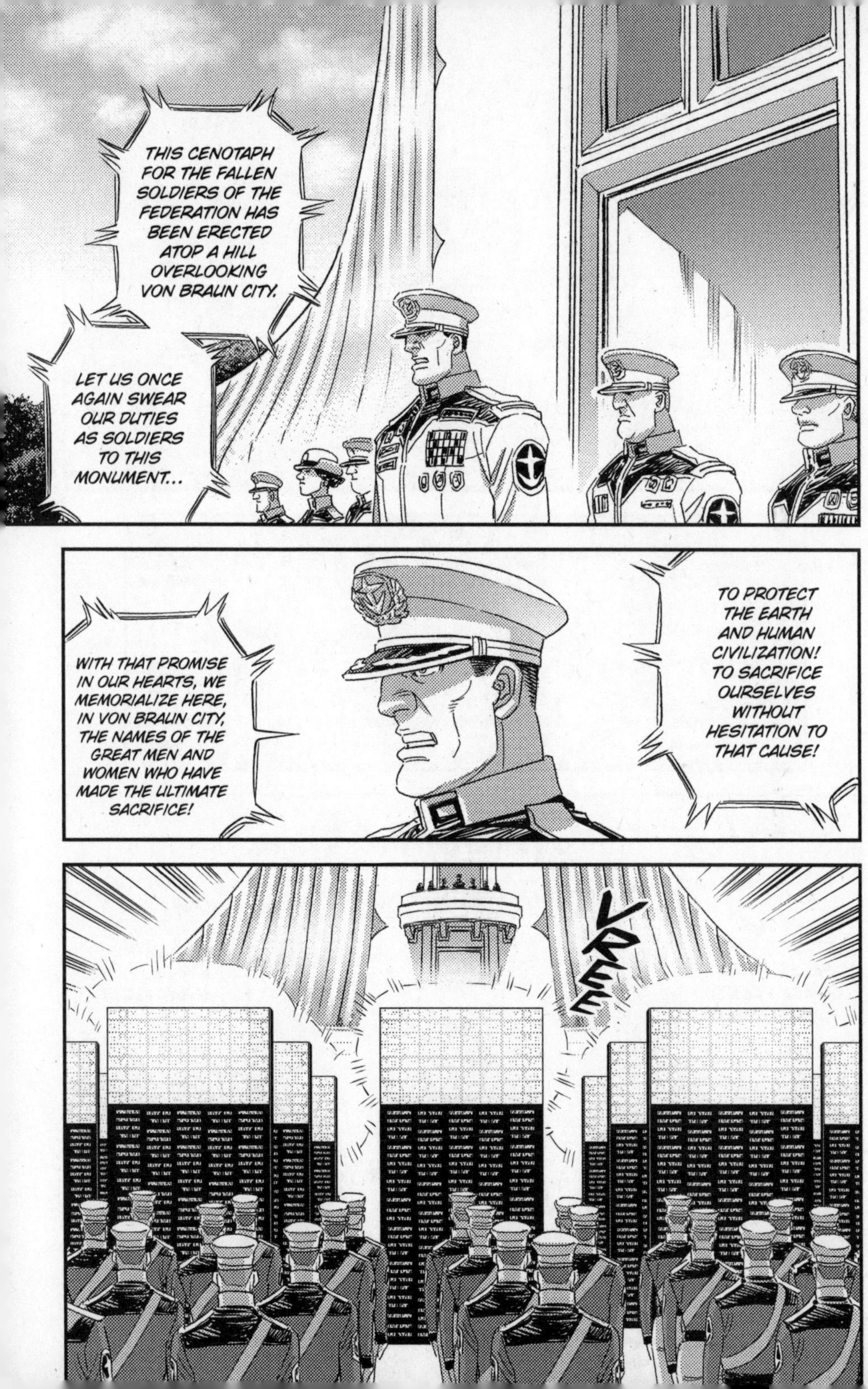
THIS CENOTAPH FOR THE FALLEN SOLDIERS OF THE FEDERATION HAS BEEN ERECTED ATOP A HILL OVERLOOKING VON BRAUN CITY.
LET US ONCE AGAIN SWEAR OUR DUTIES AS SOLDIERS TO THIS MONUMENT...
TO PROTECT THE EARTH AND HUMAN CIVILIZATION! TO SACRIFICE OURSELVES WITHOUT HESITATION TO THAT CAUSE!
WITH THAT PROMISE IN OUR HEARTS, WE MEMORIALIZE HERE, IN VON BRAUN CITY, THE NAMES OF THE GREAT MEN AND WOMEN WHO HAVE MADE THE ULTIMATE SACRIFICE!
VREEE

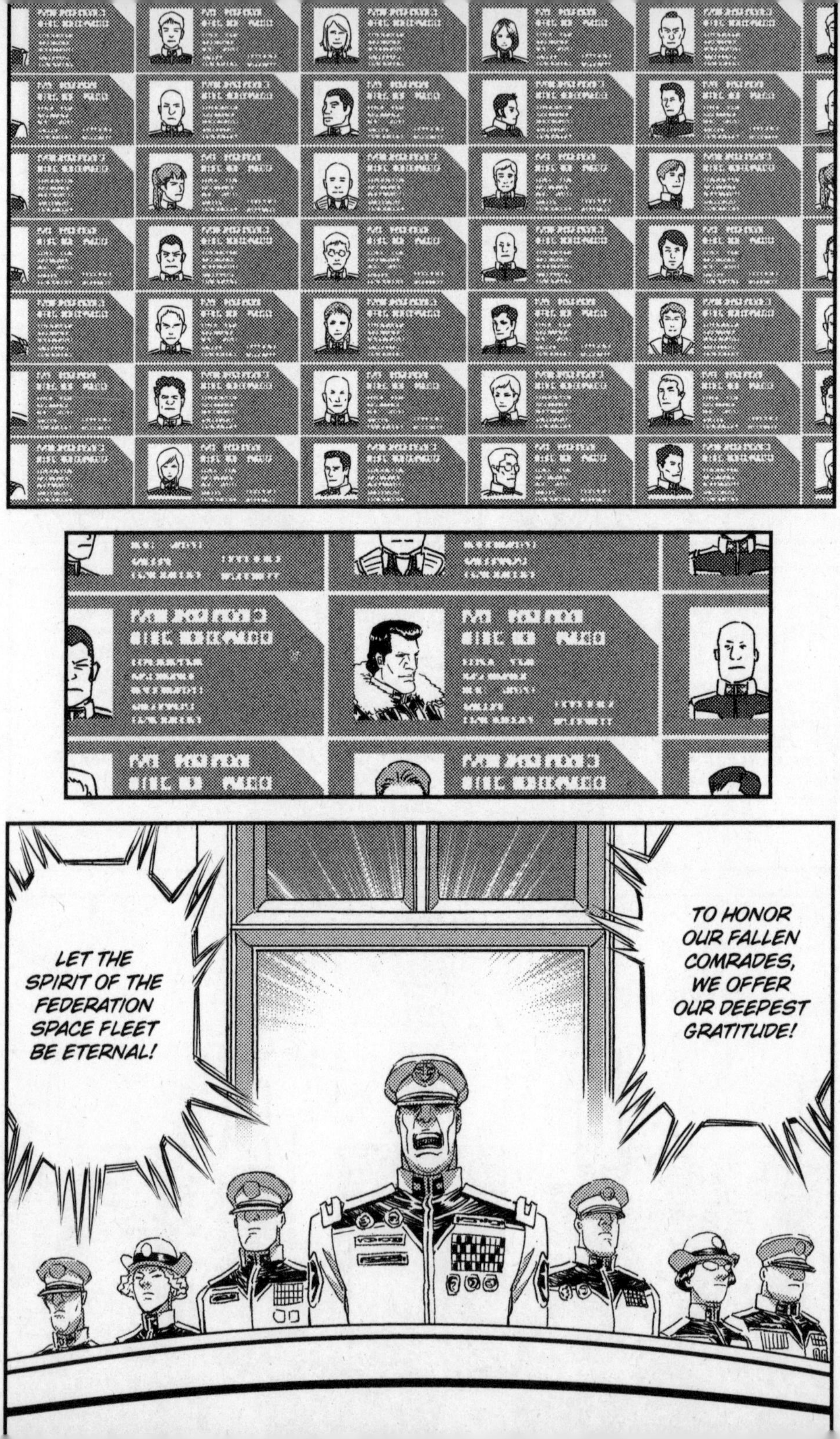
TO HONOR OUR FALLEN COMRADES, WE OFFER OUR DEEPEST GRATITUDE!
LET THE SPIRIT OF THE FEDERATION SPACE FLEET BE ETERNAL!

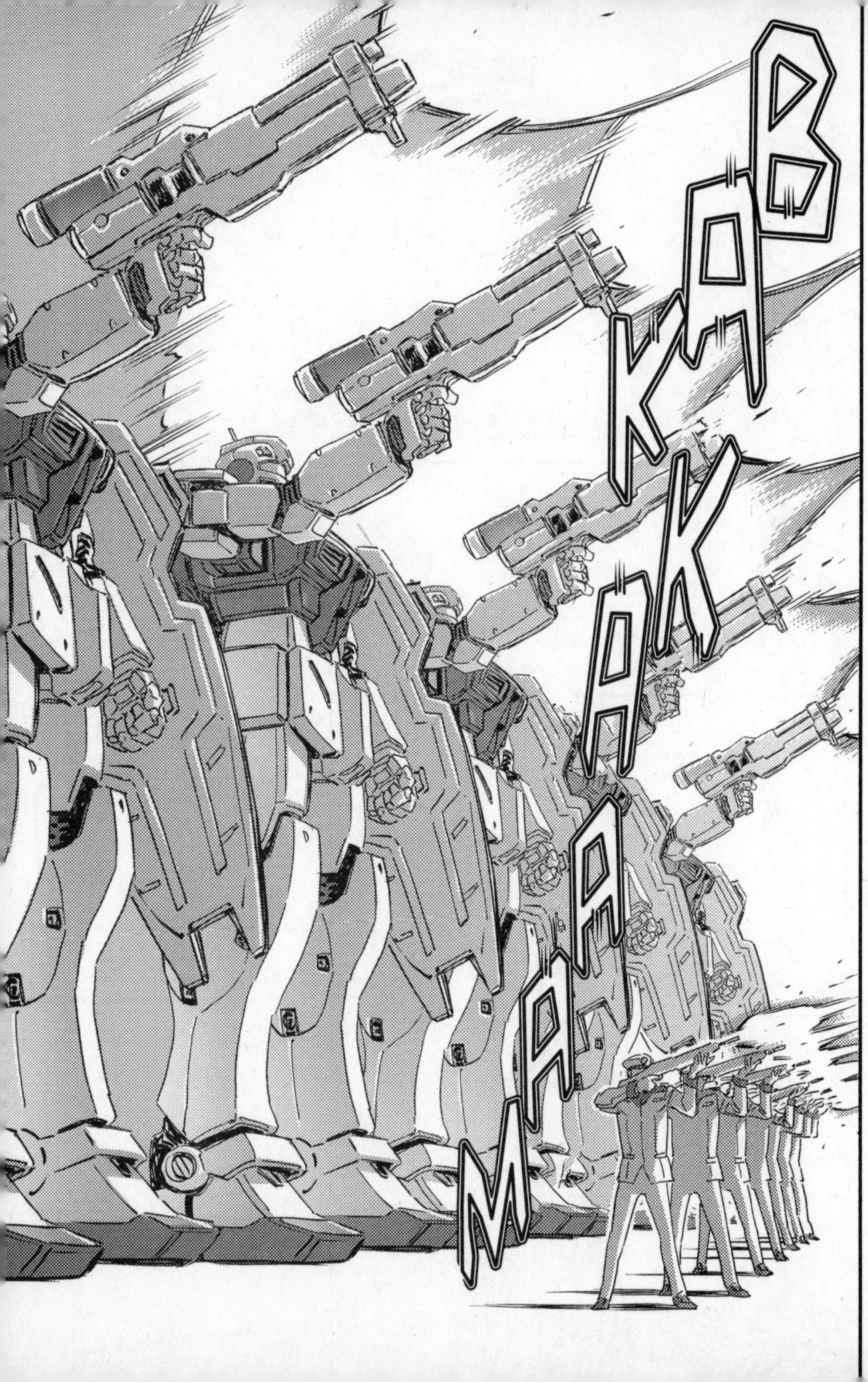
BKAKKAAAAM

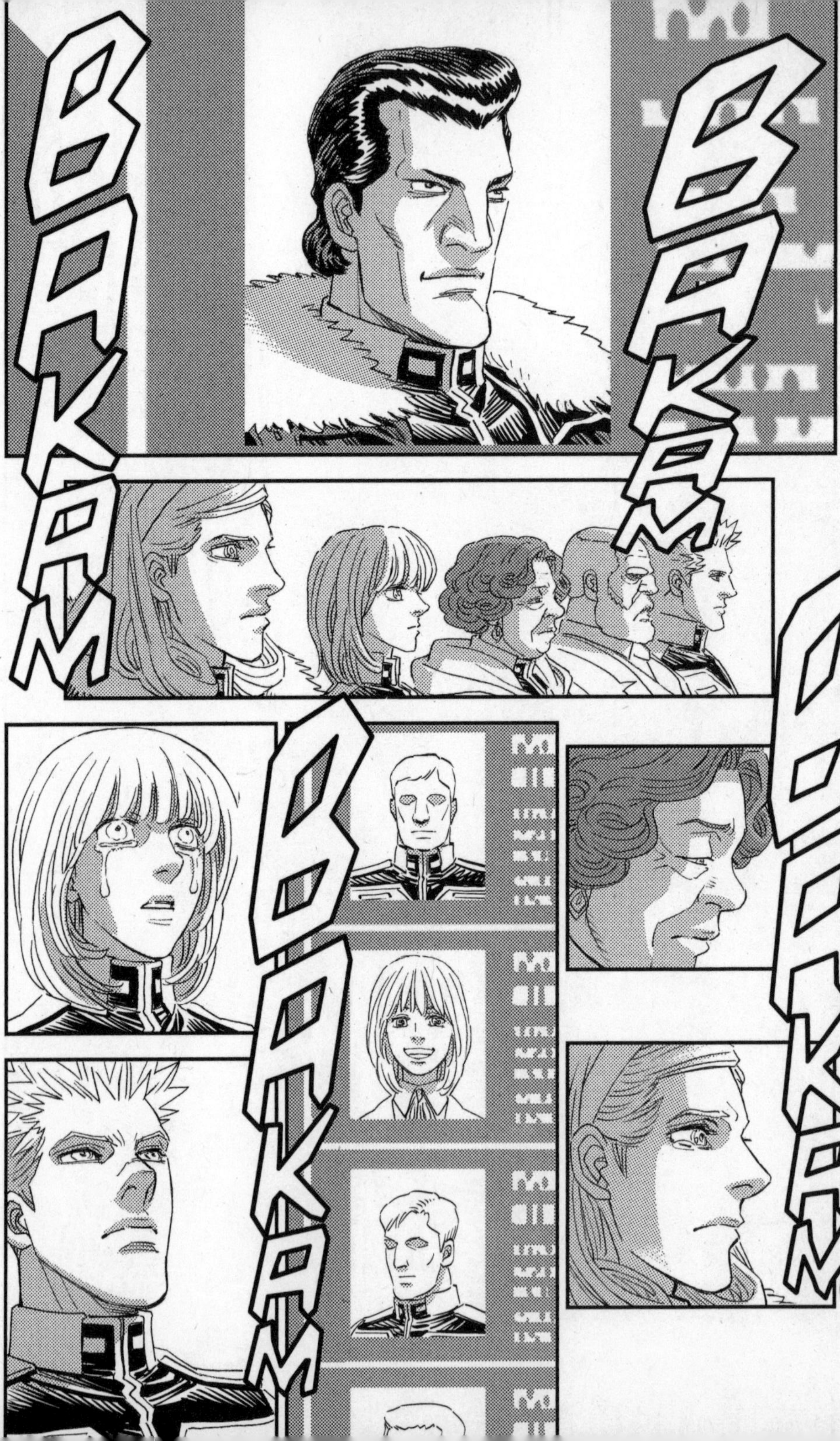
BAKAM
BAKAM
BAKAM
BAKAM

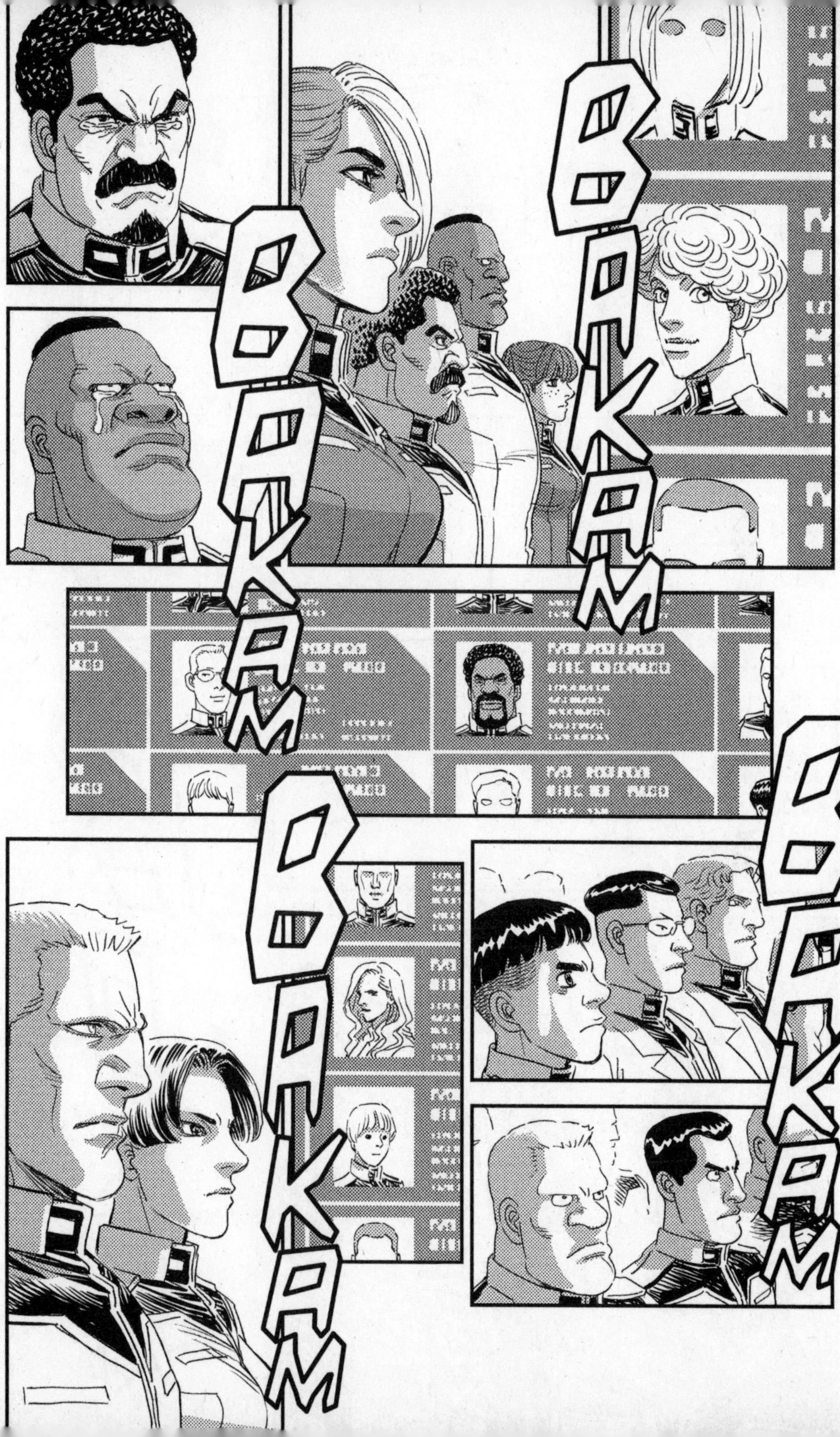
BAKAM
BAKAM
BAKAM
BAKAM

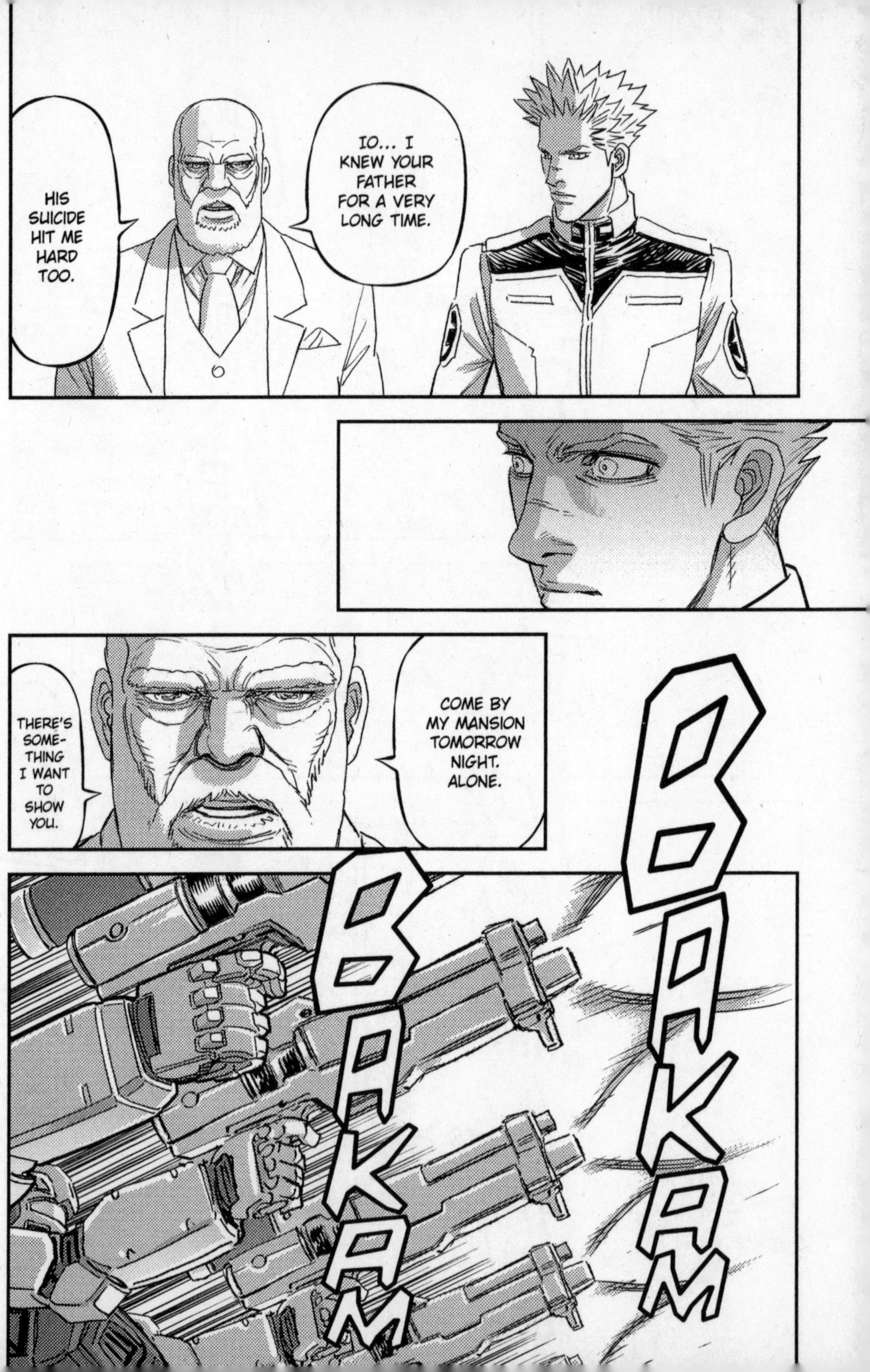
IO... I KNEW YOUR FATHER FOR A VERY LONG TIME.
HIS SUICIDE HIT ME HARD TOO.
COME BY MY MANSION TOMORROW NIGHT. ALONE.
THERE'S SOME-THING I WANT TO SHOW YOU.
BAKAM
BAKAM

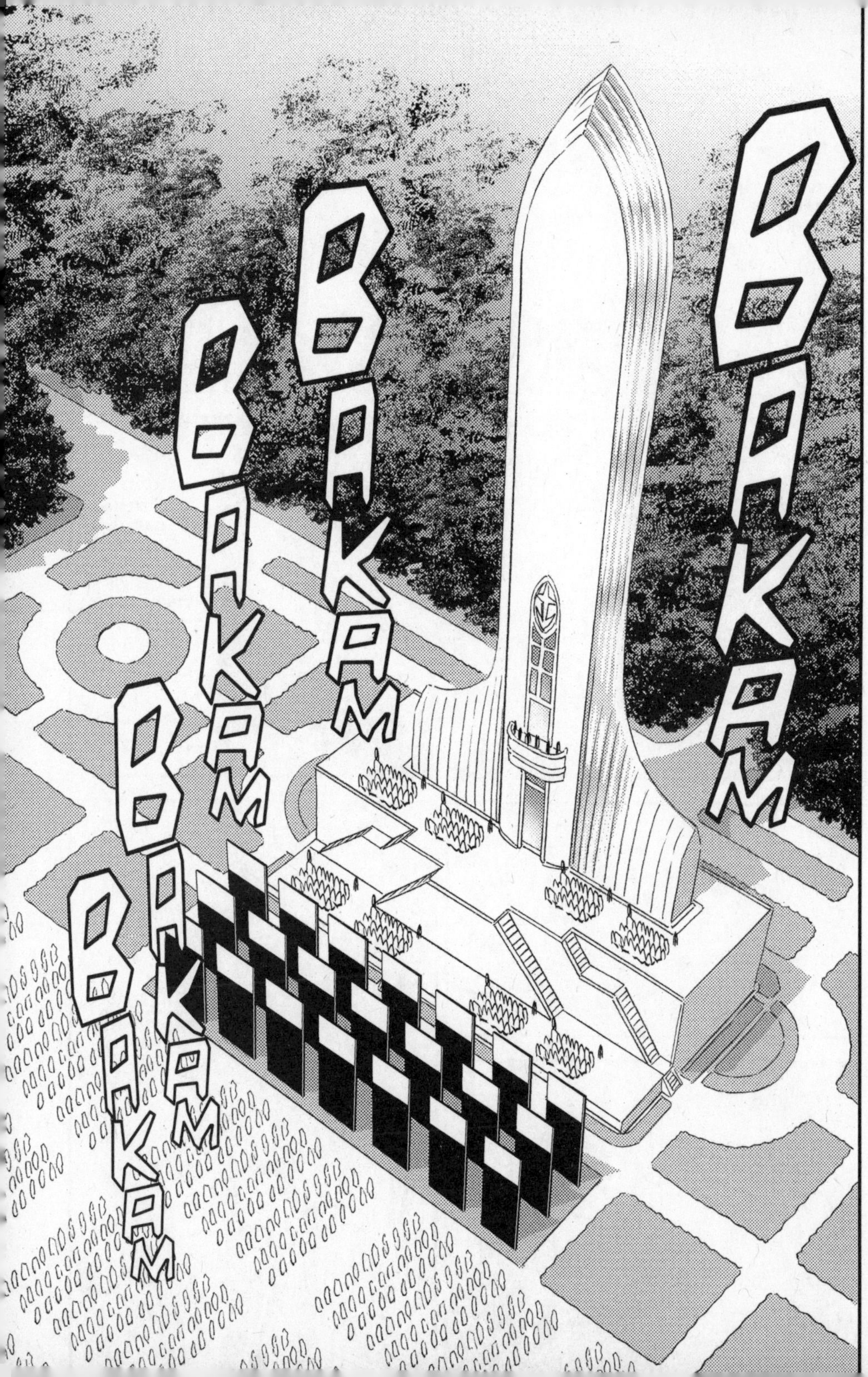
BAKAM
BAKAM
BAKAM
BAKAM
BAKAM

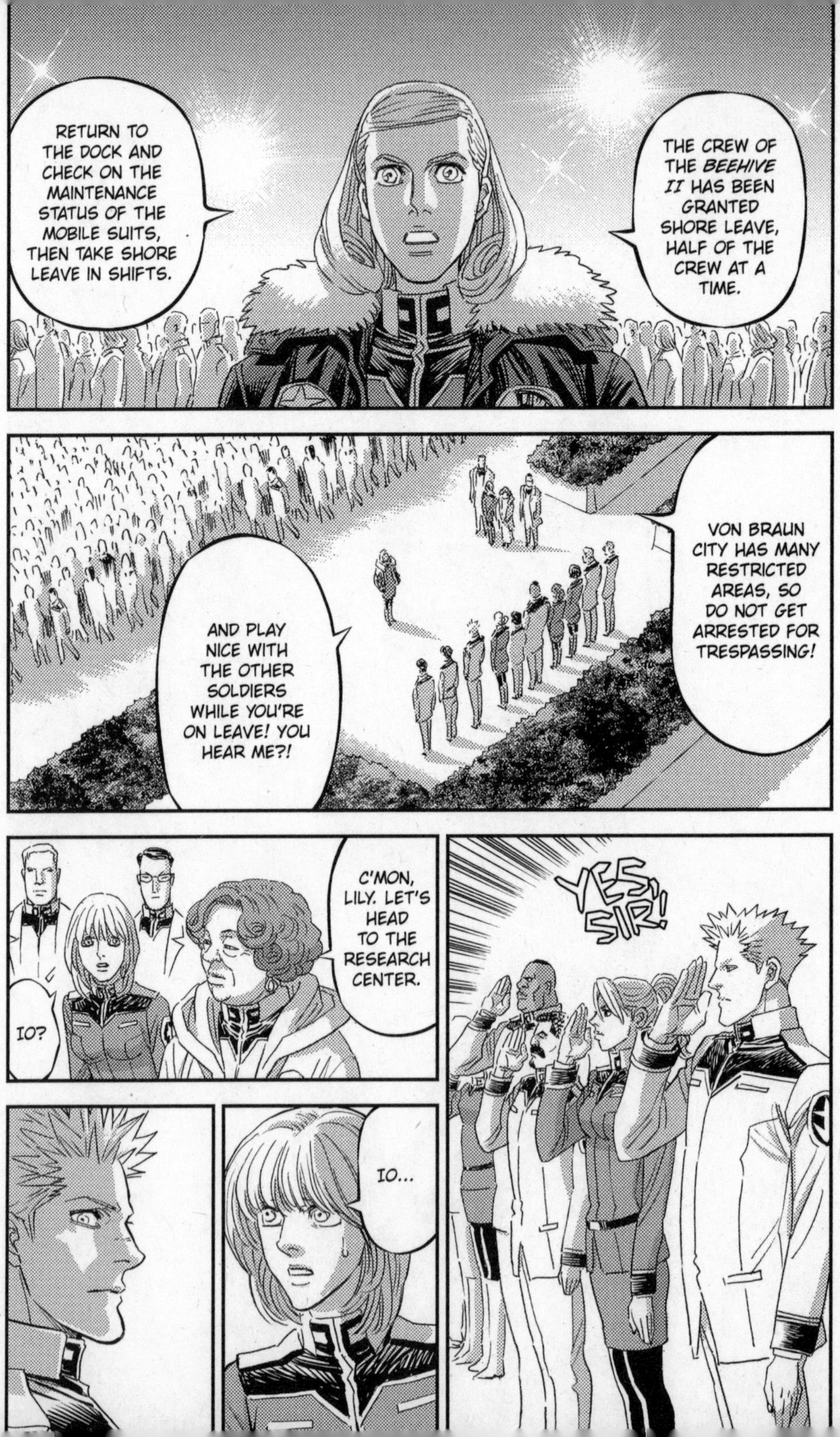
THE CREW OF THE *BEEHIVE II* HAS BEEN GRANTED SHORE LEAVE, HALF OF THE CREW AT A TIME.
RETURN TO THE DOCK AND CHECK ON THE MAINTENANCE STATUS OF THE MOBILE SUITS, THEN TAKE SHORE LEAVE IN SHIFTS.
VON BRAUN CITY HAS MANY RESTRICTED AREAS, SO DO NOT GET ARRESTED FOR TRESPASSING!
AND PLAY NICE WITH THE OTHER SOLDIERS WHILE YOU'RE ON LEAVE! YOU HEAR ME?!
YES, SIR!
C'MON, LILY. LET'S HEAD TO THE RESEARCH CENTER.
IO?
IO...

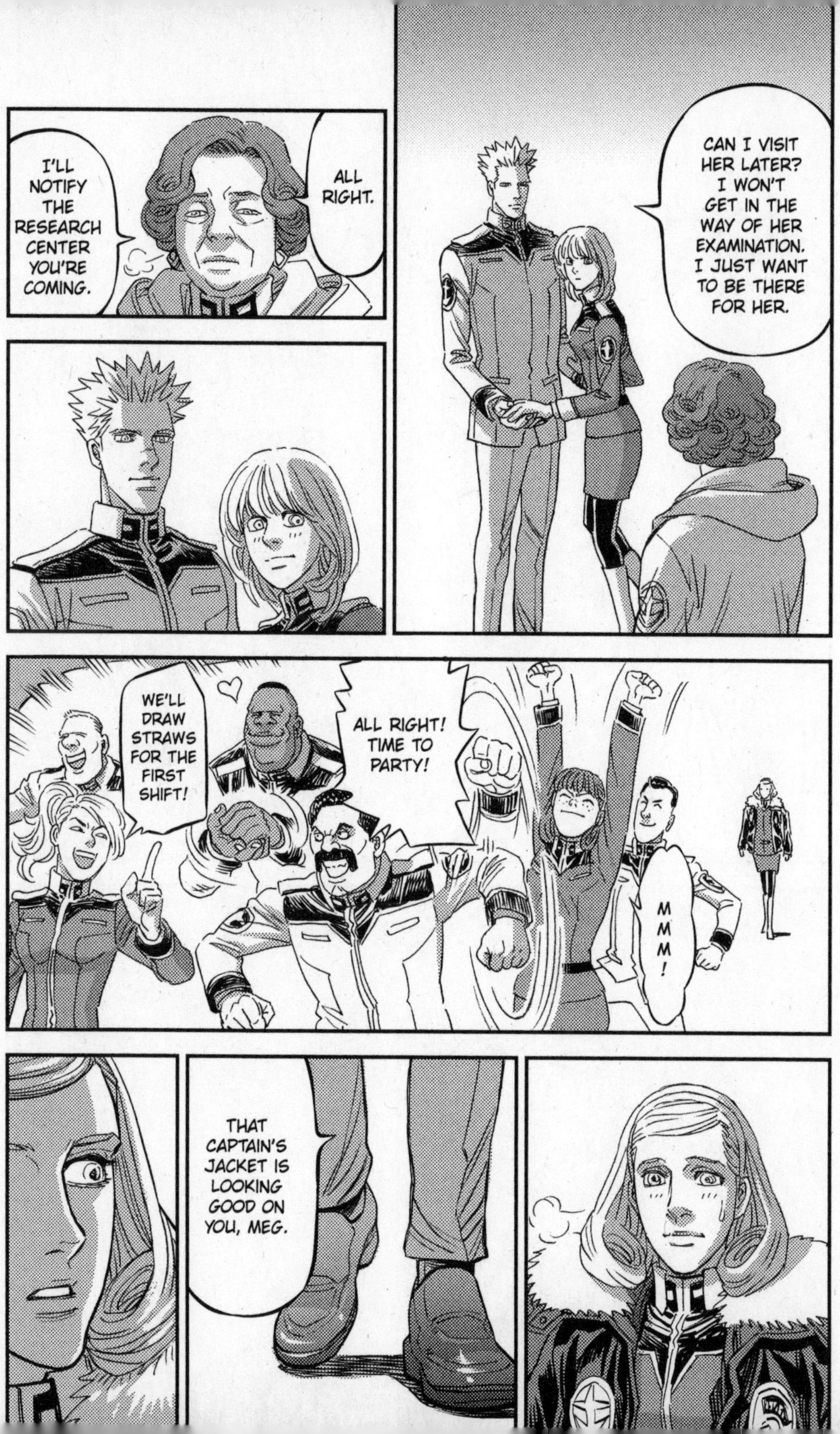
CAN I VISIT HER LATER? I WON'T GET IN THE WAY OF HER EXAMINATION. I JUST WANT TO BE THERE FOR HER.
ALL RIGHT.
I'LL NOTIFY THE RESEARCH CENTER YOU'RE COMING.
ALL RIGHT! TIME TO PARTY!
MMM!
WE'LL DRAW STRAWS FOR THE FIRST SHIFT!
THAT CAPTAIN'S JACKET IS LOOKING GOOD ON YOU, MEG.

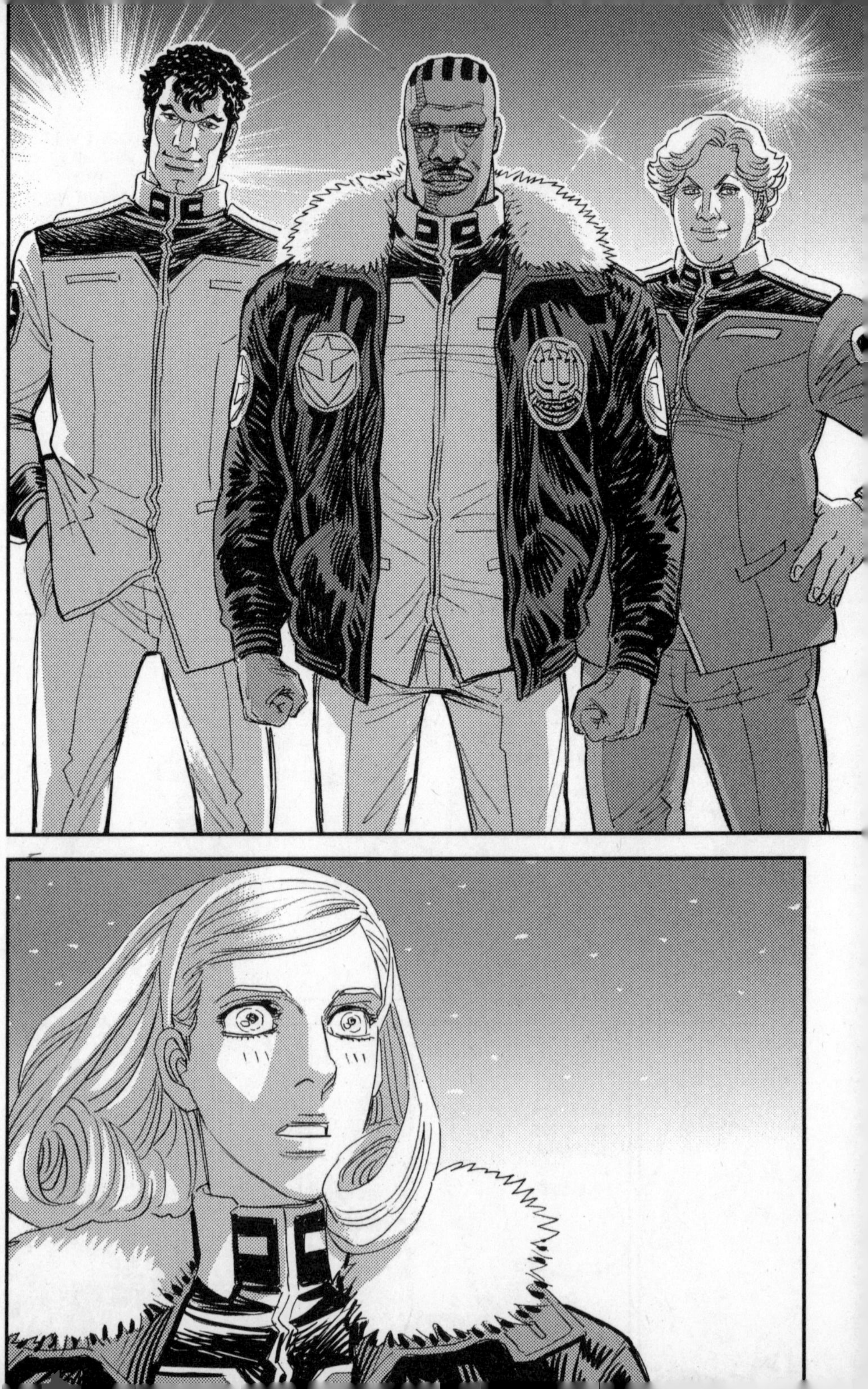

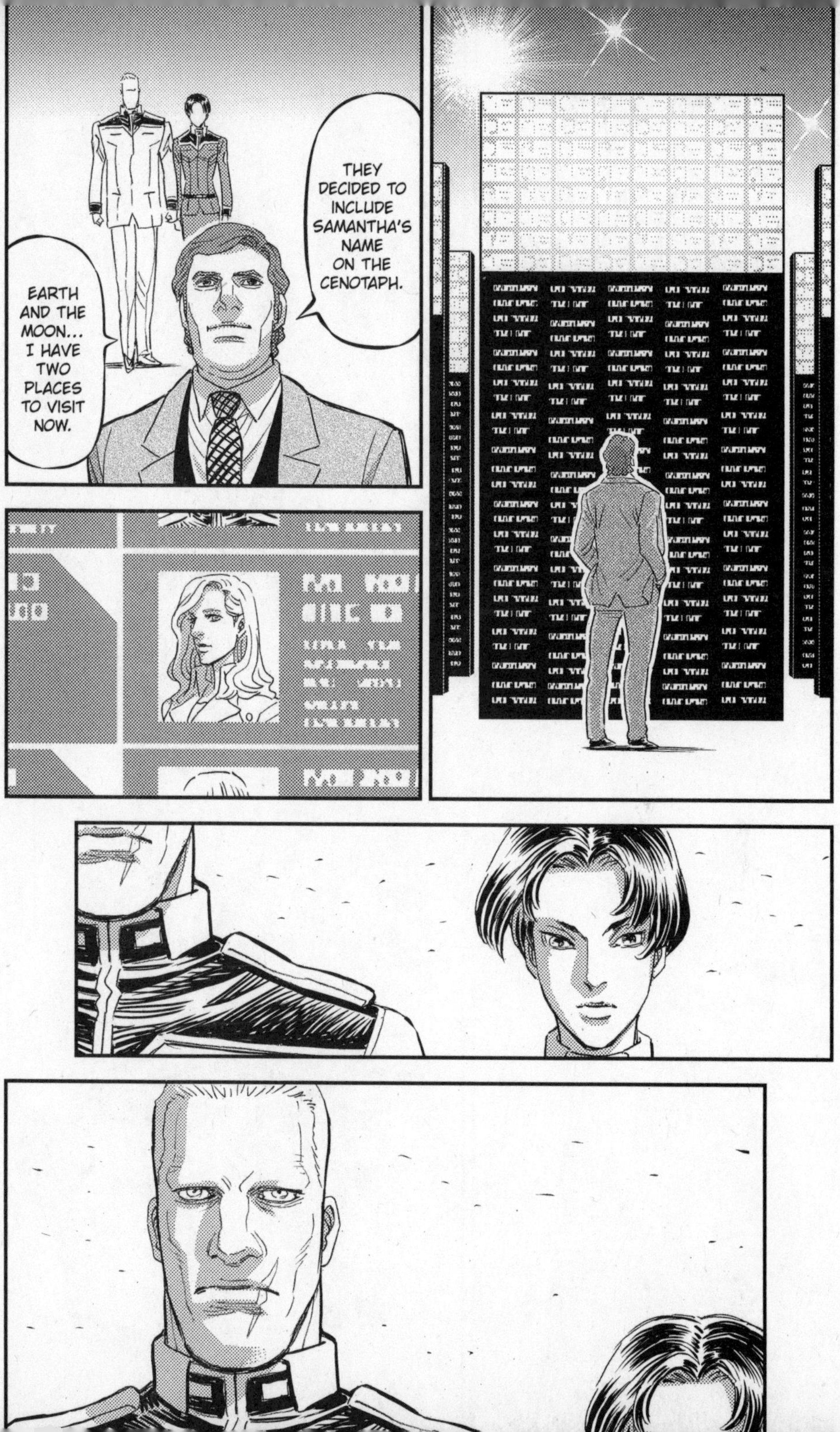
THEY DECIDED TO INCLUDE SAMANTHA'S NAME ON THE CENOTAPH.
EARTH AND THE MOON... I HAVE TWO PLACES TO VISIT NOW.

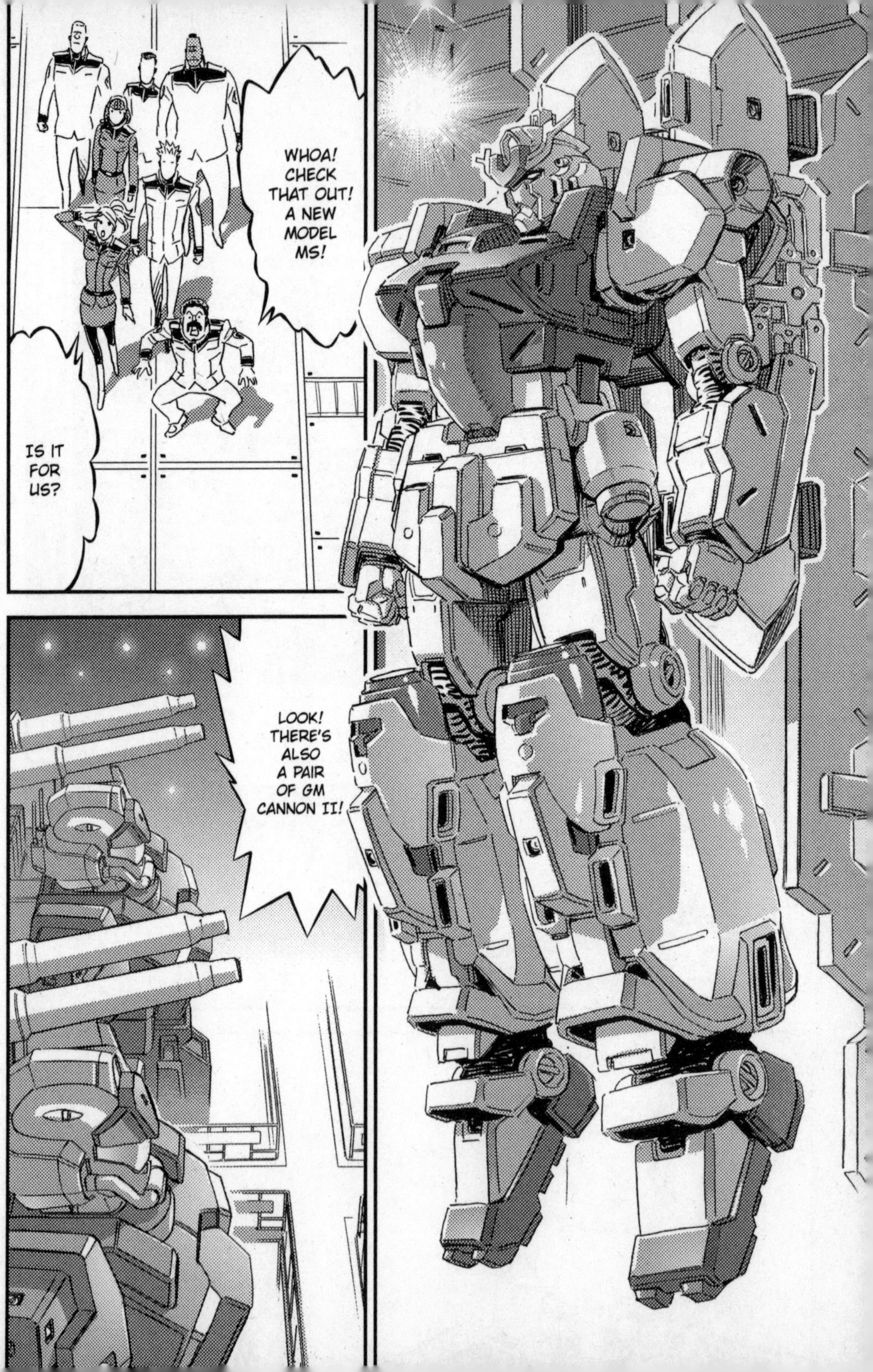
WHOA! CHECK THAT OUT! A NEW MODEL MS!
IS IT FOR US?
LOOK! THERE'S ALSO A PAIR OF GM CANNON II!

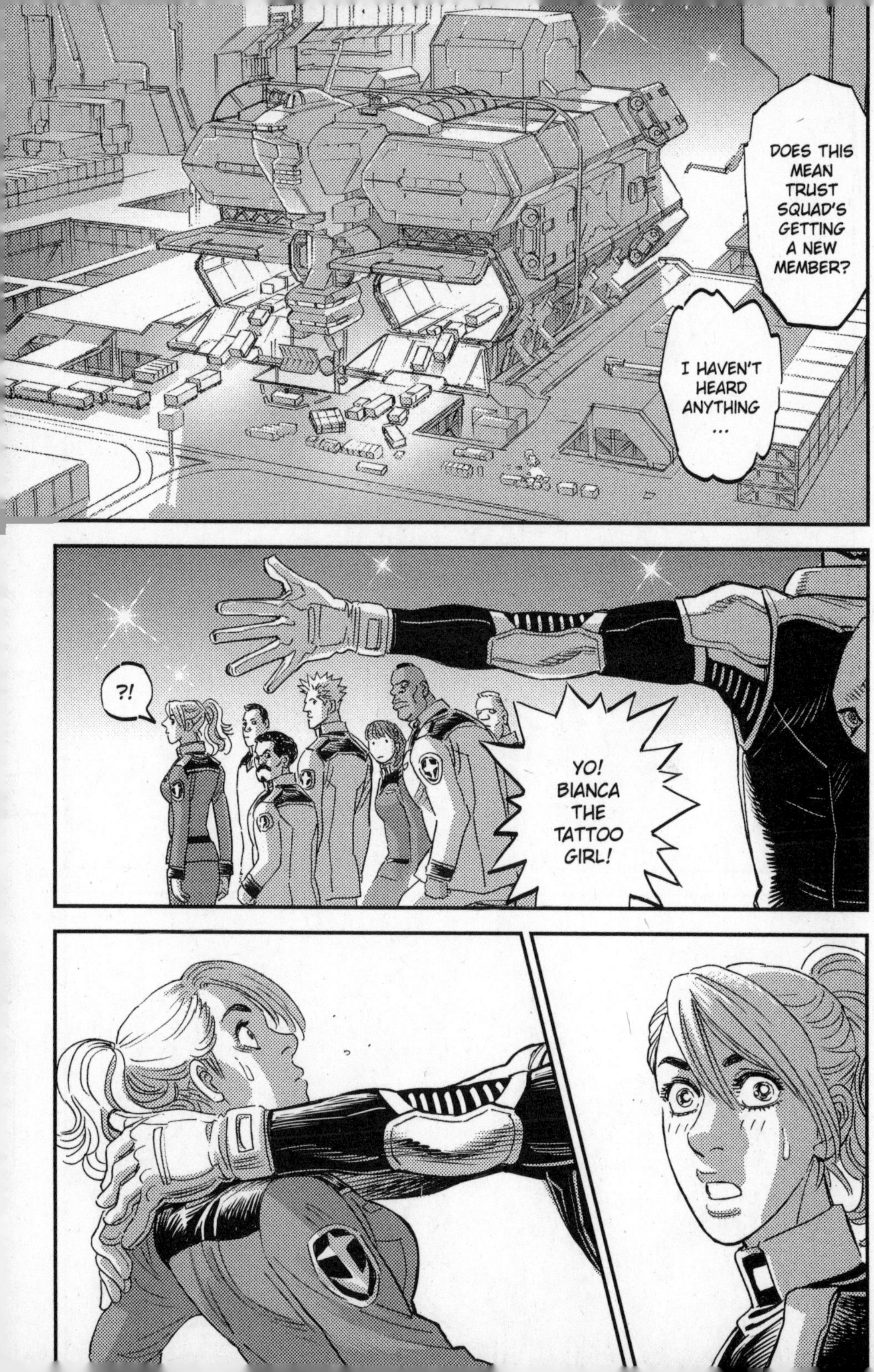
DOES THIS MEAN TRUST SQUAD'S GETTING A NEW MEMBER?
I HAVEN'T HEARD ANYTHING ...
YO! BIANCA THE TATTOO GIRL!
?!

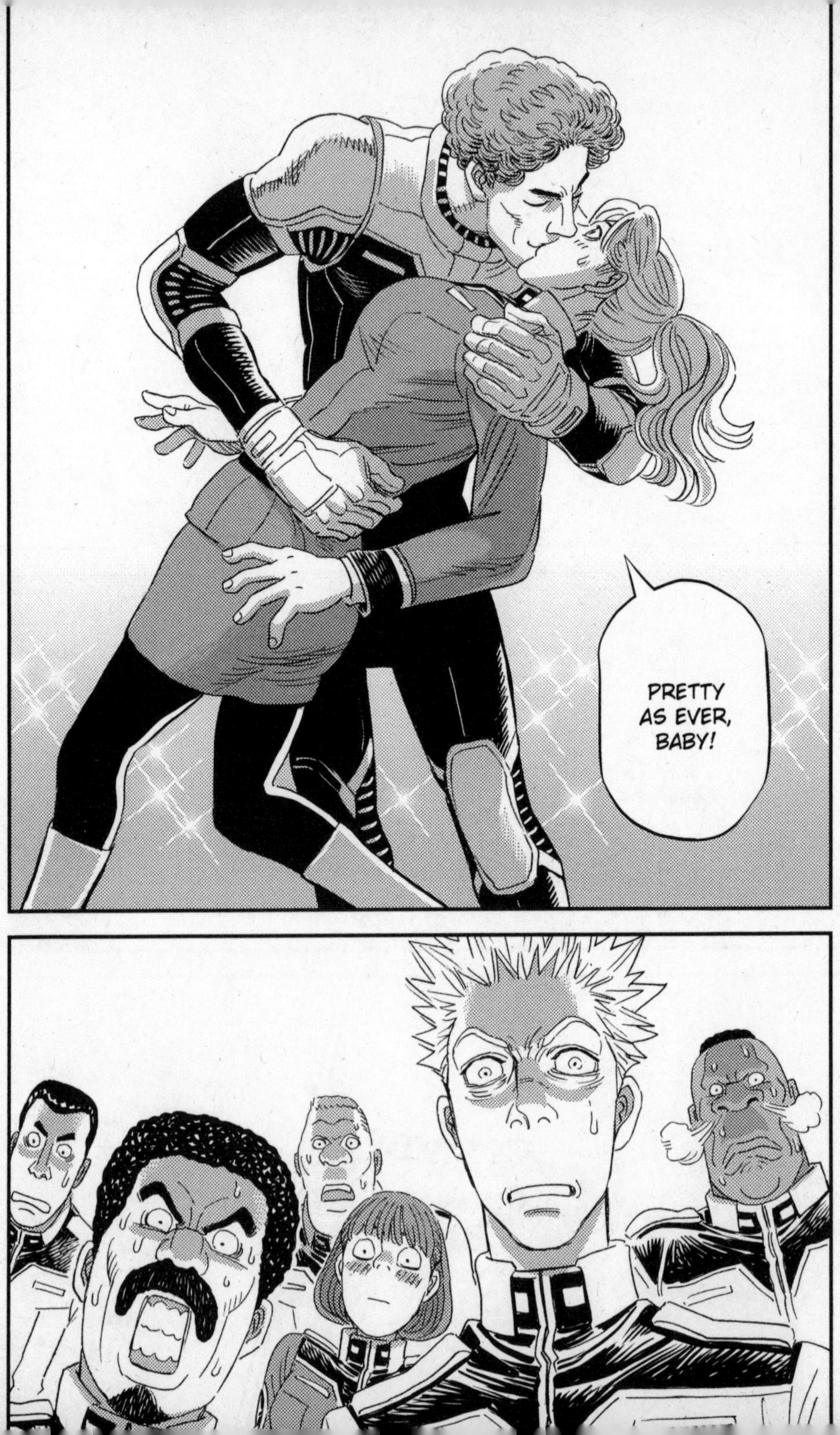
PRETTY AS EVER, BABY!

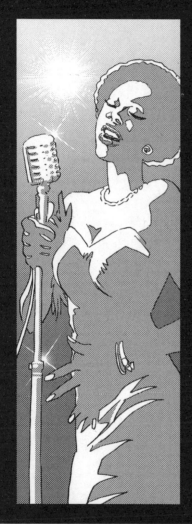

MOBILE SUIT GUNDAM THUNDERBOLT | **CHAPTER 163**

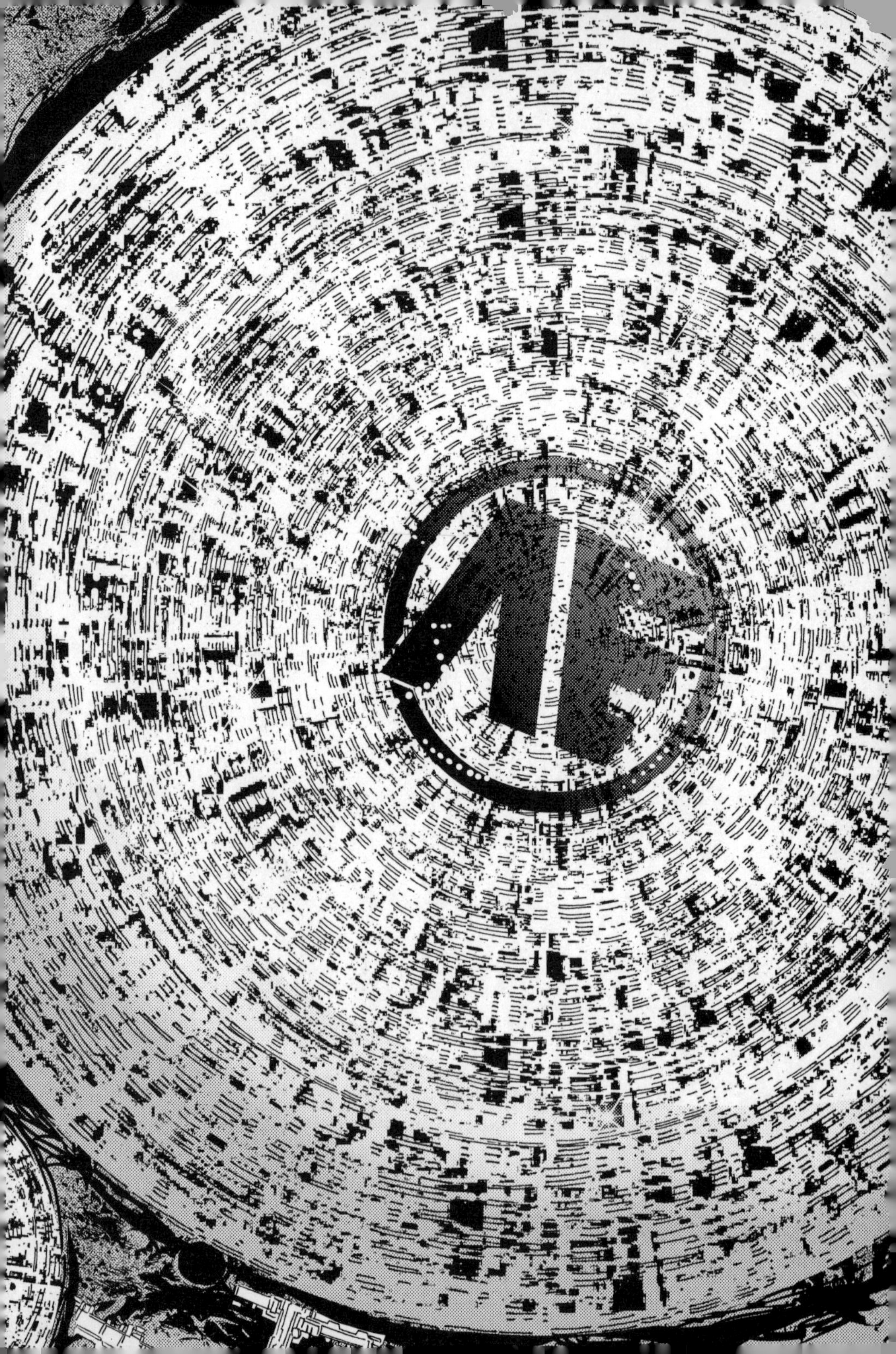

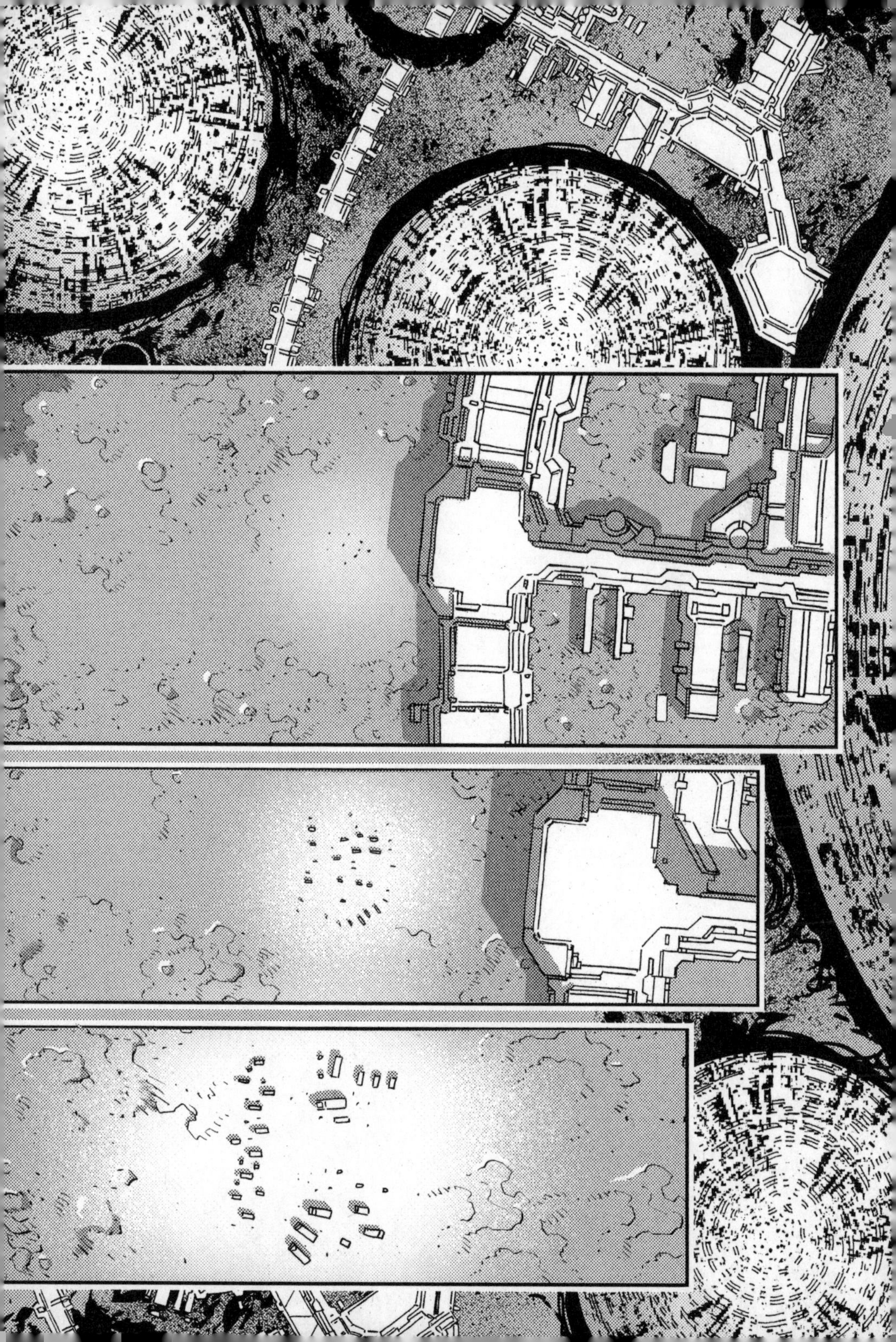

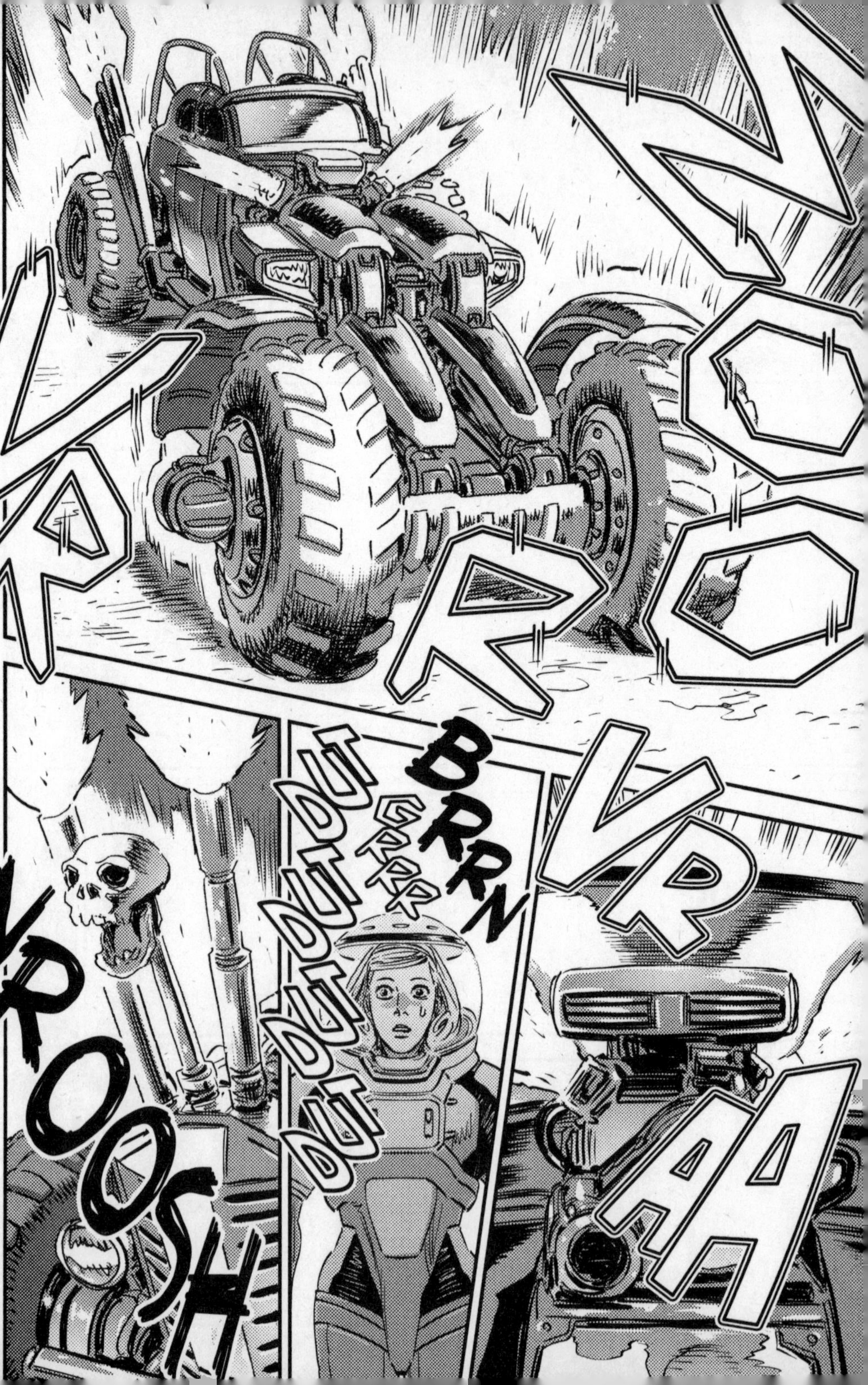
VAROO
VRAA
BRRRN
GRRRR
JUDDUDDUDD
VROOSH

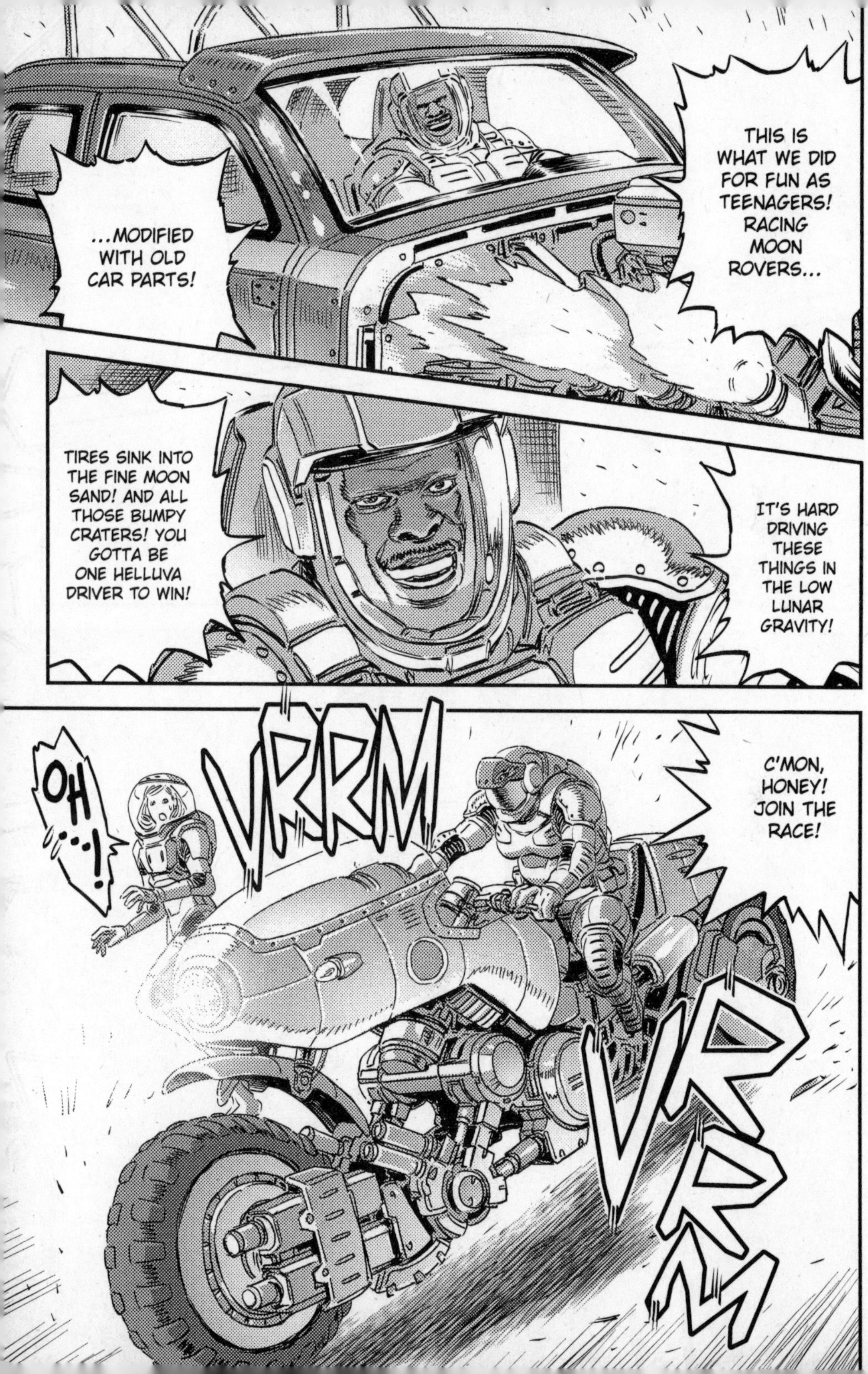
THIS IS WHAT WE DID FOR FUN AS TEENAGERS! RACING MOON ROVERS...
...MODIFIED WITH OLD CAR PARTS!
IT'S HARD DRIVING THESE THINGS IN THE LOW LUNAR GRAVITY!
TIRES SINK INTO THE FINE MOON SAND! AND ALL THOSE BUMPY CRATERS! YOU GOTTA BE ONE HELLUVA DRIVER TO WIN!
C'MON, HONEY! JOIN THE RACE!
VRRM
OH...!
VRRM

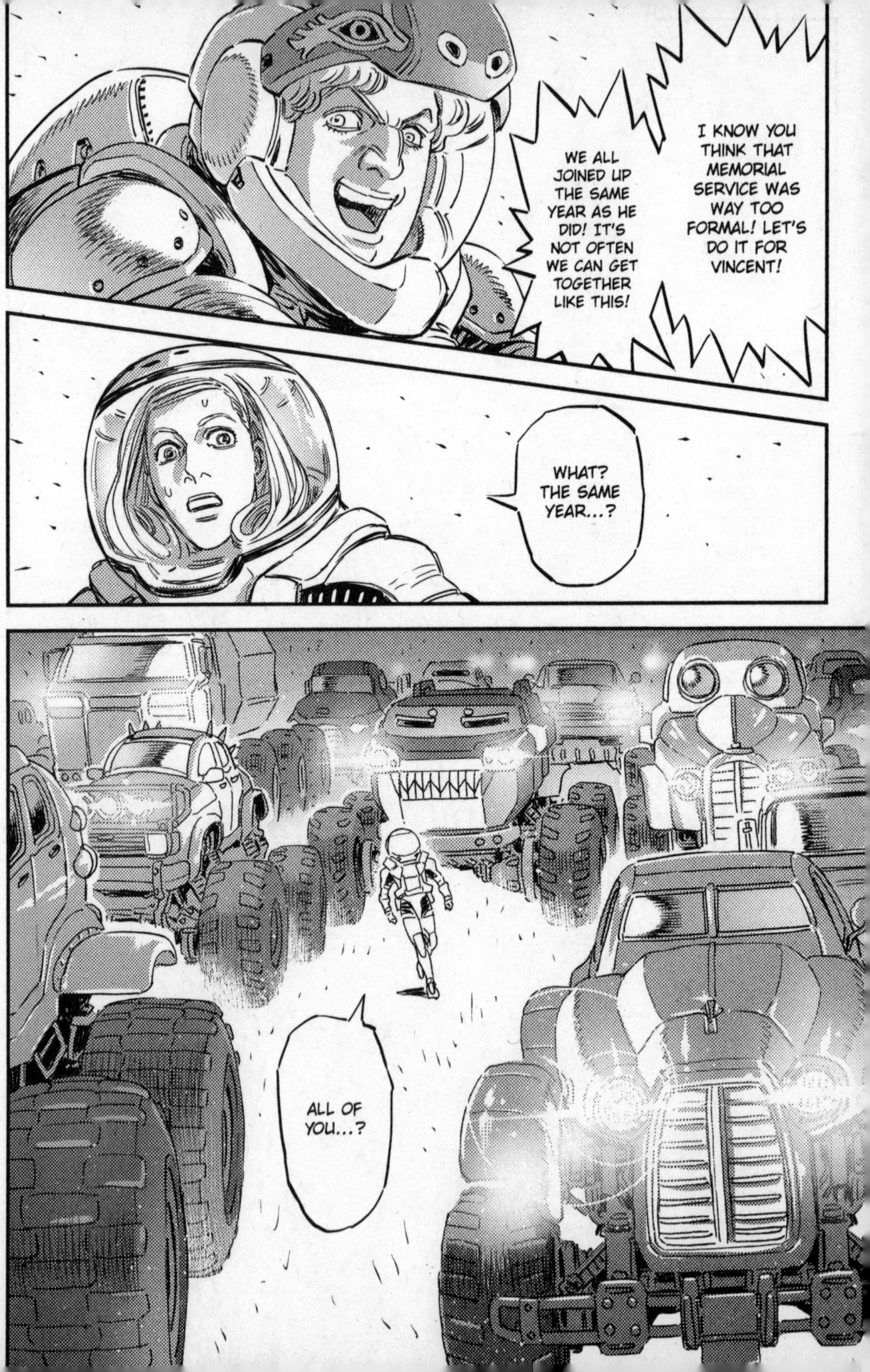
I KNOW YOU THINK THAT MEMORIAL SERVICE WAS WAY TOO FORMAL! LET'S DO IT FOR VINCENT!
WE ALL JOINED UP THE SAME YEAR AS HE DID! IT'S NOT OFTEN WE CAN GET TOGETHER LIKE THIS!
WHAT? THE SAME YEAR...?
ALL OF YOU...?

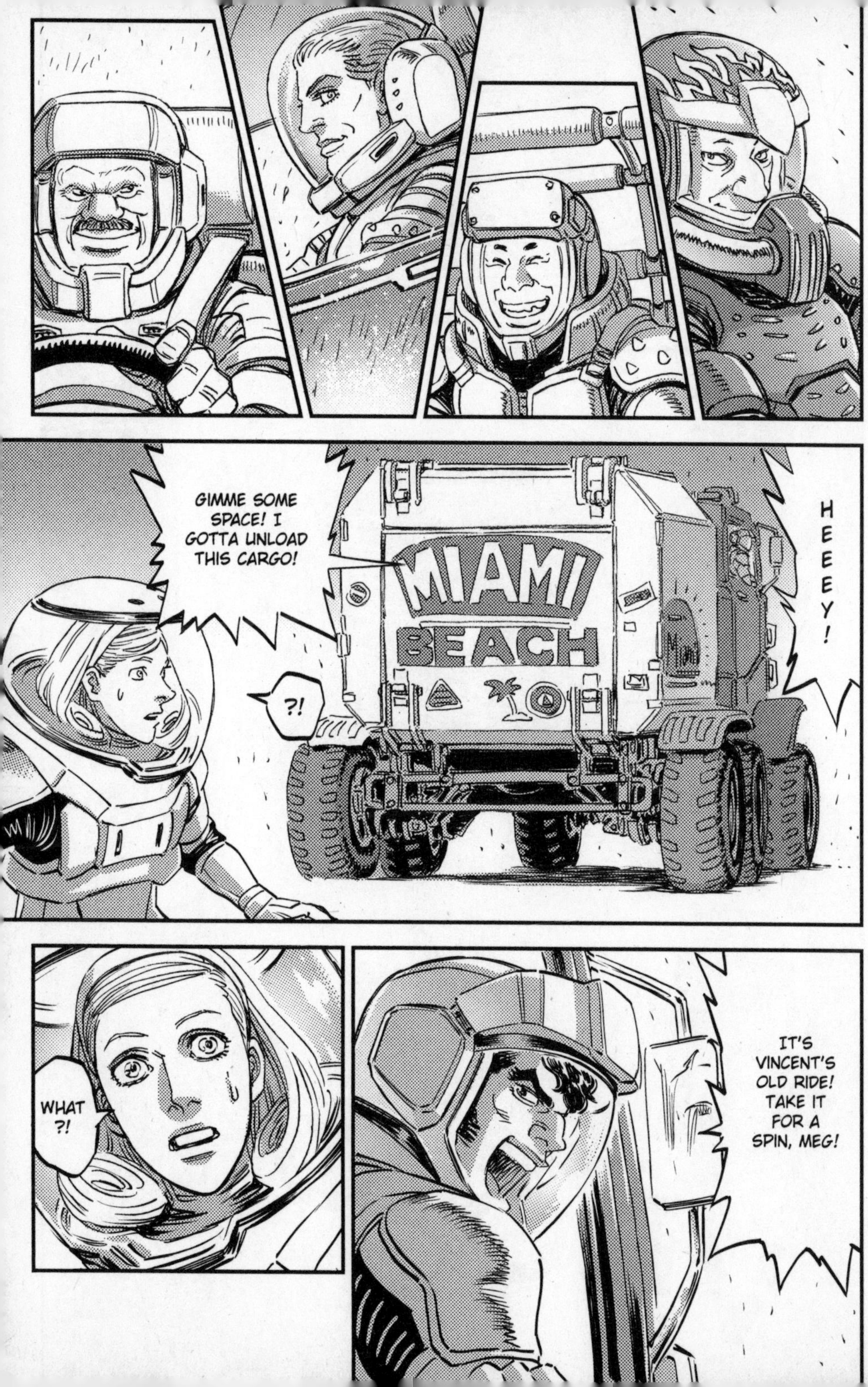
HEEEY!
GIMME SOME SPACE! I GOTTA UNLOAD THIS CARGO!
MIAMI BEACH
?!
IT'S VINCENT'S OLD RIDE! TAKE IT FOR A SPIN, MEG!
WHAT ?!

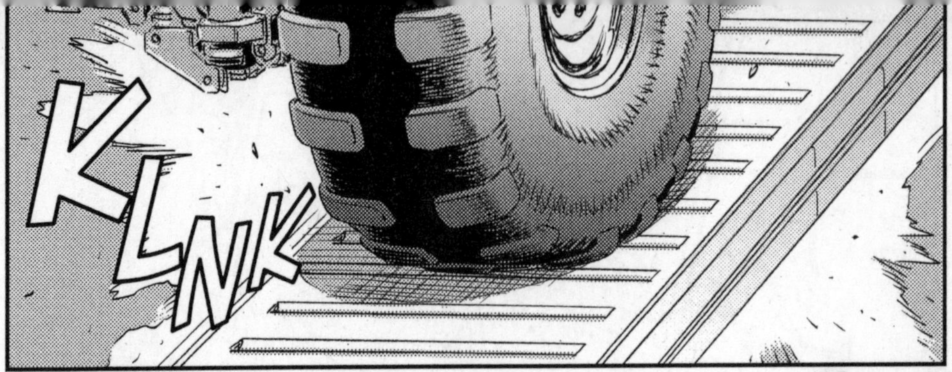
KLNK
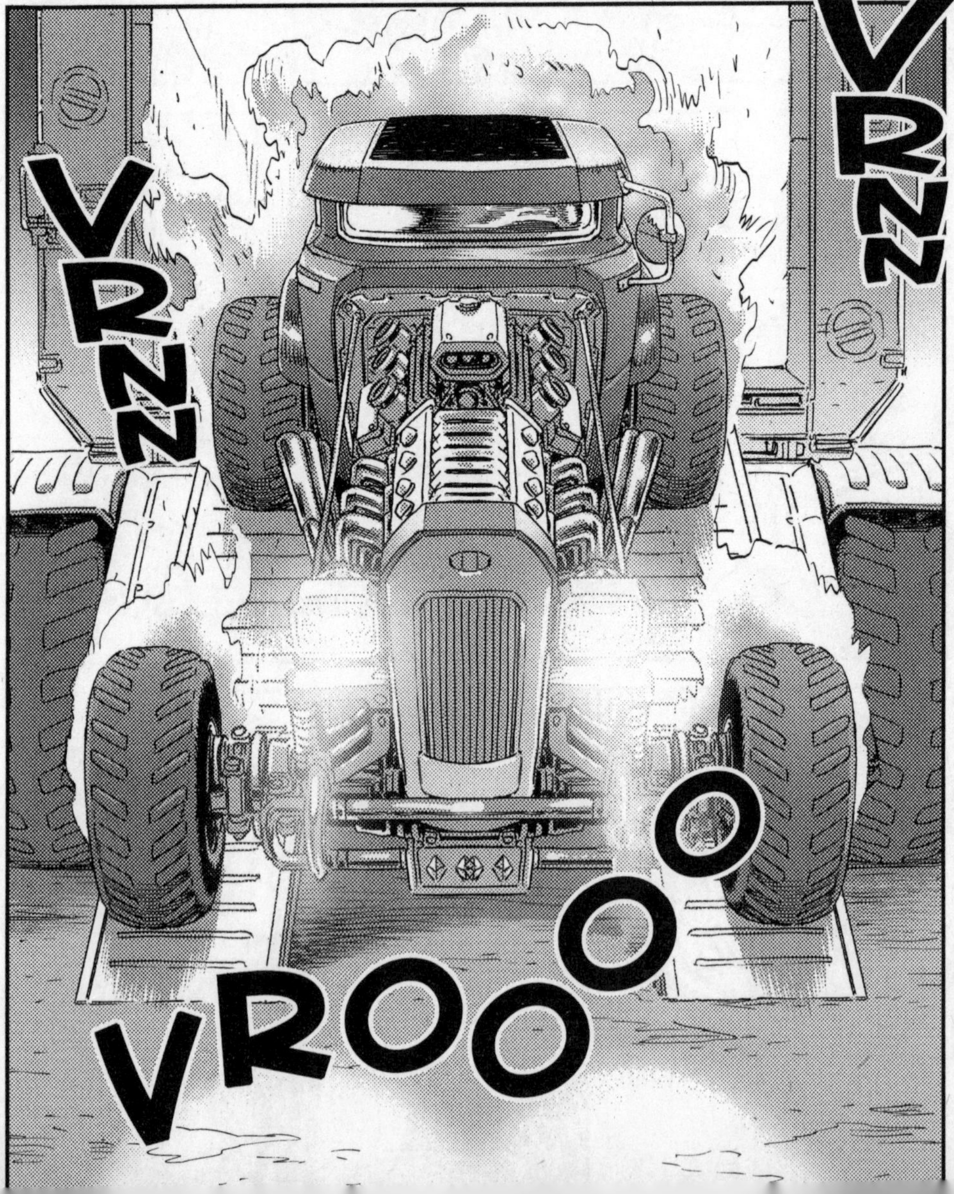
VRNN
VRNN
VROOOO

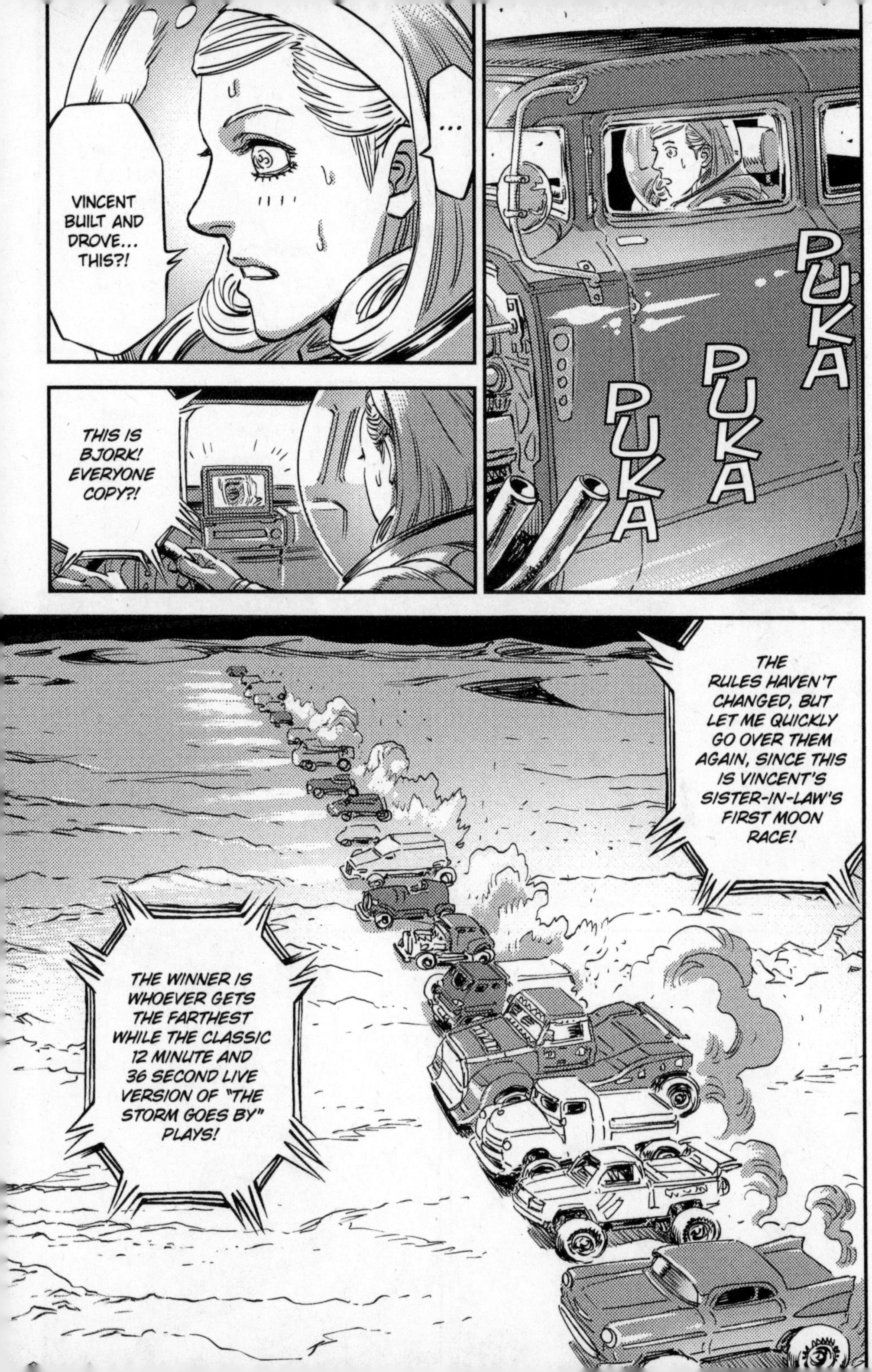
PUKA
PUKA
PUKA
...
VINCENT BUILT AND DROVE... THIS?!
THIS IS BJORK! EVERYONE COPY?!
THE RULES HAVEN'T CHANGED, BUT LET ME QUICKLY GO OVER THEM AGAIN, SINCE THIS IS VINCENT'S SISTER-IN-LAW'S FIRST MOON RACE!
THE WINNER IS WHOEVER GETS THE FARTHEST WHILE THE CLASSIC 12 MINUTE AND 36 SECOND LIVE VERSION OF "THE STORM GOES BY" PLAYS!

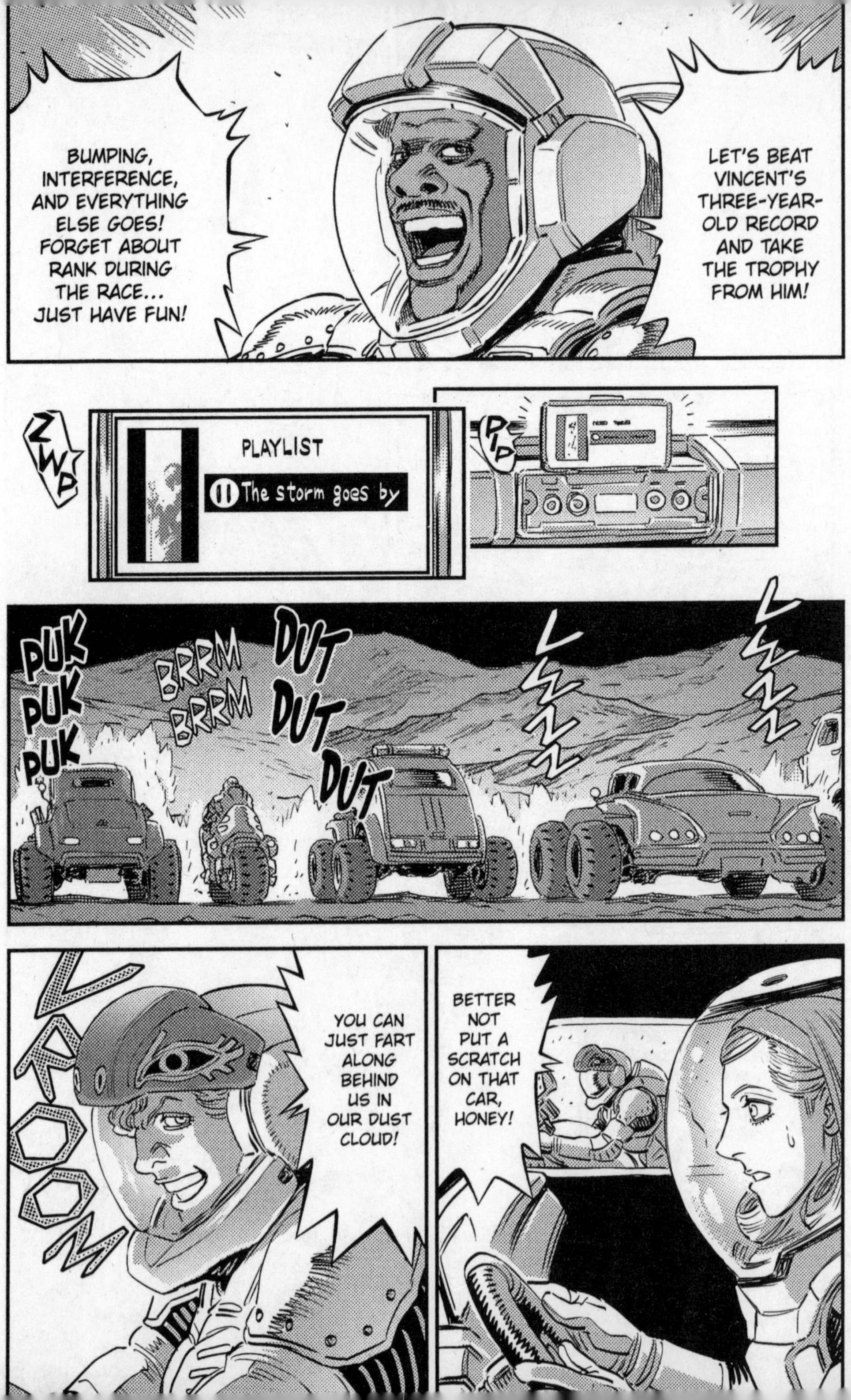
LET'S BEAT VINCENT'S THREE-YEAR-OLD RECORD AND TAKE THE TROPHY FROM HIM!
BUMPING, INTERFERENCE, AND EVERYTHING ELSE GOES! FORGET ABOUT RANK DURING THE RACE... JUST HAVE FUN!
PIP
ZWP
PLAYLIST
The storm goes by
VWNN
VWNN
DUT DUT DUT
BRRM BRRM
PUK PUK PUK
BETTER NOT PUT A SCRATCH ON THAT CAR, HONEY!
YOU CAN JUST FART ALONG BEHIND US IN OUR DUST CLOUD!
VROOOM

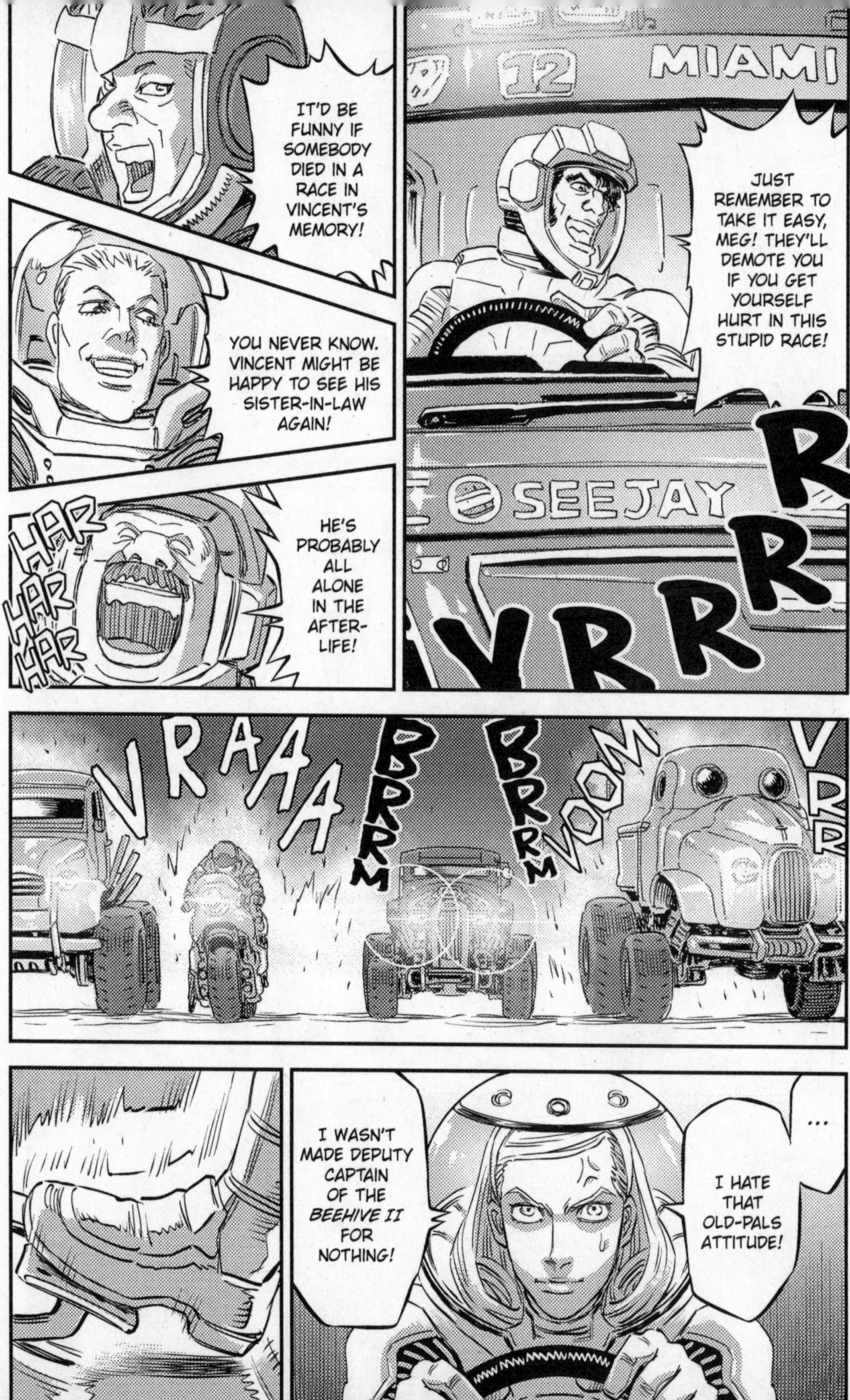

MIAMI
12
JUST REMEMBER TO TAKE IT EASY, MEG! THEY'LL DEMOTE YOU IF YOU GET YOURSELF HURT IN THIS STUPID RACE!
SEEJAY
VRRRRR
IT'D BE FUNNY IF SOMEBODY DIED IN A RACE IN VINCENT'S MEMORY!
YOU NEVER KNOW. VINCENT MIGHT BE HAPPY TO SEE HIS SISTER-IN-LAW AGAIN!
HE'S PROBABLY ALL ALONE IN THE AFTER-LIFE!
HAR HAR HAR HAR
VRR
VOOM
BRRRM
BRRRM
VRAAA
...
I HATE THAT OLD-PALS ATTITUDE!
I WASN'T MADE DEPUTY CAPTAIN OF THE *BEEHIVE II* FOR NOTHING!

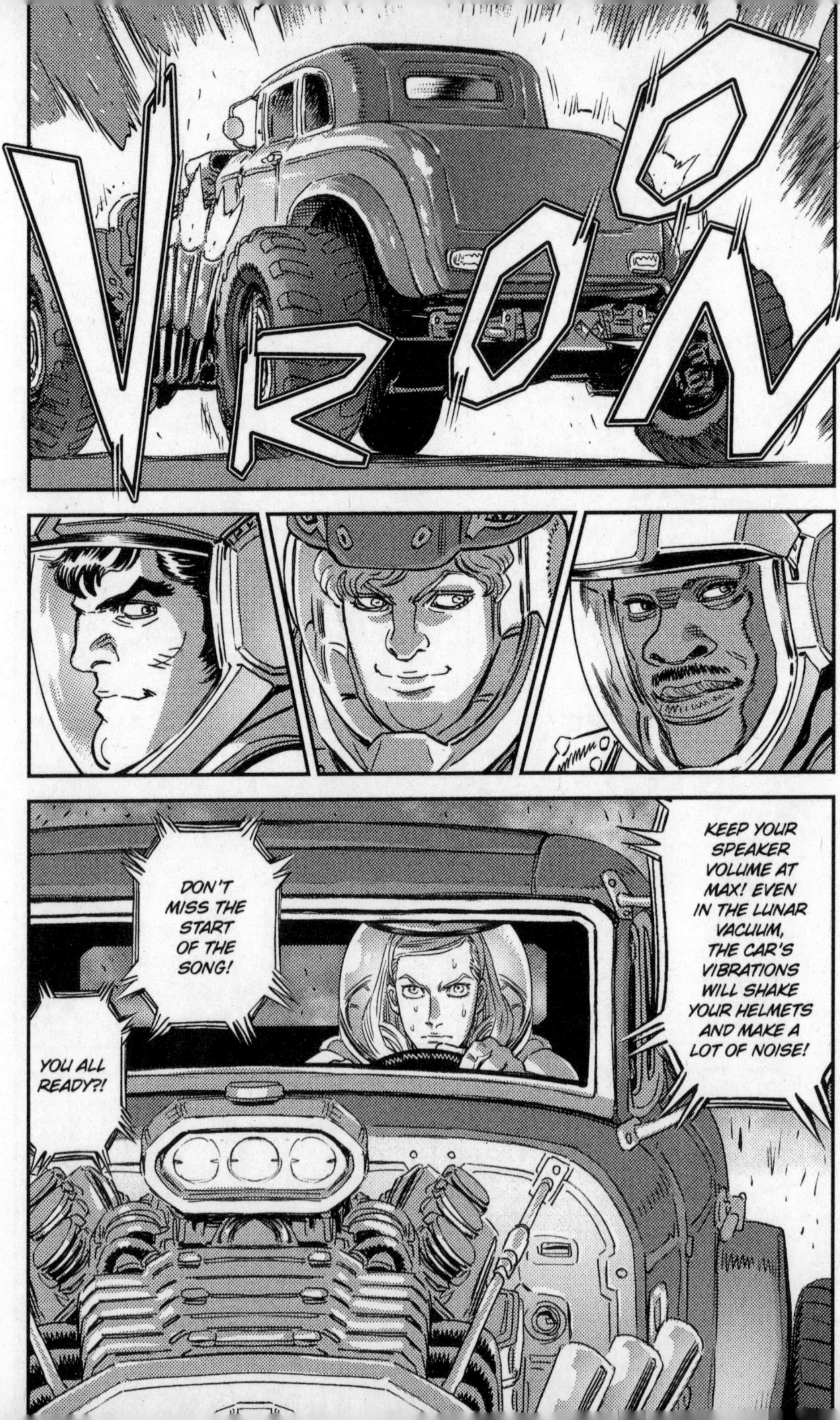
VROOOM
KEEP YOUR SPEAKER VOLUME AT MAX! EVEN IN THE LUNAR VACUUM, THE CAR'S VIBRATIONS WILL SHAKE YOUR HELMETS AND MAKE A LOT OF NOISE!
DON'T MISS THE START OF THE SONG!
YOU ALL READY?!

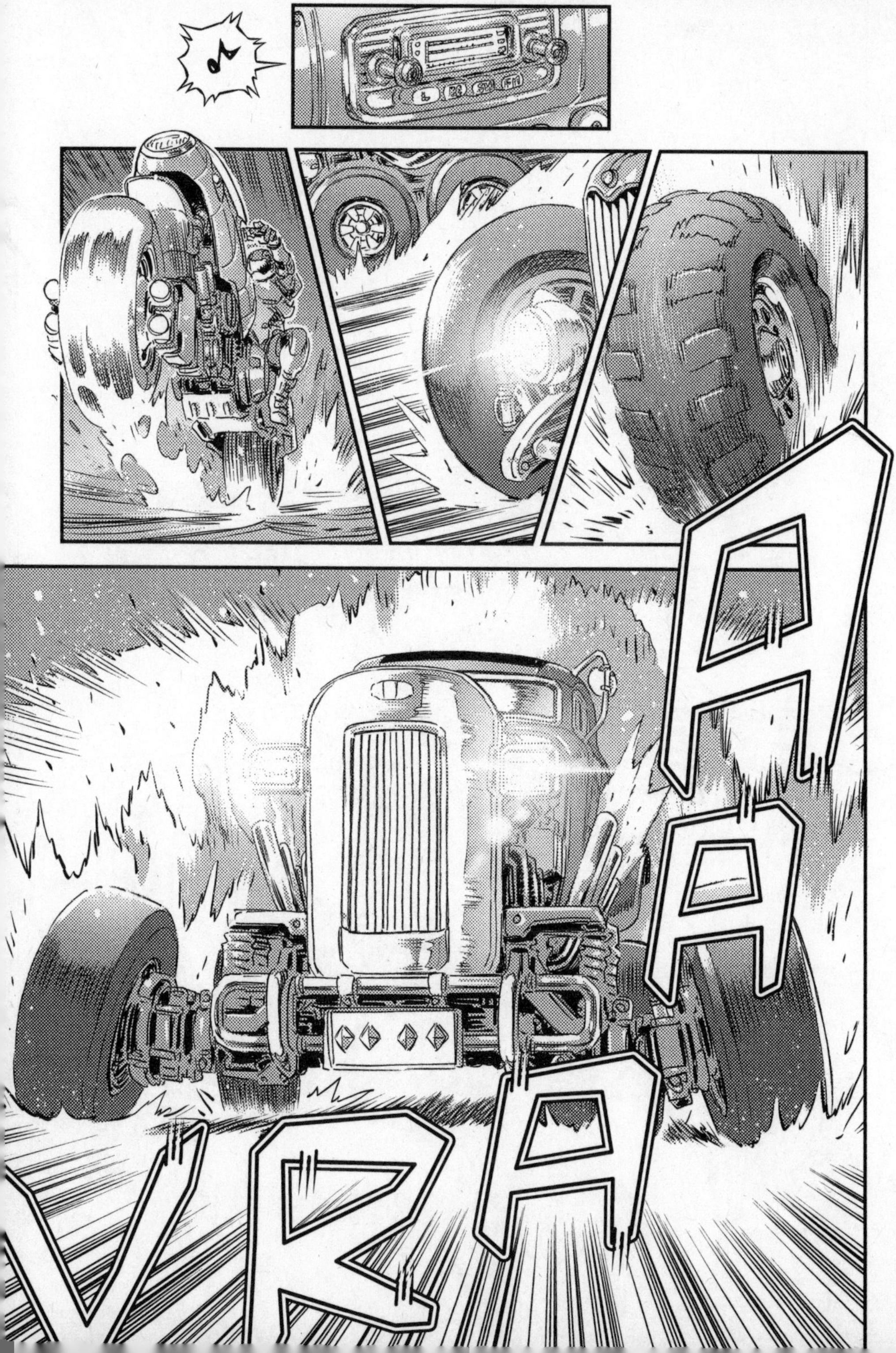
VRAAA

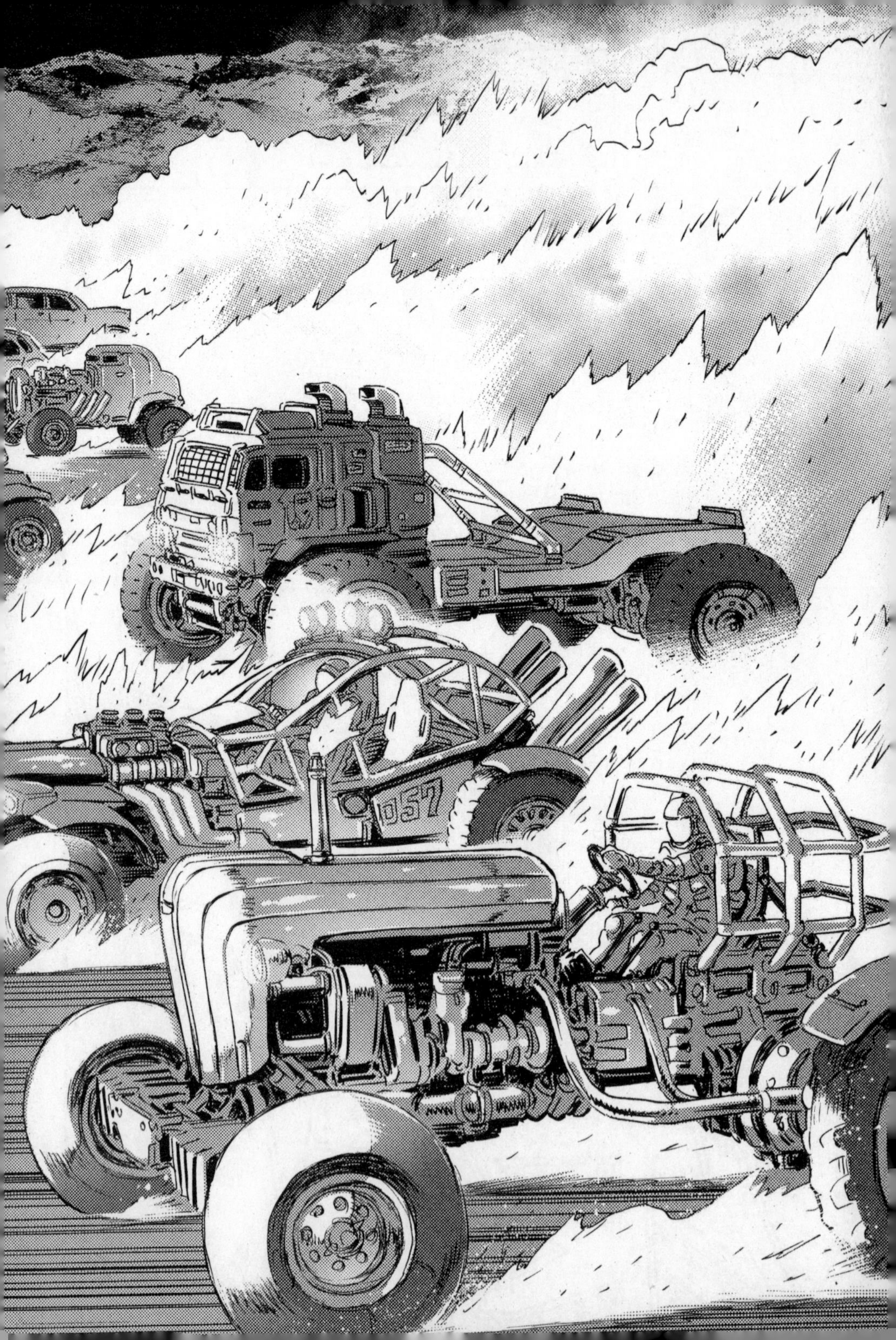
057

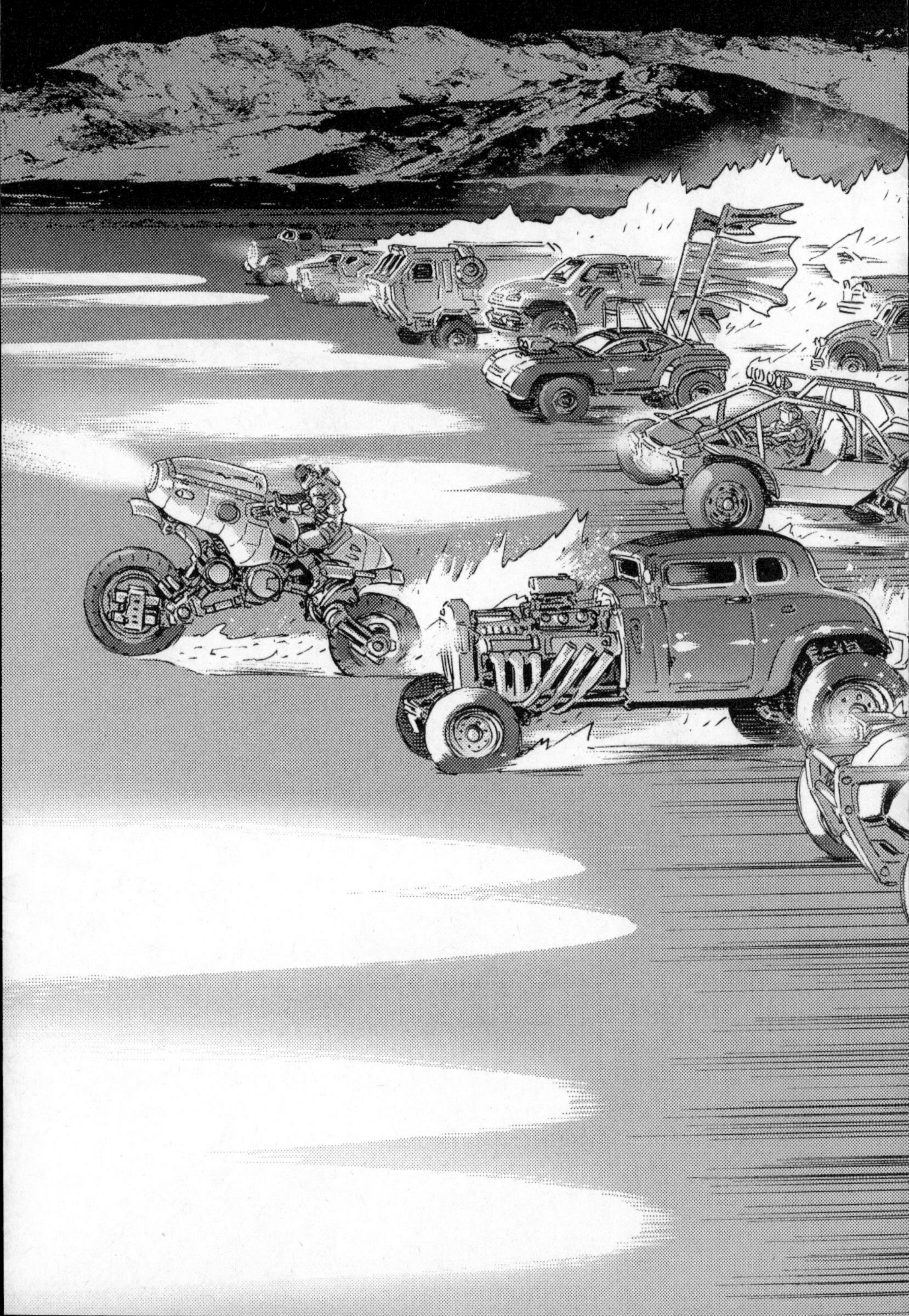

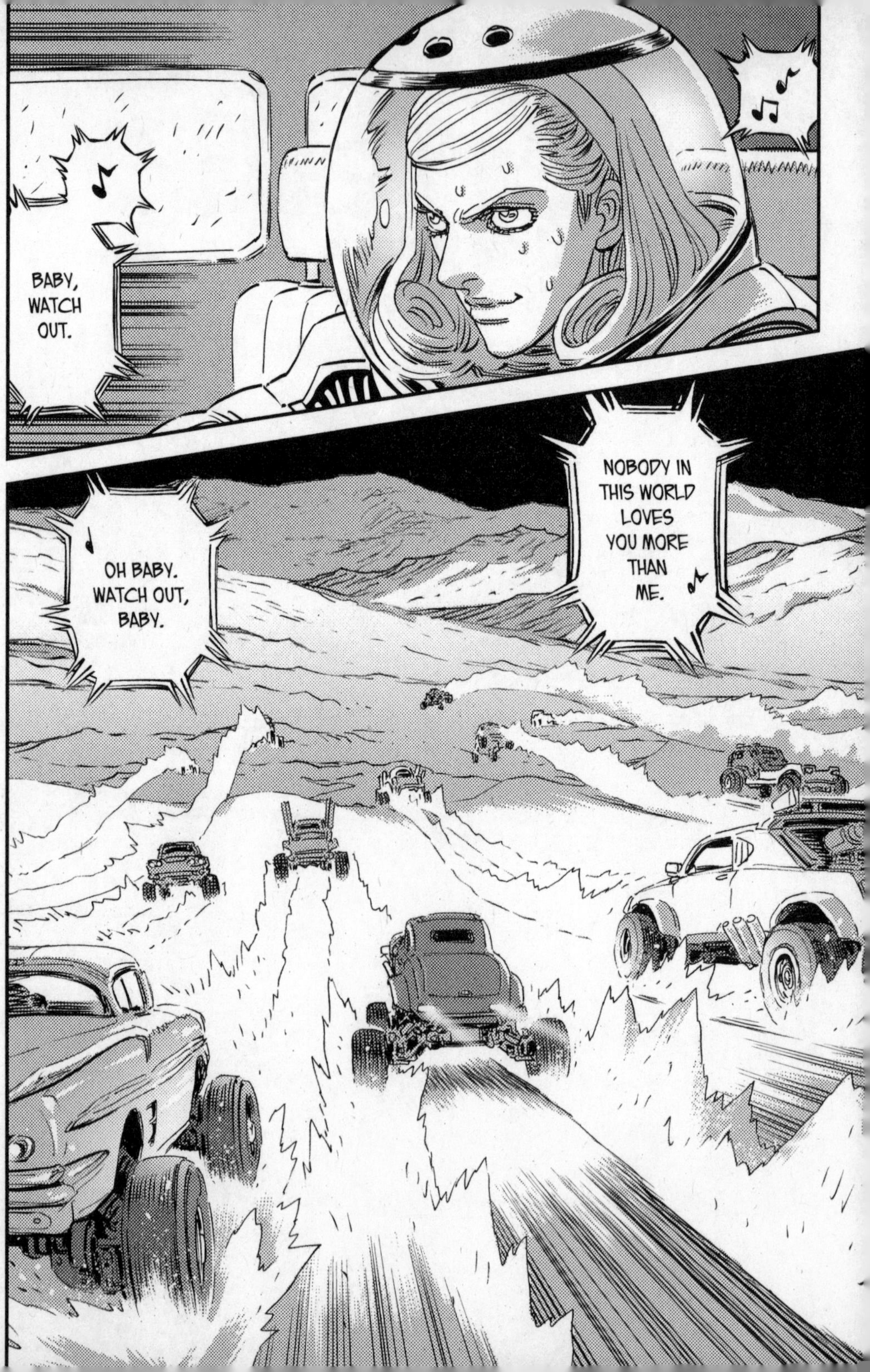
BABY, WATCH OUT.
NOBODY IN THIS WORLD LOVES YOU MORE THAN ME.
OH BABY. WATCH OUT, BABY.

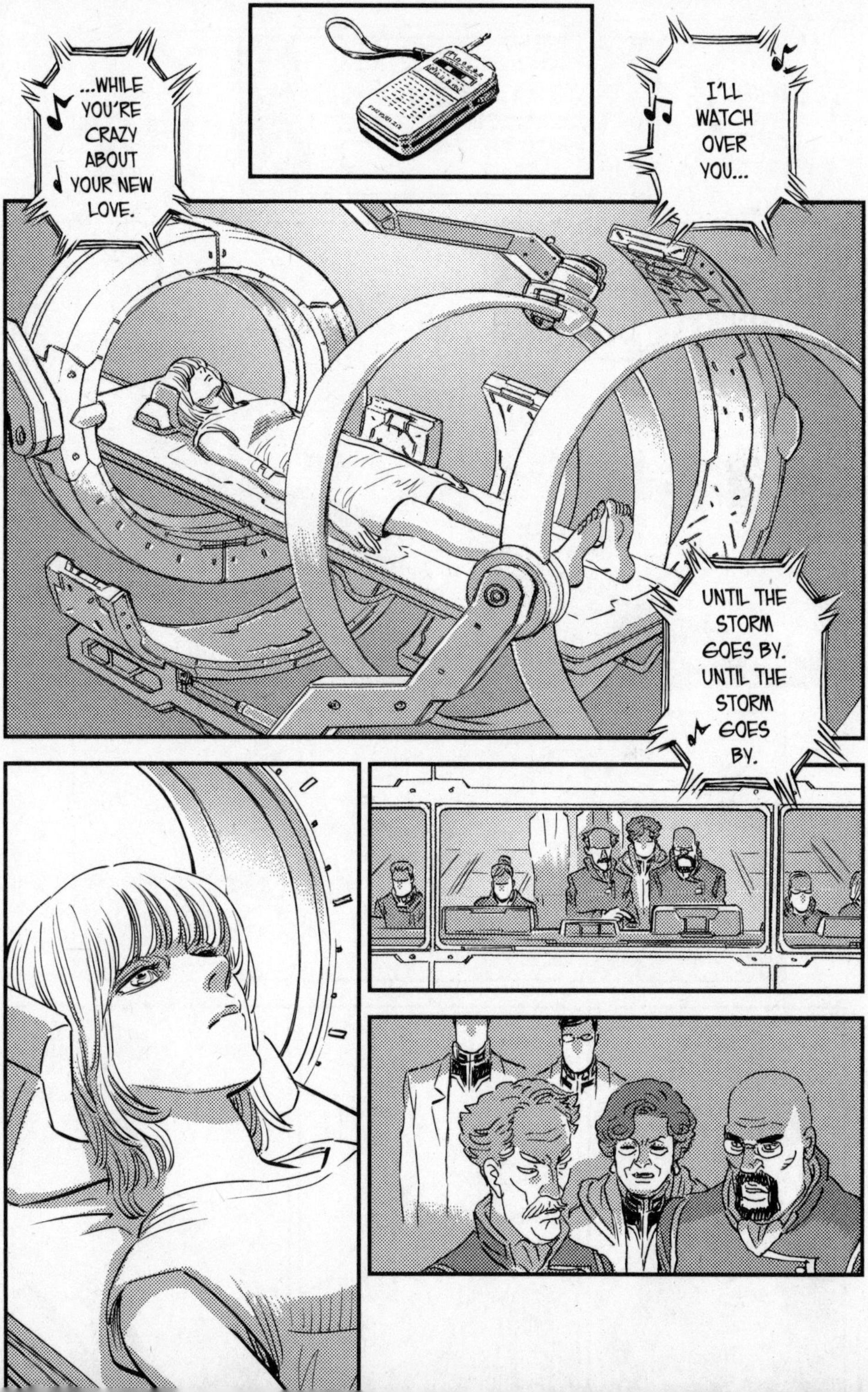
I'LL WATCH OVER YOU...
...WHILE YOU'RE CRAZY ABOUT YOUR NEW LOVE.
UNTIL THE STORM GOES BY. UNTIL THE STORM GOES BY.

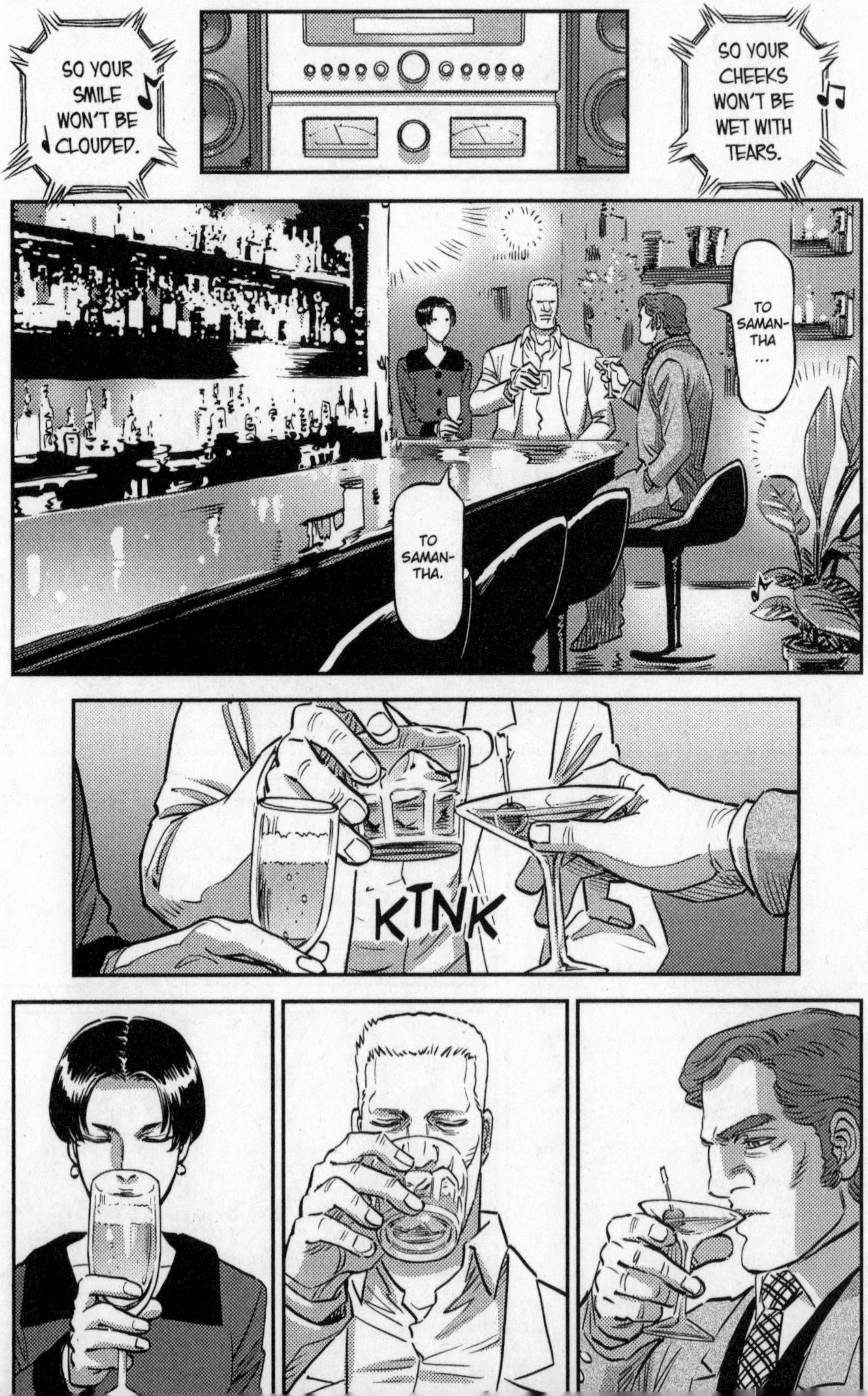
SO YOUR CHEEKS WON'T BE WET WITH TEARS.
SO YOUR SMILE WON'T BE CLOUDED.
TO SAMANTHA...
TO SAMANTHA.
KINK

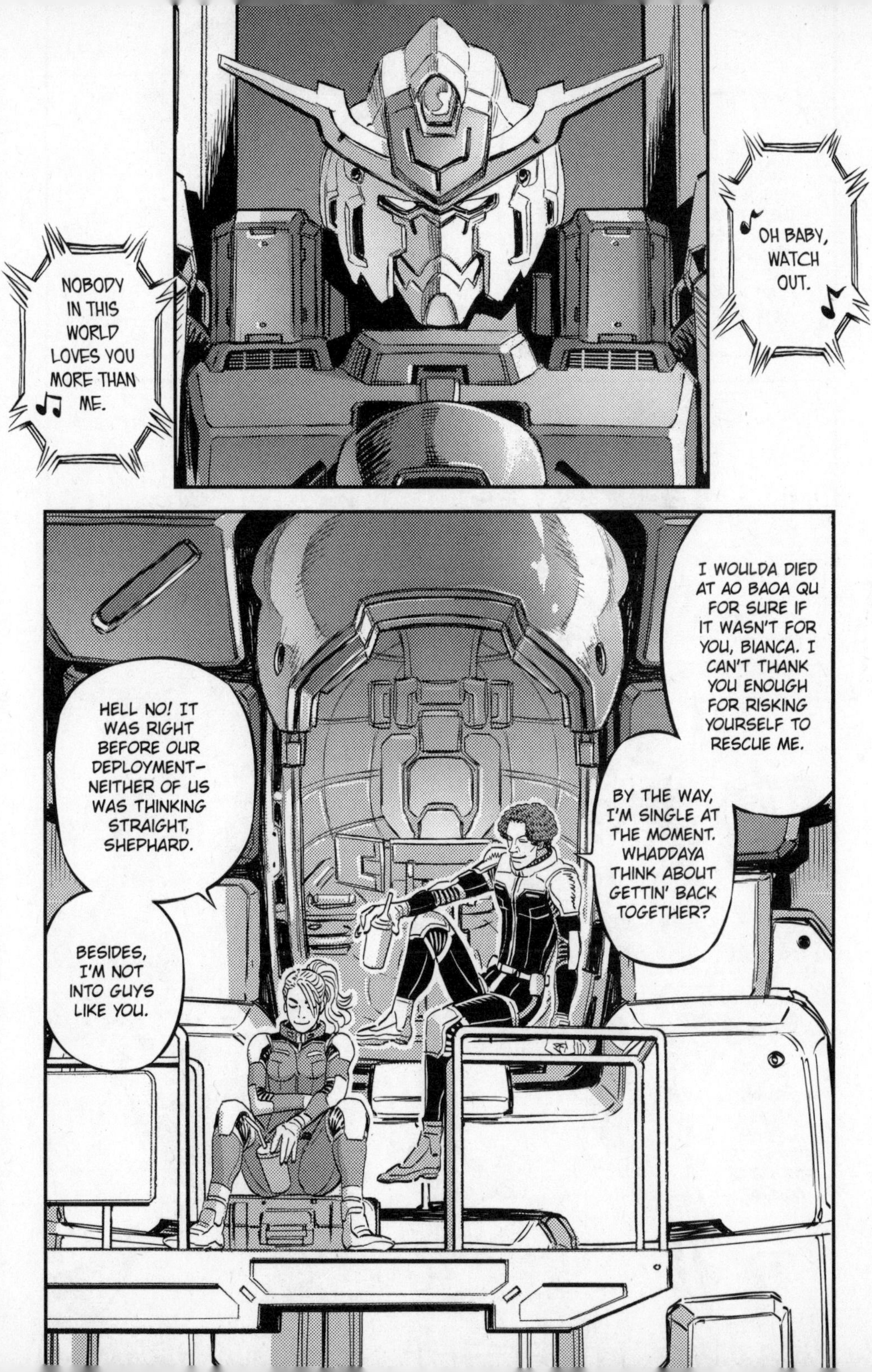
♪ OH BABY, WATCH OUT. ♪
NOBODY IN THIS WORLD LOVES YOU MORE THAN ♫ ME.
I WOULDA DIED AT AO BAOA QU FOR SURE IF IT WASN'T FOR YOU, BIANCA. I CAN'T THANK YOU ENOUGH FOR RISKING YOURSELF TO RESCUE ME.
BY THE WAY, I'M SINGLE AT THE MOMENT. WHADDAYA THINK ABOUT GETTIN' BACK TOGETHER?
HELL NO! IT WAS RIGHT BEFORE OUR DEPLOYMENT-NEITHER OF US WAS THINKING STRAIGHT, SHEPHARD.
BESIDES, I'M NOT INTO GUYS LIKE YOU.

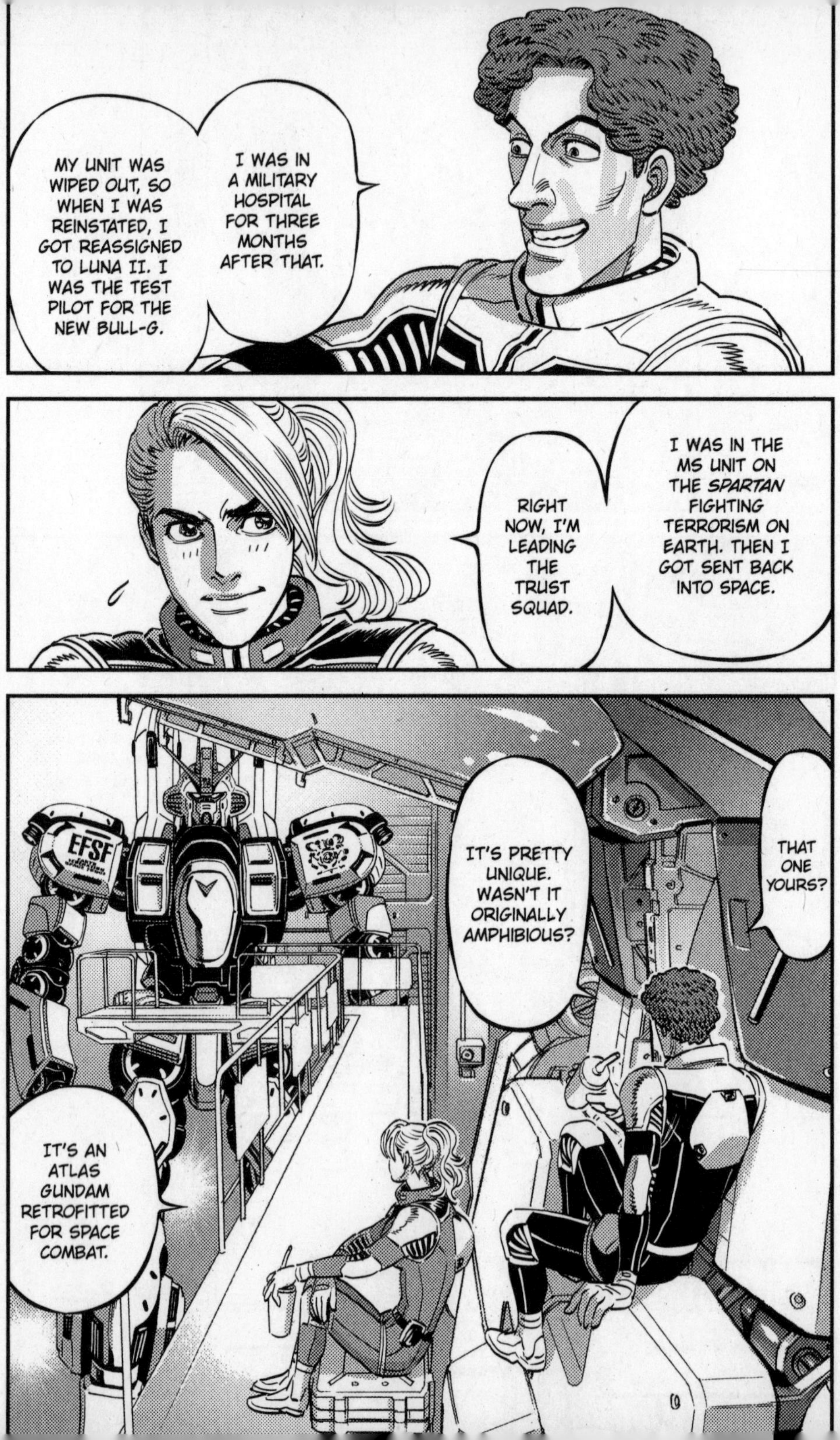
I WAS IN A MILITARY HOSPITAL FOR THREE MONTHS AFTER THAT.
MY UNIT WAS WIPED OUT, SO WHEN I WAS REINSTATED, I GOT REASSIGNED TO LUNA II. I WAS THE TEST PILOT FOR THE NEW BULL-G.
I WAS IN THE MS UNIT ON THE *SPARTAN* FIGHTING TERRORISM ON EARTH. THEN I GOT SENT BACK INTO SPACE.
RIGHT NOW, I'M LEADING THE TRUST SQUAD.
THAT ONE YOURS?
IT'S PRETTY UNIQUE. WASN'T IT ORIGINALLY AMPHIBIOUS?
EFSF
IT'S AN ATLAS GUNDAM RETROFITTED FOR SPACE COMBAT.

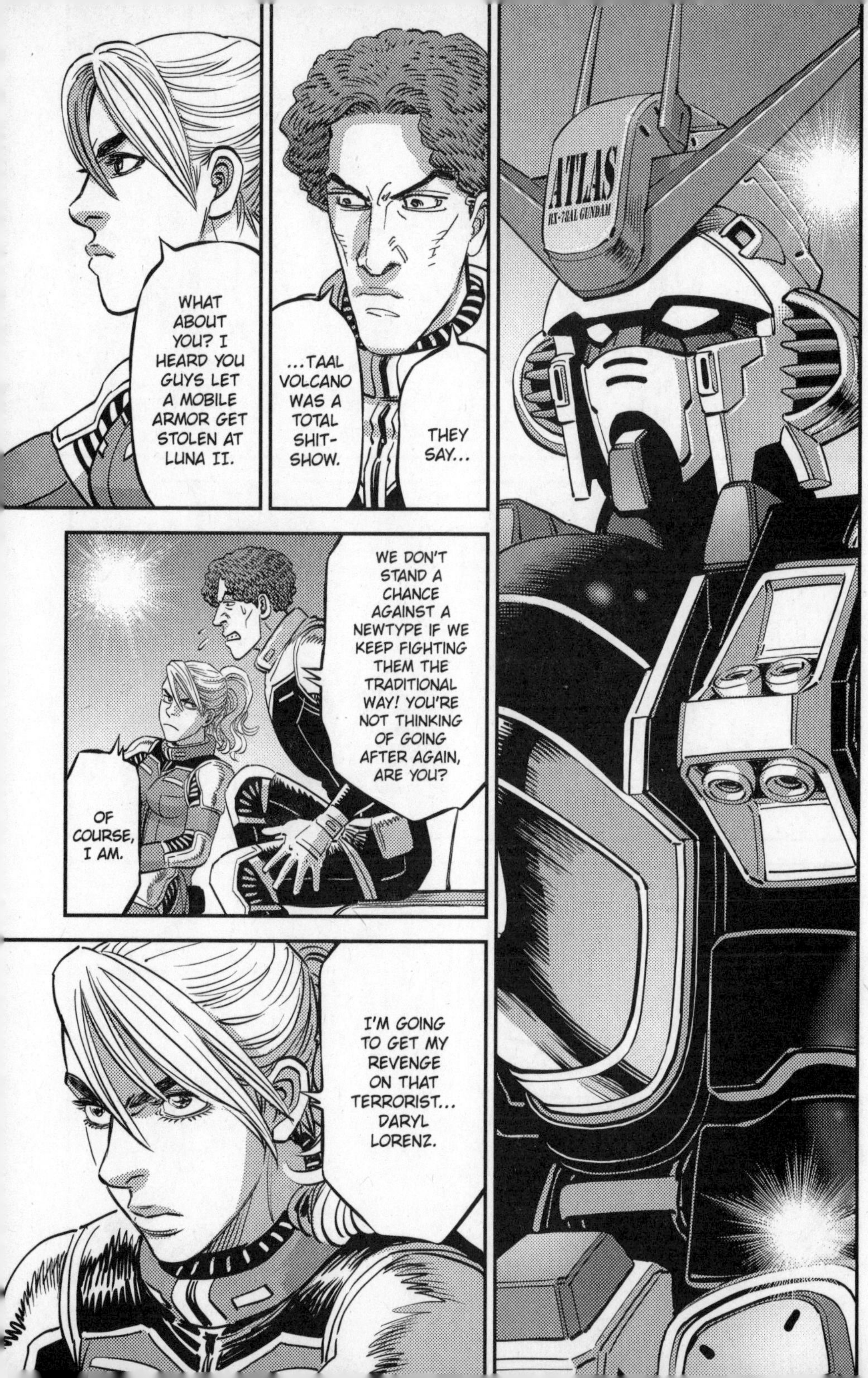
ATLAS
RX-78AL GUNDAM
THEY SAY...
...TAAL VOLCANO WAS A TOTAL SHIT-SHOW.
WHAT ABOUT YOU? I HEARD YOU GUYS LET A MOBILE ARMOR GET STOLEN AT LUNA II.
WE DON'T STAND A CHANCE AGAINST A NEWTYPE IF WE KEEP FIGHTING THEM THE TRADITIONAL WAY! YOU'RE NOT THINKING OF GOING AFTER AGAIN, ARE YOU?
OF COURSE, I AM.
I'M GOING TO GET MY REVENGE ON THAT TERRORIST... DARYL LORENZ.

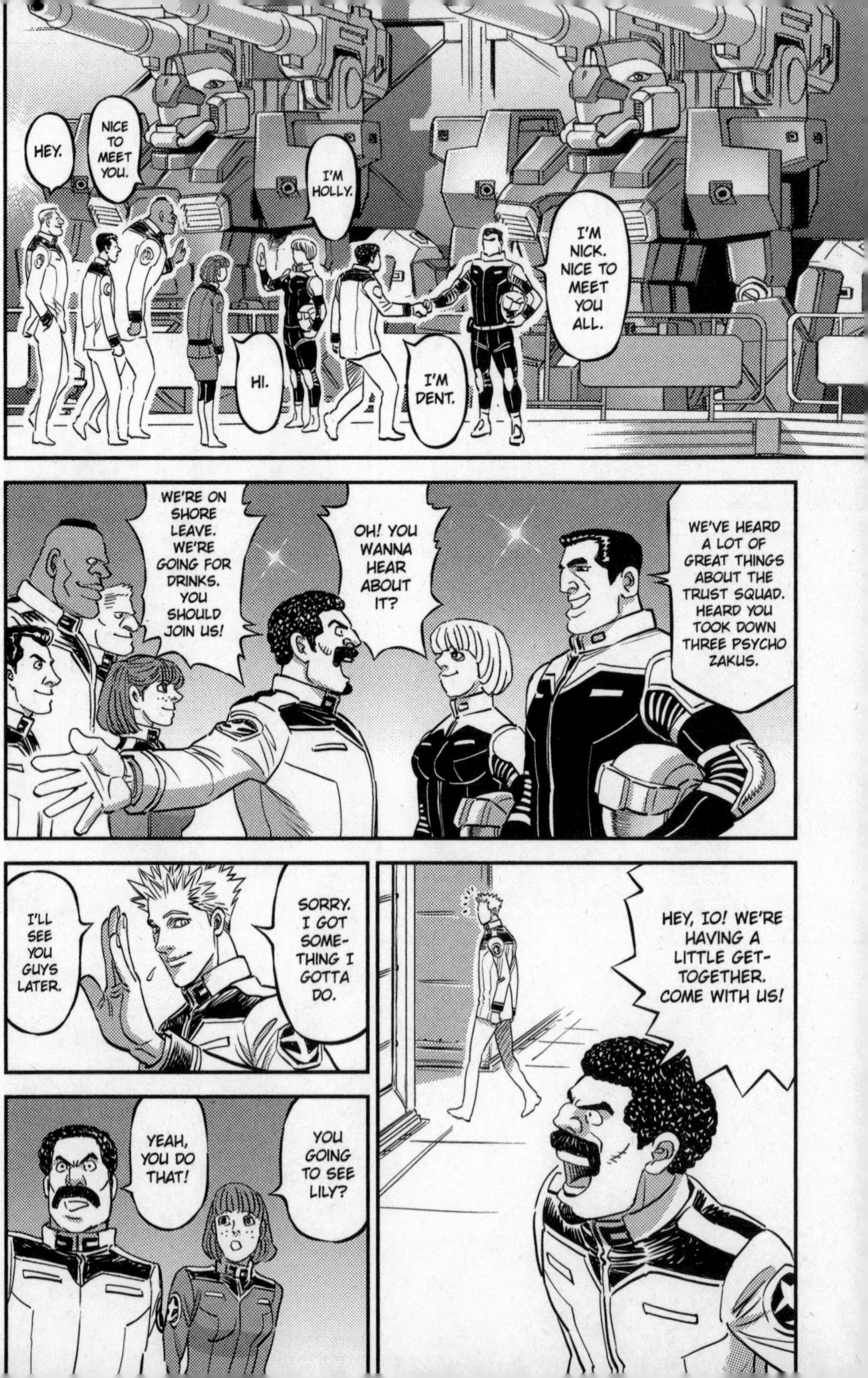
I'M NICK. NICE TO MEET YOU ALL.
I'M DENT.
I'M HOLLY.
HI.
NICE TO MEET YOU.
HEY.
WE'VE HEARD A LOT OF GREAT THINGS ABOUT THE TRUST SQUAD. HEARD YOU TOOK DOWN THREE PSYCHO ZAKUS.
OH! YOU WANNA HEAR ABOUT IT?
WE'RE ON SHORE LEAVE. WE'RE GOING FOR DRINKS. YOU SHOULD JOIN US!
HEY, IO! WE'RE HAVING A LITTLE GET-TOGETHER. COME WITH US!
SORRY. I GOT SOMETHING I GOTTA DO.
I'LL SEE YOU GUYS LATER.
YOU GOING TO SEE LILY?
YEAH, YOU DO THAT!

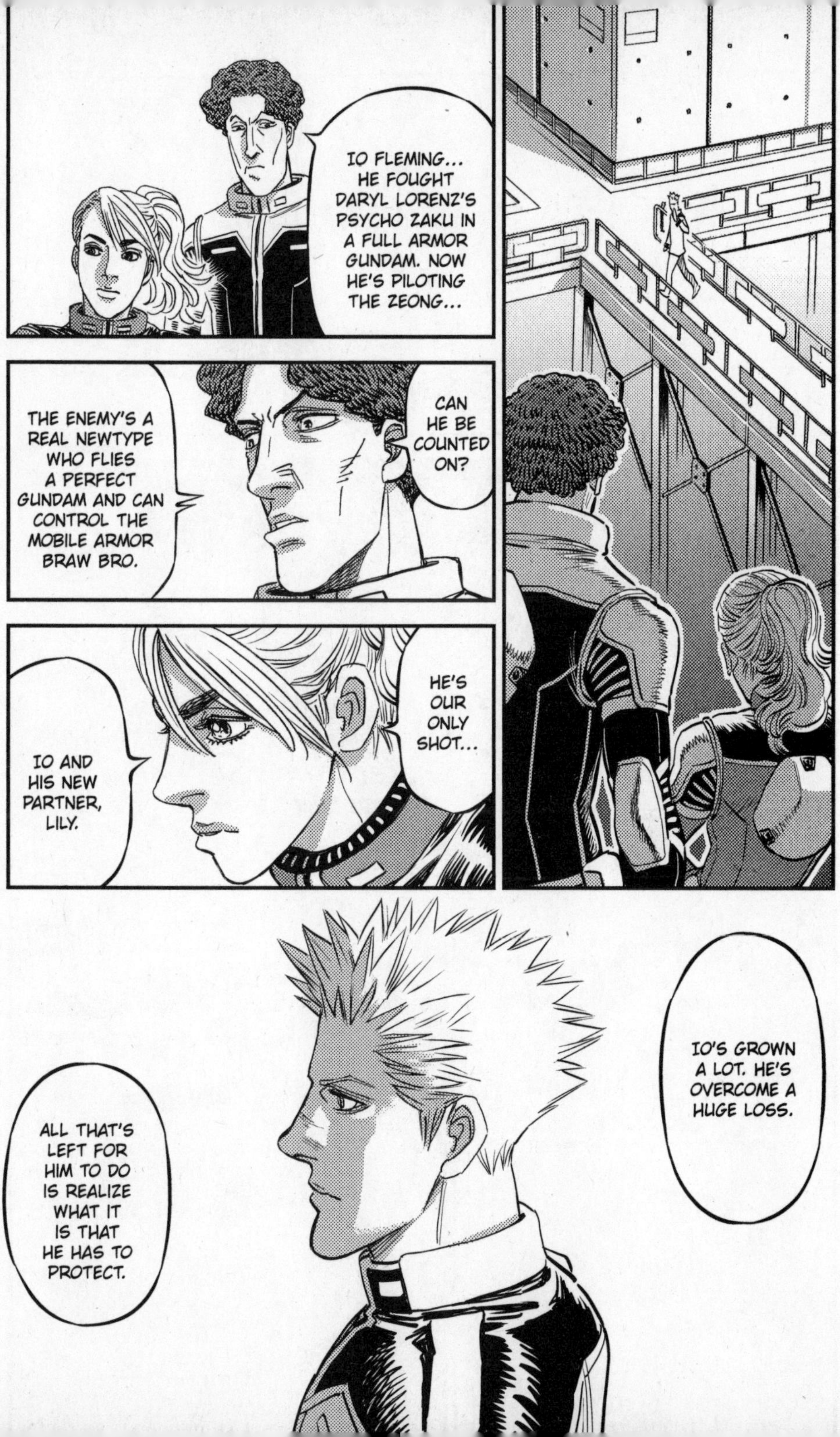
IO FLEMING... HE FOUGHT DARYL LORENZ'S PSYCHO ZAKU IN A FULL ARMOR GUNDAM. NOW HE'S PILOTING THE ZEONG...
CAN HE BE COUNTED ON?
THE ENEMY'S A REAL NEWTYPE WHO FLIES A PERFECT GUNDAM AND CAN CONTROL THE MOBILE ARMOR BRAW BRO.
HE'S OUR ONLY SHOT...
IO AND HIS NEW PARTNER, LILY.
IO'S GROWN A LOT. HE'S OVERCOME A HUGE LOSS.
ALL THAT'S LEFT FOR HIM TO DO IS REALIZE WHAT IT IS THAT HE HAS TO PROTECT.

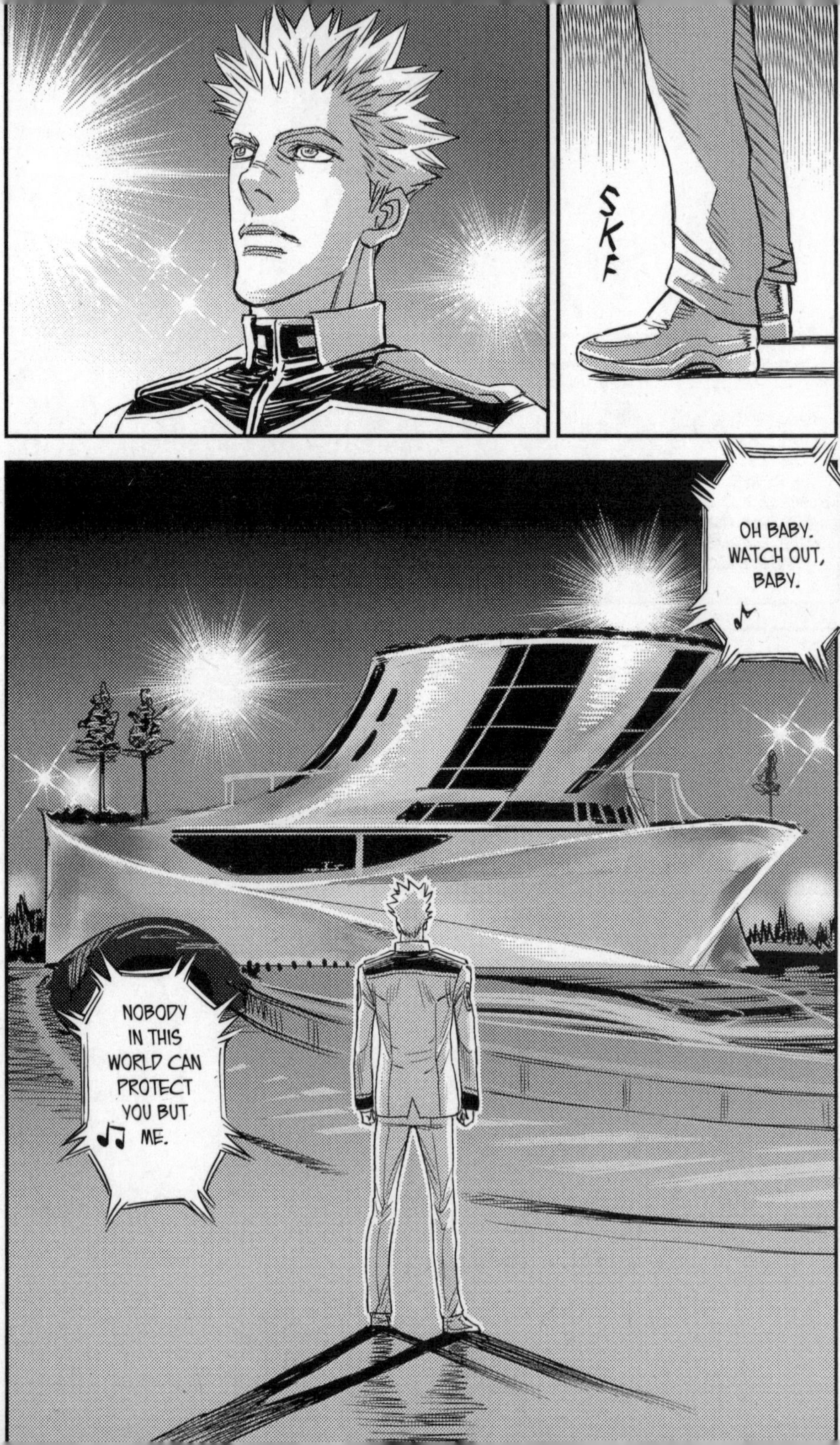
SKF
OH BABY. WATCH OUT, BABY. ♪
NOBODY IN THIS WORLD CAN PROTECT YOU BUT ♫ ME.

MOBILE SUIT GUNDAM THUNDERBOLT

CHAPTER 164

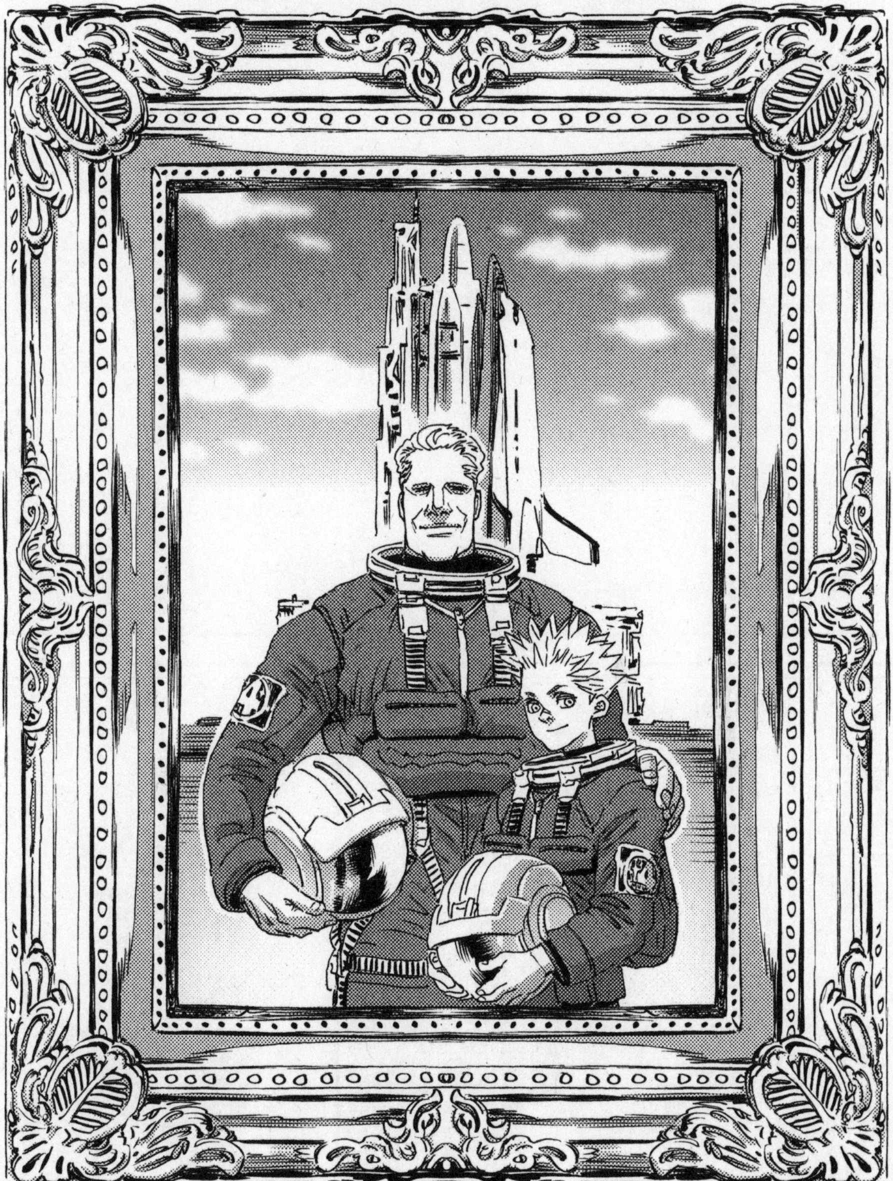

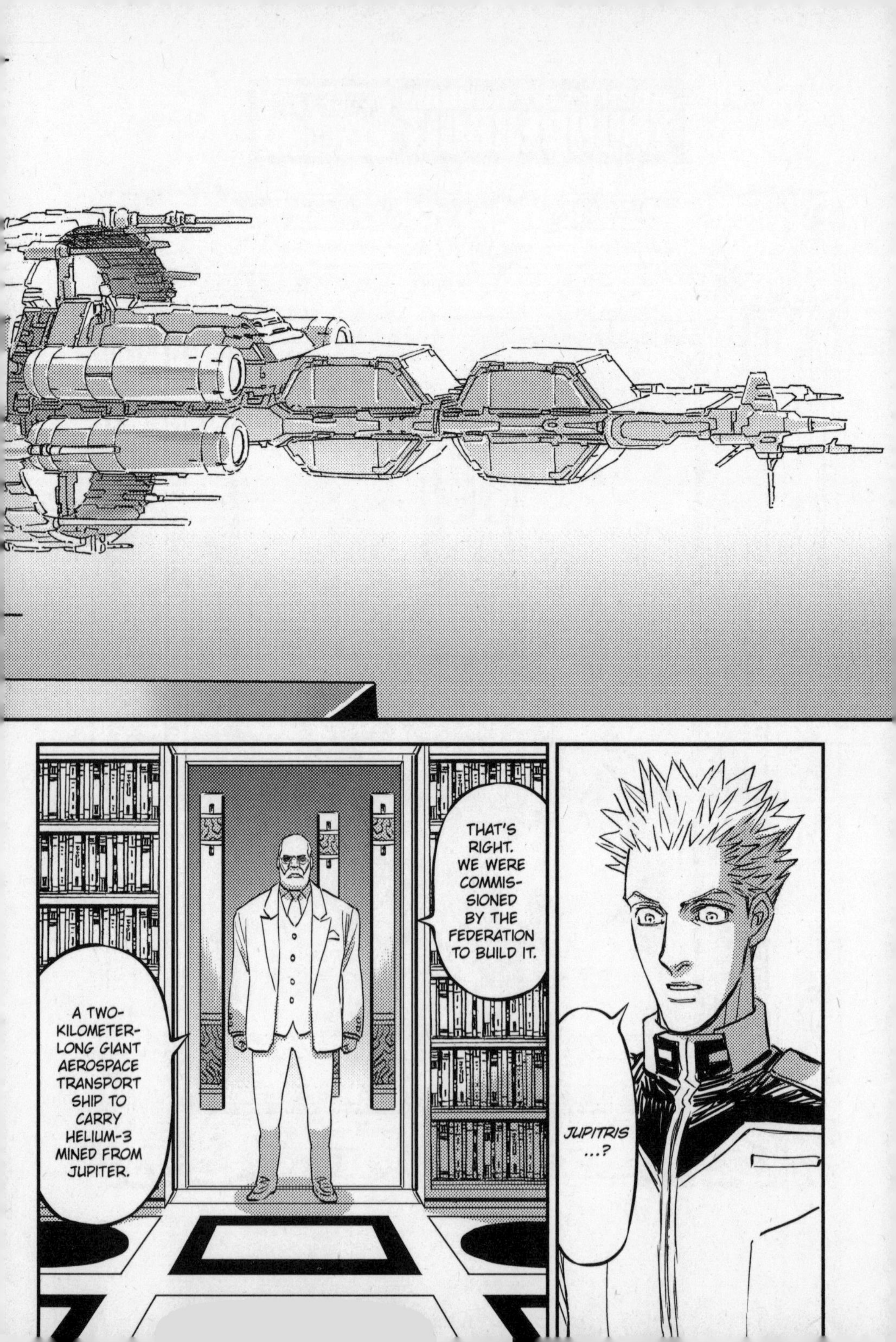
JUPITRIS ...?
THAT'S RIGHT. WE WERE COMMISSIONED BY THE FEDERATION TO BUILD IT.
A TWO-KILOMETER-LONG GIANT AEROSPACE TRANSPORT SHIP TO CARRY HELIUM-3 MINED FROM JUPITER.

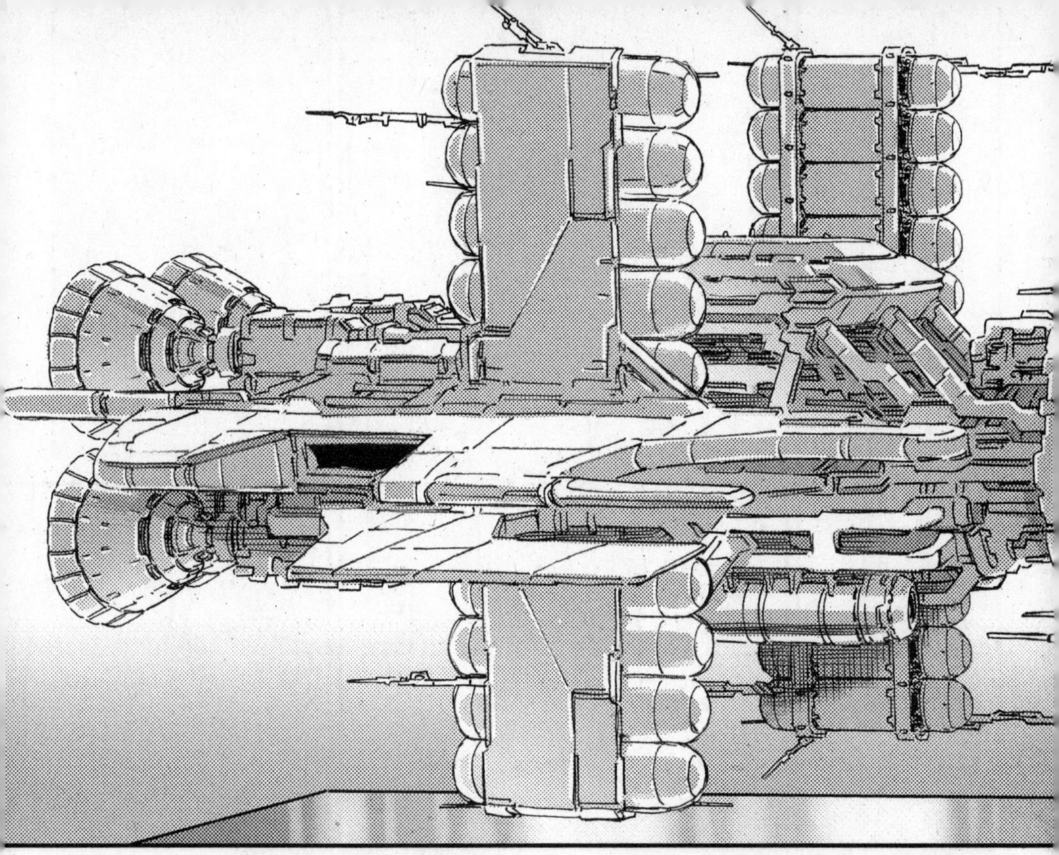

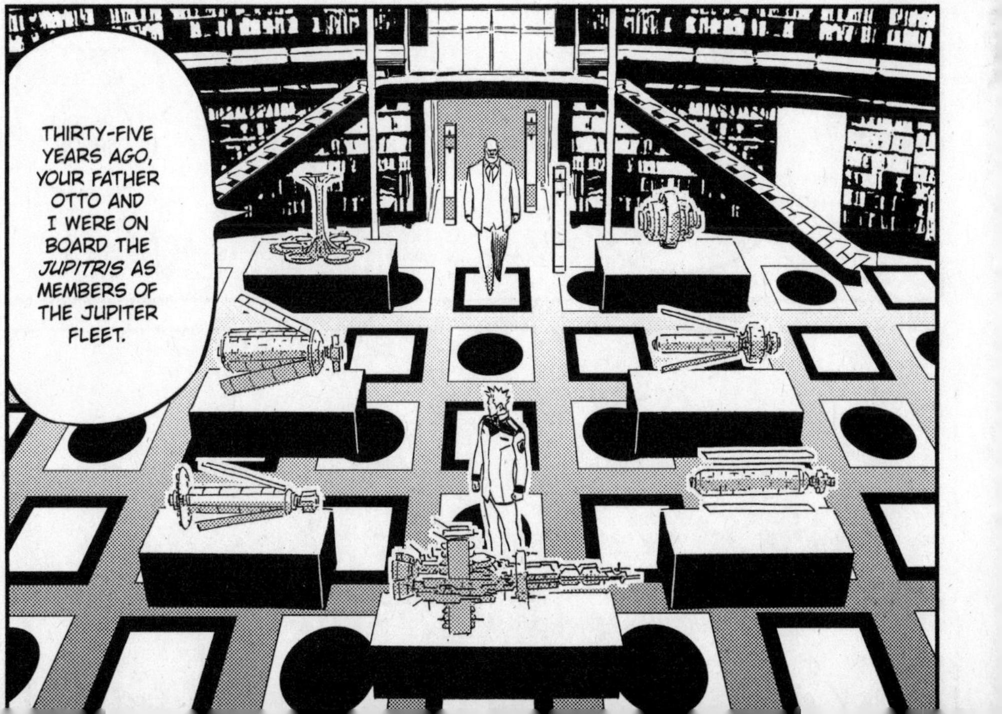
THIRTY-FIVE YEARS AGO, YOUR FATHER OTTO AND I WERE ON BOARD THE *JUPITRIS* AS MEMBERS OF THE JUPITER FLEET.

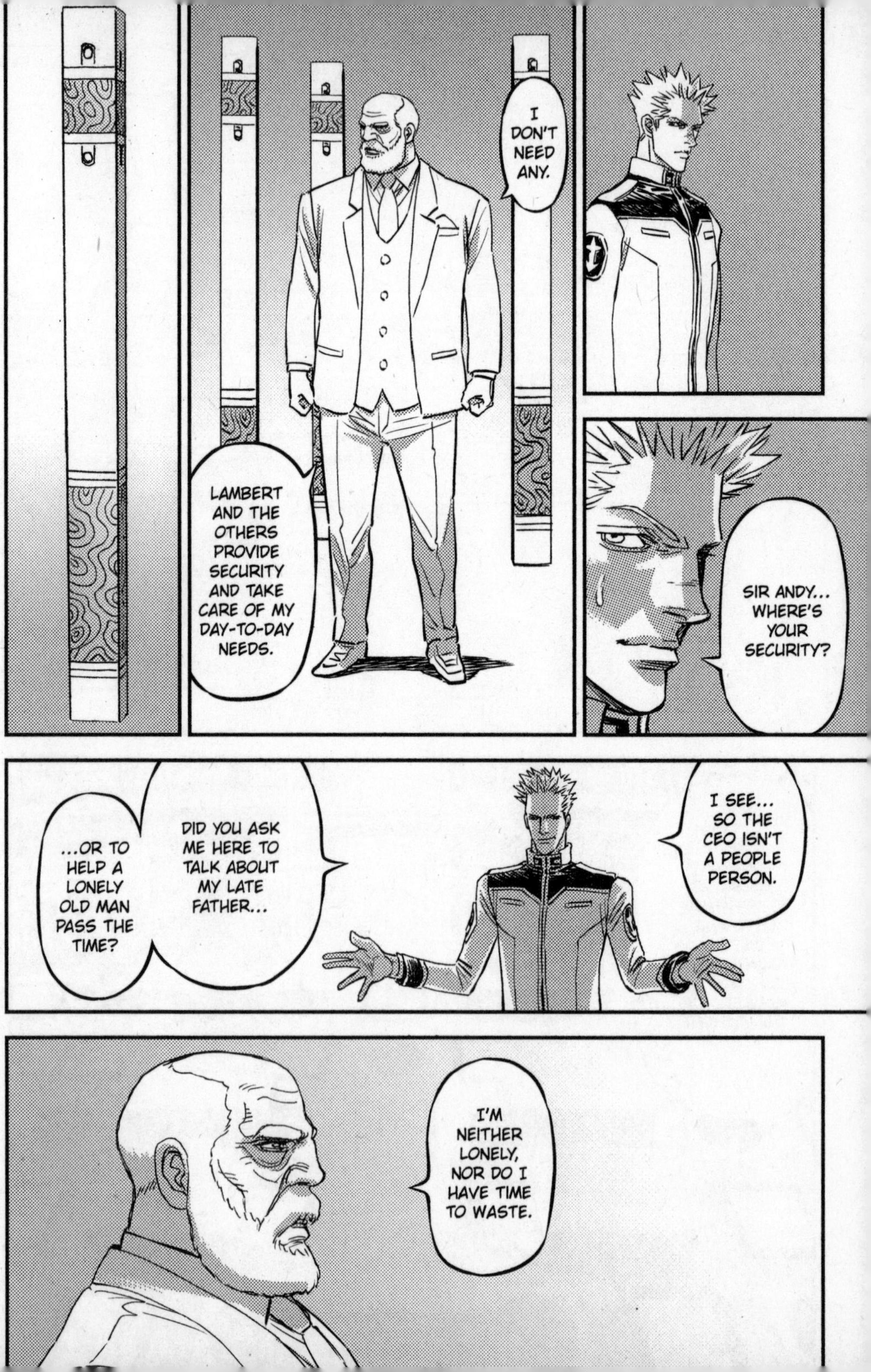
SIR ANDY... WHERE'S YOUR SECURITY?
I DON'T NEED ANY.
LAMBERT AND THE OTHERS PROVIDE SECURITY AND TAKE CARE OF MY DAY-TO-DAY NEEDS.
I SEE... SO THE CEO ISN'T A PEOPLE PERSON.
DID YOU ASK ME HERE TO TALK ABOUT MY LATE FATHER...
...OR TO HELP A LONELY OLD MAN PASS THE TIME?
I'M NEITHER LONELY, NOR DO I HAVE TIME TO WASTE.

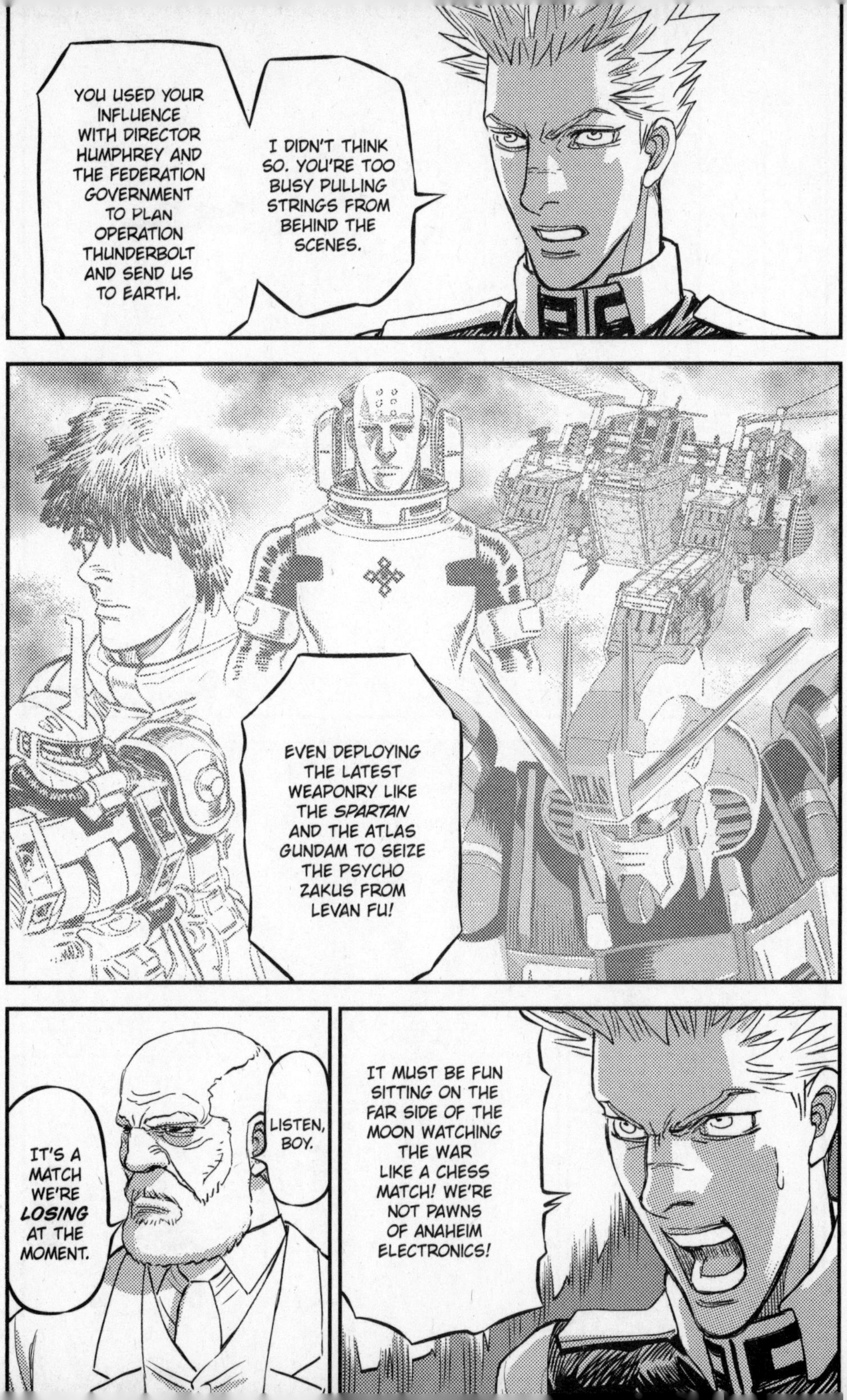
I DIDN'T THINK SO. YOU'RE TOO BUSY PULLING STRINGS FROM BEHIND THE SCENES.
YOU USED YOUR INFLUENCE WITH DIRECTOR HUMPHREY AND THE FEDERATION GOVERNMENT TO PLAN OPERATION THUNDERBOLT AND SEND US TO EARTH.
EVEN DEPLOYING THE LATEST WEAPONRY LIKE THE *SPARTAN* AND THE ATLAS GUNDAM TO SEIZE THE PSYCHO ZAKUS FROM LEVAN FU!
IT MUST BE FUN SITTING ON THE FAR SIDE OF THE MOON WATCHING THE WAR LIKE A CHESS MATCH! WE'RE NOT PAWNS OF ANAHEIM ELECTRONICS!
LISTEN, BOY.
IT'S A MATCH WE'RE ***LOSING*** AT THE MOMENT.

FOLLOW ME.

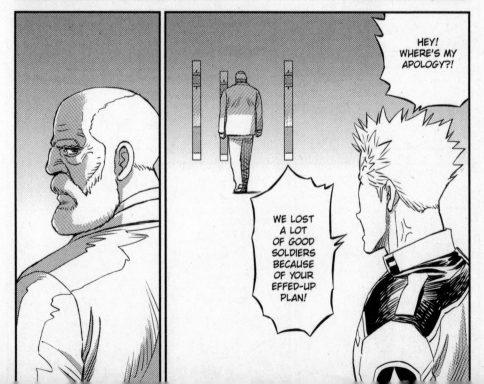

HEY! WHERE'S MY APOLOGY?!

WE LOST A LOT OF GOOD SOLDIERS BECAUSE OF YOUR EFFED-UP PLAN!

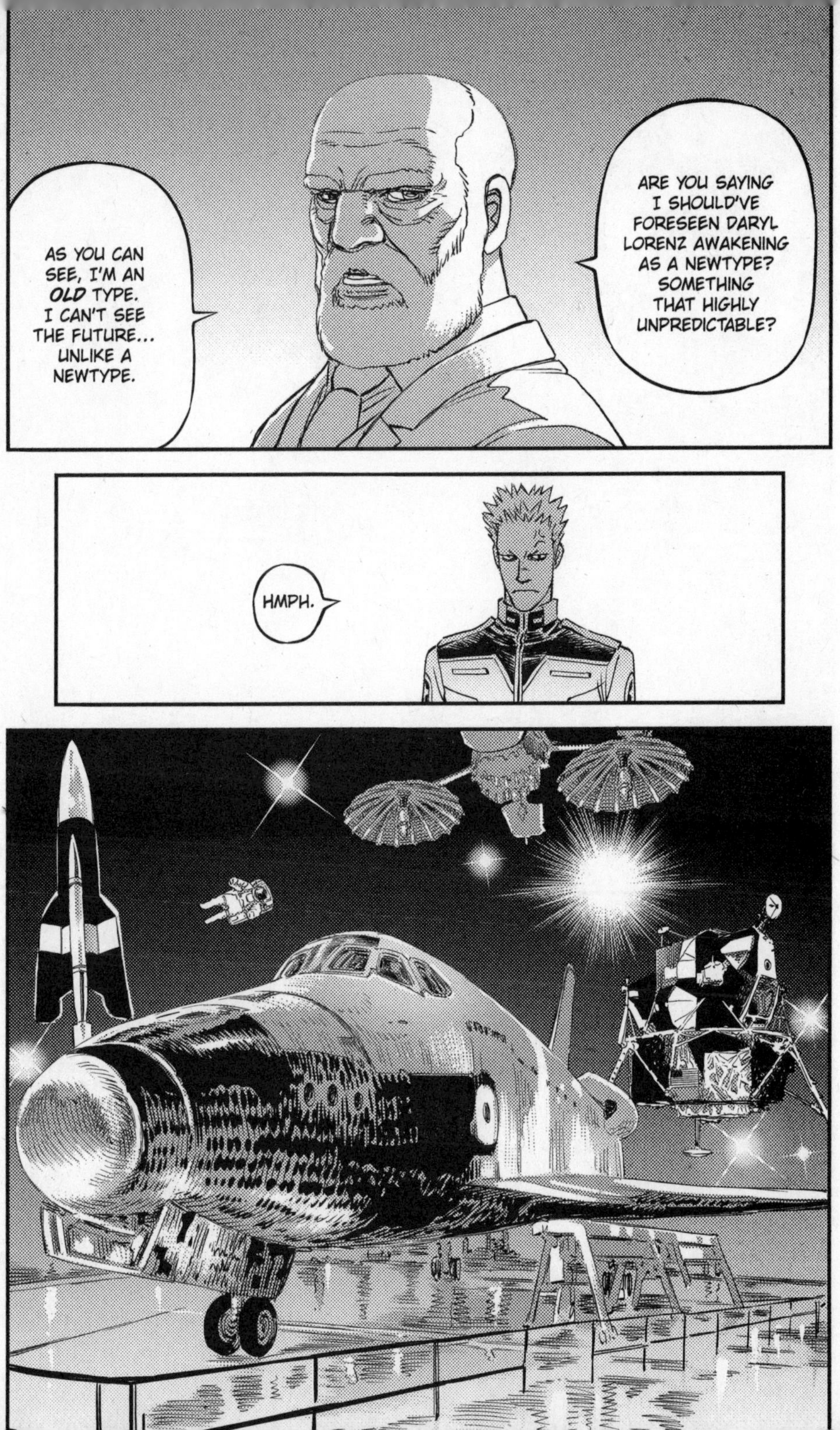
ARE YOU SAYING I SHOULD'VE FORESEEN DARYL LORENZ AWAKENING AS A NEWTYPE? SOMETHING THAT HIGHLY UNPREDICTABLE?
AS YOU CAN SEE, I'M AN *OLD* TYPE. I CAN'T SEE THE FUTURE... UNLIKE A NEWTYPE.
HMPH.

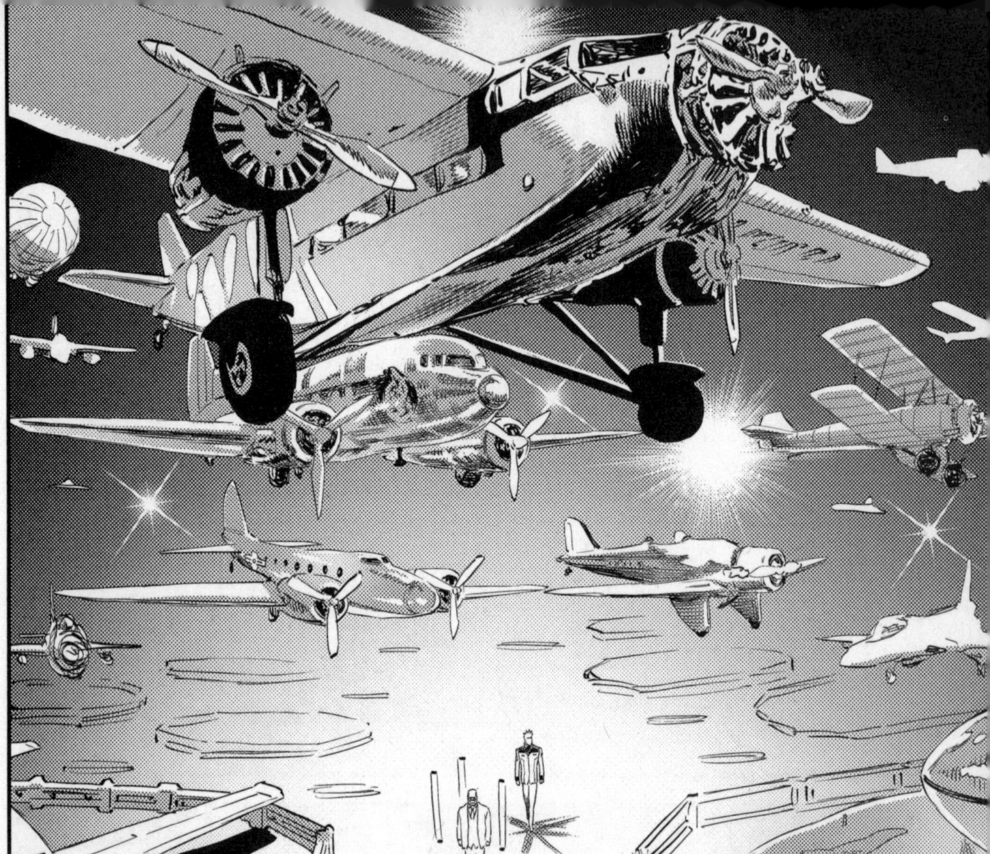
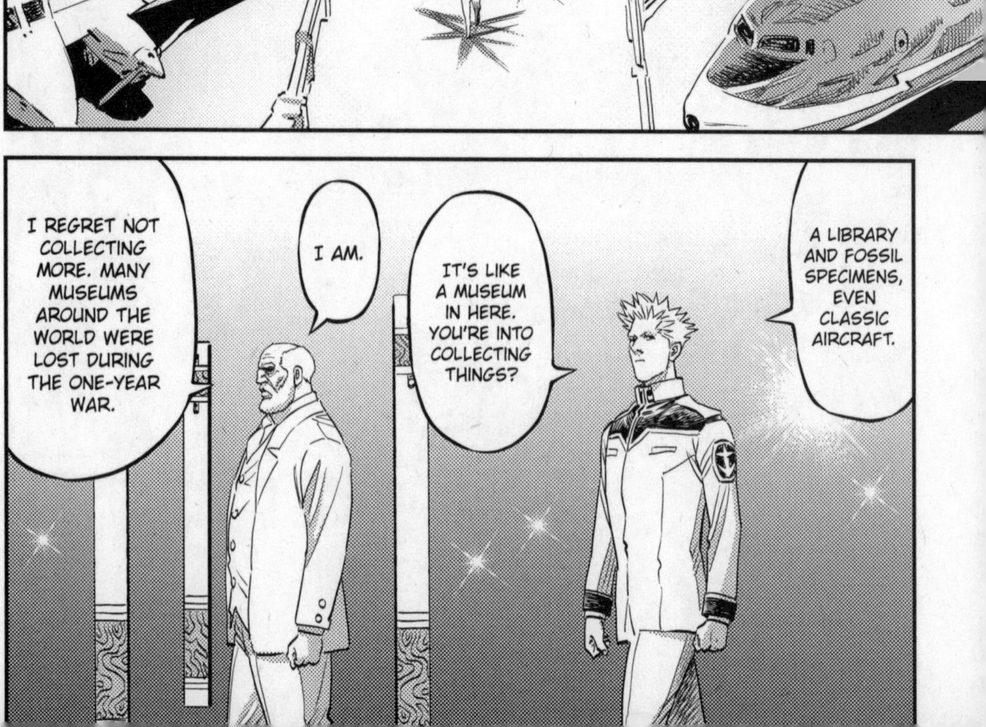
A LIBRARY AND FOSSIL SPECIMENS, EVEN CLASSIC AIRCRAFT.
IT'S LIKE A MUSEUM IN HERE. YOU'RE INTO COLLECTING THINGS?
I AM.
I REGRET NOT COLLECTING MORE. MANY MUSEUMS AROUND THE WORLD WERE LOST DURING THE ONE-YEAR WAR.

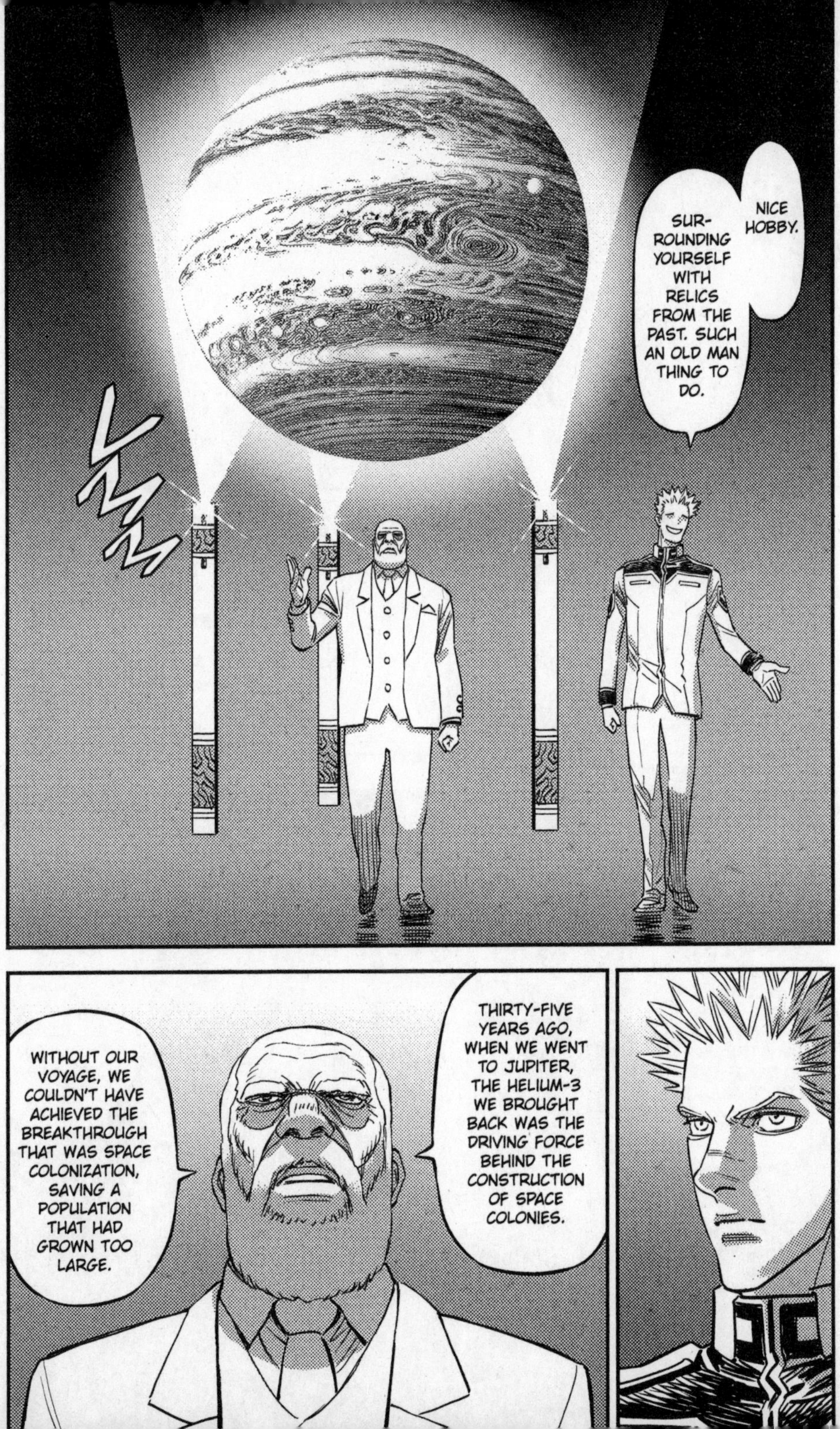
VMM
NICE HOBBY. SUR-ROUNDING YOURSELF WITH RELICS FROM THE PAST. SUCH AN OLD MAN THING TO DO.
THIRTY-FIVE YEARS AGO, WHEN WE WENT TO JUPITER, THE HELIUM-3 WE BROUGHT BACK WAS THE DRIVING FORCE BEHIND THE CONSTRUCTION OF SPACE COLONIES.
WITHOUT OUR VOYAGE, WE COULDN'T HAVE ACHIEVED THE BREAKTHROUGH THAT WAS SPACE COLONIZATION, SAVING A POPULATION THAT HAD GROWN TOO LARGE.

YOUR FATHER OTTO HAD THE DIFFICULT RESPONSIBILITY OF BRINGING THE CREW TOGETHER AS THE MISSION COMMANDER.

I ASSISTED HIM AS AN ENGINEER. WE TRUSTED EACH OTHER. WE WERE FRIENDS.

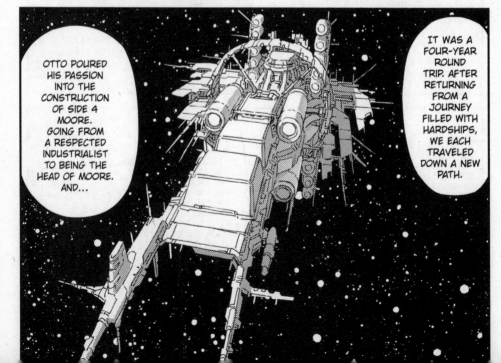

IT WAS A FOUR-YEAR ROUND TRIP. AFTER RETURNING FROM A JOURNEY FILLED WITH HARDSHIPS, WE EACH TRAVELED DOWN A NEW PATH.

OTTO POURED HIS PASSION INTO THE CONSTRUCTION OF SIDE 4 MOORE. GOING FROM A RESPECTED INDUSTRIALIST TO BEING THE HEAD OF MOORE. AND...

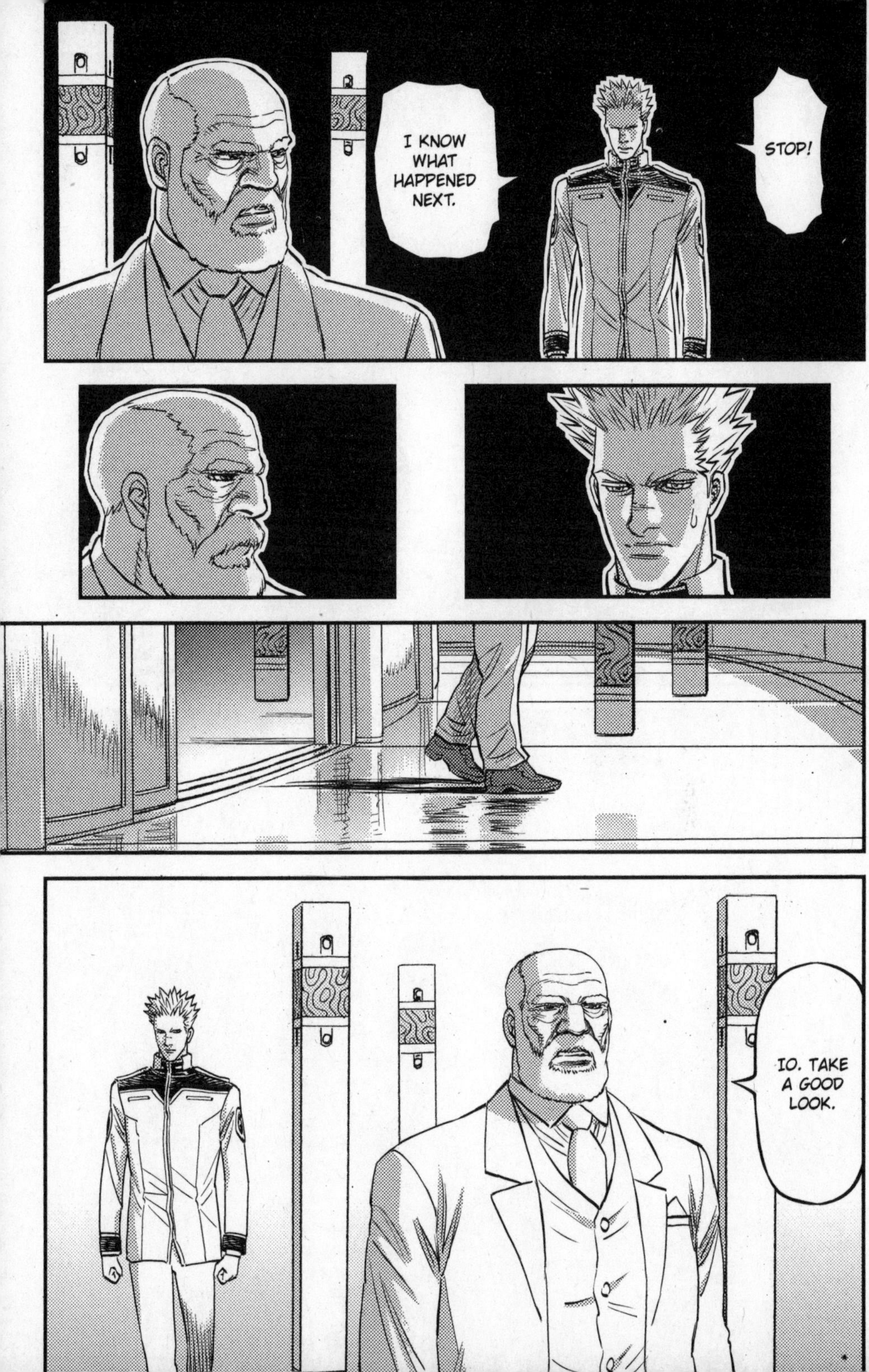
STOP!
I KNOW WHAT HAPPENED NEXT.
IO. TAKE A GOOD LOOK.

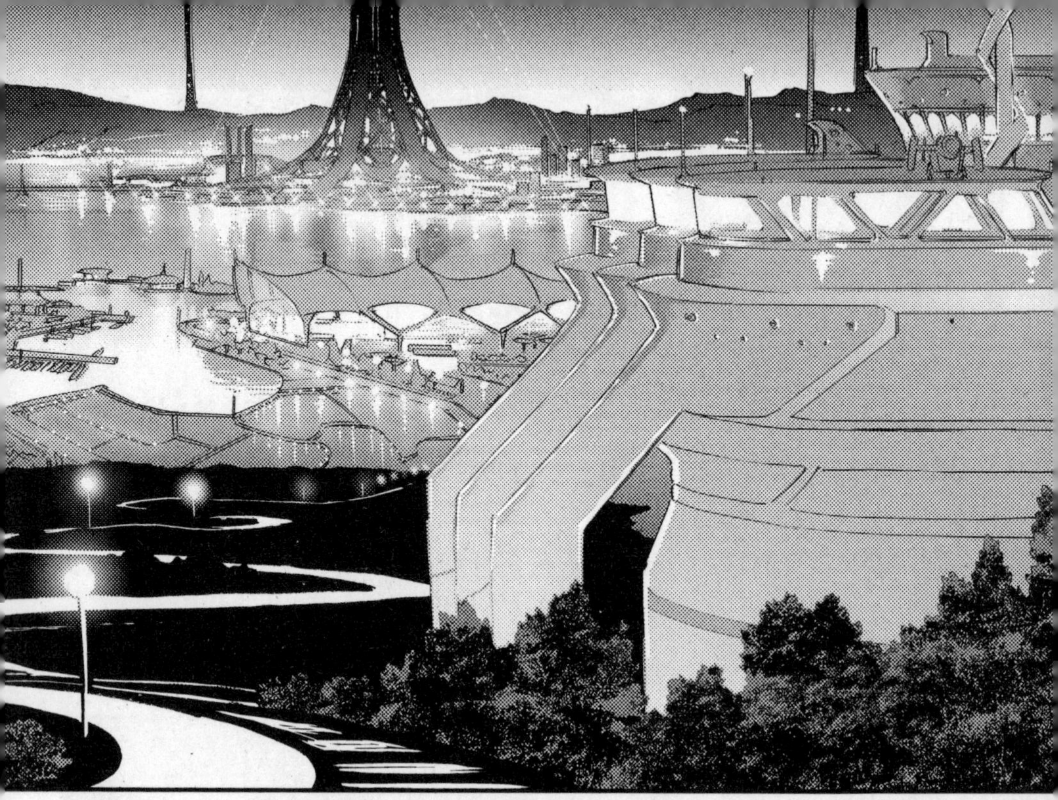
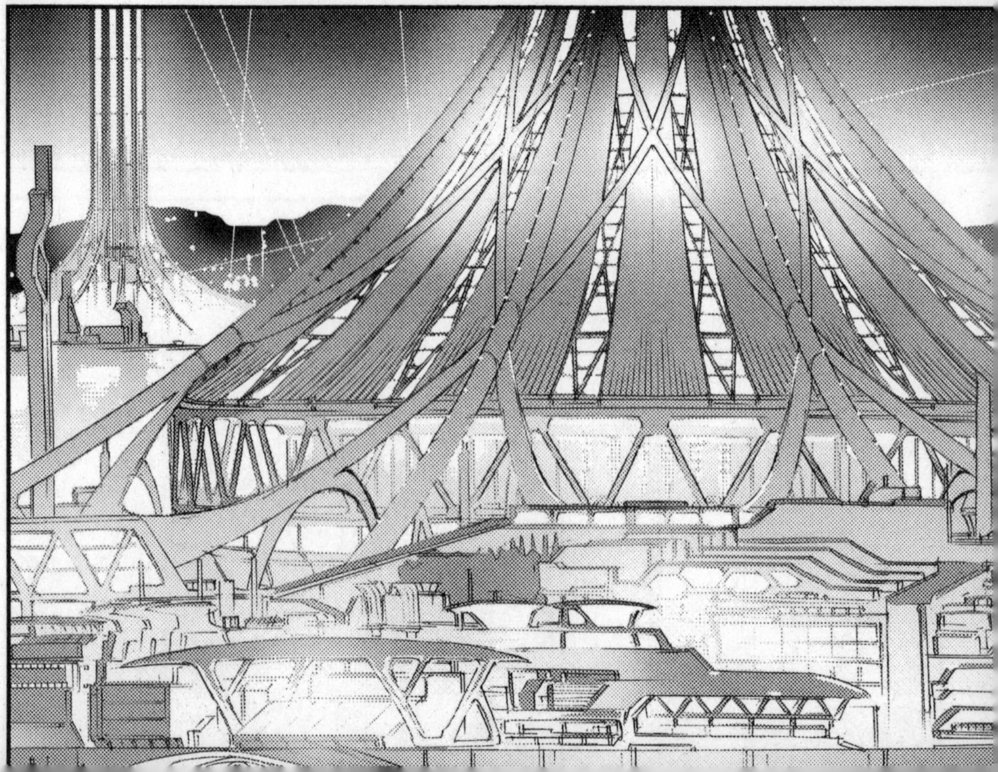

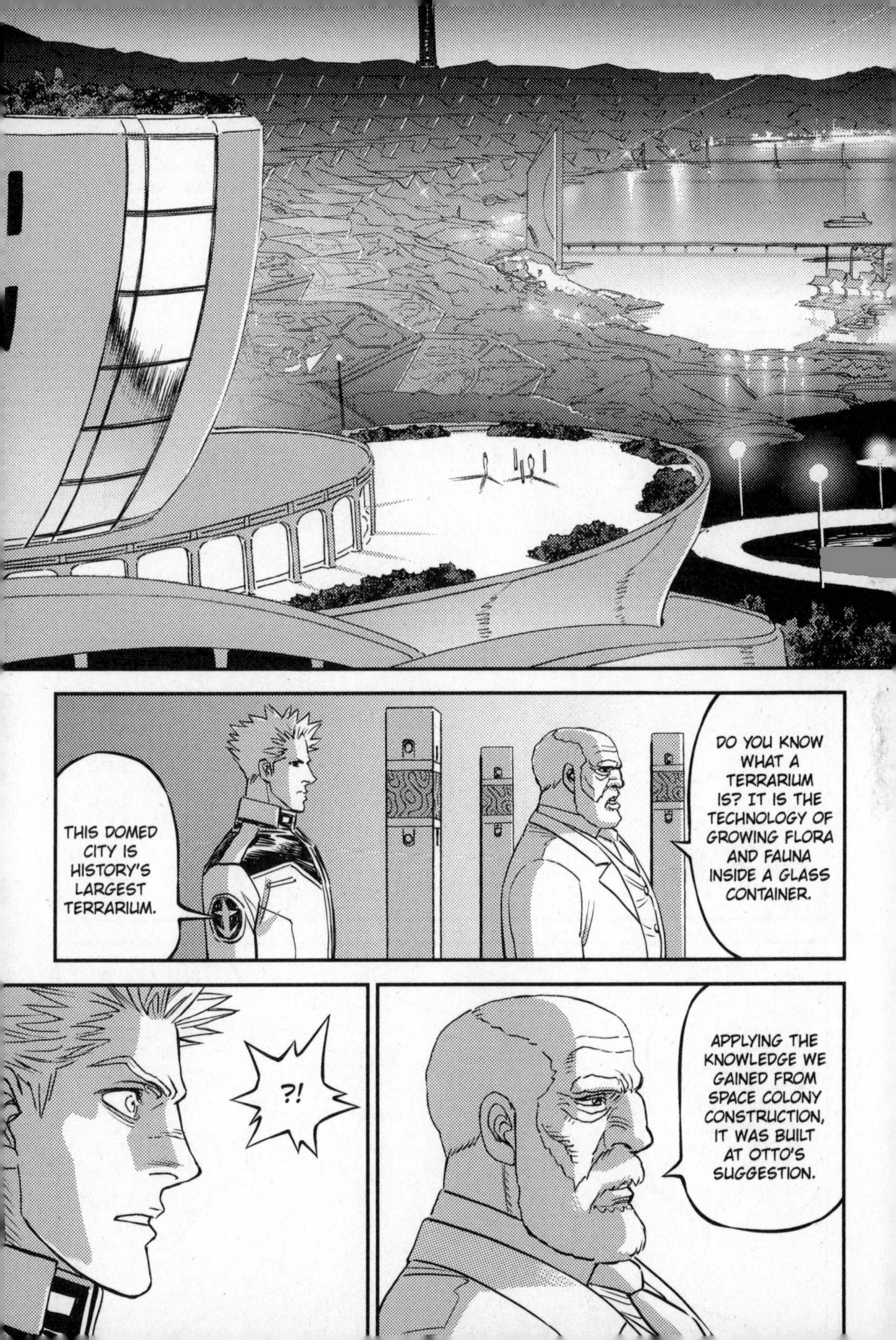
DO YOU KNOW WHAT A TERRARIUM IS? IT IS THE TECHNOLOGY OF GROWING FLORA AND FAUNA INSIDE A GLASS CONTAINER.
THIS DOMED CITY IS HISTORY'S LARGEST TERRARIUM.
APPLYING THE KNOWLEDGE WE GAINED FROM SPACE COLONY CONSTRUCTION, IT WAS BUILT AT OTTO'S SUGGESTION.
?!

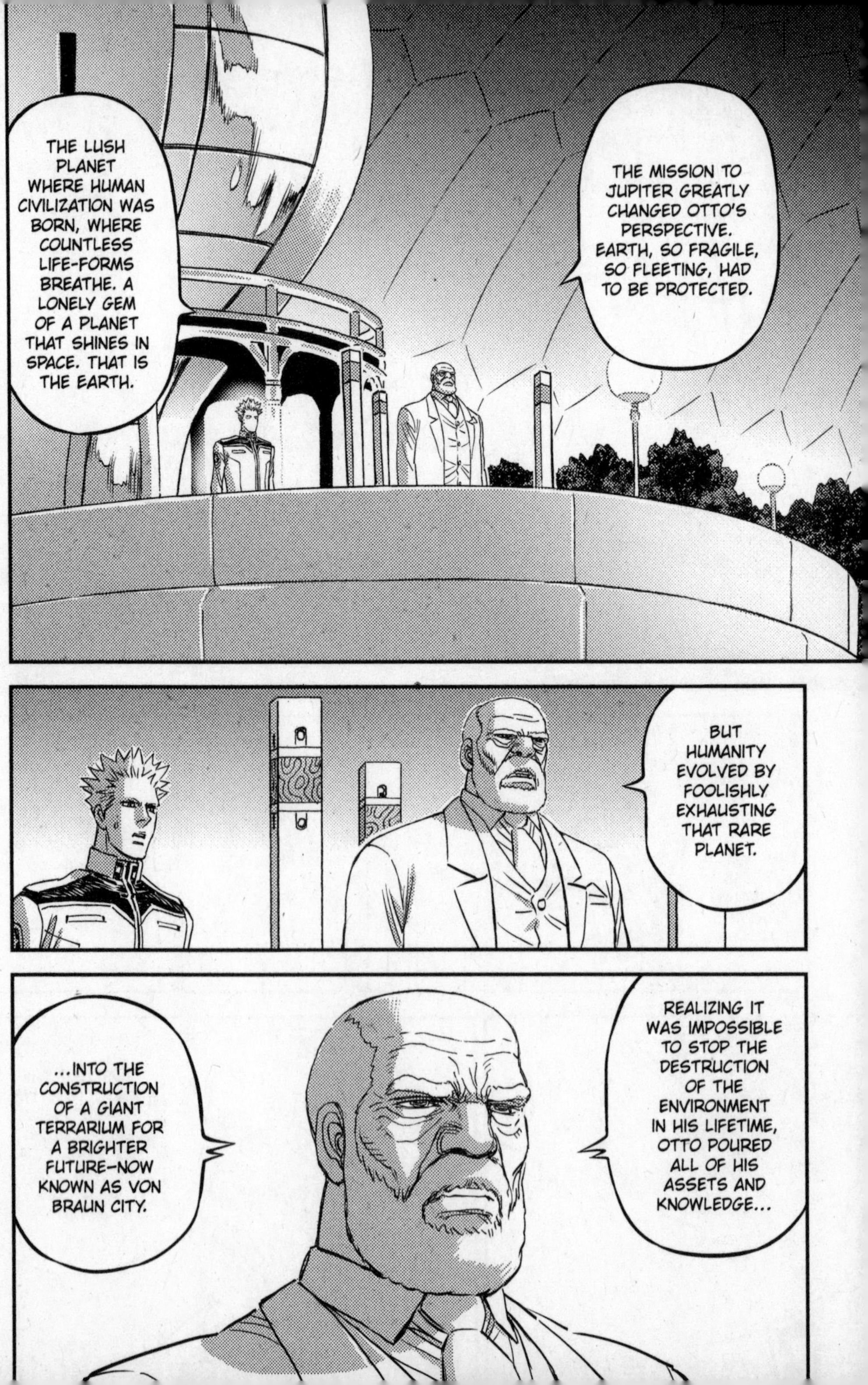
THE MISSION TO JUPITER GREATLY CHANGED OTTO'S PERSPECTIVE. EARTH, SO FRAGILE, SO FLEETING, HAD TO BE PROTECTED.
THE LUSH PLANET WHERE HUMAN CIVILIZATION WAS BORN, WHERE COUNTLESS LIFE-FORMS BREATHE. A LONELY GEM OF A PLANET THAT SHINES IN SPACE. THAT IS THE EARTH.
BUT HUMANITY EVOLVED BY FOOLISHLY EXHAUSTING THAT RARE PLANET.
REALIZING IT WAS IMPOSSIBLE TO STOP THE DESTRUCTION OF THE ENVIRONMENT IN HIS LIFETIME, OTTO POURED ALL OF HIS ASSETS AND KNOWLEDGE...
...INTO THE CONSTRUCTION OF A GIANT TERRARIUM FOR A BRIGHTER FUTURE—NOW KNOWN AS VON BRAUN CITY.

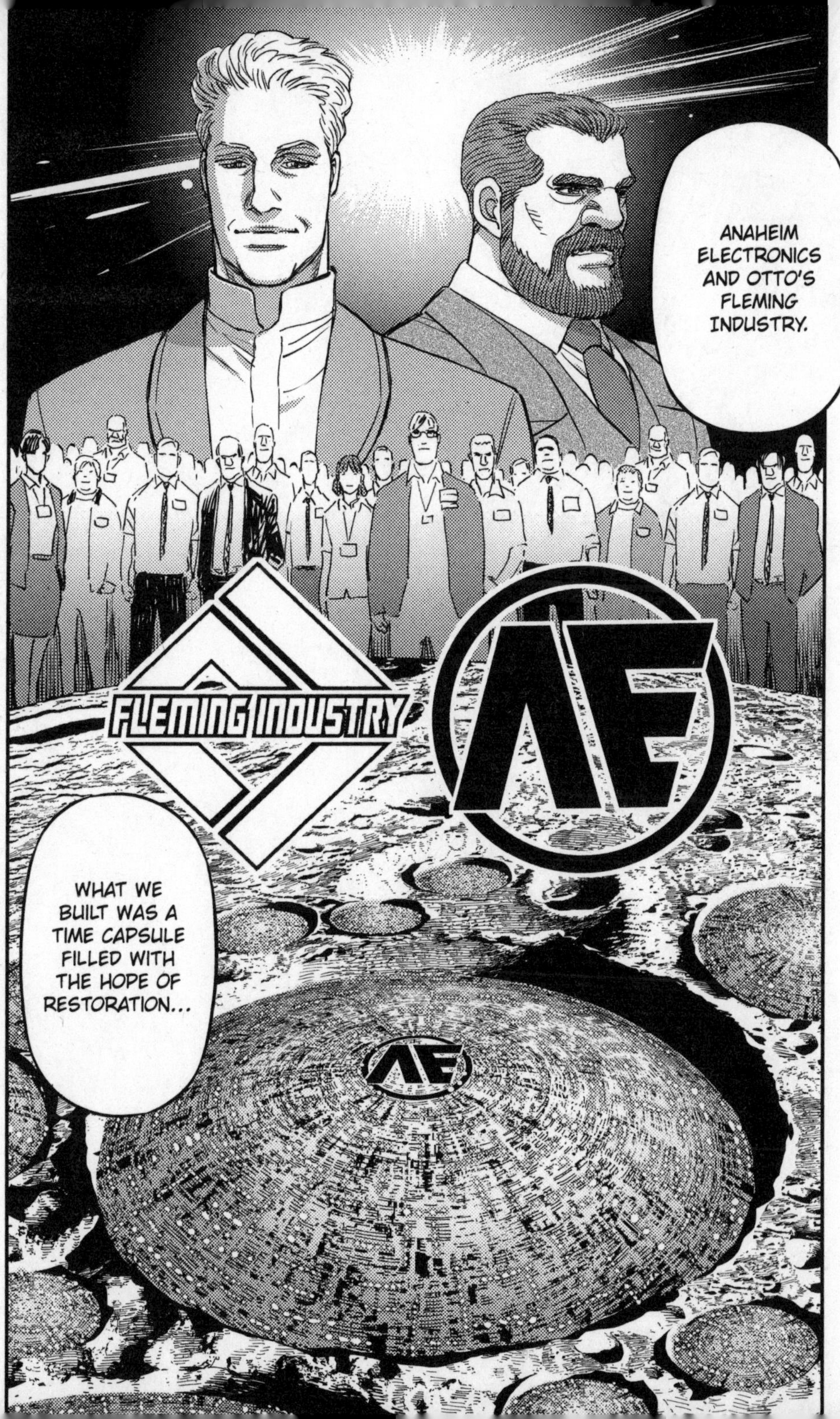
ANAHEIM ELECTRONICS AND OTTO'S FLEMING INDUSTRY.
FLEMING INDUSTRY
AE
WHAT WE BUILT WAS A TIME CAPSULE FILLED WITH THE HOPE OF RESTORATION...

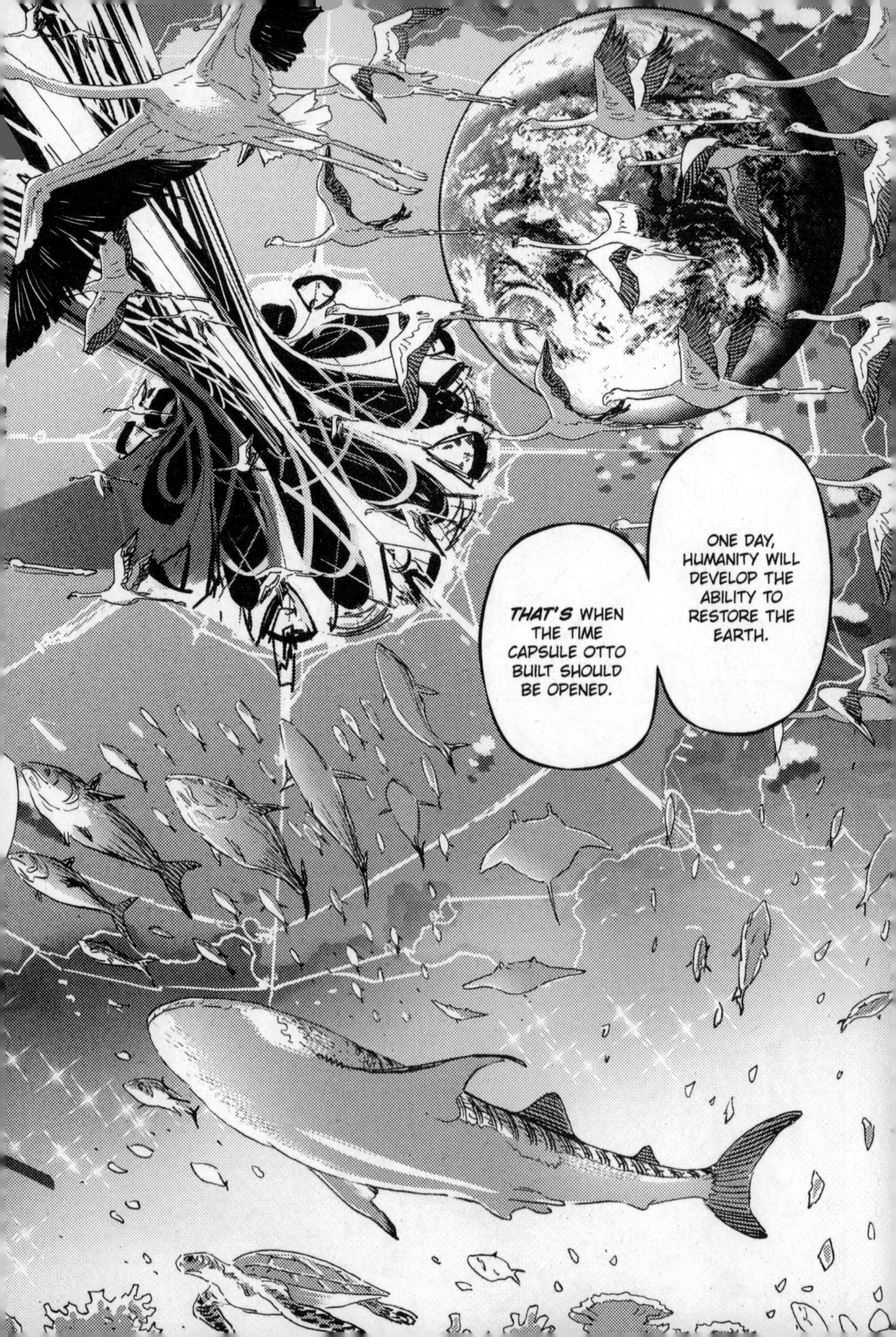
ONE DAY, HUMANITY WILL DEVELOP THE ABILITY TO RESTORE THE EARTH.
THAT'S WHEN THE TIME CAPSULE OTTO BUILT SHOULD BE OPENED.

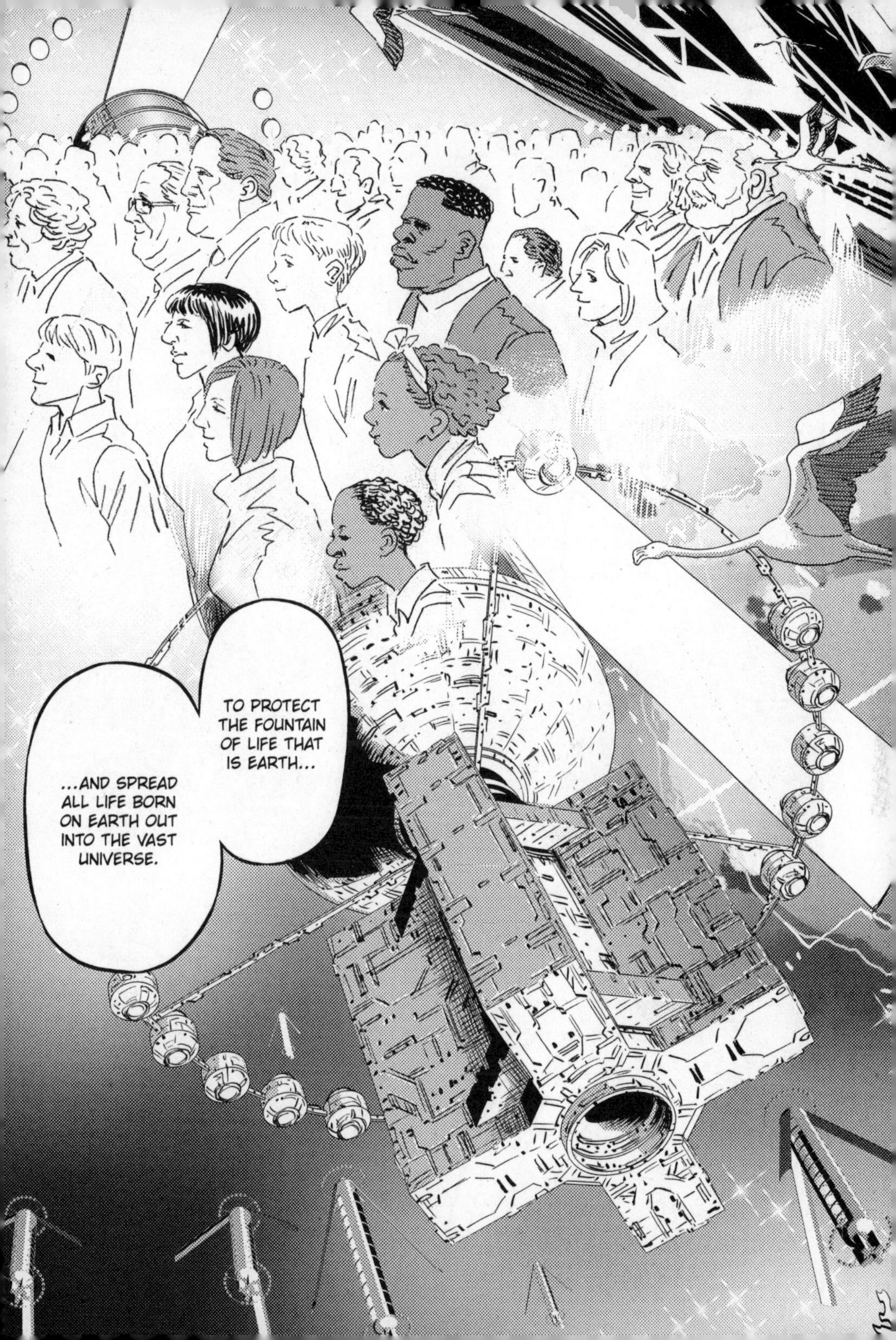
TO PROTECT THE FOUNTAIN OF LIFE THAT IS EARTH...
...AND SPREAD ALL LIFE BORN ON EARTH OUT INTO THE VAST UNIVERSE.

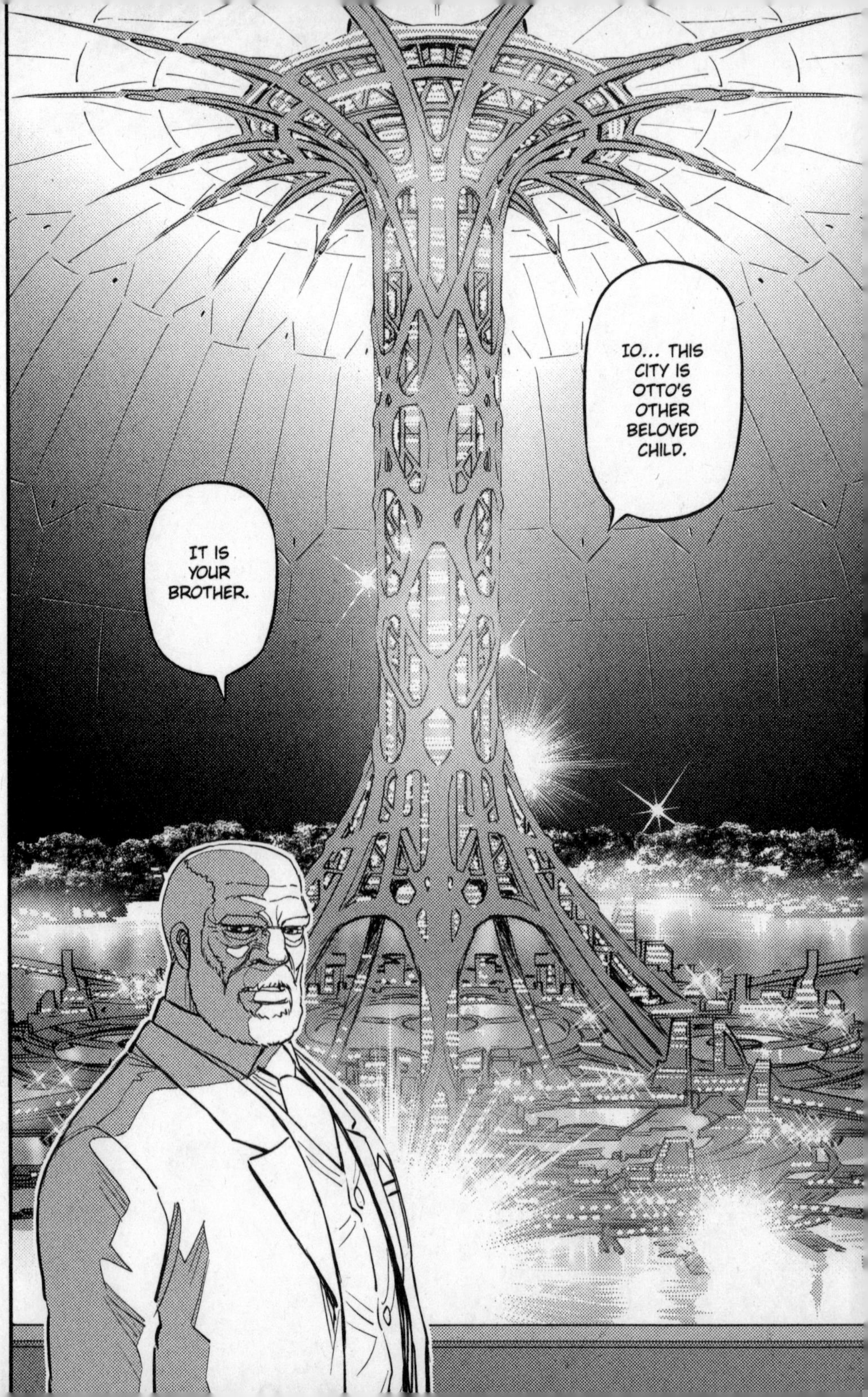
IO... THIS CITY IS OTTO'S OTHER BELOVED CHILD.
IT IS YOUR BROTHER.

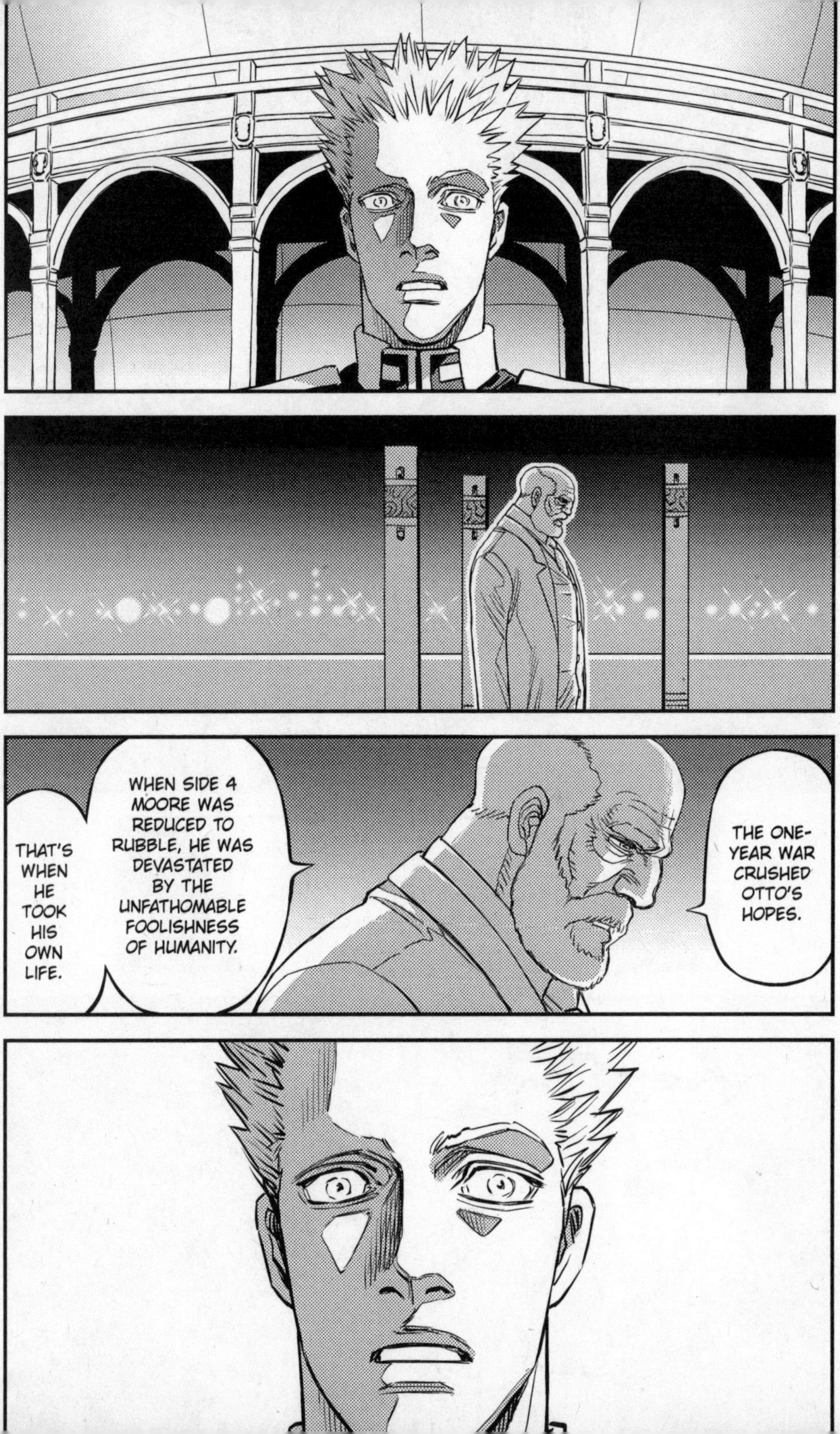
THE ONE-YEAR WAR CRUSHED OTTO'S HOPES.
WHEN SIDE 4 MOORE WAS REDUCED TO RUBBLE, HE WAS DEVASTATED BY THE UNFATHOMABLE FOOLISHNESS OF HUMANITY.
THAT'S WHEN HE TOOK HIS OWN LIFE.

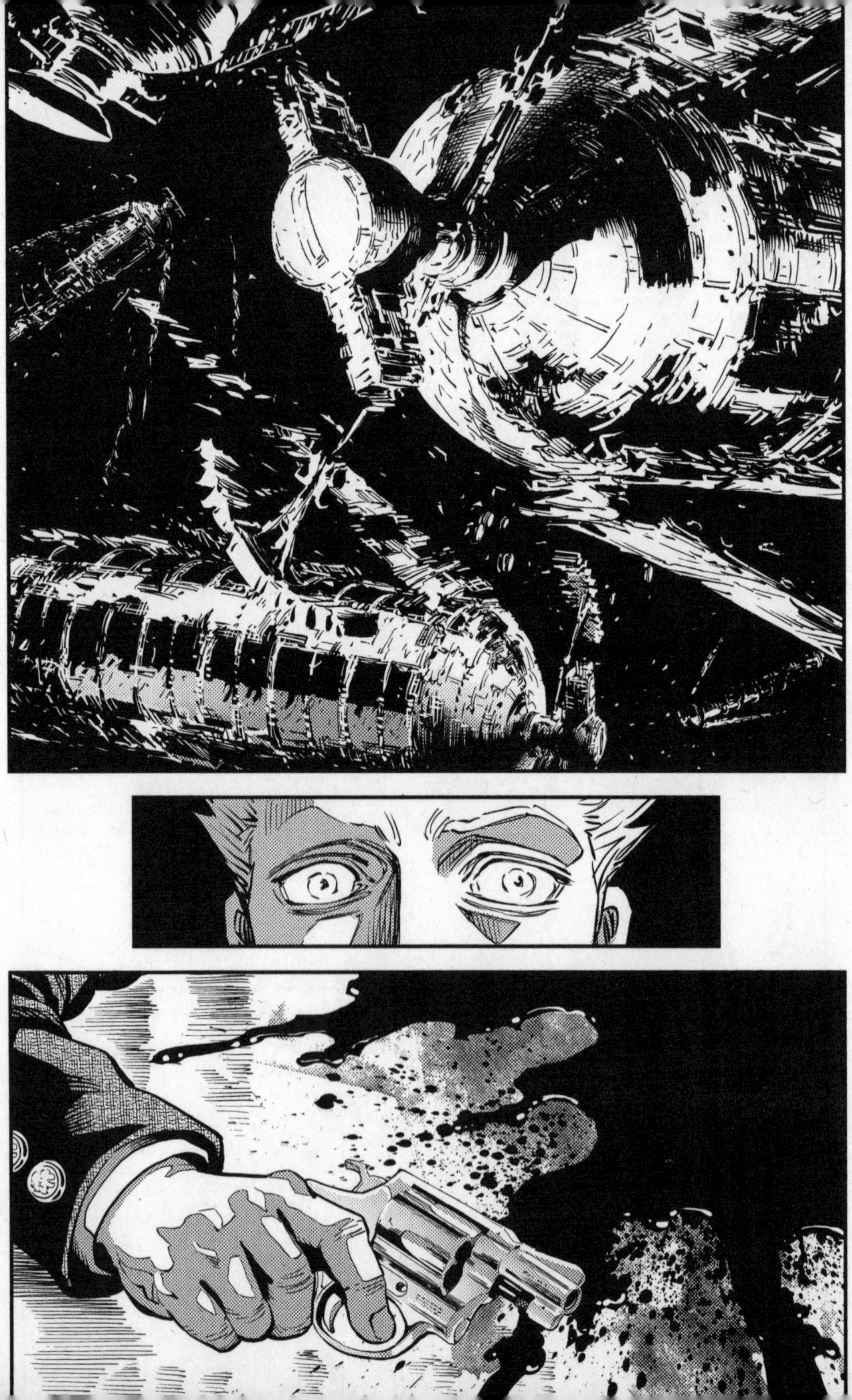

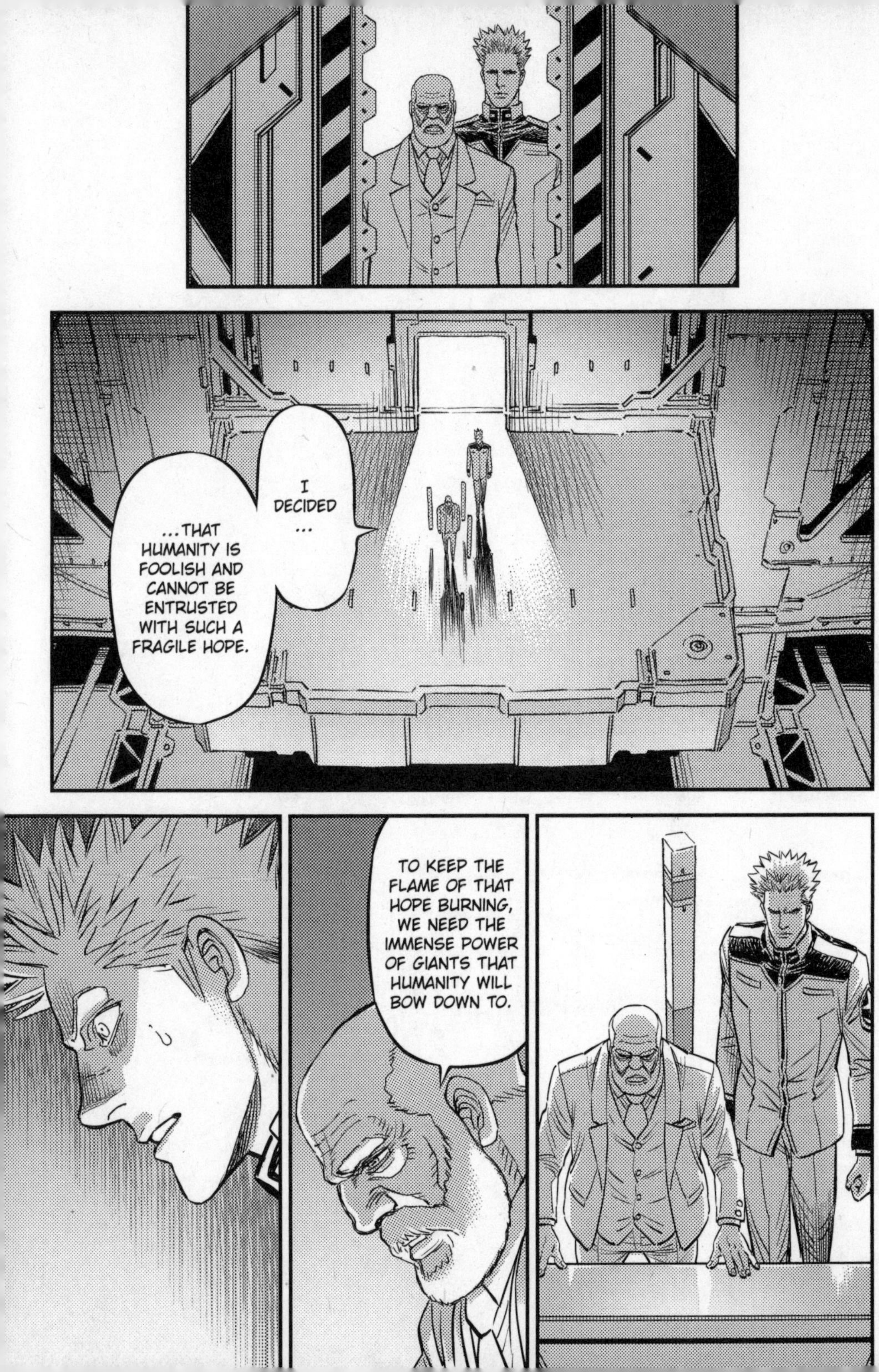
I DECIDED ...
...THAT HUMANITY IS FOOLISH AND CANNOT BE ENTRUSTED WITH SUCH A FRAGILE HOPE.
TO KEEP THE FLAME OF THAT HOPE BURNING, WE NEED THE IMMENSE POWER OF GIANTS THAT HUMANITY WILL BOW DOWN TO.

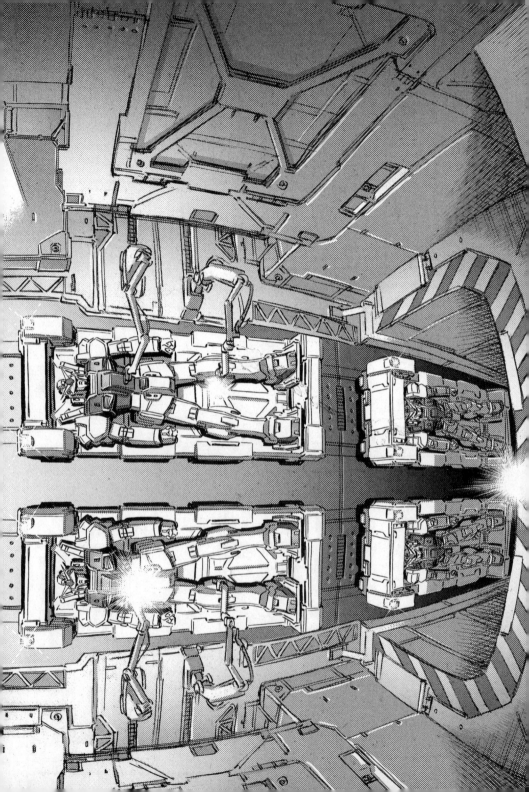

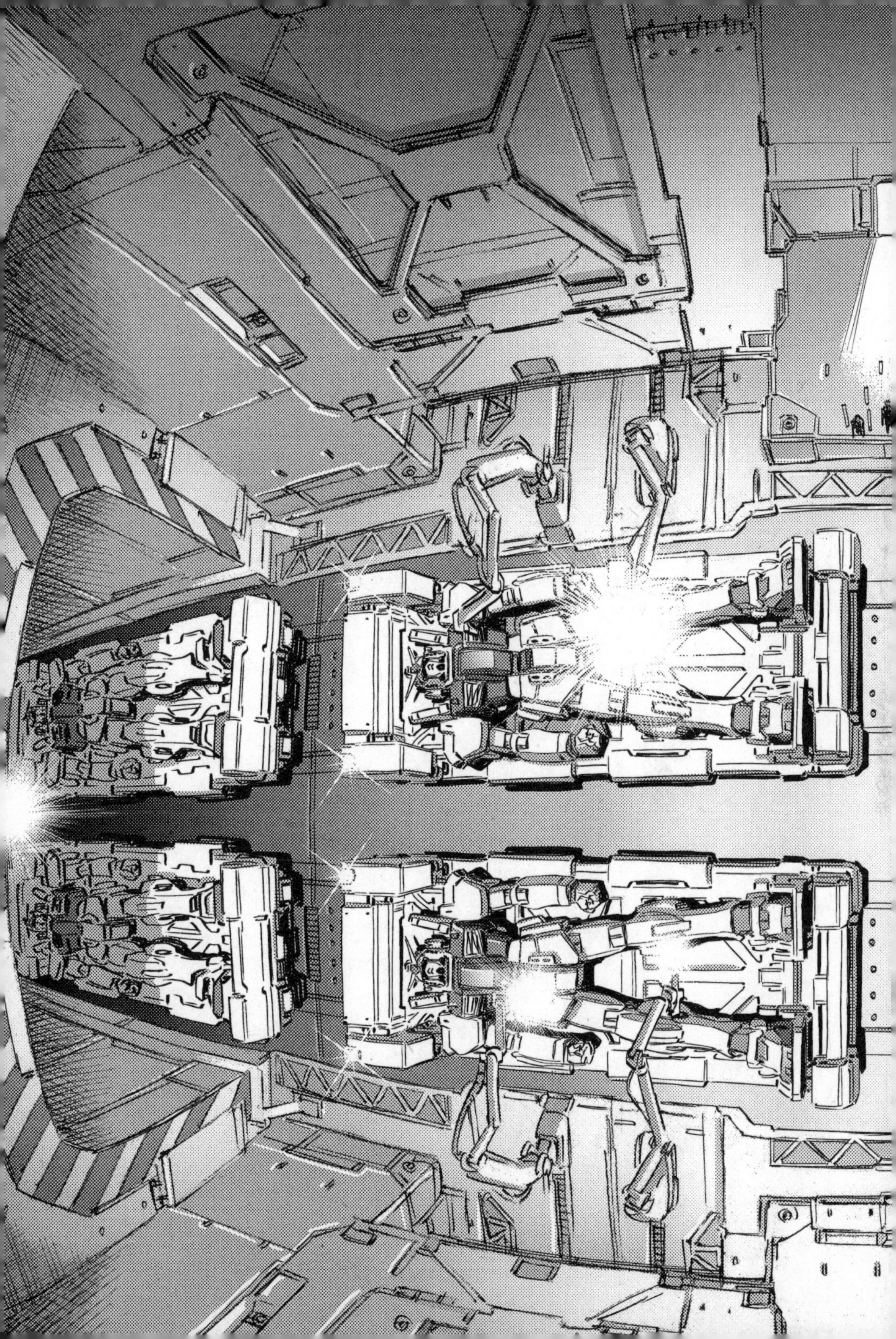

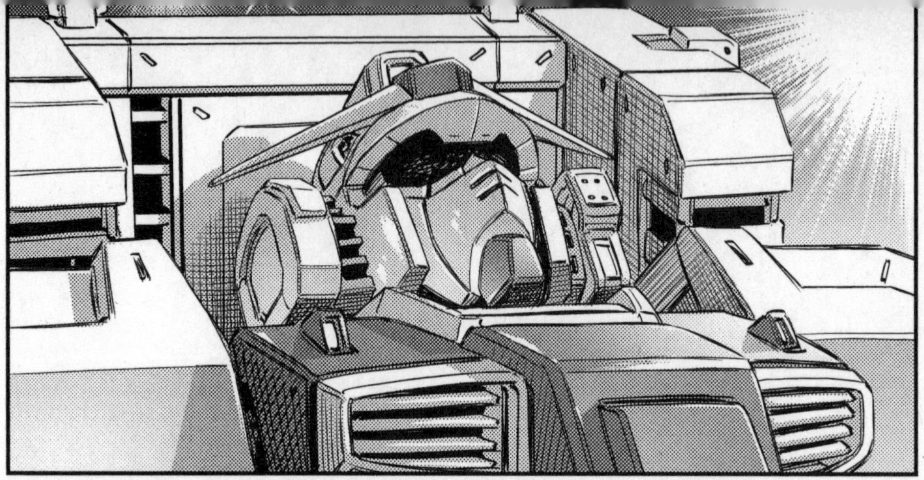
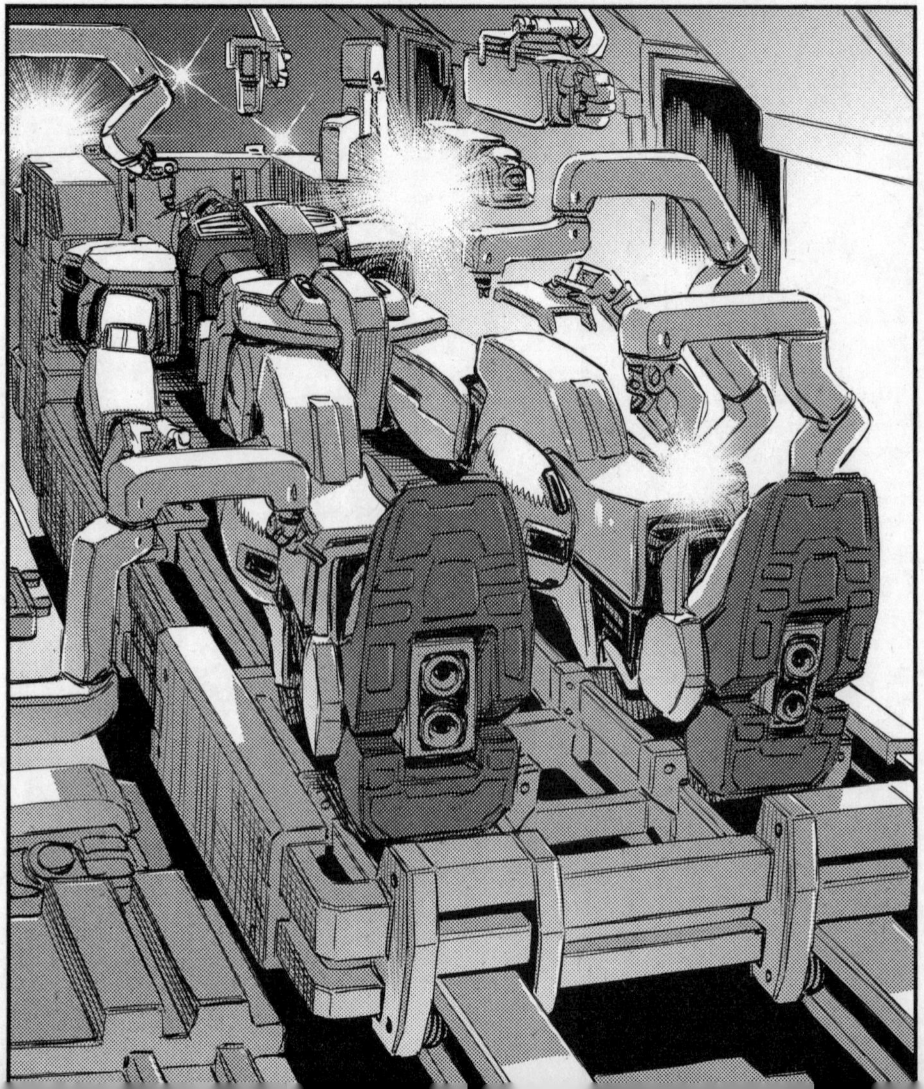

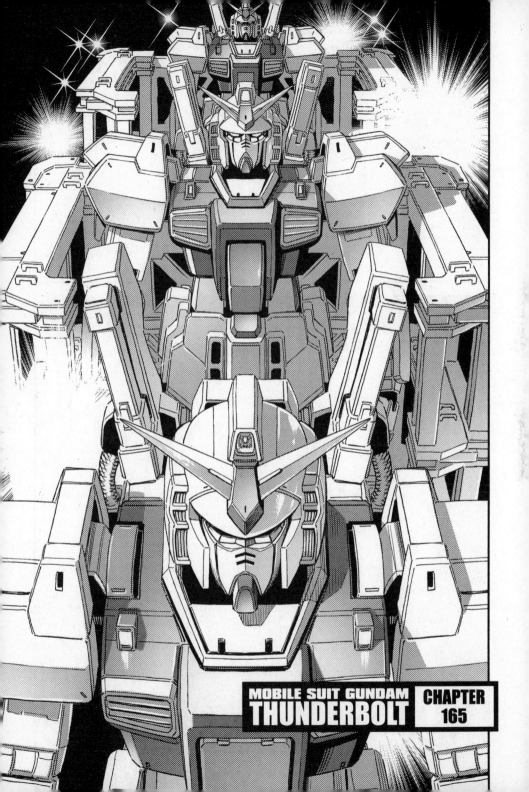

MOBILE SUIT GUNDAM THUNDERBOLT **CHAPTER 165**

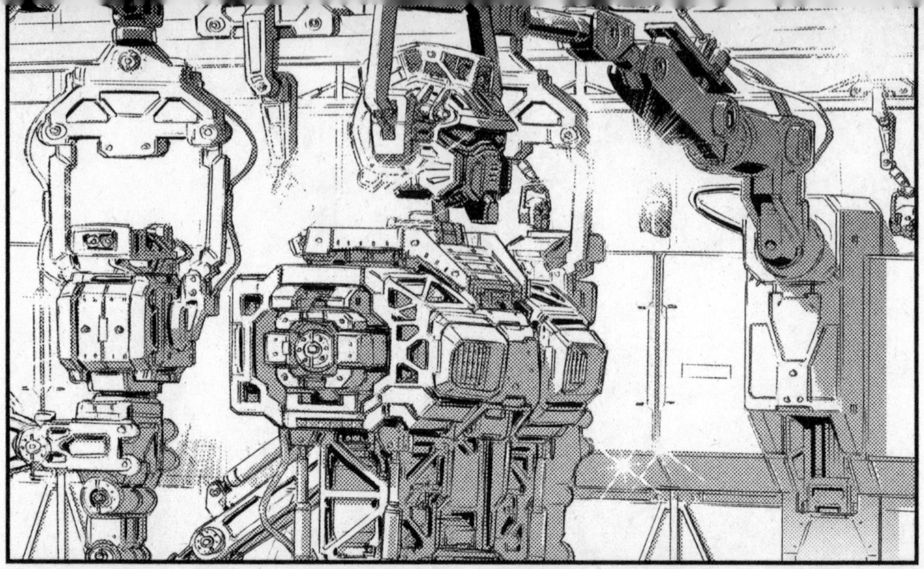

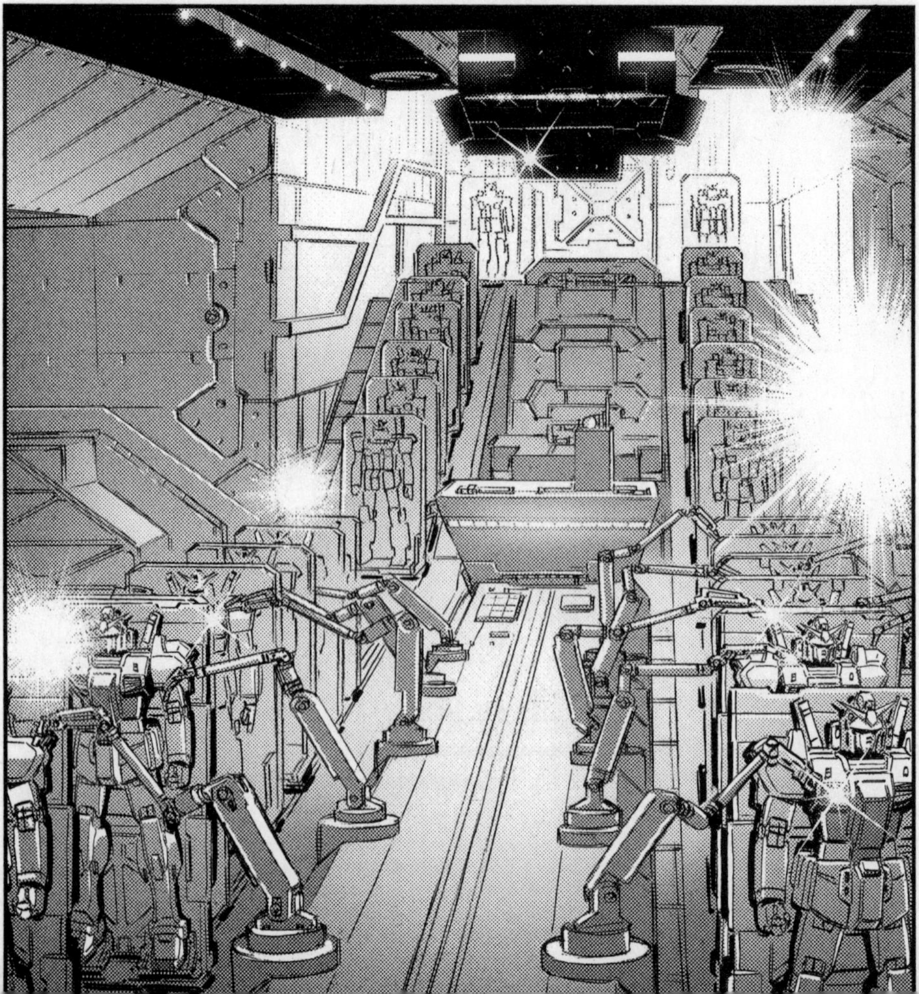

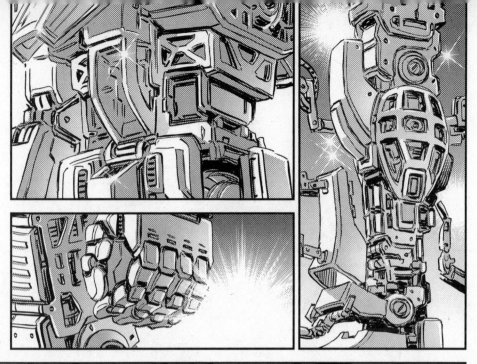

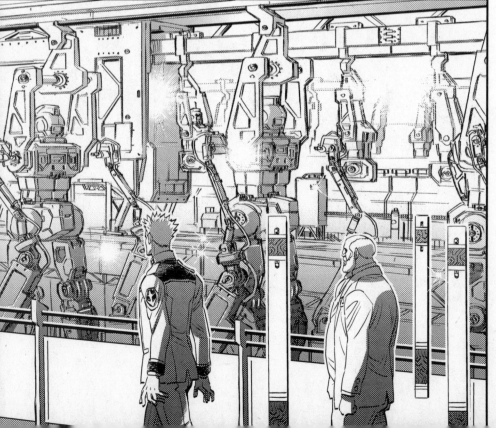

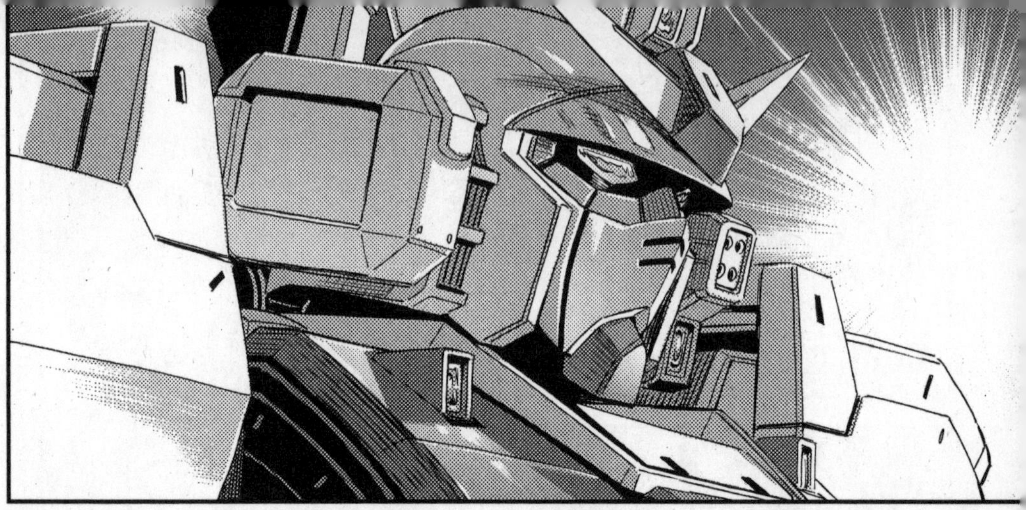
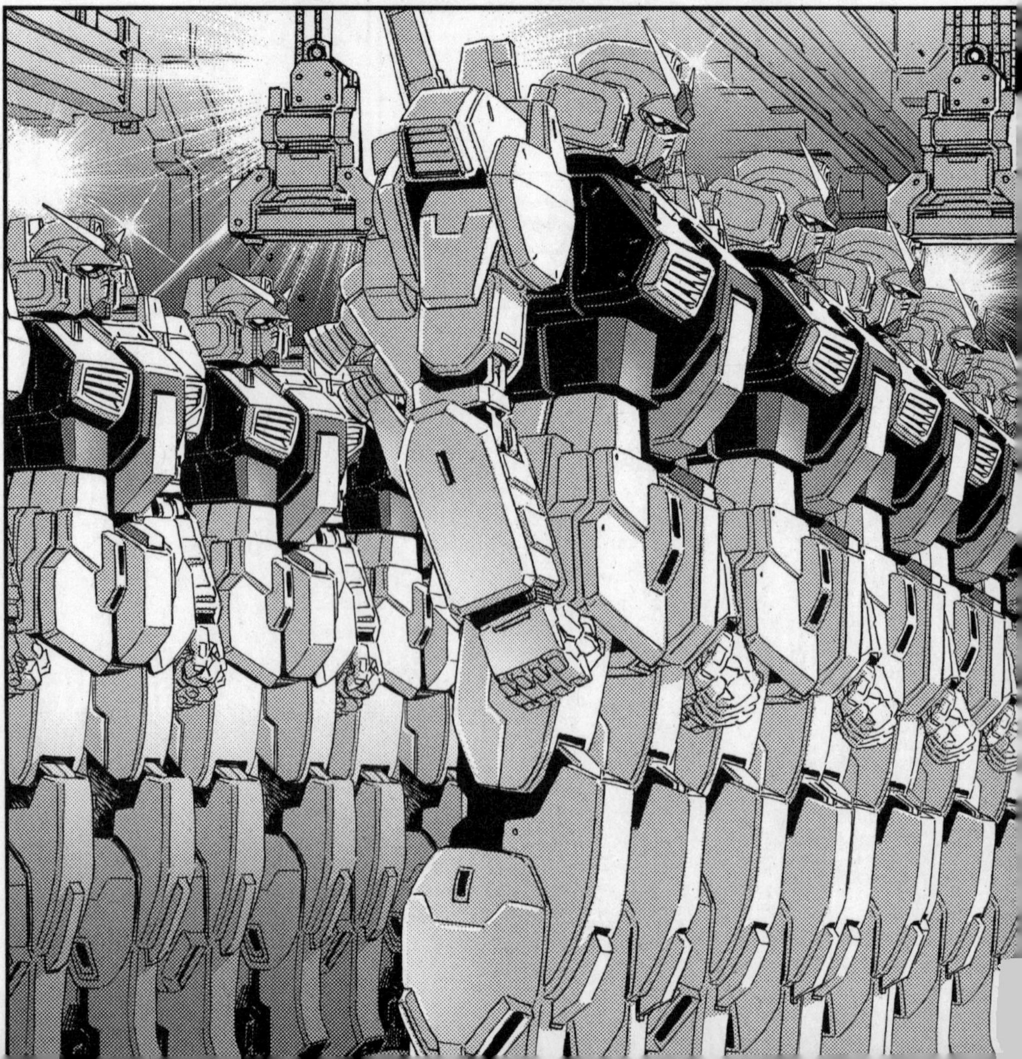

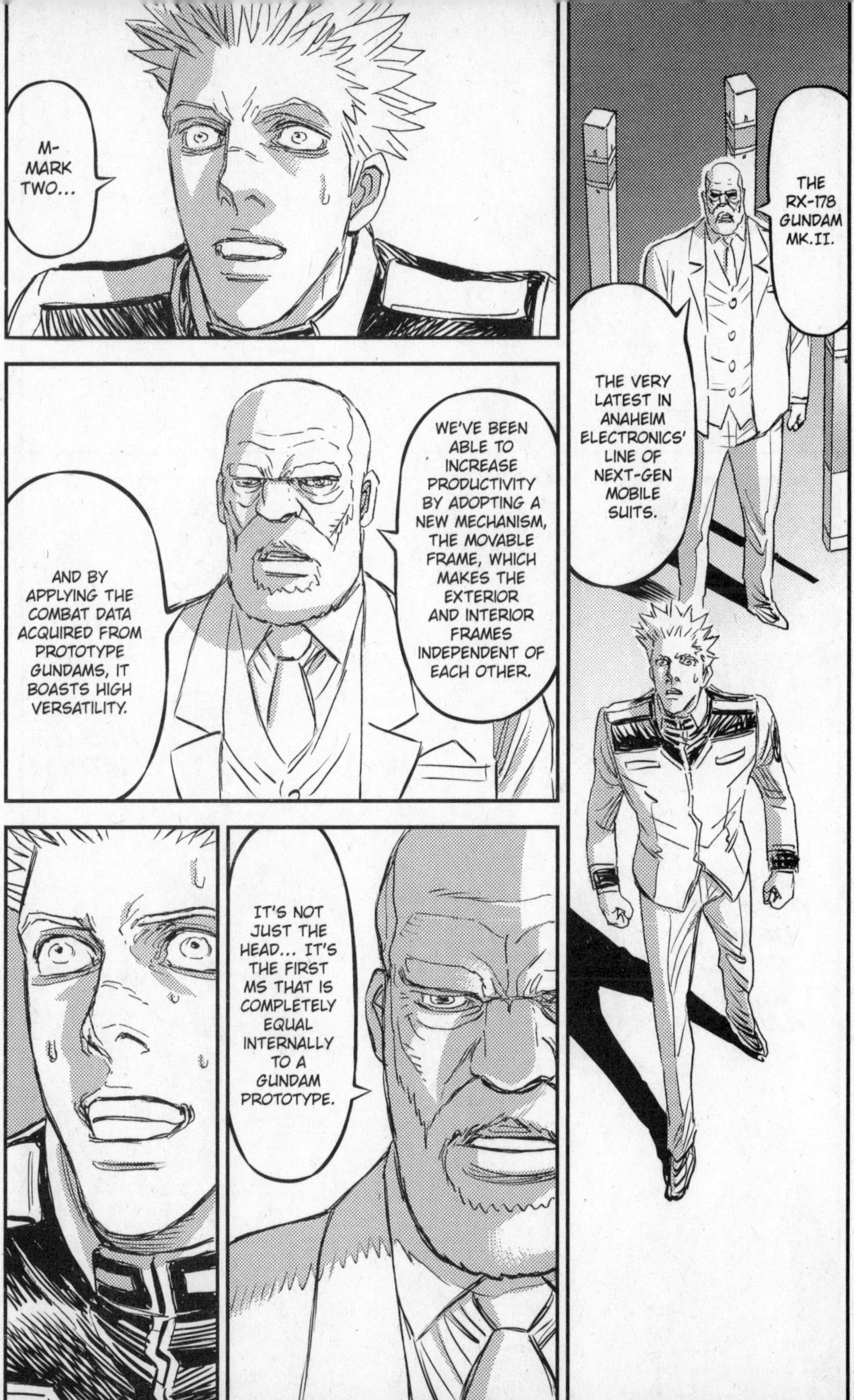
THE RX-178 GUNDAM MK.II.
THE VERY LATEST IN ANAHEIM ELECTRONICS' LINE OF NEXT-GEN MOBILE SUITS.
M-MARK TWO...
WE'VE BEEN ABLE TO INCREASE PRODUCTIVITY BY ADOPTING A NEW MECHANISM, THE MOVABLE FRAME, WHICH MAKES THE EXTERIOR AND INTERIOR FRAMES INDEPENDENT OF EACH OTHER.
AND BY APPLYING THE COMBAT DATA ACQUIRED FROM PROTOTYPE GUNDAMS, IT BOASTS HIGH VERSATILITY.
IT'S NOT JUST THE HEAD... IT'S THE FIRST MS THAT IS COMPLETELY EQUAL INTERNALLY TO A GUNDAM PROTOTYPE.

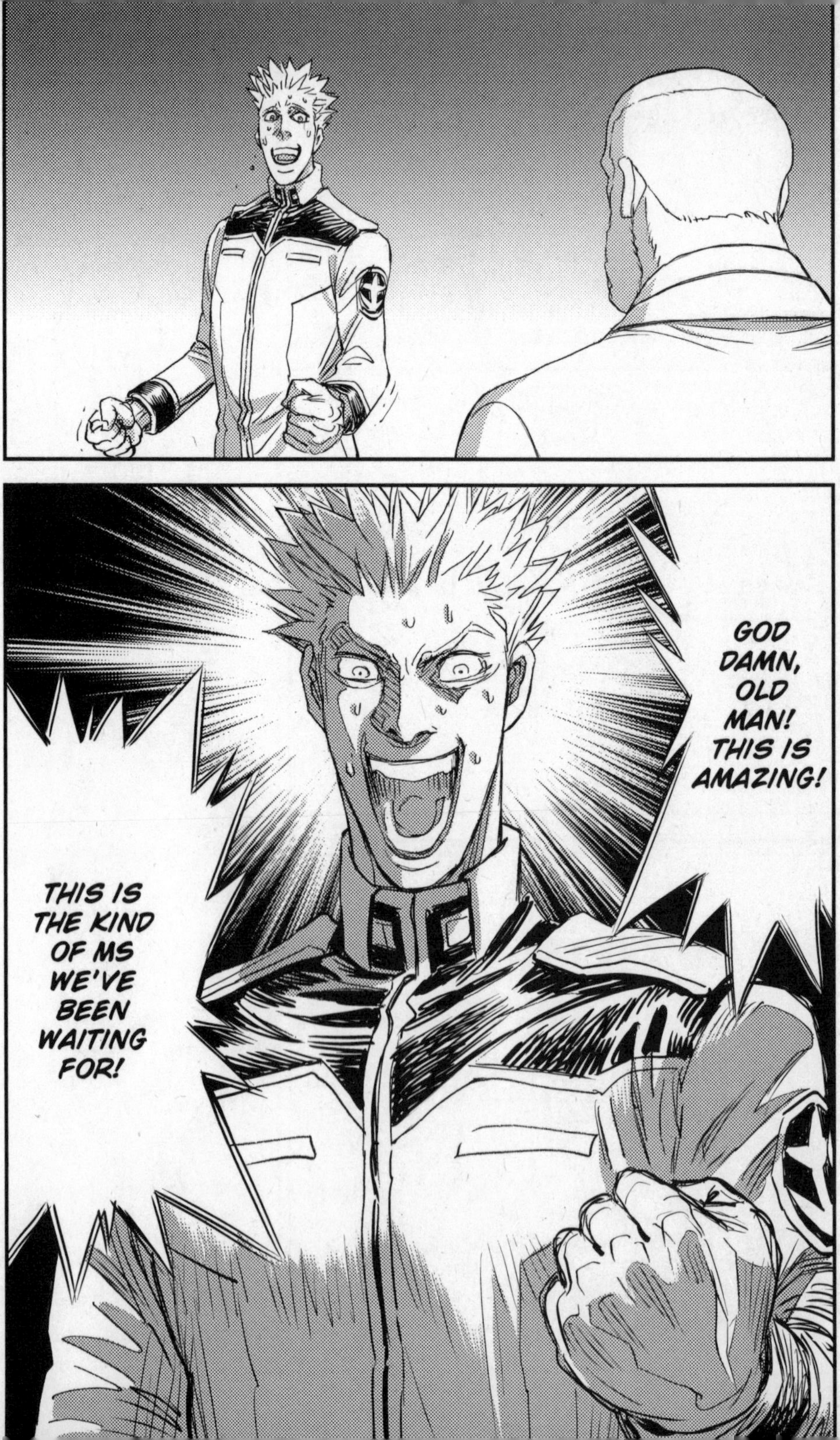
GOD DAMN, OLD MAN! THIS IS AMAZING!
THIS IS THE KIND OF MS WE'VE BEEN WAITING FOR!

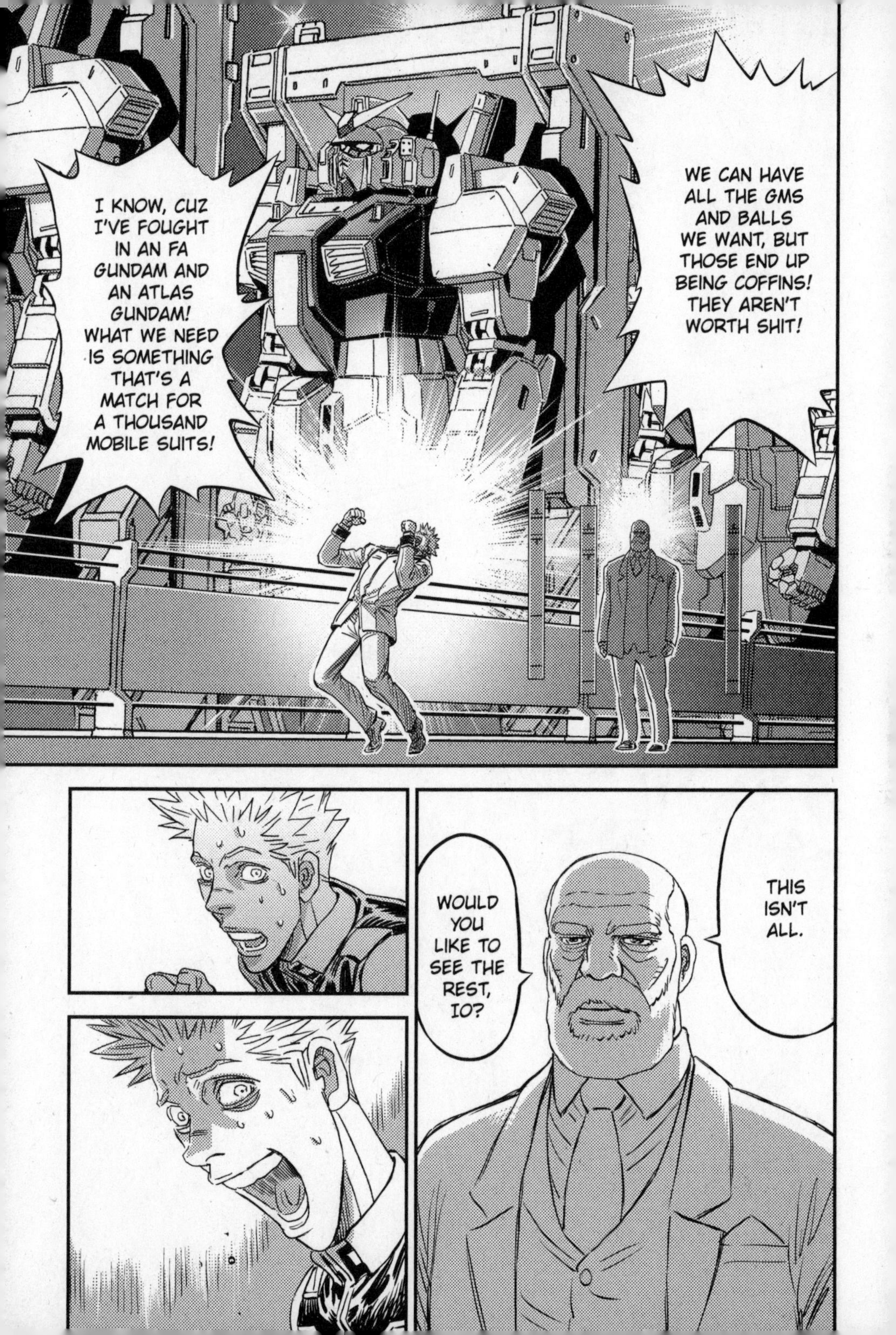
WE CAN HAVE ALL THE GMS AND BALLS WE WANT, BUT THOSE END UP BEING COFFINS! THEY AREN'T WORTH SHIT!
I KNOW, CUZ I'VE FOUGHT IN AN FA GUNDAM AND AN ATLAS GUNDAM! WHAT WE NEED IS SOMETHING THAT'S A MATCH FOR A THOUSAND MOBILE SUITS!
THIS ISN'T ALL.
WOULD YOU LIKE TO SEE THE REST, IO?

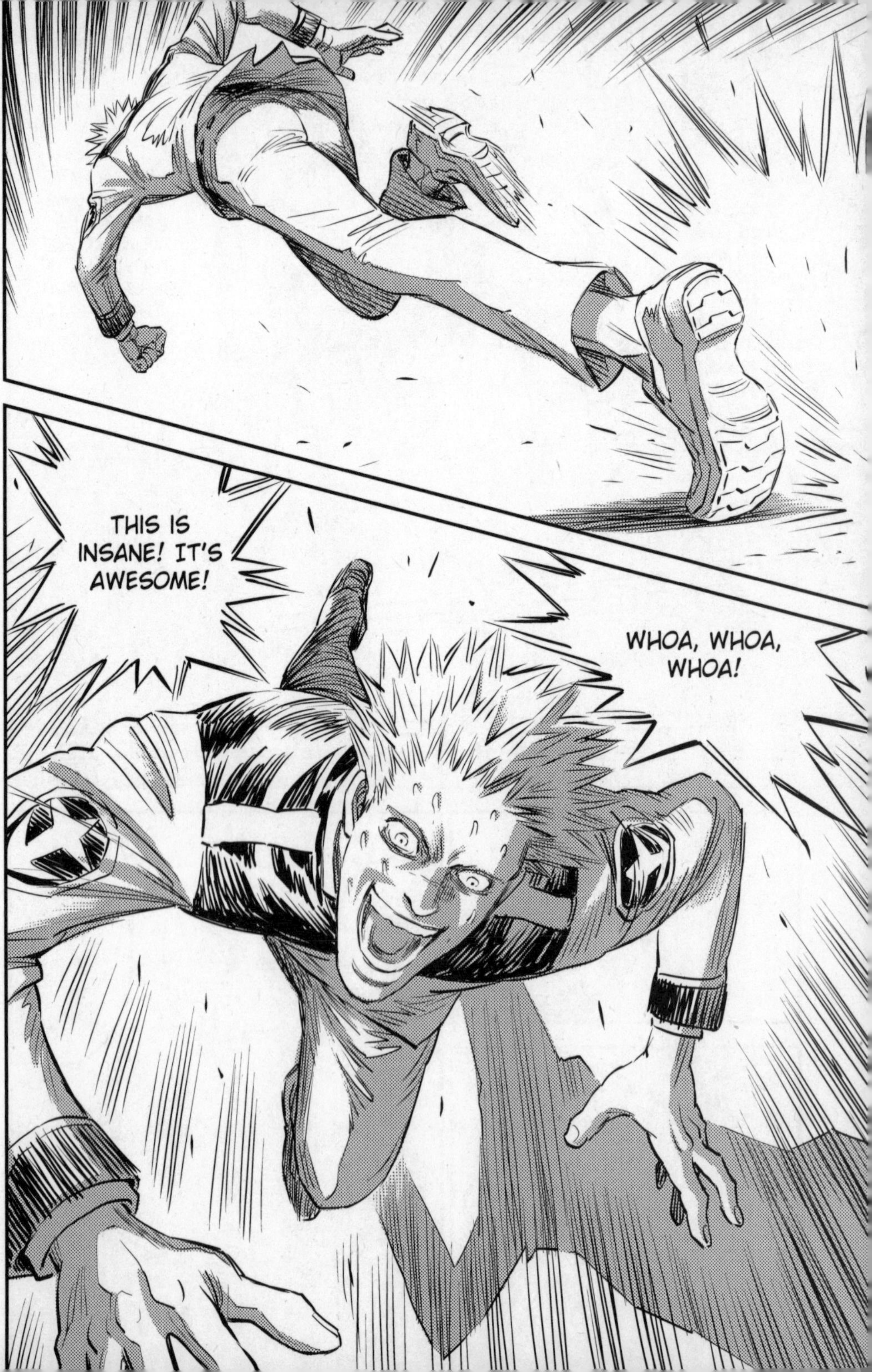
WHOA, WHOA, WHOA!
THIS IS INSANE! IT'S AWESOME!

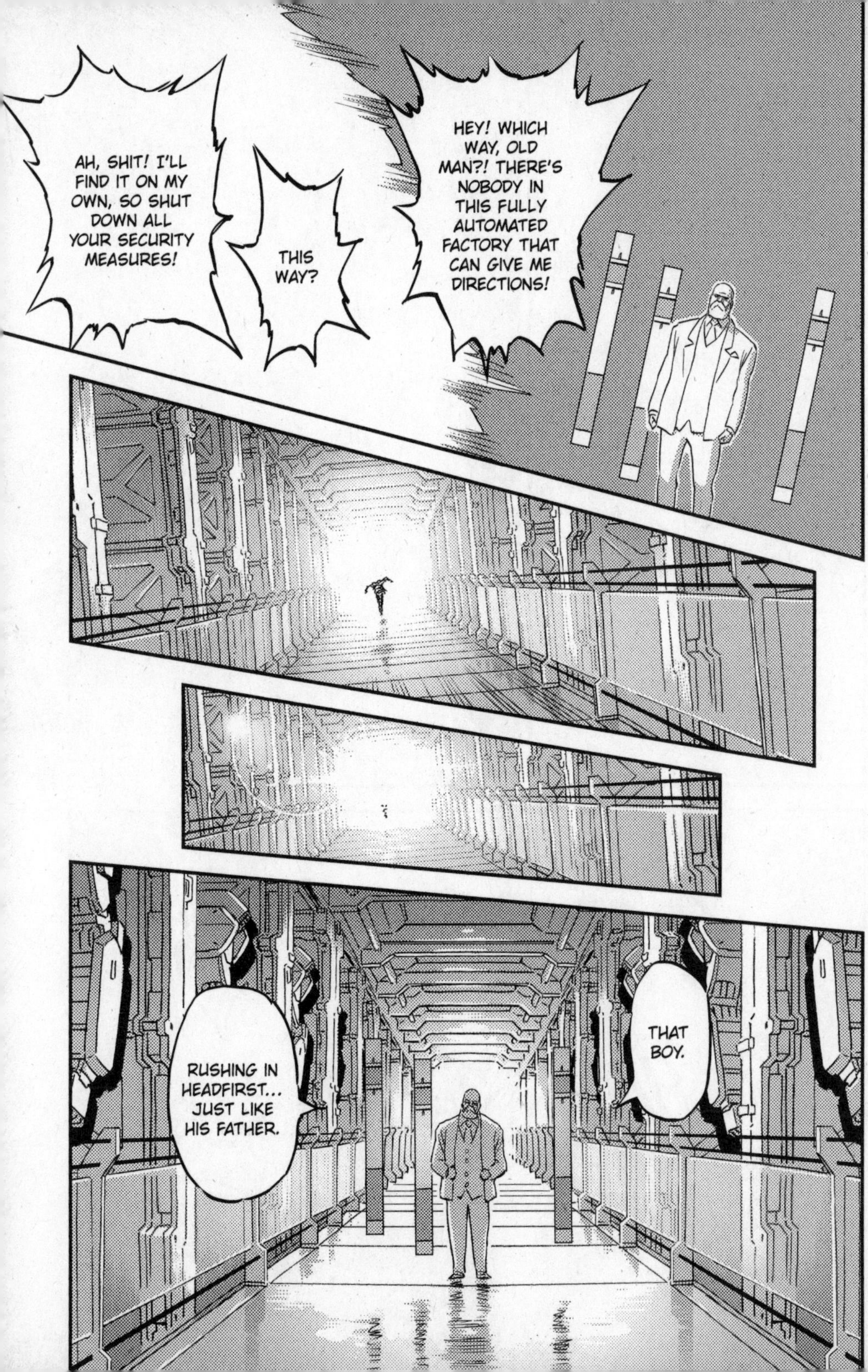
HEY! WHICH WAY, OLD MAN?! THERE'S NOBODY IN THIS FULLY AUTOMATED FACTORY THAT CAN GIVE ME DIRECTIONS!
THIS WAY?
AH, SHIT! I'LL FIND IT ON MY OWN, SO SHUT DOWN ALL YOUR SECURITY MEASURES!
THAT BOY.
RUSHING IN HEADFIRST... JUST LIKE HIS FATHER.

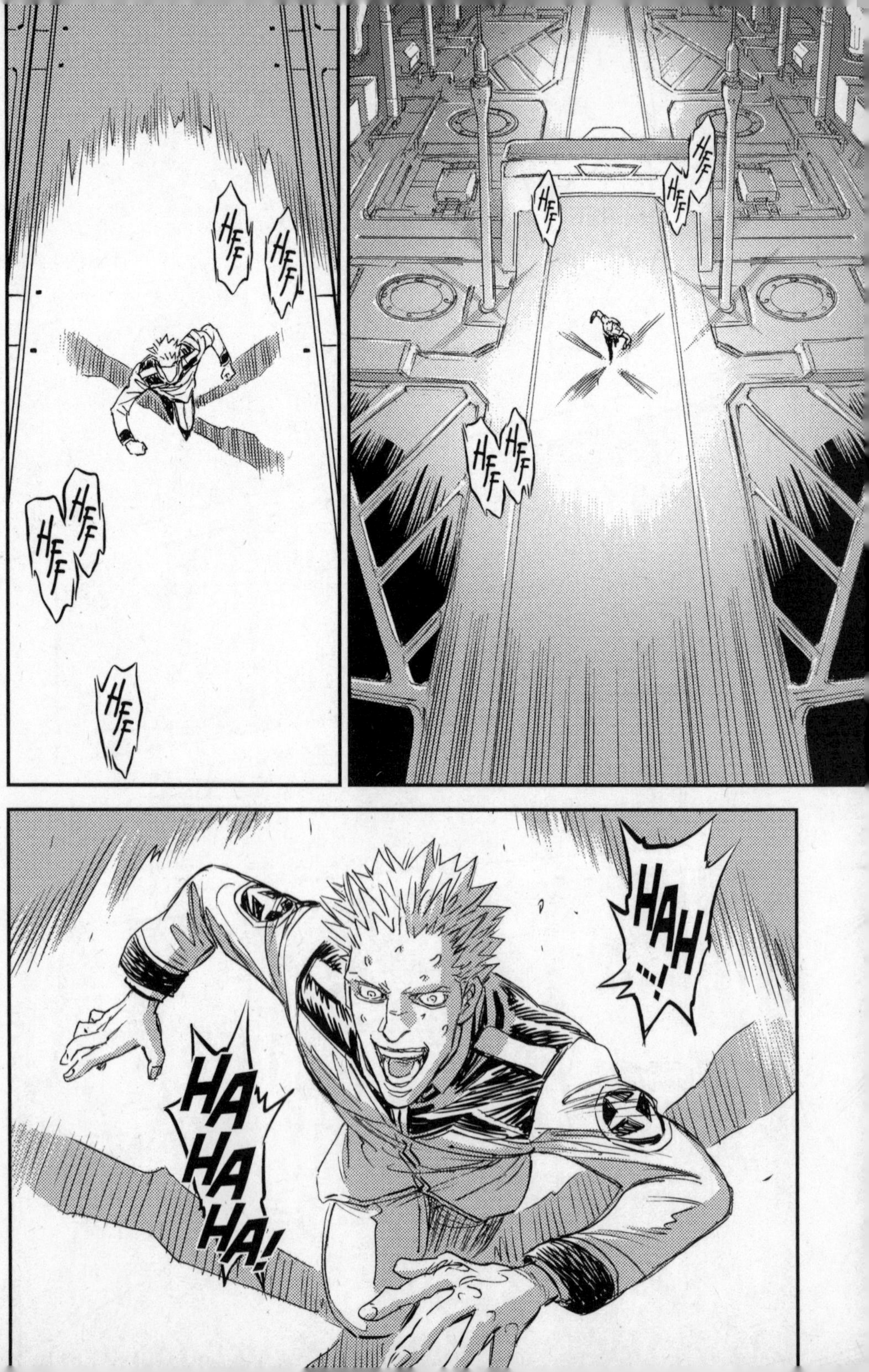
HFF
HFF
HFF
HFF
HFF
HFF
HFF
HFF
HFF
HFF
HAH...!
HA HA HA HA!

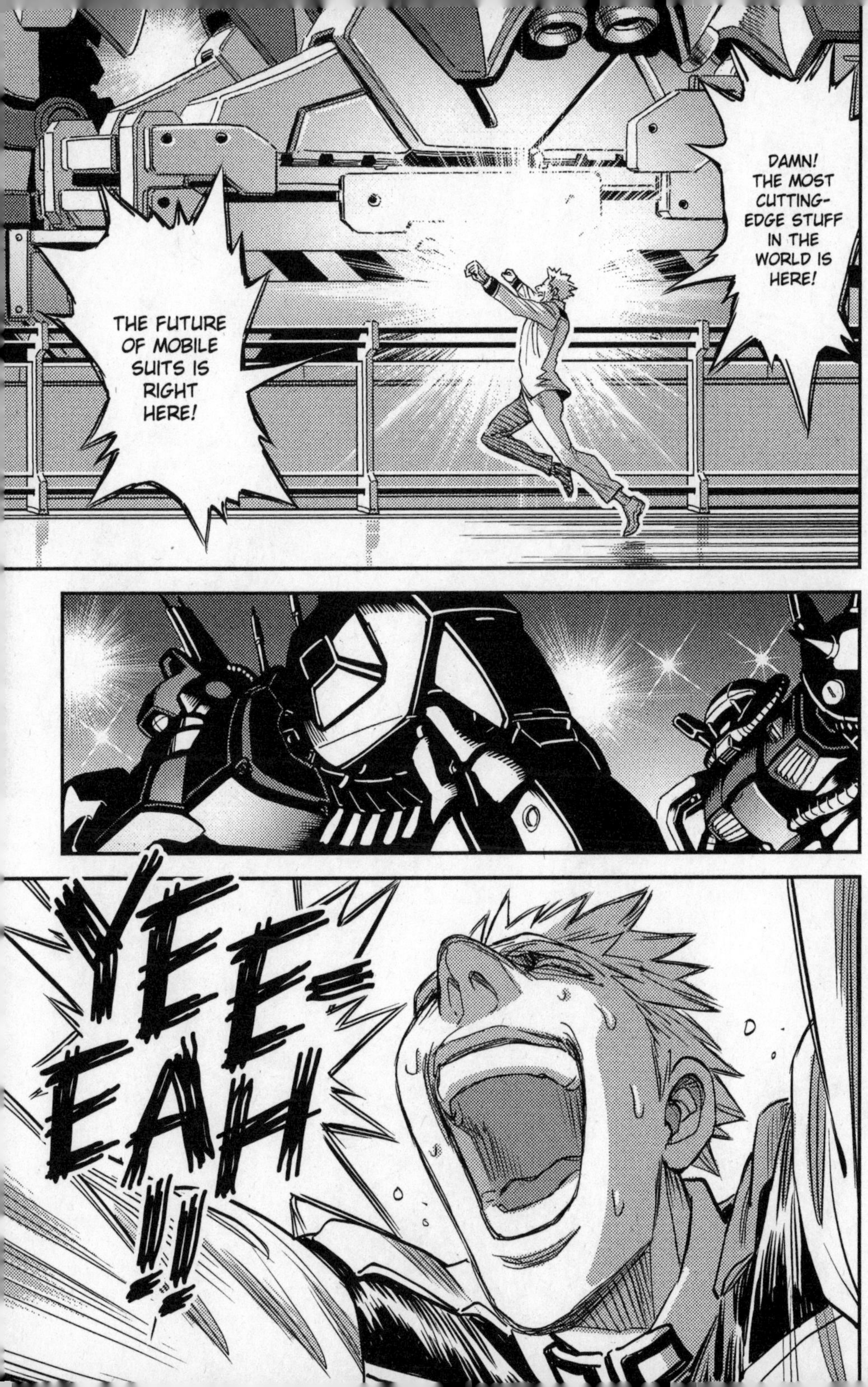
DAMN! THE MOST CUTTING-EDGE STUFF IN THE WORLD IS HERE!
THE FUTURE OF MOBILE SUITS IS RIGHT HERE!
YEE-EAH!!

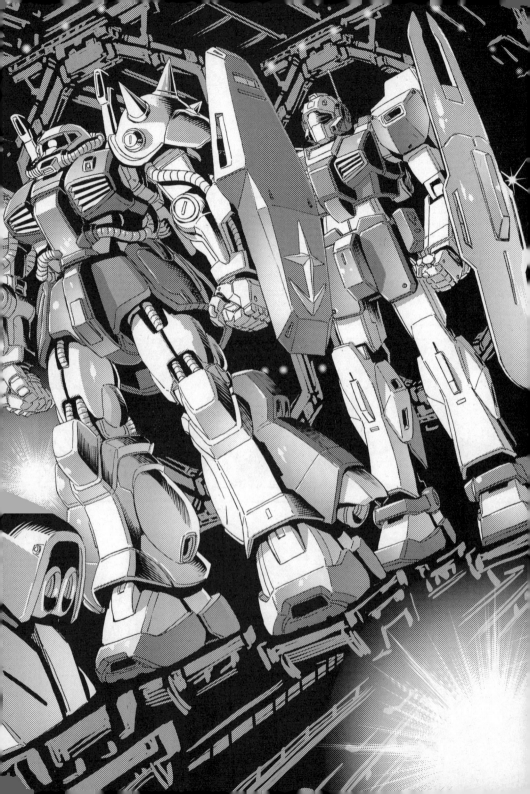

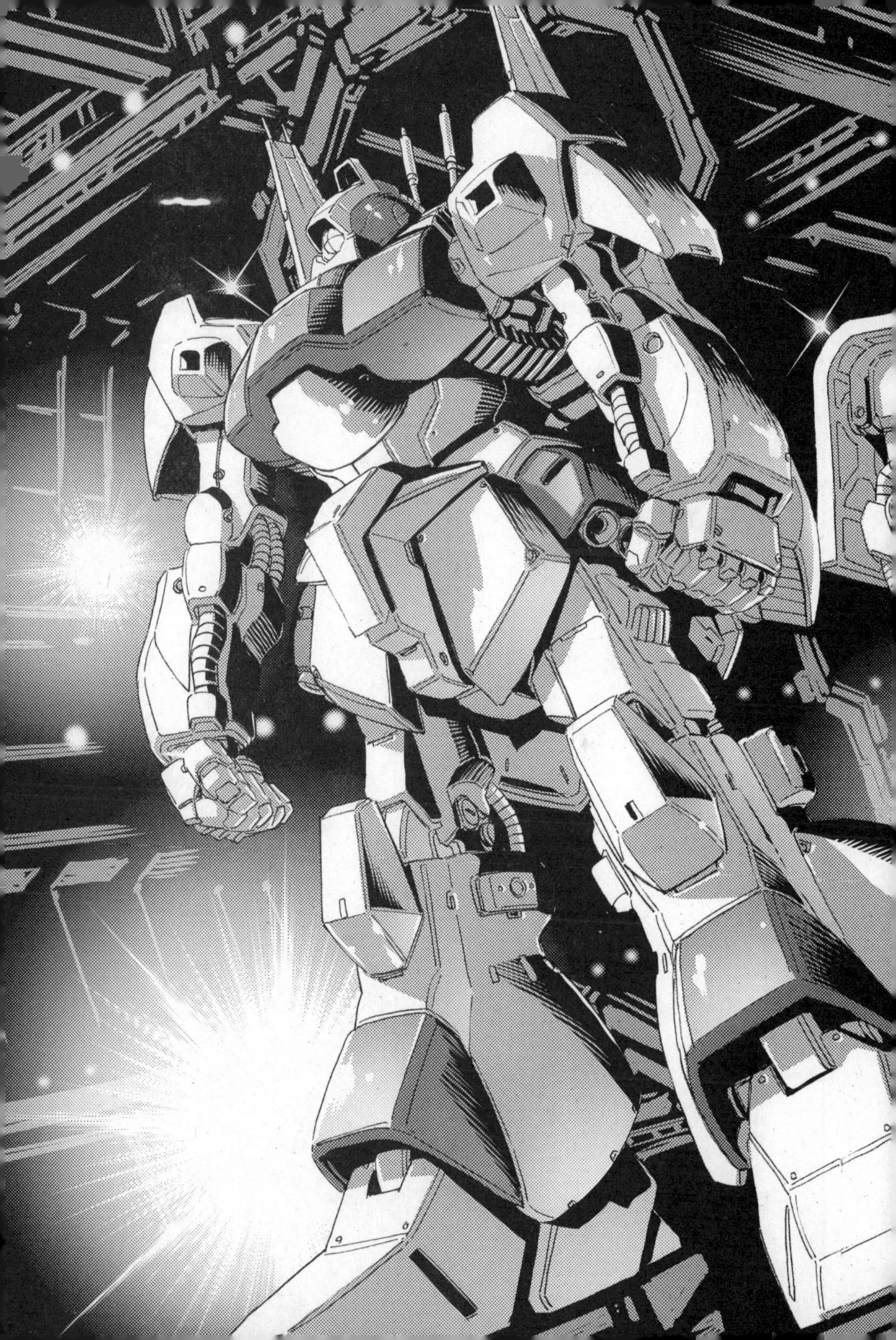

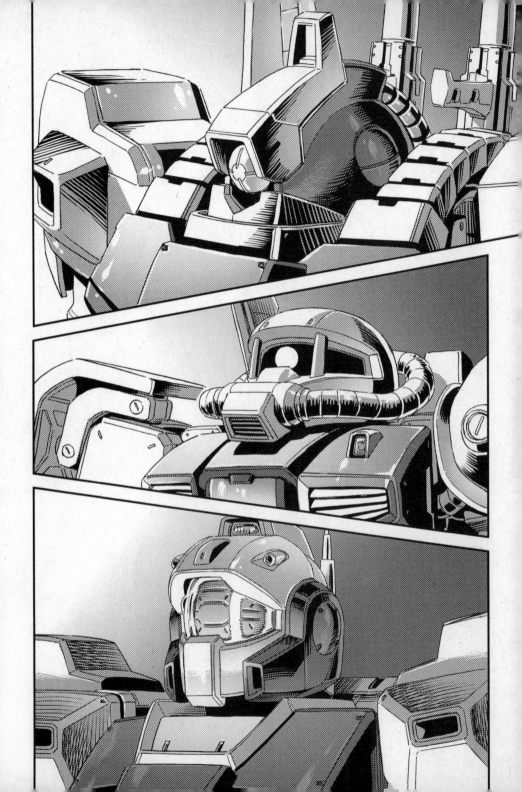

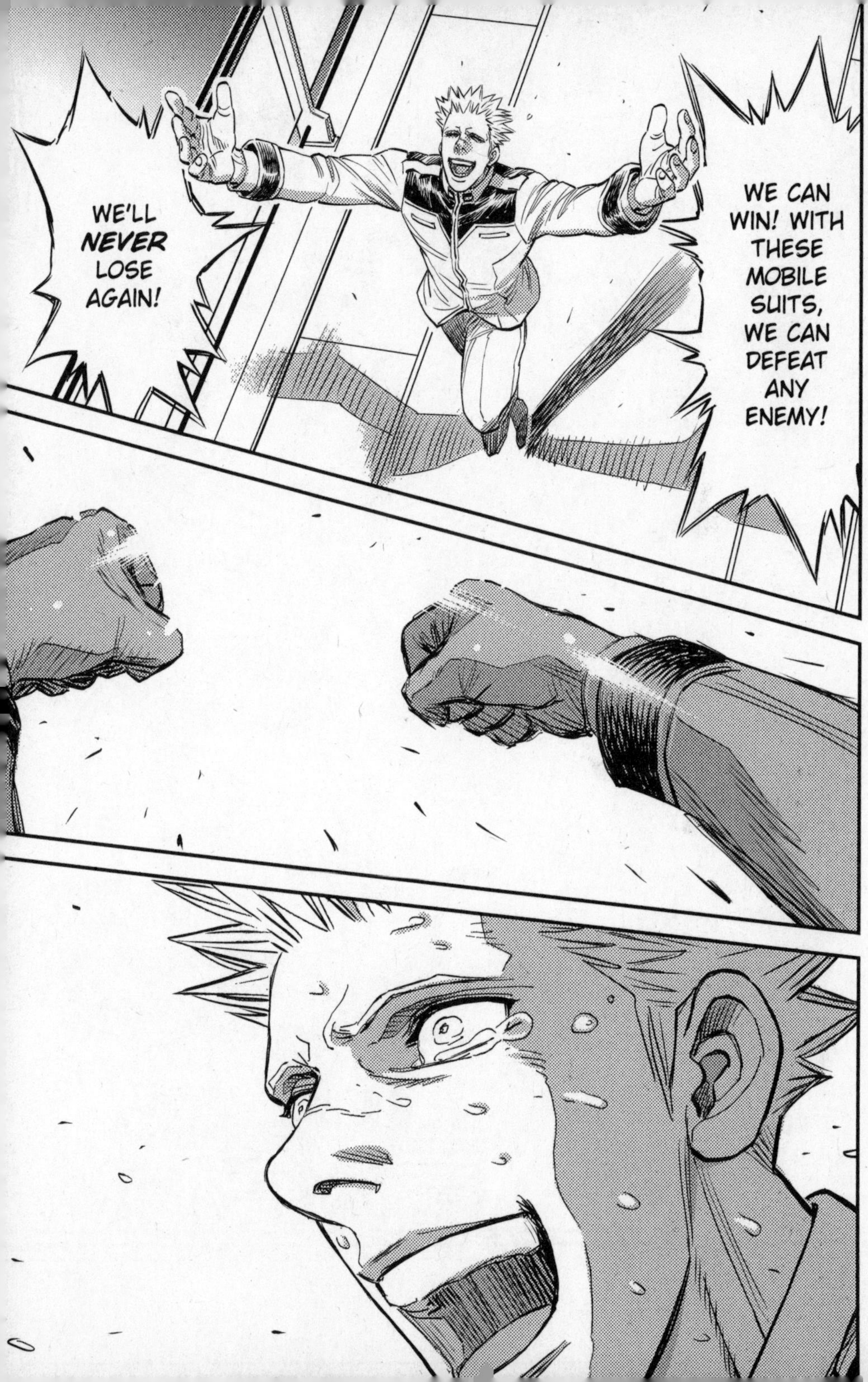
WE CAN WIN! WITH THESE MOBILE SUITS, WE CAN DEFEAT ANY ENEMY!
WE'LL NEVER LOSE AGAIN!

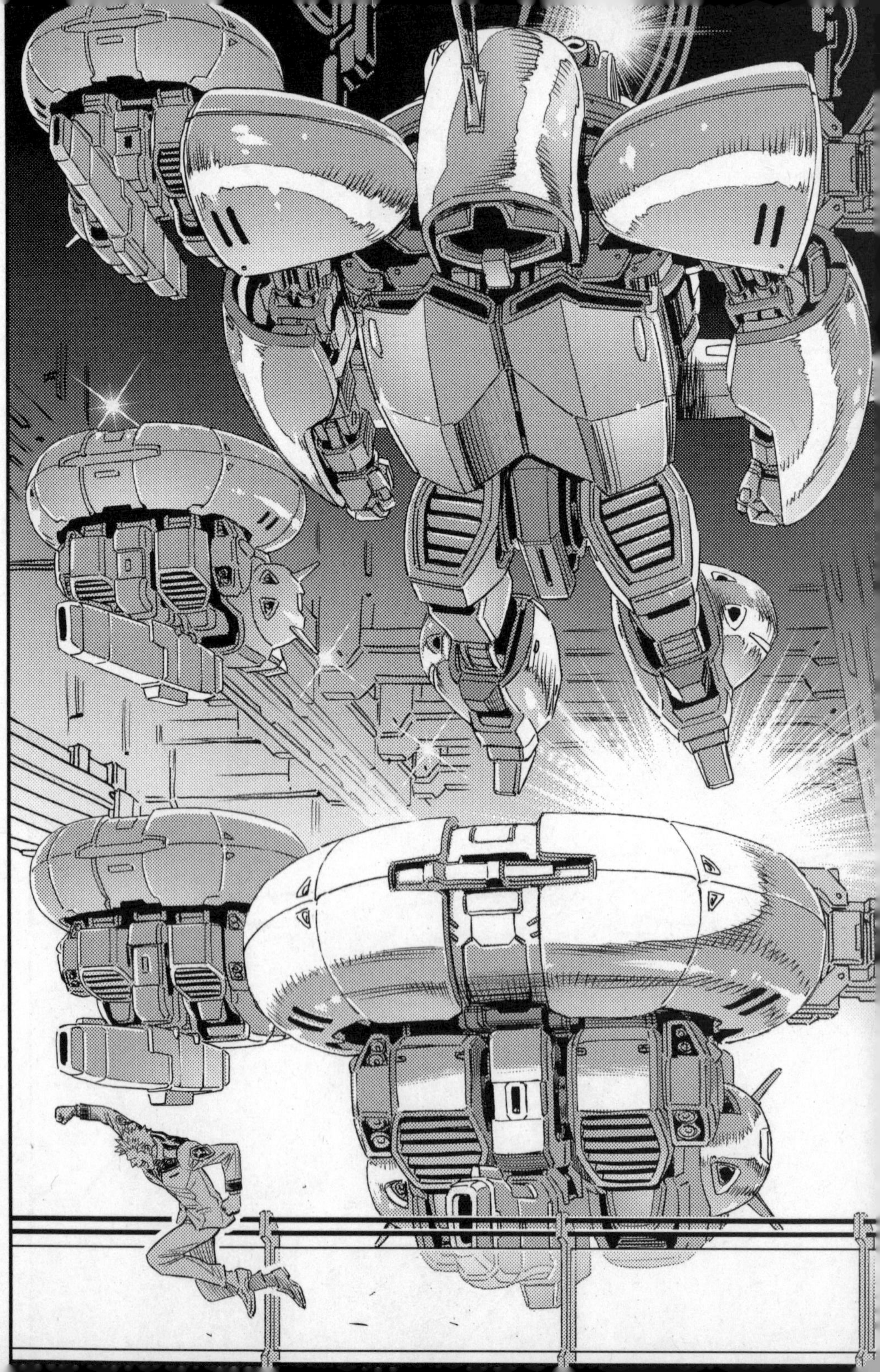

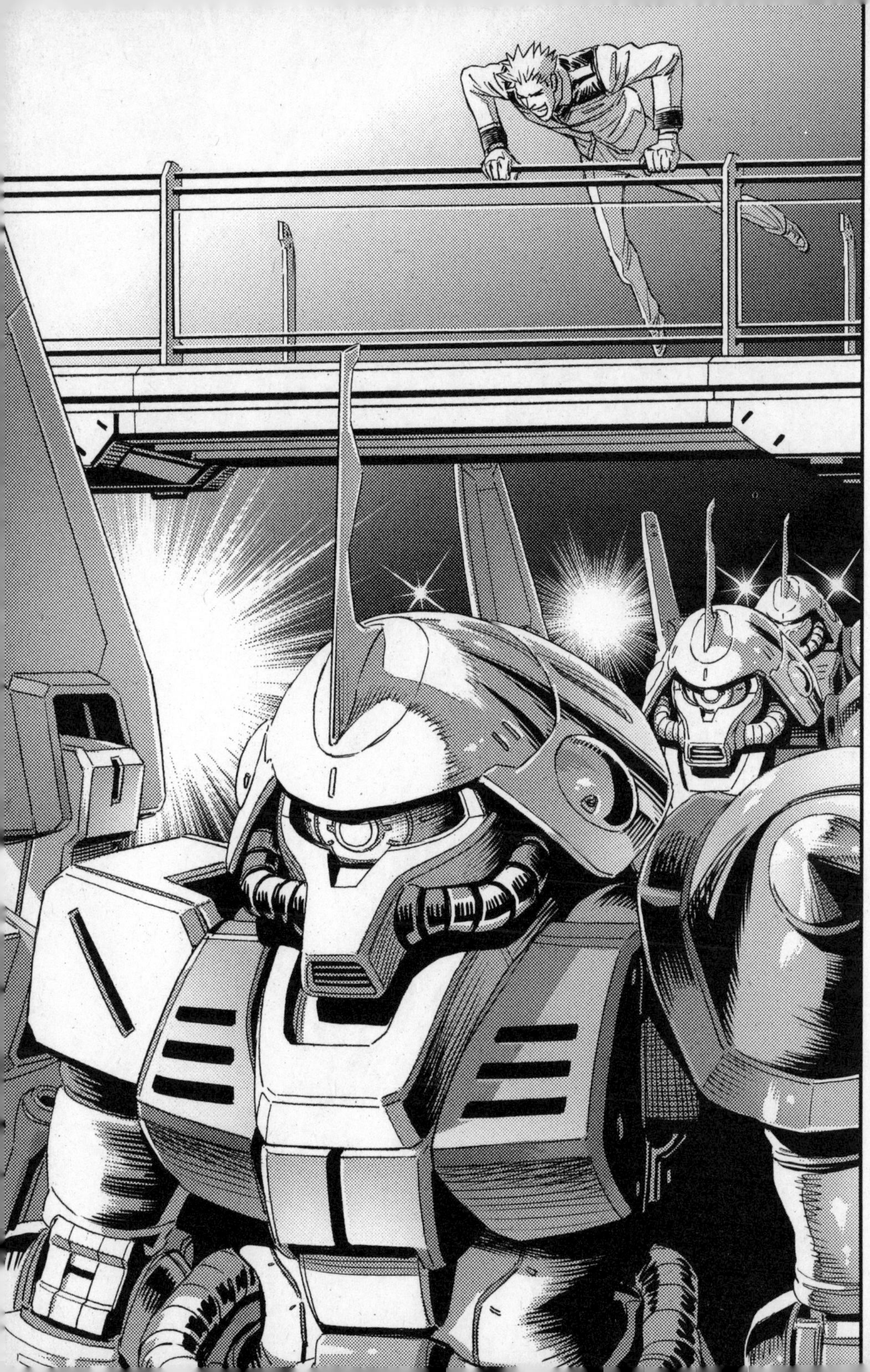

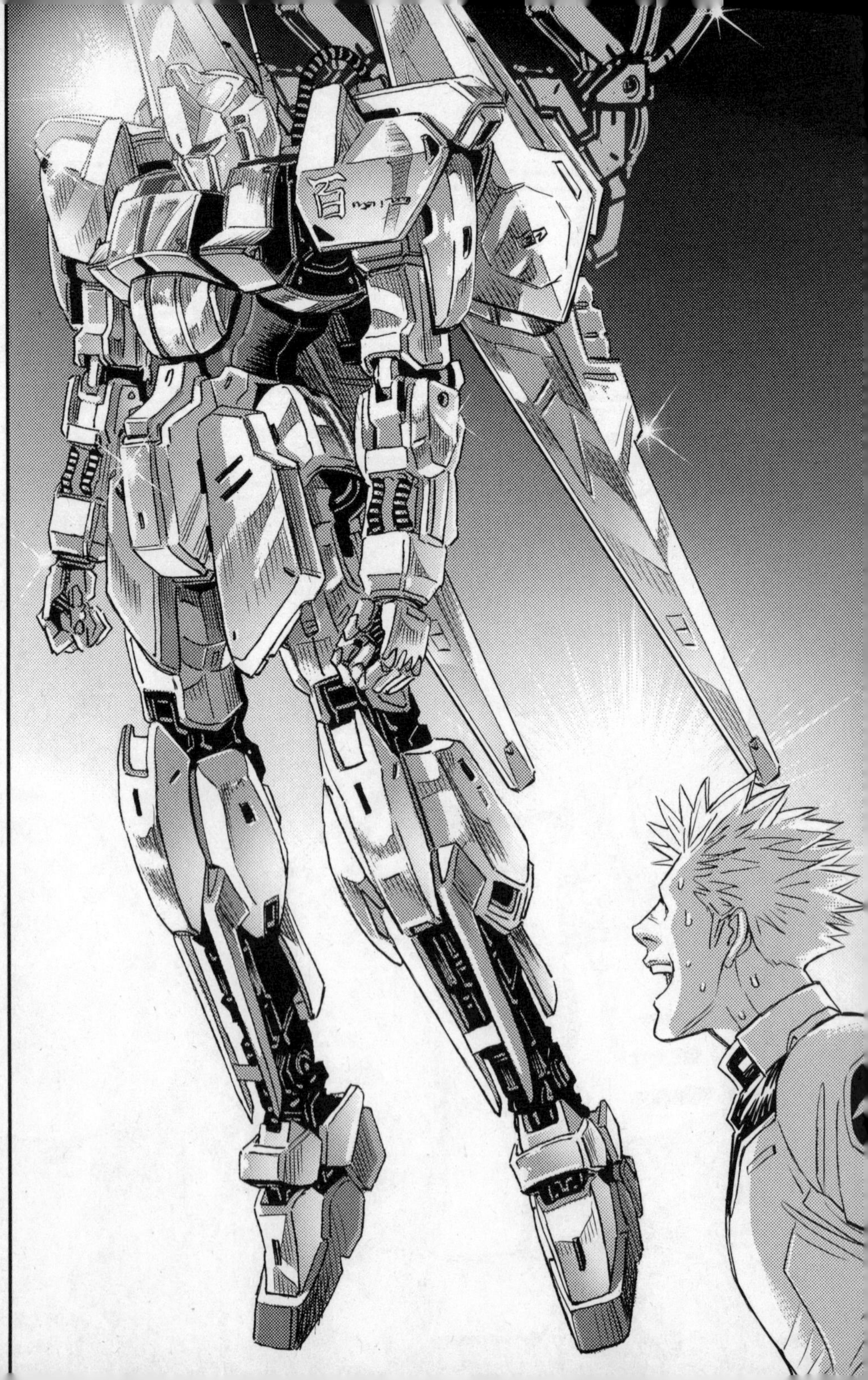
百

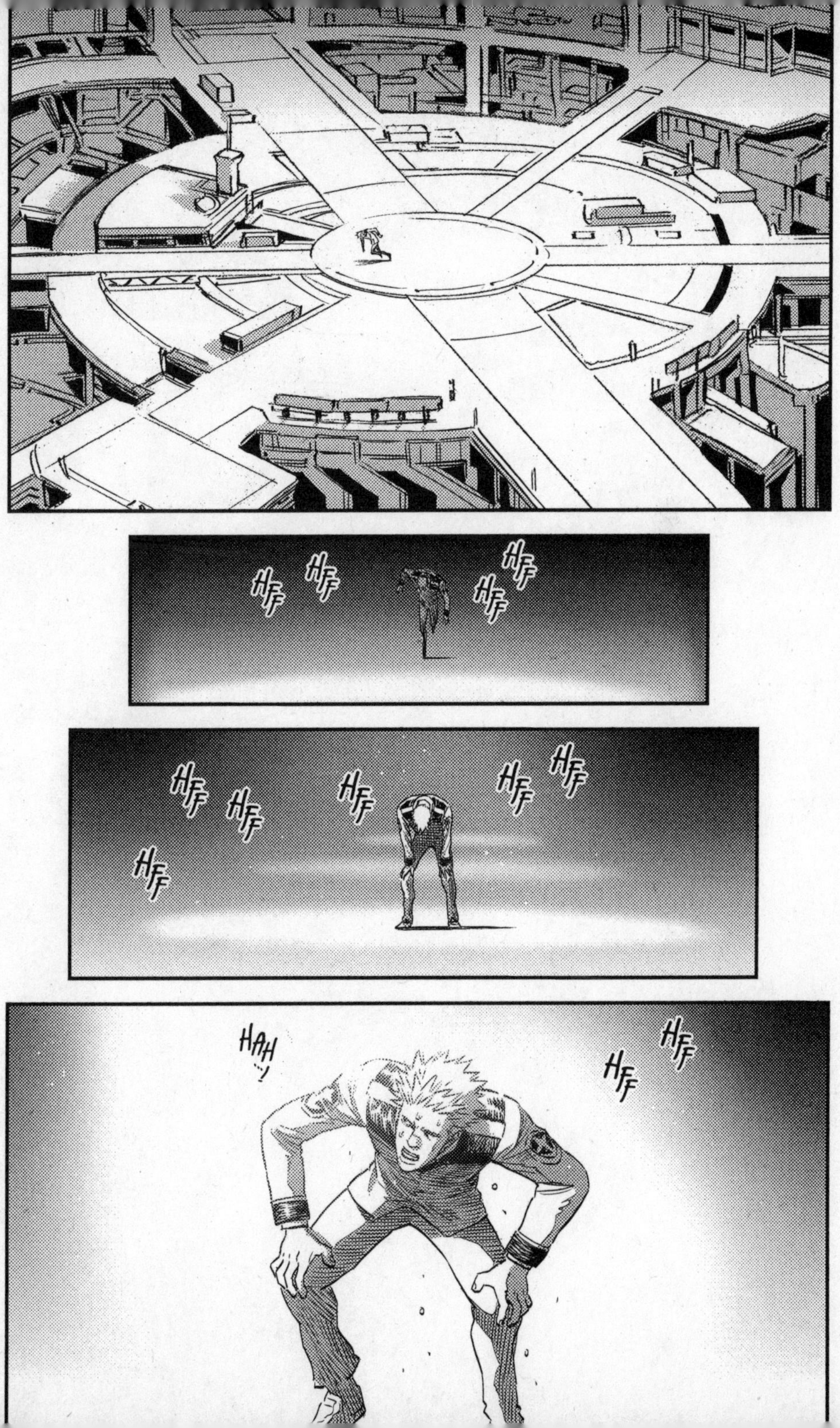
HFF
HFF
HFF
HFF
HFF
HFF
HFF
HFF
HFF
HFF
HFF
HFF
HAH…!

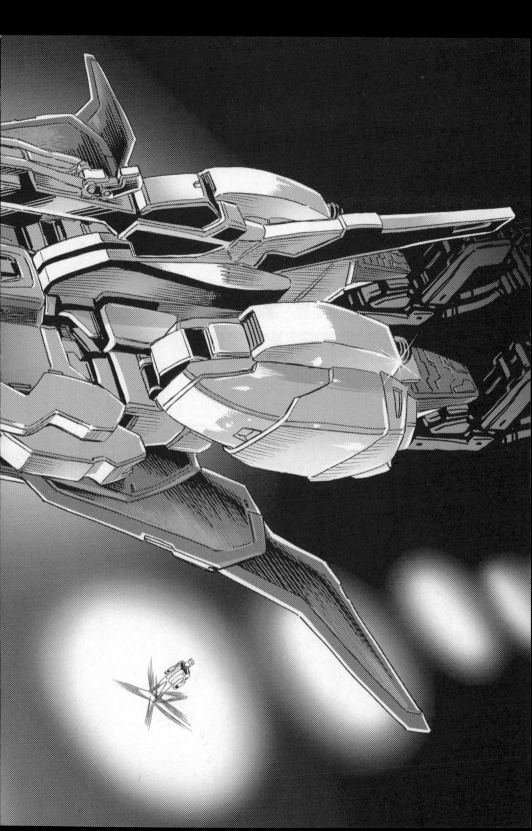

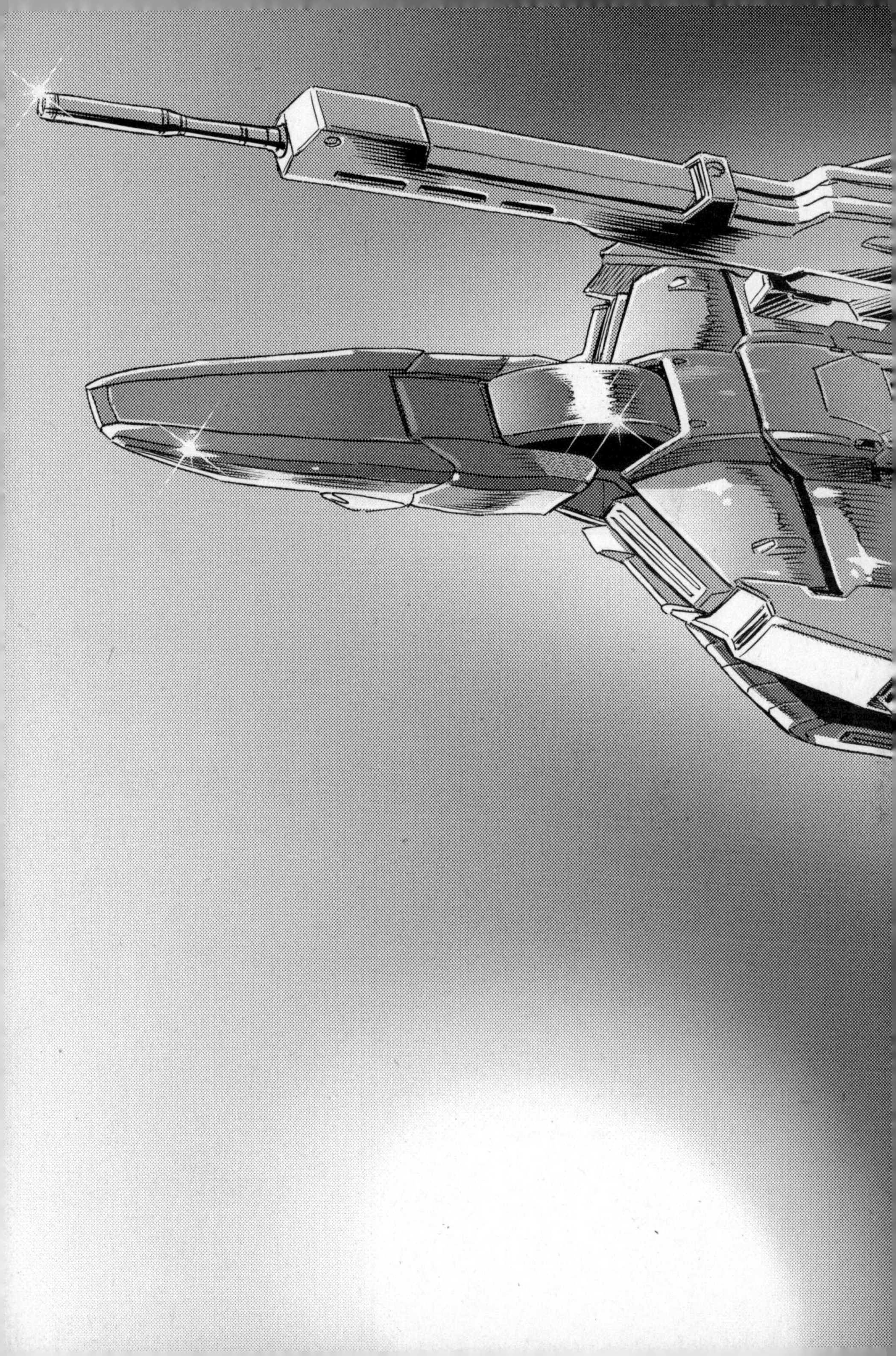

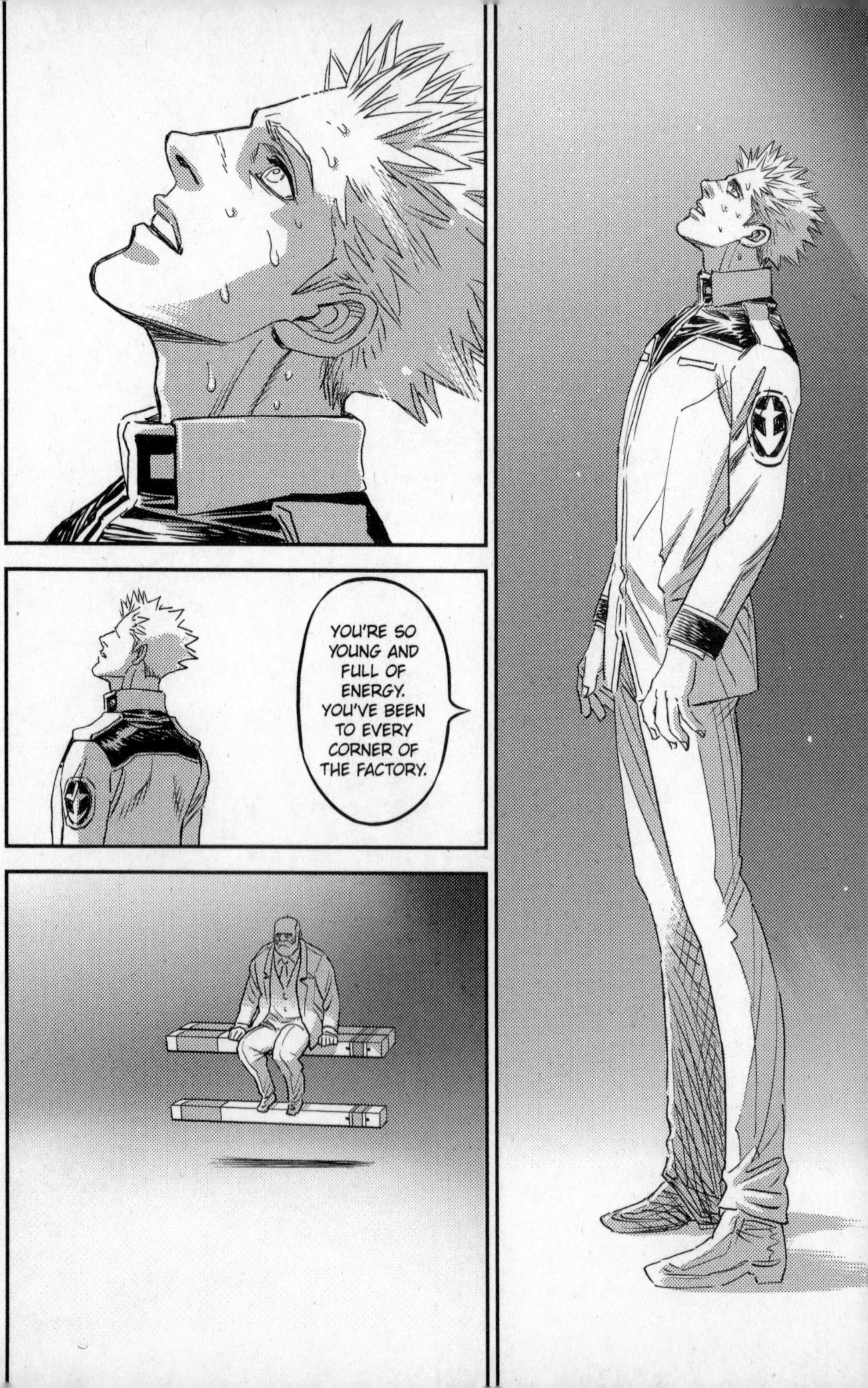
YOU'RE SO YOUNG AND FULL OF ENERGY. YOU'VE BEEN TO EVERY CORNER OF THE FACTORY.

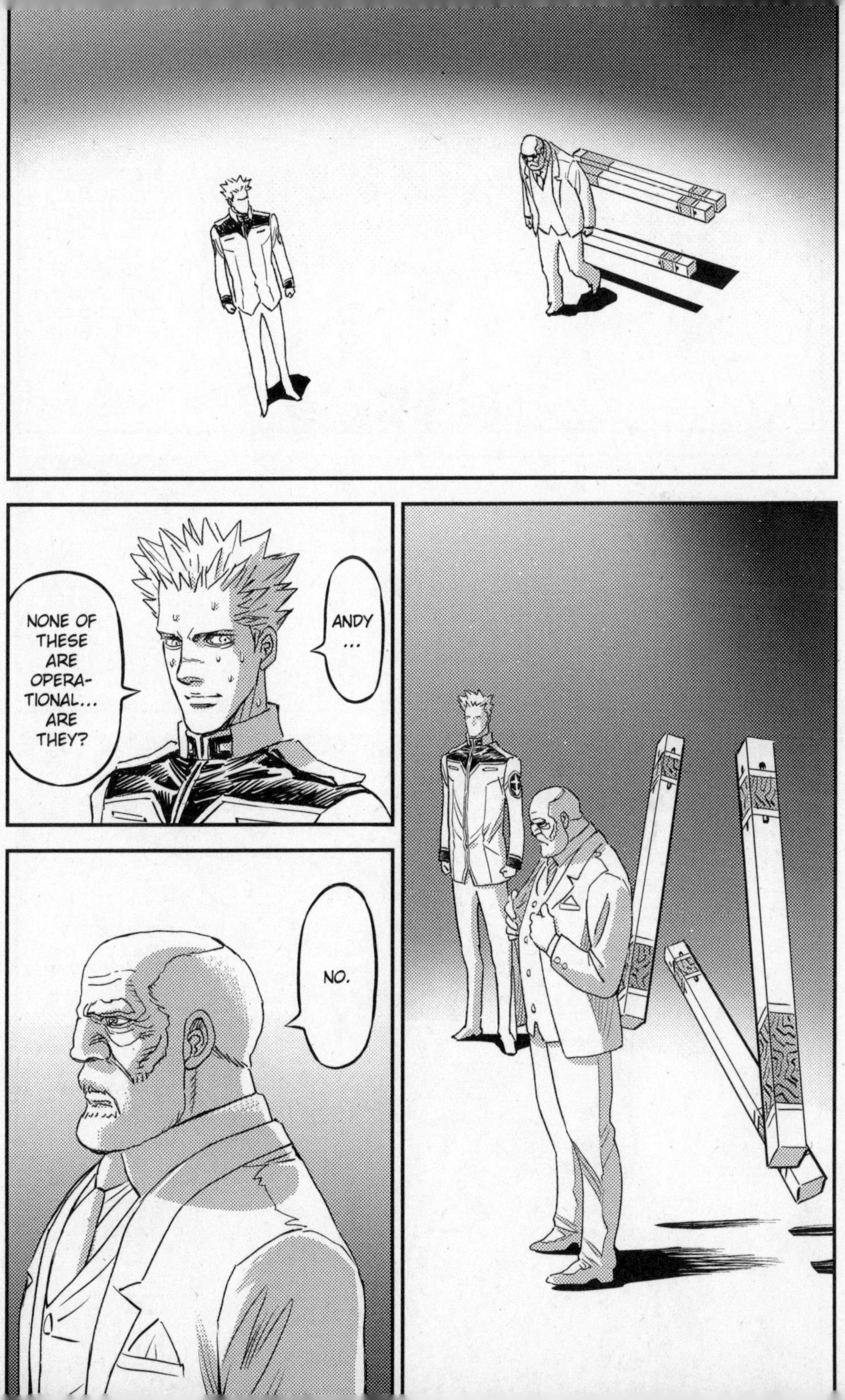
ANDY...
NONE OF THESE ARE OPERATIONAL... ARE THEY?
NO.

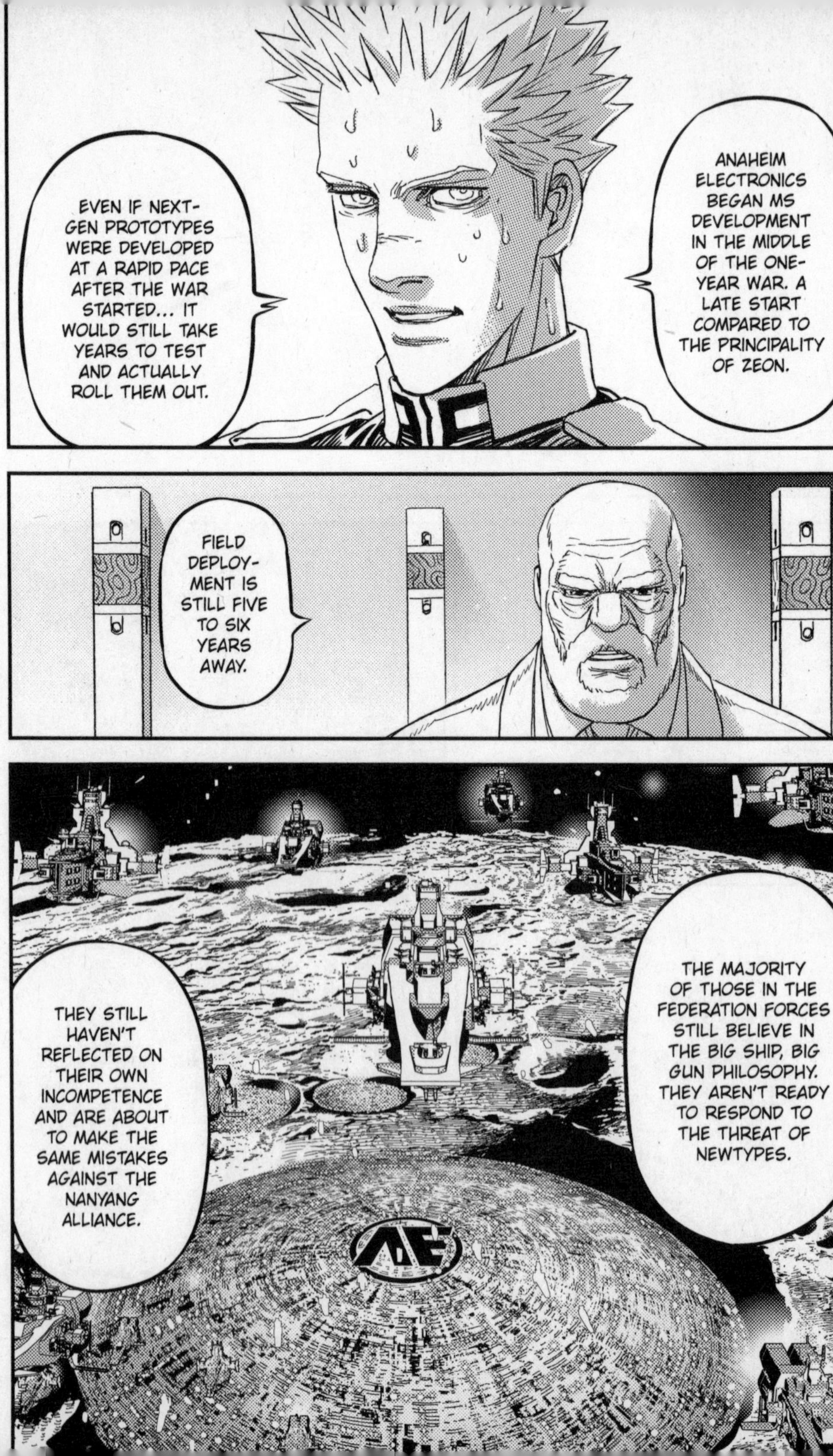
ANAHEIM ELECTRONICS BEGAN MS DEVELOPMENT IN THE MIDDLE OF THE ONE-YEAR WAR. A LATE START COMPARED TO THE PRINCIPALITY OF ZEON.
EVEN IF NEXT-GEN PROTOTYPES WERE DEVELOPED AT A RAPID PACE AFTER THE WAR STARTED... IT WOULD STILL TAKE YEARS TO TEST AND ACTUALLY ROLL THEM OUT.
FIELD DEPLOY-MENT IS STILL FIVE TO SIX YEARS AWAY.
THE MAJORITY OF THOSE IN THE FEDERATION FORCES STILL BELIEVE IN THE BIG SHIP, BIG GUN PHILOSOPHY. THEY AREN'T READY TO RESPOND TO THE THREAT OF NEWTYPES.
THEY STILL HAVEN'T REFLECTED ON THEIR OWN INCOMPETENCE AND ARE ABOUT TO MAKE THE SAME MISTAKES AGAINST THE NANYANG ALLIANCE.

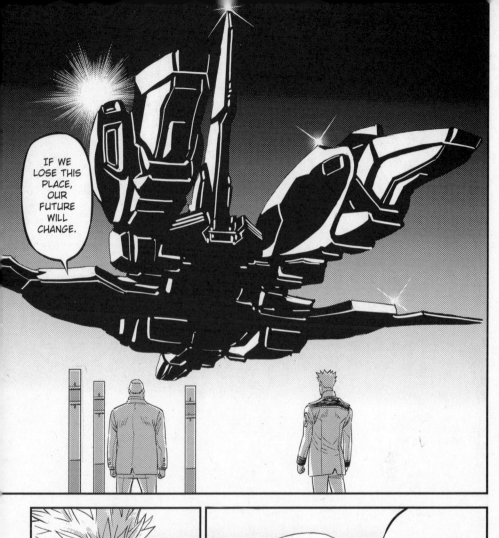

IF WE LOSE THIS PLACE, OUR FUTURE WILL CHANGE.

MANY PLANT AND ANIMAL SPECIES WERE LOST ON EARTH IN THE ONE-YEAR WAR. VON BRAUN CITY IS THE ONLY TERRARIUM THAT STILL PRESERVES EARTH'S ENVIRONMENT.

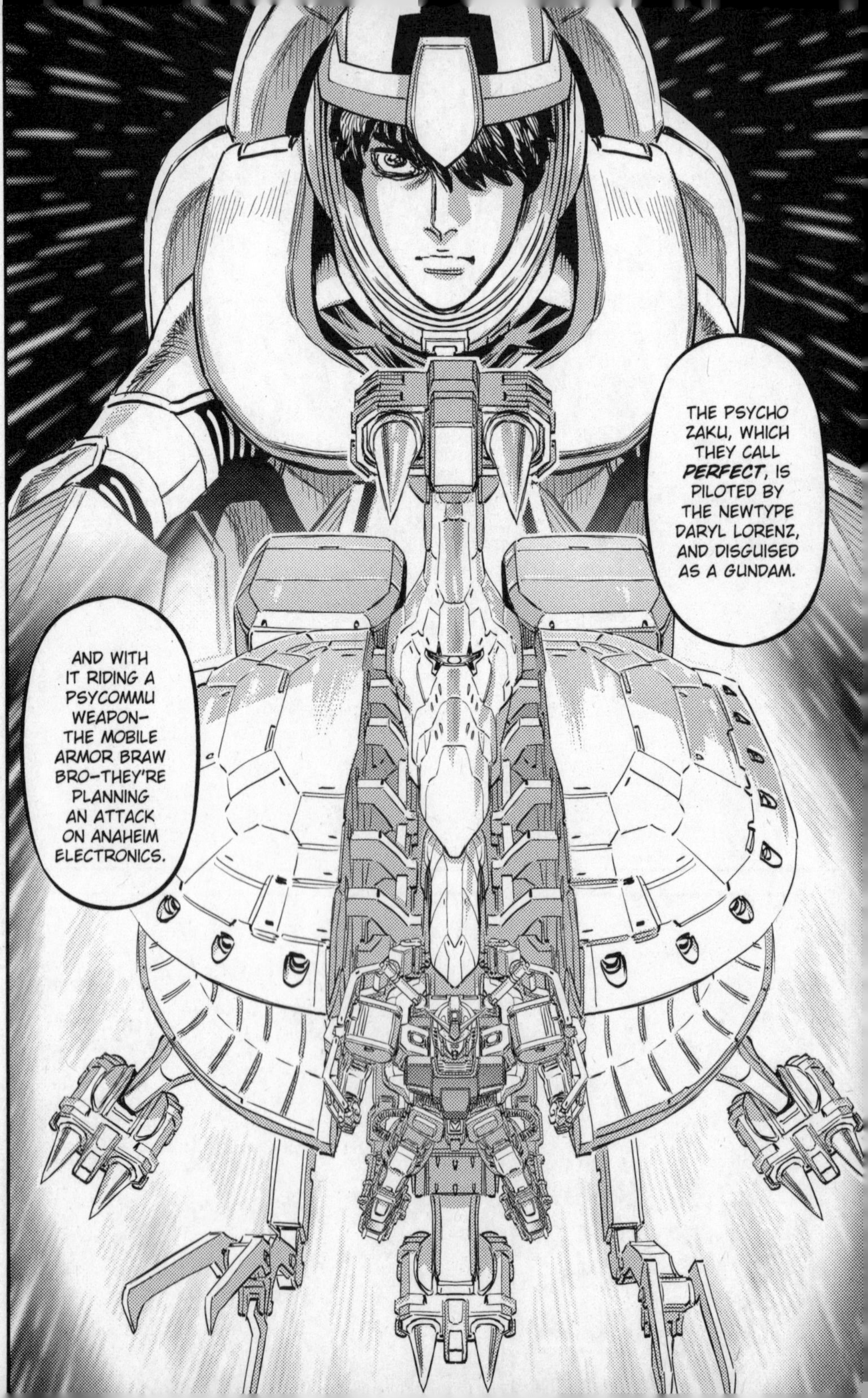
THE PSYCHO ZAKU, WHICH THEY CALL *PERFECT*, IS PILOTED BY THE NEWTYPE DARYL LORENZ, AND DISGUISED AS A GUNDAM.
AND WITH IT RIDING A PSYCOMMU WEAPON—THE MOBILE ARMOR BRAW BRO—THEY'RE PLANNING AN ATTACK ON ANAHEIM ELECTRONICS.

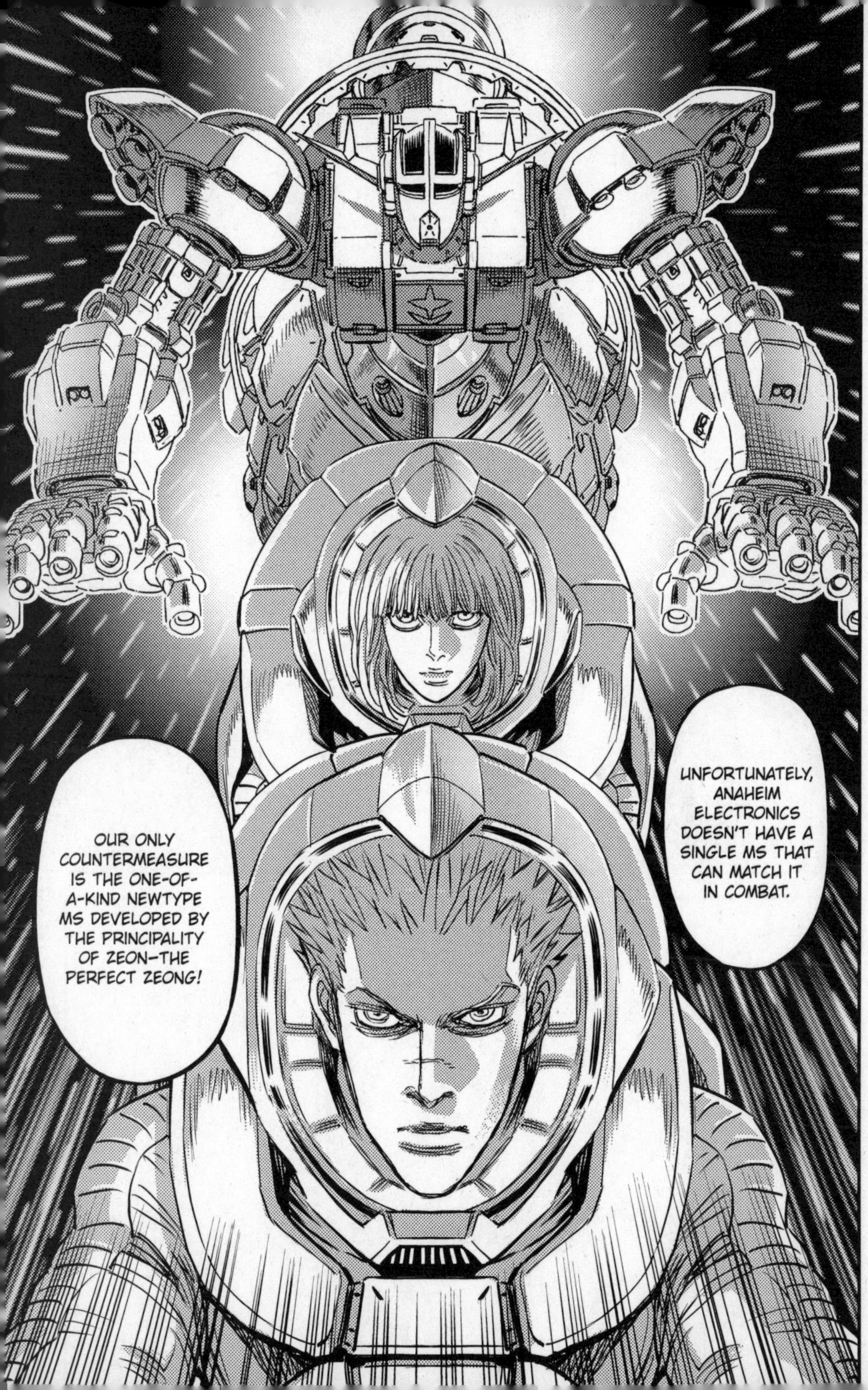
UNFORTUNATELY, ANAHEIM ELECTRONICS DOESN'T HAVE A SINGLE MS THAT CAN MATCH IT IN COMBAT.
OUR ONLY COUNTERMEASURE IS THE ONE-OF-A-KIND NEWTYPE MS DEVELOPED BY THE PRINCIPALITY OF ZEON—THE PERFECT ZEONG!

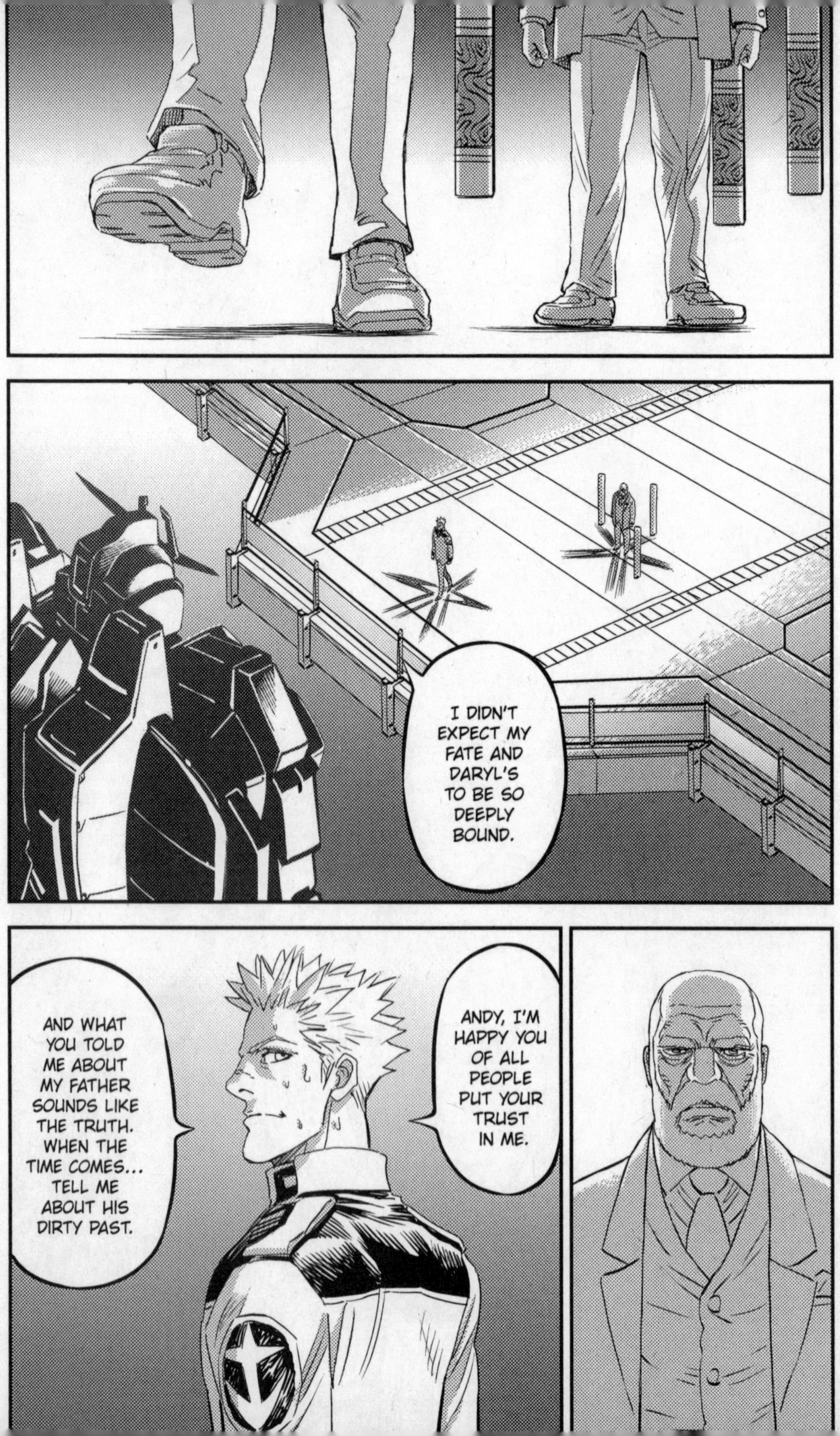
I DIDN'T EXPECT MY FATE AND DARYL'S TO BE SO DEEPLY BOUND.
ANDY, I'M HAPPY YOU OF ALL PEOPLE PUT YOUR TRUST IN ME.
AND WHAT YOU TOLD ME ABOUT MY FATHER SOUNDS LIKE THE TRUTH. WHEN THE TIME COMES... TELL ME ABOUT HIS DIRTY PAST.

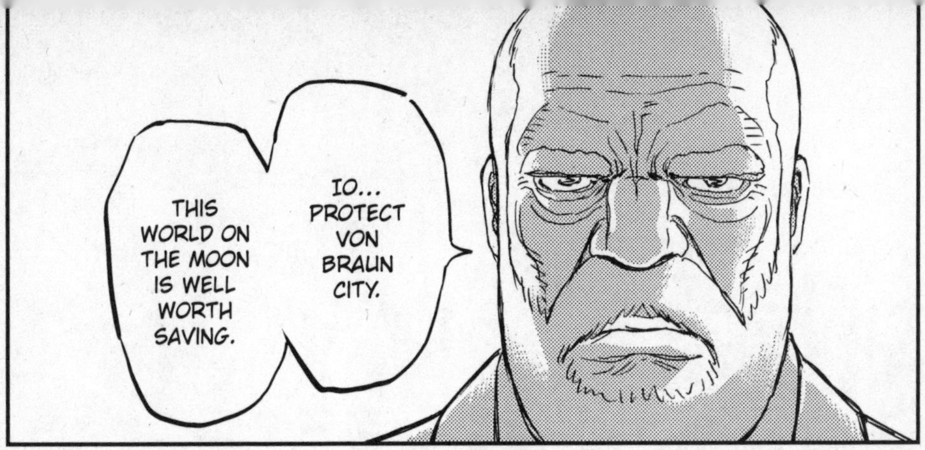
TO... PROTECT VON BRAUN CITY.
THIS WORLD ON THE MOON IS WELL WORTH SAVING.

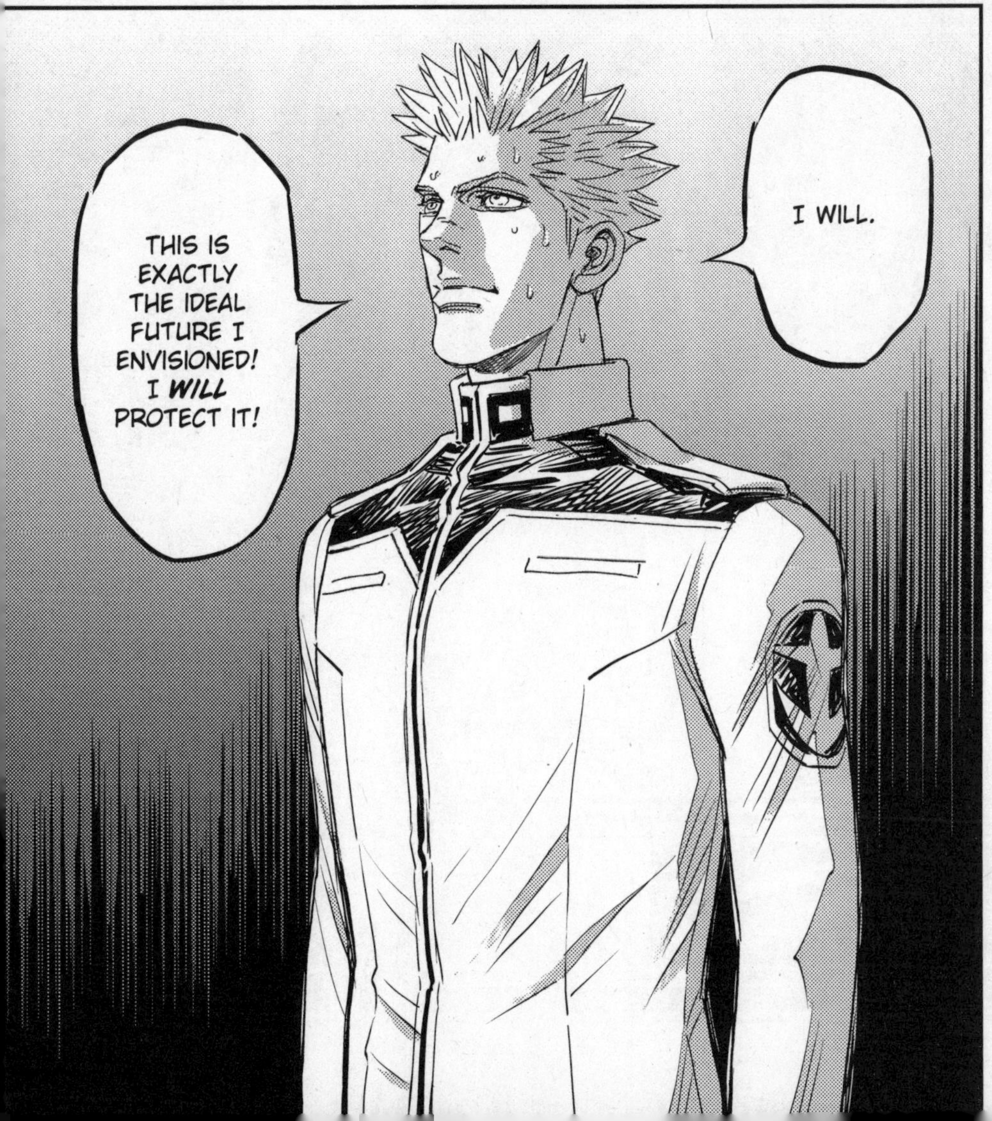
I WILL.
THIS IS EXACTLY THE IDEAL FUTURE I ENVISIONED! I *WILL* PROTECT IT!

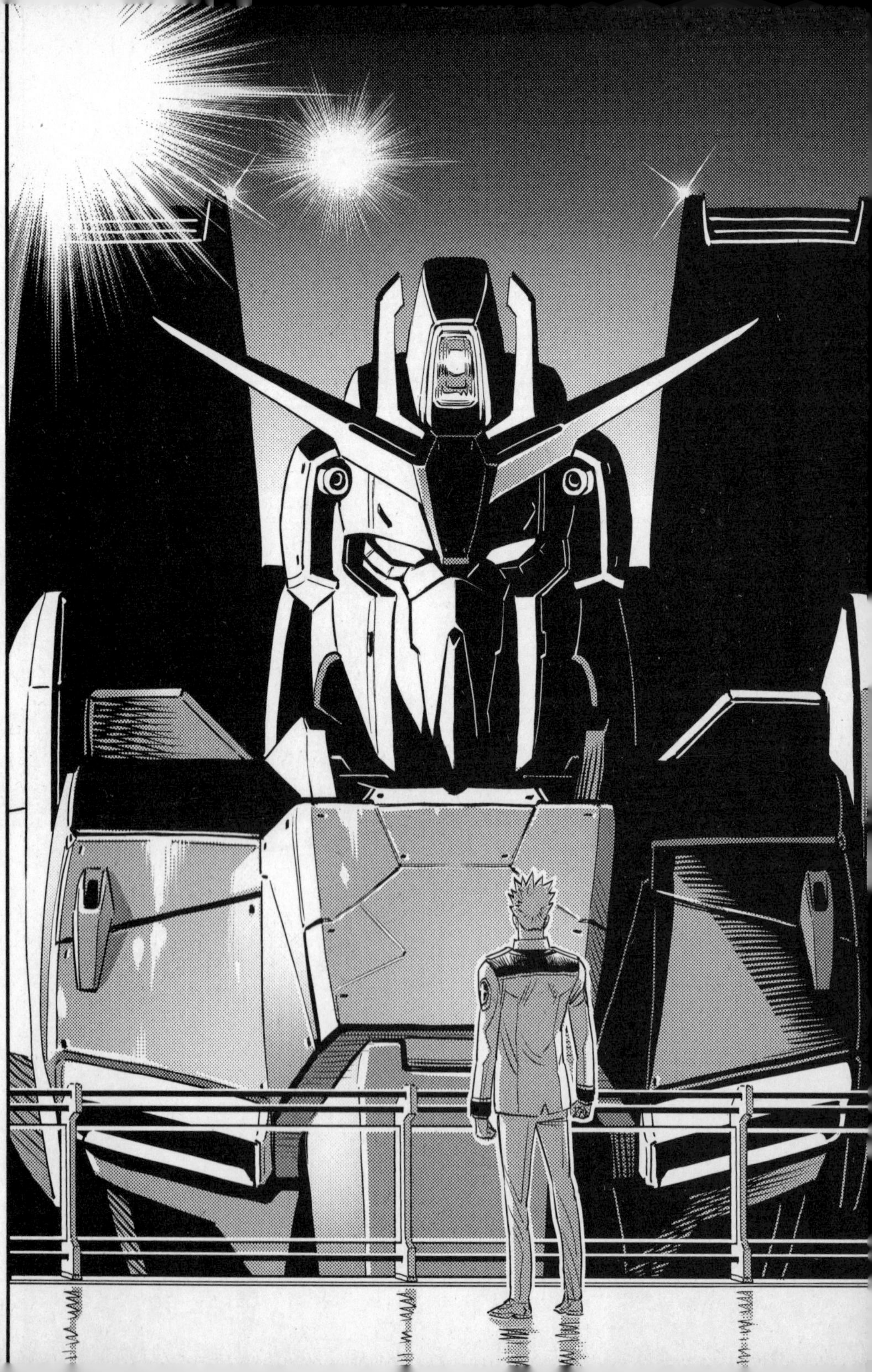

MOBILE SUIT GUNDAM - THUNDERBOLT - VOL. 19 - END

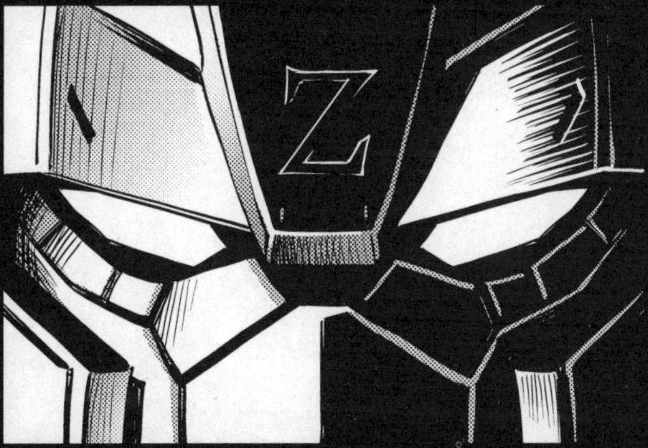
Z

TO BE CONTINUED

STUDIO TOA S.P.A

Executive Director   **Yasuo Ohtagaki**

Special Thanks   **Mizuki Sakura**
umegrafix
Digital Noise Ltd.

MOBILE SUIT GUNDAM
THUNDERBOLT 19

VIZ Signature Edition

STORY AND ART **YASUO OHTAGAKI**
Original Concept by **HAJIME YATATE** and **YOSHIYUKI TOMINO**

Translation **JOE YAMAZAKI**
English Adaptation **STAN!**
Touch-up Art & Lettering **EVAN WALDINGER**
Cover & Design **SHAWN CARRICO**
Editor **MIKE MONTESA**

MOBILE SUIT GUNDAM THUNDERBOLT Vol. 19 by Yasuo OHTAGAKI
Original Concept by Hajime YATATE, Yoshiyuki TOMINO
© 2012 Yasuo OHTAGAKI
© SOTSU·SUNRISE
All rights reserved.
Original Japanese edition published by SHOGAKUKAN.
English translation rights in the United States of America,
Canada, the United Kingdom, Ireland, Australia and New Zealand
arranged with SHOGAKUKAN.

ORIGINAL COVER DESIGN / Yoshiyuki SEKI for VOLARE inc.

EDITORIAL COOPERATION / Shinsuke HIRAIWA (Digitalpaint.jp)

Printed in the U.S.A.

Published by VIZ Media, LLC
P.O. Box 77010
San Francisco, CA 94107

10 9 8 7 6 5 4 3 2 1
First printing, March 2023

VIZ MEDIA
viz.com

VIZ SIGNATURE
vizsignature.com

Hey! You're Reading in the Wrong Direction!

This is the **end** of this graphic novel!

To properly enjoy this VIZ graphic novel, please turn it around and begin reading from **right to left.** Unlike English, Japanese is read right to left, so Japanese comics are read in reverse order from the way English comics are typically read.

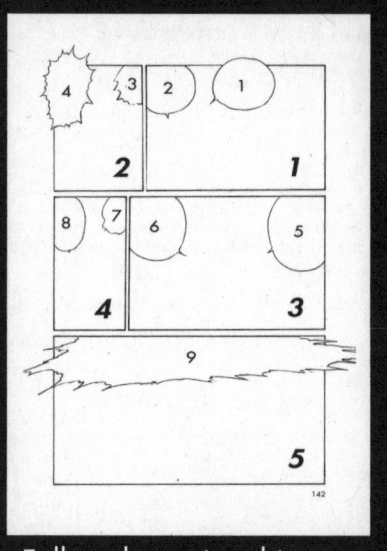

Follow the action this way

This book has been printed in the original Japanese format in order to preserve the orientation of the original artwork. Have fun with it!